SUMTER
AFTER THE FIRST SHOTS

SUMTER
AFTER THE FIRST SHOTS

The Untold Story of America's Most Famous Fort
until the End of the Civil War

DEREK SMITH

STACKPOLE
BOOKS

For my mother, Willene Marsh Smith,
who fostered my love of books and history

Published by
STACKPOLE BOOKS
5067 Ritter Road
Mechanicsburg, PA 17055
www.stackpolebooks.com

Printed in the United States of America

10 9 8 7 6 5 4 3 2 1

FIRST EDITION

Library of Congress Cataloging-in-Publication Data

Smith, Derek, 1956 November 3-
 Sumter after the first shots : the untold story of America's most famous fort until the end of the Civil War / Derek Smith. — First edition.
     pages cm
 Includes bibliographical references and index.
 ISBN 978-0-8117-1614-7
1. Fort Sumter (Charleston, S.C.)—History—19th century. 2. Charleston (S.C.)—History—Civil War, 1861-1865. I. Title.
 F279.C48F687 2015
 975.7'91503—dc23
         2015003769

CONTENTS

Introduction ix

Prologue 1
Chapter 1   "I Have Possession of Sumter" 11
Chapter 2   Dueling Blue Bloods and Whispers of Mutiny—
              1862 37
Chapter 3   A Gathering of Leviathans—1863 61
Chapter 4   Du Pont's Attack—"A Grand and Imposing
              Spectacle" 75
Chapter 5   "He May Knock Fort Sumter to Pieces" 101
Chapter 6   "I Could Scarcely Restrain My Tears" 125
Chapter 7   "Hold the Fort to the Last" 147
Chapter 8   "I Will Assault Sumter Tonight" 169
Chapter 9   "Sumter . . . Laughs at Her Enemy" 195
Chapter 10   "Fort Sumter Can Be Taken at Any Time"—1864 . . . 233
Chapter 11   "They Have Killed Me, Captain . . . " 261
Chapter 12   "God Has Laid Us Very Low"—1865 291
Epilogue   The Postwar Years 317

Glossary 327
Fort Sumter Timeline of Events 329
Notes 333
Bibliography 357
Index 365

"While Greece has her Thermopylae, England her Waterloo, the United States her Yorktown, South Carolina has her Fort Sumter."

—GEN. B. H. RUTLEDGE'S ADDRESS ON THE UNVEILING OF
THE CONFEDERATE MONUMENT IN CHARLESTON,
NOVEMBER 30, 1882

INTRODUCTION

"If everyone took a piece of the fort home with them there wouldn't be much left pretty soon, would there?" The tanned skipper of the Fort Sumter tour boat smiled at me from behind his sunglasses as he gently scolded me for my indiscretion in picking up an unidentifiable piece of rusted metal from inside Sumter's walls. It was 1968, and I was a fifth grader and budding Civil War buff on a field trip to Charleston from my hometown of Bishopville, South Carolina, some two hours inland.

Up to that point it had been a wonderful day, visiting one of America's most beautiful cities, hanging with some high school kids also on the trip, and spending my lawn-mowing money on a souvenir magazine in the fort's gift shop. After all, this was Fort Sumter, where the war began. But the captain's mild reprimand was rattling to an eleven year old, and I dropped my metal treasure before reboarding the tour boat.

I admit that more than four decades later, and with four books on the conflict under my belt, Fort Sumter's defining moment still is the historic April 1861 bombardment that propelled North and South into the jaws of the beast. But there is so much more to Sumter's story. It began on April 14, 1861—the day after the Union garrison surrendered to end the artillery pounding—and is a forgotten but fascinating saga of the struggle that needs to be dusted off.

Fort Sumter would be the site of more battle action than any other place in the Civil War. On no other bloodied ground—not Gettysburg, Antietam, or Shiloh—was the combat as relentless and deadly and daily as the campaign by the Federals to reclaim the fort and the Confederate defenders to hold it.

The great armies immortalized little-known towns or crossroads like Franklin, Fredericksburg, Resaca, Manassas, and Pea Ridge. On the waters, men died in legendary clashes such as the *Monitor* and *Virginia*, the *Kearsarge* versus the *Alabama*, or Admiral Farragut's smashing "damn the torpedoes" thrust into Mobile Bay. Yet nowhere, from Chancellorsville to Vicksburg to Bentonville, did the war's hourglass tremble for days and months on end as it did to the thunder of guns over Charleston Harbor and the brick fort at its mouth. On no other patch of American real estate did the public and the press on both sides focus more, almost daily, attention than the violent drama of Fort Sumter.

To the North it represented a slap in the face by the traitors who had dared rebellion and seized it. This embarrassment could only be soothed by the U.S. flag once again waving over her walls, the rebels put in their place and punished by Union military might. For the South, Sumter was its keystone of defiance against the Union. The beating heart of the rebellion, it had to be held at any cost. Thus the fort quickly became a symbolic icon that blue and gray dearly coveted, their duel for it paid in blood, iron, and reputations. Political and military leaders recognized the vast importance of possessing Sumter, the Confederates' prolonged defense of the fort building and shattering careers of admirals and generals. Retaking Sumter would bring glory beyond wildest dreams to the Union Caesar who achieved it, whoever he might be.

The reality was much different for the South—holding the fort was paramount to Confederate morale, especially in the war's early years, as well as in preventing the Yanks from seizing Charleston, an obviously bigger calamity since the latter was one of the South's major seaports despite the blockade. With so much at stake, human frailties came into play; hot-blooded chivalry, jealousy, raw ambitions, incompetency, and vices shaped Sumter's story as much as endurance, gallantry, and sacrifice.

Writing to a friend on February 5, 1864, Lt. George E. Dixon, commander of the soon-to-be famous Confederate submarine *H.L. Hunley*, noted that nowhere else was the conflict as endless and ongoing as the South Carolina coast. He was concerned that comrades in his old company of the 21st Alabama Infantry might think he was on a cushy assignment and had forgotten them. If there was "any post of honor or fame where there is any danger," Dixon wrote, "I think it must be Charleston, for if you wish to see war every day and night, this is the place to see it." Dixon would be dead less than two weeks later, but no one could dispute his assessment: Much of the action always centered on Fort Sumter.[1]

The United States arrayed the most modern and fearsome weaponry of the age against the fort and its defenders. Monitors were the latest technology for warships, and the rifled guns were the most accurate and powerful artillery mankind had created to that time. Both sides also experimented with submerged mines or "torpedoes"—especially the Confederates. All were forerunners of weapons with much greater killing power in the decades to come.

All that said, the Confederates estimated that Union guns—army and navy—poured some 3,500 tons of metal on Fort Sumter while the Southerners held it. Could the little chunk of iron I found there so many years ago have been a few ounces of anger fired by a Reb or Yank? In the long-ago imagination of a young boy, I will always believe that it was.

This is its story.

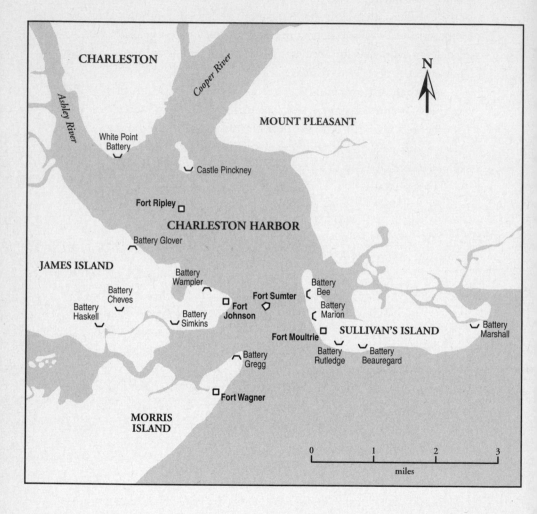

CHARLESTON

Ashley River

Cooper River

MOUNT PLEASANT

N

White Point
Battery

Castle Pinckney

Fort Ripley ▢

CHARLESTON HARBOR

Battery Glover

JAMES ISLAND

Battery
Wampler

Fort Sumter

Battery
Bee

Battery
Cheves

Battery
Haskell

Battery
Simkins

▢ **Fort
Johnson**

Battery
Marion

SULLIVAN'S ISLAND

Battery
Marshall

Fort Moultrie ▢

Battery
Gregg

Battery
Rutledge

Battery
Beauregard

▢ **Fort Wagner**

**MORRIS
ISLAND**

0   1   2   3

miles

PROLOGUE

It was the week of Christmas, and the distant lights of the city twinkled like stars fallen into the harbor's dark water, beckoning with their promise of pretty belles, lively music, and good cheer from many a bottle. To the eighty-four or so U.S. soldiers commanded by Maj. Robert Anderson, however, the holiday spirit in Charleston, South Carolina, was tainted by the viperous rhetoric and shocking action of traitors.

South Carolina had seceded from the Union six days earlier, and on that Wednesday night of December 26, 1860, Anderson's two companies of troops were evacuating Fort Moultrie on Sullivan's Island, silently pushing their small boats off the moon-shadowed beach and into the unknown. Rising in the distance about a mile away was their destination, Fort Sumter, situated in the middle of the harbor mouth, a stately and stoutly built brick outpost still incomplete more than thirty years after construction was begun. It had neither fired nor received a shot in battle, but the coming four and a half years would make this seemingly insignificant structure the most famous fort in American history. These laurels were yet to be earned that chilly night as Anderson's soldiers labored across the channel in three separate crossings, narrowly avoiding detection from the Southerners' patrol vessels.

South Carolina's secession had been a defiant response to the November election of Abraham Lincoln, the first Republican president. Now several other Southern states were poised to follow the Carolinians into disunion, Lincoln's ascendency sparking a fuse of sectional conflict that had been boiling for decades over states' rights, including slavery. If the top had not yet been blown off the teakettle, it soon would be.

A lanky, gaunt Kentuckian—like Lincoln—Anderson was fifty-five but appeared older even by the standards of the day. His father, Richard, had been a Continental army officer in the Revolution, was wounded,

1

Prewar view of Charleston, South Carolina.
HARPER'S ENCYCLOPEDIA OF UNITED STATES HISTORY, VOL. 2

and was captured when the British took Charleston in 1780. Graduating West Point in 1825, his son was no stranger to battle either, an old-school artillerist who had tasted combat in the Black Hawk War, fought the Seminoles in Florida's swamps, and who was twice recognized for gallantry in the conflict with Mexico, where he had been wounded. Anderson also knew the Charleston area well, having served at Moultrie in 1845–46. With secession fever seething, his assignment to this rebellion hotbed was a calculated move to possibly soothe tensions, since Anderson had proslavery views and his wife, Eliza, was from Georgia. Anderson initially established his headquarters at Moultrie, but soon realized his position there was untenable if the Southerners decided to attack. As December faded, he learned that the Carolinians were possibly planning to occupy Sumter. He decided that he had to act and, despite no direct orders to do so, he moved his troops to Sumter, spiking cannon and burning gun carriages left behind at Moultrie.[1] Named for South Carolina's Revolutionary War hero Thomas "The Gamecock" Sumter, the five-sided brick fort was one of a series of coastal installations that had been slated for construction by the U.S. government after the War of 1812. Work on the fort began in 1829 but was inconsistent and slow.

Built on a shoal on an artificial rock foundation composed of tons of New England granite, it took engineers and laborers some ten years to raise the foundation above water. The walls rose fifty feet and were made of Carolina gray brick varying in thickness from five to ten feet. The bricks were laid with mortar, cement, and a concrete mixture of oyster shells and cement. A sally port on the gorge opened onto a stone quay, or wharf, and pier. At the water's edge on the fort's other faces, the rock foundation sloped gently to the base of the walls.[2]

Anderson's bold move to Sumter further inflamed the Southerners but was generally praised in the North. "Charleston was . . . thrown into a state of the wildest excitement" the *Charleston Mercury* noted, adding that people "immediately sought the steeples and cupolas of the public buildings, and telescopes were brought into active requisition, to gratify the general curiosity." As his troops settled in behind its walls, both sides began girding for possible hostilities, Anderson knowing that he could only hold out for so long without reinforcements and supplies.

Oddly enough, his decision to occupy Sumter initially was a preventative measure to possibly *avoid* conflict. Anderson realized that if he was assailed and trapped at Moultrie he would have to fight back, and war would likely be inevitable. By abandoning Moultrie and going to Sumter, which was surrounded by water, he knew that his troops would be more secure and that the Carolinians might think twice before attacking such a formidable fortress. It was a gamble, and its success was totally dependent on the government sending him more men and rations. Grimly, the Federals noted that Sumter contained sixty-six cannon, but only fifteen were mounted and ready for combat should they be needed.

Within days the Federals also noticed construction beginning on batteries on Morris and Sullivan's Islands. Yet other than hot rhetoric and electric excitement, there was no real action until January 9, 1861, when the steamer *Star of the West* was fired on by the Carolinians while trying to reach Sumter. The vessel had come from New York with supplies and about 200 troops for Anderson's garrison but was driven off by the brief cannonade.

That day and those thereafter brought a flurry of nation-rattling decisions the likes of which had not been experienced since the American colonies broke ties with the British Empire. Mississippi seceded on the ninth, Florida following on the tenth. Alabama joined them the next day

Fort Sumter in tranquil glory before the war.

and Georgia on the nineteenth. Louisiana came aboard on the twenty-sixth and Texas on February 1. In Montgomery, Alabama, representatives from these rogue states (other than Texas, whose delegates were late) provisionally established the Confederate States of America on February 4, and a few days later elected Jefferson Davis president of the new republic; Montgomery was its first capital.[3]

These were volatile and uncertain times. Days before the *Star of the West* had been fired on, the *Columbia*, another steamship bound for Charleston from New York, anchored outside the harbor and in full sight of Fort Sumter on January 19 without molestation from the Southern guns, which were daily becoming more numerous in menacing Anderson's garrison. However, unlike the *Star of the West*, the *Columbia* was not a military threat and had a number of Southern passengers aboard, as well as a correspondent for the Boston-based *Atlantic Monthly*, a popular national magazine.

After noon that day, the tide was favorable for the *Columbia* to enter the harbor and proceed to the city. To the south was the lean and low form of Morris Island and its fine lighthouse. To the north of the harbor mouth was Sullivan's Island with its higher sand dunes, a scattering of beach cottages, and the barely visible walls and cannon of Fort Moultrie, where a weathered palmetto flag wafted in the lazy breeze.

"And here in the midst of all things, apparent master of all things, at the entrance to the harbor proper . . . frowned Fort Sumter," the *Atlantic* reporter wrote. It was, he said, "a huge and lofty and solid mass of brick-work and stone embrasures, all rising from a foundation of ragged granite boulders washed by the tides. The port-holes were closed; a dozen or so of monstrous cannon peeped from the summit; two or three sentinels paced slowly along the parapet; the stars and stripes blew out from the lofty flag-staff. . . . Its whole air is massive, commanding and formidable."[4]

Behind the big walls, Anderson and his troops had to feel profoundly alone, especially after their wives and children departed by a northbound ship on February 3. The men were discouraged by the *Star of the West* fiasco and unsure of ever again seeing their loved ones as a hostile world seemingly closed in around them. On March 1, three days before Lincoln's inauguration, an officer with whom Anderson was quite familiar arrived in Charleston, but his mission was not remotely to aid the Union soldiers at Sumter. Confederate brigadier general P. G. T. Beauregard had been sent from Montgomery by Jefferson Davis to take charge of the South Carolina troops in and around Charleston.[5]

Peering through a glass across the water at Fort Sumter some three miles away, the forty-two-year-old Beauregard must have recalled the days when Anderson had been his artillery instructor at West Point. And for a brief time after his graduation, the Louisianan had been Anderson's assistant at the academy. To now turn some of this training—as well as his guns—against his old friend and teacher was difficult, as was the possibility of having to fire on the flag under which he had served and spilt blood. But Beauregard had sided with the Confederacy and was a disciplined officer whose instructions were clear: If the Northerners refused to evacuate Sumter, he was to take it.[6]

With nerves tightening, Lincoln was inaugurated in Washington on March 4 and did not mince words about the threat of conflict: "In your hands, my dissatisfied countrymen, and not in mine, is the momentous issue of civil war. . . . You can have no conflict without being yourselves the aggressors." But his speech also appealed to the Southerners as fellow Americans with a shared history. "We are not enemies but friends," he said. "Though passion may have strained, it must not break our bonds of affection. The mystic chords of memory, stretching from every battlefield and patriot grave to every living heart and hearthstone all over this broad land, will yet swell the chorus of the Union when again touched, as surely they will be, by the better angels of our nature."

The day after the inauguration, Lincoln learned that Anderson likely had only enough supplies to last about six weeks. The next three weeks would be a torturous journey for the new president as the rival states seemingly spiraled toward war. Through all of this unrelenting pressure, the new president pondered a course; sleepless nights, severe headaches, and at least one fainting spell punctuated the awful burden of leadership.[7]

In early April, Lincoln decided to send a naval relief expedition to Sumter. The vessels would include the steam transport *Baltic* with rations and other supplies for the garrison. It would be escorted by warships with troops aboard, but these would not be authorized to go into action unless the Confederates tried to stop the lightly armed *Baltic*. The mission would be commanded by navy captain Gustavus V. Fox. On April 6, Lincoln notified South Carolina governor Francis W. Pickens about the relief effort, stating that it was to "supply Fort Sumter with provisions only, and that if such attempt be not resisted, no effort to throw in men, arms, or ammunition will be made," unless there was "an attack on the fort." In Montgomery, the Confederate authorities debated this development and came to their own momentous decision: Beauregard was to force Sumter's surrender, with authority to open fire, before the relief vessels arrived. Beauregard also was told that under "no circumstances are you to allow provisions to be sent to Fort Sumter."[8]

Beauregard sent an April 11 dispatch to Anderson demanding the fort's surrender, but Anderson refused, replying that he would be starved out in a few days anyway. More correspondence and negotiations came to nothing, and the Southerners' patience had finally worn down, especially with the relief ships likely nearing Charleston. About 3:20 AM on Friday, April 12, Anderson was notified that the bombardment would commence in one hour. At 4:30 AM Capt. George S. James, commanding a mortar battery at Fort Johnson on James Island, ordered a signal gun fired—the first shot of the war—and by sunrise, batteries at Johnson, Cummings Point, and Fort Moultrie were blasting Fort Sumter, which did not immediately retaliate. "I do not pretend to go to sleep," Mary Chesnut wrote in her now-famous diary of that momentous night in Charleston. "How can

I? . . . At half-past four, the heavy booming of a cannon. I sprang out of bed. And on my knees—prostrate—I prayed as I never prayed before."[9]

Captain Fox and the *Baltic*, meanwhile, had reached the waters off Charleston about the time Anderson was told of the impending attack. The relief vessels had become separated in the voyage south, and Fox found only the armed cutter *Harriet Lane* present when the *Baltic* arrived. The little force was soon joined by the sloop of war *Pawnee*, but Fox awaited—and needed—the frigate *Powhatan* and her sixteen guns, as well as the sloop of war *Pocahontas*, if he was to make a dash into the harbor. Three tugs to be used in ferrying provisions to Sumter also had yet to appear. In the absence of these warships and the tugs, Fox and the Union officers and men on the assembled three vessels had to wait and watch the pyrotechnics as projectiles slashed the lightening, but cloudy sky.[10]

By 5:00 AM, Sumter was receiving fire from all of the forty-three guns pointed at it. Anderson, however, held his fire until 7:00 AM, about the time the *Pawnee* arrived. Capt. Abner Doubleday, the garrison's second-in-command, aimed Sumter's first shot at the Confederates' "Iron Battery" near Cummings Point. The Union gunners had only 700 rounds of ammunition, and their rapid rate of fire that morning prompted Anderson by noon to use only six guns, to save his rounds.

The Confederates used "hot shot," or super-heated projectiles, and succeeded in setting the fort's barracks afire three times during the day. Each time the Federals were able to quell the blaze. Throughout the day, the Northerners cast hopeful glances at the three U.S. ships anchored off the bar, expecting action from them at some point. Anderson tried signaling them, but Fox's vessels remained idle, still awaiting the arrival of the other ships.

The bombardment and Sumter's answers tapered off about 7:00 PM and a heavy rain set in, as if the man-made lightning had ruptured the heavens. Confederate mortars kept up their shelling overnight, firing at fifteen-minute intervals. Despite rough seas, rain, and wind, the defenders anticipated small boats from the Union ships attempting to bring in food and other supplies. When this didn't happen, some of the soldiers' exhaustion and frustration boiled over in the form of curses hurled at the sailors.[11]

Sumter had sustained significant damage but, surprisingly, no serious casualties—five men had been slightly injured. Many guns were disabled

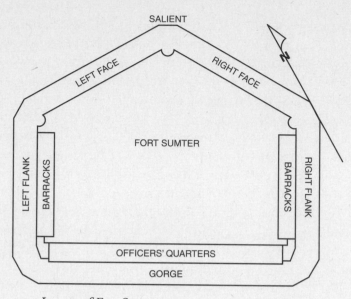

Layout of Fort Sumter. FORT SUMTER NATIONAL MONUMENT

and the barracks partially burned. The south and southwest walls had been punished by the Morris Island batteries as had the front facing Sullivan's Island, and the mortars' arcing rounds had torn up the fort's interior.

Saturday, April 13, dawned sunny and clear, revealing Sumter's battle scars, and the artillery duel was resumed. Confederate cannoneers on Sullivan's Island again used hot shot, which produced dramatic results shortly after 8:00 AM when thick smoke and tongues of flame could be seen lofting from the officers' quarters. The Southerners raised a shout of triumph as they watched the smoke swath the fort, and increased the intensity of their shelling, knowing the garrison was in trouble. The blaze spread from the barracks to the hospital and then threatened the magazine and its 300 barrels of gunpowder. Desperately, the defenders hauled dozens of barrels out of the magazine and into a casemate where they were covered in wet blankets; some barrels were thrown into the harbor. Still the flames licked higher, the dirty fog thickening, but Sumter was still firing, although only about one round every ten minutes due to the loss of powder. By 11:00 AM, some of the men sprawled on the parade ground, clutching handkerchiefs to their faces, while others crowded into casemates, all gasping for air. Watching smoke shroud Sumter, some Charlestonians believed the men must surely be suffocated, and some of the Southern troops, realizing what the garrison must be enduring, cheered every shot launched by Anderson's gunners. The fort's flagstaff and huge garrison flag were shot down about 1:00 PM, but the standard was hoisted again shortly afterward on an improvised staff, the defenders cheering its rise. Their enthusiasm was short-lived, however, as the danger of the magazine exploding, smothering smoke, and hellish heat inside the walls prompted Anderson to raise a white flag at about 2:00 PM. The fort had been under almost continuous bombardment for nearly thirty-four hours and had been hit by some 1,800 projectiles, Doubleday estimated.[12] Incredibly, there were still no deaths and only a few minor injuries on either side.

Gustavus Fox and his trio of vessels continued to watch history being made from their anchorage outside the bar. All through Saturday, Fox remained idle still awaiting the arrival of the other ships. The *Pocahontas* finally reached Fox that Saturday afternoon, and its skipper brought more disappointing news. Due to confused orders, the *Powhatan* had been sent with a force to relieve Fort Pickens in Florida. A recipe of bad weather, miscommunication, and a lack of coordination had doomed the Union naval effort to relieve Sumter. An officer on the *Pawnee* noted that "we witnessed the sad spectacle of the fall of our flag, which we were so impotent to assist. In vain we looked for its reappearance over the fort."

Arrangements for the fort's surrender—or "evacuation" as Anderson termed it—took up much of the rest of the day. Beauregard would allow Anderson and his troops to offer a one hundred-gun salute to the U.S. flag before they left the fort on Sunday. The Southerners would then provide the steamer *Isabel* to take Anderson and his soldiers out to Fox's ships, and the Federals would board the *Baltic* for the voyage north.[13]

CHAPTER 1

"I Have Possession of Sumter"

Sunday, April 14, 1861

A Northern visitor to Charleston in late January 1861 was watching a drill of home guards—or reservists—practicing basic cavalry maneuvers. A local "malicious citizen," as the Yankee described him, joked that the horsemen, some with silver hair and whiskers, were "in training to take Fort Sumter by charging upon it at low water." In reality, the work was done by the big guns and hot shot.[1]

The city itself had been awash with exultation since Anderson raised the white flag—church bells gonging, excited mobs cavorting in the streets, and Beauregard the toast of every bar and parlor. Despite the revelry it seemed like everyone was up early on Sunday, all who could crowding aboard anything that wouldn't sink to get closer to the hazy pancake of a fort at the harbor's throat. "The bay was alive with floating craft of every description, filled with people from all parts of the South, in their holiday attire," wrote Doubleday. The weary Union garrison also rose early, the men packing their baggage and preparing to board the *Isabel*.[2]

Indeed, Sumter remained a dangerous place that Sunday, with flames still smoldering out of control. The fort's upper works had been heavily damaged, the officers' quarters and the roofs of the two enlisted men's barracks destroyed in the bombardment and resulting fires. While it was a beautiful, sunny spring day, smoke hovered over the debris-cluttered

11

parade ground, sparks and glowing embers fluttering through the air. In the bombardment's aftermath, there still was the immediate threat of the fort's magazines exploding. A number of Charleston firemen and some fire engines had been ferried out to the fort after the surrender and managed to control many of the hot spots, although they had not been totally suppressed. Ignoring the hazards, a cluster of newspapermen, politicians, and others had been admitted to the fort to see the damage and talk to Anderson, who received them amiably. The Carolinians sent in bags of mail for the Federals that had been withheld for weeks. A supply of brandy was also sent in, much to the pleasure of the Union officers. At some point, Anderson showed the Southerners the location of mines that had been placed for the fort's defense. He also gave Sumter's keys to Capt. Samuel Ferguson, one of Beauregard's aides.[3]

The garrison was supposed to depart the fort at 11:00 AM, but the ceremony was delayed and the first gun did not bark the initial salute until almost 2:00 PM. As the cannons were readied on the barbette, or top tier of the fort, Doubleday was uneasy; with the ashes and cinders flying about, this was no place to be handling powder and ammunition. Sure enough, on the seventeenth salute, a gun fired prematurely—possibly due to a spark that settled in the muzzle—causing momentary chaos. One soldier, Pvt. Daniel Hough, of Company E, 1st U.S. Artillery, had his right arm blown off. Within seconds, fire from the discharge flickered into a pile of cartridges nearby, igniting them. The blast hurled five Union men into the air, injuring all of them. Hough died instantly, the first fatality of the hours-old conflict. The wounded were placed on mattresses and carried to safety, where they were treated by Anderson's surgeon, Dr. Samuel W. Crawford, as well as several physicians among the Carolinians.[4]

Despite the tragedy, the ceremony was resumed, although shortened to a fifty-gun salute. Thus it was not until about 4:00 PM that Anderson, the garrison flag tucked under his arm, led his somber troops out of the fort, their band playing "Yankee Doodle" and "Hail to the Chief." Three of the five soldiers wounded in the cannon mishap were able to leave with their comrades. The other two, Pvts. Edward Galway and George Fielding, also of Company E, 1st Artillery, were too badly hurt and were soon taken to a Charleston hospital. Ironically, Galway had been one of the few soldiers slightly wounded in the bombardment.

As the bluecoats marched down the wharf and settled into the *Isabel*, the first Confederate troops to formally occupy Sumter filed through the sally port. This honor was given to Company B of the 1st South Carolina Artillery Battalion, led by Capt. James H. Hallonquist, and the Palmetto Guard, a volunteer company under Capt. George B. Cuthbert. Hallonquist's superior, Ohio-born Lt. Col. Roswell S. Ripley of the 1st South Carolina Artillery, would be Sumter's first Confederate commander.[5] Among Hallonquist's forty soldiers were Lt. John C. Mitchel and his men, who had likely done more than any others in the bombardment to cause Anderson's surrender, firing the hot shot from Moultrie that set the garrison's quarters ablaze. Mitchel would play a major role in the rest of Sumter's story.

Bearing the ensign of Cuthbert's troops was Edmund Ruffin, the secessionist fireball from Virginia who was instantly recognizable due to his lion-like white mane. Ruffin had been made an honorary private with the Palmetto Guard—which had manned guns at Cummings Point on Morris Island—and had jerked a lanyard to send a Columbiad shell at Sumter in the war's opening moments. In the latter stages of the shelling, with smoke wafting skyward from the blazing barracks, Cuthbert's boys cheered every shot fired from Sumter toward Fort Moultrie—a tribute to the bravery of Anderson and his garrison—even as they continued to slam the fort with their own cannon.

The selection of the Palmetto Guard was not cut-and-dried. The Morris Island commander suggested that Cuthbert's company and the other volunteer units there draw for the honor within hours of Anderson's capitulation. Cuthbert decided not to participate in this, and the officers of the other units declined as well, following his example. The commander then selected "the Palmettos," as a news account called them, for the honor.

The Palmettos were obviously quite honored to occupy Sumter that first night, Cuthbert describing it as the "highest compliment ever bestowed upon any volunteer corps in the history of our State" and an event that would "always be held by them in grateful remembrance." The *Mercury* stated that while it would have been a historic compliment to any troops allowed to be the first Confederates to occupy Sumter, there was no question that the companies of Hallonquist and Cuthbert deserved the honor. "In respect to what company has a claim to most distinction for services rendered," the paper said, "there is no possible doubt in the world that there can be but two claimants [*sic*]. . . . The service . . . by these two companies was marked and conspicuous beyond all comparison." The Palmettos drew rations for three days for their assignment at Sumter.[6]

As the Confederate celebration began, Anderson and his men were no closer to home than near the end of Sumter's wharf. The various delays—including the loading of the troops, which wasn't completed until sundown, and Dr. Crawford's caring for the wounded—meant that the *Isabel* had missed the tide to cross the bar. Thus, the Federals had to sit on the ship and endure the hoopla over their downfall. Despite the no-choice presence of the ousted garrison, the Carolinians continued with their victory ceremony. The Confederate and Palmetto flags were hoisted simultaneously; Beauregard's aide, Captain Ferguson, raised the seven-starred Confederate national banner while Lt. Col. F. J. Moses Jr. and members of the Palmetto Guard hoisted their flag with its red star and large black palmetto tree against a white background, representing the state. The sight of the new flags over Sumter prompted yells and cheers, the shrill of boat whistles and artillery blasts booming across the harbor. There were "tremendous shouts of applause . . . from the vast multitude of spectators," Doubleday recalled, "and all the vessels and steamers, with one accord, made for the fort."

Through all of this, Beauregard had been conspicuously absent, not wanting to possibly embarrass Anderson, his old friend. Cuthbert's men joined in the pageantry, but soon had more pressing business to take care of than basking in their glory. The fires in the fort lingered, and after they were dismissed they joined the city firemen in battling the flames. "I wish to take no laurels from the . . . members of the fire-engine companies . . . but truth requires that I should state that, from the moment of their being disbanded within the walls of the fort, the Palmetto Guard worked incessantly at the engines until after midnight," Cuthbert reported. "The fire had been more destructive . . . than the shot and shells," Ruffin recorded. "And the fire was still going on, finding fuel in the timbers covered by fallen brick and smaller rubbish."[7]

Aboard the Union relief vessels, the sight of the Stars and Stripes being lowered and replaced by the "so called Confederate flag" as one U.S. officer put it, was a depressing and frustrating scene. Yet amid the artillery salutes honoring Sumter's fall, lookouts on the USS *Pawnee* had

*Confederate general
P. G. T. Beauregard.*
AUTHOR'S COLLECTION

been savvy enough to take the bearings of various batteries on Morris and Sullivan's Islands for future reference. The body of the unfortunate Private Hough, meanwhile, was buried in the parade ground with military honors by the Confederates shortly after the accident. He had been the "first victim of the sad explosion which took place while Major Anderson was engaged in saluting his flag," Cuthbert noted.[8]

"I have possession of Sumter," Beauregard wrote to Confederate secretary of war Leroy P. Walker on the night of the fourteenth. "Quarters in ruins. Interior of fort damaged. Armament still effective against entrance to channel." Anderson and his soldiers, meanwhile, spent a cheerless night aboard the *Isabel*, waiting for the incoming tide so they could finally depart this long nightmare. Early on the morning of Monday, April 15, the ship eased away from Sumter, some of the Federals seeing the fort for the last time as it shrank in the distance. Among those who would eventually return was Capt. John G. Foster of the U.S. Engineers. He would be a prominent player in the coming drama to be played out around Charleston over the next four years.

As the *Isabel* passed the northern end of Morris Island, some Rebel soldiers lined the beach in silence, their heads uncovered, honoring Anderson and his men. The chivalry certainly did not extend to the crews and troops on Fox's vessels anchored outside the harbor. Beauregard noted that "expressions of scorn at the apparent cowardice of the fleet in not attempting to rescue so gallant an officer and his command were upon the lips of all." The Southern papers also were scathing in their condemnation of the inaction of the little fleet. "It was fully expected . . . that these mighty men of war off our bar (all manned at the North, and by Northern men), would have made at least some effort to have relieved their distressed comrades in Fort Sumter," the *Mercury* railed. Fox's vessels had not ventured in even as Sumter fought courageously, "commanding the admiration even of her enemies. . . . There still immovable, without one single effort to relieve him [Anderson], stood this Northern fleet, until actually all round in the ranks men began, from the very bitterness of scorn, to mingle expressions of sympathy for the beleaguered fortress, with imprecations of contempt upon the dastard[ly] conduct of their Northern friends." Adding to the aggravation of the Union tars, the *Pawnee* and *Baltic* had collided on Sunday night, both damaged but still seaworthy.[9]

About noon, the *Isabel* reached the *Baltic* and the Federals began to board the Union ship; the steamer *Clinch* followed with the garrison's baggage. The transfer was completed by 4:00 PM; Anderson's men were "received with great sympathy and feeling" by the navy and army personnel on the transport, Doubleday recorded. In short order, Anderson allowed his garrison flag—its thirty-three stars even then representing in part the states in rebellion—to be raised over the vessel and "as it blew out from the main truck of the *Baltic* it was saluted by the United States steamers and greeted by three times three cheers from the crews of the vessels," related an officer on the *Pawnee*. This timeless moment on the waters off Charleston was a tough, defiant response to a tough, defiant act—the latter a shockingly treasonous one, any true Union man would tell you. As the *Baltic* and the rest of the little fleet lifted anchor and veered north late that afternoon, both of the newly chosen sides knew that Fort Sumter had become a symbol that each desperately wanted to claim.[10]

In Sumter, the first night of its occupation by the Southerners had been an anxious one as fires still crackled in the barracks ruins and the threat of a magazine detonating still very much existed. Charleston firefighters, assisted by some of the soldiers, struggled "with great exertions" throughout much of Monday before the blazes were extinguished.

Beauregard noted on the seventeenth that the "gallant fire companies" were "at their pumps night and day, although aware that close by them was a magazine filled with thirty thousand pounds of powder, with a shot-hole through the wall of its anteroom." The *Mercury* reported on the sixteenth that Sumter "was entirely free from danger. The firemen deserve great credit for their faithful and timely service." The Confederates also had a chance to inspect the result of their artillery's handiwork against the fort. "The walls outside were thickly sprinkled with marks of cannon balls, which had not penetrated more than from six to eighteen inches, and had nowhere made a breach," Ruffin noted.

Charleston itself remained kindled with nervous exhilaration on Monday, much of it fed by speculation about the intent of the Union ships perched on the horizon. "The people are in a state of great excitement, but more with reference to the movements of the fleet than from invasion," a *New York Herald* reporter wrote from the city that day. "In fact, they rather court such an emergency. The general sentiment is fight."[11]

There was a changing of the guard at Sumter that Monday as the Palmetto Guard contingent was relieved by another company of the 1st South Carolina Artillery Battalion, seventy-five soldiers led by Lt. Alfred Moore Rhett. Before departing, three of Cuthbert's men placed a "neat and appropriate head-piece" at Private Hough's grave. "The performance of this sacred duty did credit to their generous hearts, and proved that Carolina chivalry exists only in combination with a spirit of reverence and magnanimity," Cuthbert said of his Palmettos. When Hallonquist received orders a day or so later to report to Brig. Gen. Braxton Bragg with the Rebel forces at Pensacola, Florida, Rhett became the fort's second-in-command under Ripley.

While his comrades waited to leave the harbor, Private Galway had died Sunday night, shortly after reaching a Charleston hospital. Private Fielding, however, survived despite serious facial wounds, recovering enough to be sent home by the Confederates in late May with a pass from Beauregard. Amid his duties on the seventeenth, Beauregard sent a letter of commendation to Charleston fire chief M. H. Nathan and Lt. Col. R. S. Duryea, an aide to Governor Pickens, who had been instrumental in controlling Sumter's fires. The general thanked Duryea, Nathan, and the men they directed for their "energy, coolness and gallantry . . . While directing the engines playing on the smouldering ruins surrounding the magazine . . . , you exposed yourselves in the most daring manner, as an explosion of the well-filled magazine might, at any moment, have occurred, destroying the lives of everyone in the vicinity."[12]

In the city itself that day, William Howard Russell, a British correspondent for *The Times* of London, marveled at the surreal atmosphere unleashed by Sumter's fall. "The streets of Charleston present some such aspect as those of Paris in the last revolution," he wrote. "Crowds of armed men singing and promenading. . . . The battle blood running through their veins—that hot oxygen which is called 'the flush of victory' on the cheek; restaurants full, revelling in bar rooms, club-rooms crowded, orgies and carousings in tavern or private house. . . . Sumter has set them distraught; never was such a victory; never such brave lads; never such a fight. There are pamphlets already full of the incident. It is a bloodless Waterloo." Some 760 miles to the north, the scene would be amazingly similar the next day. When the *Baltic* reached New York City on a sunny and breezy April 18, Anderson and his men were roundly welcomed as triumphant warriors despite their defeat. "The shipping dipped their flags as the *Baltic* came up the bay, and every possible demonstration of enthusiasm greeted the returning heroes of Fort Sumter," said the April 19 *New York Times*. Guns in the harbor forts blasted salutes and clanging bells accented the cheering of growing throngs as the ship neared the docks. From the *Baltic*'s foremast fluttered the tattered U.S. flag that had flown over Forts Moultrie and Sumter, the *New York Herald* noted. From the mizzenmast flew the ragged banner Anderson had lowered at the surrender, a piece of the flagstaff still attached.

The excitement of the crowds that had gathered on the wharves, ferries, and other vessels intensified when word spread that the major himself was aboard, his men drawn up in ranks on the quarterdeck. Anderson stood on the wheelhouse, "dressed in uniform, wrapped in his military overcoat, and looking careworn and fatigued," but returning the salutations of the people, the *Herald* said. There was a massive rally for the Sumter soldiers in Union Square three days later. Portraits of Anderson soon adorned store windows while medals with his likeness were struck across the North. On May 15, Lincoln appointed Anderson a brigadier general in the Regular Army, exemplifying the high regard with which he was held in the Union.[13]

Across the South, Anderson's former colleague Beauregard was the man of the hour, the Confederacy's first war hero. The Rebel Ulysses was showered with praise by Jefferson Davis and other government officials, star-struck belles sending adoring letters to him scented with flirty remarks and requests for buttons from his tunic. The Confederate Congress issued a resolution on May 4 thanking the Louisianan and the Charleston troops for their gallantry and accomplishments in overwhelming Sumter. Beauregard basked in his achievements and the resulting adulation that were certainly the zenith of his more than two decades as a soldier to that point. Fluent in French due to his Creole upbringing and heritage, he was a handsome and exotic addition to Charleston society, cutting a dashing figure in his tailored gray uniforms. Graduating second in the West Point class of 1838, he had served as a lieutenant of engineers on the staff of Maj. Gen. Winfield Scott in the Mexican War, twice brevetted for gallantry. He was appointed superintendent of the Military Academy in January 1861 but relieved five days later, apparently due to his Southern sympathies. A few weeks later, he resigned his army commission and by March 1 had been appointed a brigadier general in the provisional Confederate army.

William Russell heard myriad snippets of conversations about Beauregard as he experienced Charleston three days after Sumter's surrender. "Our little Creole friend, by the bye, is popular beyond description," he penned. "There are all kinds of doggerel rhymes in his honour—one with a refrain—'With cannon and musket, with shell and petard [a small bomb], We salute the North with our Beau-regard'—is much in favour."[14]

Almost immediately after the fires in the fort were quelled, the Confederates, under the overall direction of Beauregard and Ripley, began to repair Sumter's battle damage. "I am now removing the tottering walls of the buildings within and clearing away all the rubbish . . . from the interior of the work, so as to render it still more formidable than it was before it was attacked," Beauregard wrote on April 17 to Secretary of War Walker. He promised to send Walker several photographs within the next day or so "taken at different points . . . , from which you can clearly understand the condition of the fort within when first occupied by us." Alfred Roman, an officer on Beauregard's staff, wrote: "And now began in earnest, without the loss of a day, the repairs, which amounted almost to the rebuilding of Fort Sumter."

Russell, meanwhile, had boarded a steamer, along with other correspondents, officers, and troops, for an April 17 trip to see the Rebel positions in and around the harbor. After a stop on Morris Island, Russell and
some of the others headed toward Fort Sumter, seeing the Confederate
flag waving over its shell-pocked walls as they approached. Inside, he saw
parties of soldiers clearing away debris. "Never did men plunge into
unknown depth of peril and trouble more recklessly than these Carolinians," the Brit noted, comparing the American conflict with the English
Civil War. "They fling themselves against the grim, black future, as the
cavaliers under Rupert may have rushed against the grim, black Ironsides." Russell also visited with some of Sumter's officers, sharing whiskey,
crackers, "many pleasant stories and boundless welcome." One young
officer complained about lack of pay, telling Russell, "I have not received
a cent since I came to Charleston for this business."[15]

Within a week of Anderson's departure, Charleston's military land-
scape already was beginning to be reshaped, and not only at Sumter. Big
guns that had ringed the harbor, their maws aimed at the fort, were now
being moved, incorporated in defensive works better designed to protect
the city and its environs from the naval and coastal assaults everyone
expected.

Sumter, already the diamond of the Confederacy, would be the hub
of the defenses, but this jewel needed some spit and polish to restore its
luster in late spring 1861. "Several companies are engaged in repairing the
damage done at . . . Sumter, the interior of which is about as ugly a standing ruin as can be well conceived," a *New York Times* reporter wrote on
April 21. "In a military point of view, the injury can hardly be said to have
impaired its defensive strength. Not a casemate has been laid open, and a
sufficient force, provided with mortars and the other necessities of . . .
resistance, would . . . give a very different account of themselves from the
brave but hopeless and ineffectual performance of Major Anderson."
Shattered carriages and chassis were replaced; the barracks were rebuilt, to
a height of one story instead of two as they had been; and the walls were
patched up. "With zeal and energy this work was done; and in less than
three weeks no vestige of the former injuries remained," Roman related.[16]

While Sumter had been restored to her pre-bombardment majesty,
there still was much backbreaking work to be done over many months to
come. The Southerners wanted to complete the fort based on the original

plans from decades earlier. They also focused on making defensive improvements to survive the firestorm that would eventually break when the United States military returned to try to reclaim this already historic piece of real estate. No one in jubilant Charleston knew when this would be, but everyone knew the clock was ticking.

On April 19, five days after Sumter's fall, President Lincoln issued a proclamation stating that a blockade of Southern ports was in effect. But this was more rhetoric than a real threat since the U.S. Navy was ill-prepared to institute such an action. At the time, the navy had some ninety vessels, only forty-two of which were commissioned—and most of these ships were scattered on assignments around the world. It would take time not only for the Union to recall existing warships for the blockade but also to build a fleet strong enough to enforce it. The area of coverage was expansive and daunting as well, with the southern coastline from the Chesapeake Bay to Key West, Florida, extending almost 900 miles, not including the Gulf of Mexico shore from western Florida to Texas. Additionally, the enemy shore presented its own challenges; the coasts of Florida and the Carolinas were checkered with sea islands, inland creeks, bays, and sounds. These waterways created an inland network, allowing shallow-draft vessels to sail north and south without entering the Atlantic.

Nevertheless, the frigate *Niagara*, the first blockader, appeared off Charleston on May 11, but one vessel was mostly useless in securing the city's four ship channels. Blockade runners entered and left Charleston with little interference during this period, bringing in military stores and other goods and leaving with holds full of cotton. Even when more U.S. ships joined the *Niagara* in the coming weeks, the blockade remained ineffective. In the first six weeks after Sumter's surrender, more than 30,000 bales of cotton were shipped out of Charleston. Between June and December 1861, more than 150 vessels arrived in the city using interior waterways rather than Charleston's main ship channel. Still, as the weeks and months passed, groceries and personal items became scarcer and more expensive on store shelves.[17]

By mid-June, there were four U.S. ships blockading Charleston, hardly enough to make any difference. In addition to the lack of ships, the navy's biggest problem in the blockade's early months was in fueling its few vessels. The ships frequently had to leave their stations to replenish their coal supplies or for repairs. The navy soon realized that if it was to sustain the blockade on the south Atlantic coast, it would need to establish a base in hostile territory, close to the action.

Despite these developments, Charlestonians in early May were excited about the release of "fine stereoscopic views" of Sumter taken in mid- to late April by a "photographist" from the firm of Osborn & Durbec. The company had obtained "special permission" to visit the fort, as well as Moultrie and sites on Morris and Sullivan's Islands. Now their work was on display and for sale under the sign of the big camera at their "Photographic & Stereographic Rooms," located at 223 King Street. The photographists also offered views of the city and various plantations.[18]

The Palmetto Guard, meanwhile, one of the first two companies to occupy Sumter after its surrender, was preparing to leave Charleston and join Confederate forces marshaling in Virginia. There was an elaborate and solemn flag ceremony on Monday, May 6, at Institute Hall as the city's ladies presented the Palmettos with a magnificent new banner they had embroidered. The banner's field was of "rich blue silk, heavily fringed with gold, and adorned with gold cord and tassels," one account stated. On one side were a palmetto tree and the company's motto in scrollwork, as well as the date of its Sumter victory. The reverse featured an elaborate wreath of oak and laurel leaves, enclosing the date of the Palmettos' founding—June 28, 1851. Captain Cuthbert accepted the banner as a band played "La Marseillaise," everyone in attendance cheering and applauding. It had been a busy few days for these soldiers. The previous Thursday, they had been fêted with another ceremony in which the company was presented with a large gold medal at Institute Hall, with Beauregard and Governor Pickens attending. The flowery speeches, toasts, and fawning by the fancy belles was about to end, however. On the night of May 9, Cuthbert led the Palmettos through Charleston's streets toward the depot of the Northeastern Railroad. The column was accompanied by hundreds of people, including many adoring ladies, and martial tunes filled the air as the young men boarded the cars and said their goodbyes. Soon the train lurched away, melting into the dark, and the merry sendoff was over.[19]

Among the other troops who left Charleston to head north during this period was Capt. William Ransom Calhoun and a company from Ripley's 1st South Carolina Artillery Battalion. Calhoun—a distant relative of the late U.S. vice president John C. Calhoun, one of the South's leading statesmen—had served well at Fort Moultrie during the bombardment. But the volcano of war was only beginning to erupt, and in the weeks after Sumter's fall, the thirty-four-year-old Calhoun received orders to outfit the battalion's Company A as a light battery. In early July, Calhoun and his troops were ordered to reinforce the Sumter garrison, but almost simultaneously received instructions via the War Department to join Confederate forces near Richmond. Now he and these men also were on their way to Virginia, where Calhoun would spend the rest of 1861. His eventual return to Charleston and the ensuing lethal controversy would shake the old city—as well as Fort Sumter—to its stately foundations.[20]

Beauregard himself was ordered to Richmond, the Confederacy's new capital, in late May and by June 2 had been placed in command of Southern forces arrayed around the vital railroad junction at Manassas, Virginia, where a Union attack was expected. Well before the emergence of Robert E. Lee, "Stonewall" Jackson, Pat Cleburne, or J. E. B. Stuart, the handsome general with the flamboyantly foreign flair was the South's Napoleon. His conquest of Sumter and the resulting popularity had earned him this new, tip-of-the-sword post which, many Southerners believed, might be the first and last battle of the conflict. Col. Richard H. Anderson, a veteran officer of the 1st South Carolina Regular Infantry—and no relation to Robert Anderson—assumed command of Confederate provisional forces in Charleston and its vicinity.

The departure of Beauregard, the Palmettos, and other units did not diminish Charleston's war preparations—or its social scene. Emma Edwards Holmes, a twenty-two-year-old belle with deep Carolina ancestry, and several other civilians were treated to a tour of Fort Sumter on June 25. Miss Holmes's first impression was that big chunks of masonry had been knocked from the walls since she visited the previous summer. Workers were busy rebuilding the officers' quarters, while the enlisted men's barracks appeared to have been completed. Over the sally port, the soldiers had placed a motto in Italian that read, "He who enters here, leaves all hope behind," paraphrasing the inscription at the entrance to hell in Dante's *Divine Comedy*. The garrison apparently believed this was a humorous touch, but Emma was not amused. In her diary that night she wrote, "I think it singularly inappropriate."

Otherwise, however, she and the other visitors were impressed by the fort. They walked among the big guns, pausing at one aimed seaward to "give Lincoln's blockaders a 'salute' if they came near enough." They also were greeted by the fort's commander, Colonel Ripley; the recently promoted Capt. Alfred Rhett, whose company was still a part of the garrison; and William Prioleau, the post surgeon. "Ripley is rather above the medium size but very stout & quite a jolly looking soldier in his loose white linen suit," Emma recalled. In the warmest months, the 1st South Carolina's officers wore the lighter uniforms, accented by brass buttons and scarlet kepis, except when they were required to wear their regulation dress uniforms.

Despite being Northern-born, the thirty-eight-year-old Ripley had been totally embraced in Charleston's social and business circles over the previous decade. After graduating near the top of his West Point class in 1843, he had fought the Seminoles in Florida and had excelled in the Mexican War, twice brevetted for gallantry. He also had written a two-volume history of the latter conflict. Ripley married into the Middleton blue bloods of Charleston in 1852 and soon afterward resigned his army commission to become a Charleston businessman. As a lieutenant colonel of state forces in 1860, he occupied Moultrie after Anderson's men evacuated the post. The honor of being Sumter's first Confederate commander showed the esteem in which he was held by the Carolinians. Ripley was also characterized by his balding pate, walrus moustache, a volcanic nature that often sparked clashes with other officers, and, in the whispered gossip along The Battery, his love for the bottle. His weaknesses, however, did not offset his competency as an engineer and artillerist.

For Emma Holmes and other visitors, the latest attraction at Sumter was a "new and substantial" flagstaff that had been erected three days before their visit, the Stars and Bars hoisted to the winds. "The flag, with the beautiful ensign flying . . . adds much to the appearance of this powerful fortress," the *Charleston Mercury* said, "which, with the heavy additions to its armament now being placed in position, make it one of the most formidable positions on this continent."[21]

The Fourth of July 1861 was a day of mixed emotions across the South since the states now were part of a new and separate nation with a warring country perched on its borders. Still, there was the chiming of church bells that morning after the usual cannon blasts from the

*Postwar photo of
Confederate brigadier
general Roswell S. Ripley.*
LIBRARY OF CONGRESS

blockaders to greet the sunrise, the latter answered by the artillery at Sumter and Moultrie. At noon at least one gun in the city barked its honors. It was a leisurely Thursday, as stores were closed and street vendors did a brisk business selling ice cream, lemonade, and gingerbread from their curbside tables. There was some confusion that afternoon when residents heard the booming of cannon in the harbor. The general reasoning was that Sumter and Moultrie were firing Independence Day salutes. The *Mercury* reported it as such, but cleared up the issue two days later after interviewing officers from both forts. Neither had fired to mark the day; Sumter was merely getting in some artillery practice. The officers added, however, that they had not waited for orders to blast salutes on June 28, the anniversary of the 1776 repulse of the British fleet by patriots at Fort Moultrie. And they would certainly not await orders before the guns thundered on December 20, the first anniversary of South Carolina's secession.

The next day, the paper ran an unrelated article praising the efforts of Ripley and the other senior officers at Charleston in bolstering the harbor defenses. Ripley was credited for his exhaustive efforts at Sumter, which was described as "the great Key of the State." The *Mercury* said the "work performed there has been prodigious, under all the circumstances. There have been great difficulties to overcome. And the officers have been thrown much, too much, on their own resources. What ingenuity, and perseverance and zeal could effect, Col. Ripley has accomplished." Of Sumter, the paper said, "This great key locks and unlocks the state. Let the lock be thoroughly oiled, and the key be kept in perfect order."[22]

In mid-July, the war's focus was even more on Virginia, where the main Union and Confederate armies were destined for the first of many major and bloody confrontations. Beauregard was there, his Sumter laurels still glittering, although he would be second-in-command to Brig. Gen. Joseph E. Johnston when the armies collided. The battle of First Bull Run—or First Manassas, as the Confederates called it—was fought on July 21 and was a clear Southern victory, though both sides suffered heavy casualties. Beauregard's comet was streaking; he and Johnston were promoted to full general on August 31, although the Creole was given the lion's share of credit for the triumph. "Where Beauregard leads, Carolina asks to be there—for we honor him and love him as our own," the *Mercury* said. In the coming weeks, one of the hottest items in Charleston would be a new lithograph of Beauregard available "at the principal Book and Jewelry stores." The likeness had "been highly commended for its truthfulness, and is, we are pleased to say, meeting with a ready sale. Every admirer of the brave Beauregard—and who in Charleston is not—will be sure to secure a copy," said one account.[23]

Among the most notable Southern losses at Bull Run were Brig. Gen. Barnard E. Bee, a Charlestonian who fell while leading a charge, and Lt. Col. Benjamin J. Johnson of Beaufort, second-in-command of the Hampton Legion. A number of other Carolinians had been killed or wounded as well, and Charleston's city hall was draped in mourning black. Twenty-one-gun salutes in honor of the victory were fired by Forts Sumter and Moultrie at noon on July 23, Emma Holmes noted in her journal, adding that flags would be flown at half-staff and guns fired hourly from 6:00 AM to sunset "in honor of the illustrious dead." The bodies of Bee, Johnson, and Col. Francis Bartow (of Savannah, also killed in the battle) arrived in Charleston by train on the twenty-sixth and were honored by thousands of mourners who lined the streets as the coffins of the heroes were conveyed to City Hall, where they lay in state. Bartow's remains continued on to Savannah later in the day.[24]

There were leadership changes in Charleston in August. Richard Anderson was promoted to brigadier and sent to Pensacola to replace Braxton Bragg, while the popular Roswell Ripley also rose to brigadier and was assigned to head the Department of South Carolina. Ripley's promotion opened up the lieutenant colonelcy of the 1st South Carolina Artillery, and William Ransom Calhoun, who was still in Virginia, was promoted to lead the battalion. Ripley's new duties meant that while he would remain in Charleston, he would have to relinquish command at Sumter. Since Calhoun was away, the post went to Alfred Rhett, the thirty-one-year-old captain who was a member of one of Carolina's most proud and well-known families.

Alfred's father was Robert Barnwell Rhett Sr., a leading "Fire-Eater," or extremist Southern politician, who also was a former U.S. congressman from the state and a candidate for president of the Confederacy. The Rhetts had become sole owners of the *Charleston Mercury* in 1858, and Alfred's older brother, Robert Barnwell Rhett Jr., was the editor; the *Mercury* was regularly the mouthpiece for the patriarch's volatile views. Alfred attended Harvard and South Carolina College, graduating from the former in 1851 and settling in as a rice planter near Charleston. Commissioned a first lieutenant in the 1st South Carolina Artillery in December 1860, Rhett ably directed a battery at Moultrie during Sumter's initial bombardment. He had a reputation as a tough, aggressive soldier who was known for his quick temper and irascible nature as well as a loud laugh. If his father was known more for his acidic oratory and pro-Southern views rather than direct action, Alfred and three of his brothers were men enough to wear the Confederate gray. Still, there was a pompous air about the family which prompted a relative to write, "the world, you know, is composed of men, women, and Rhetts."[25]

While these personal dramas were unfolding in Charleston, the Union navy took a major step to strengthen the blockade. The South Atlantic Blockading Squadron, commanded by Capt. Samuel F. Du Pont, and the North Atlantic Blockading Squadron, led by Flag Officer Louis M. Goldsborough, were both created in September 1861. Du Pont's fleet was responsible for blanketing the more than 500 miles of coastline from Cape Canaveral, Florida, to the South and North Carolina border. Thus it fell to Du Pont to shut down enemy shipping at the three key ports on the south Atlantic seaboard: Charleston, Savannah, and Fernandina, Florida. He already was engaged in planning a strike to capture a location on the southern coast for use as a Union naval base.[26]

The work of the Confederates to thistle Charleston's entrance with foreboding defenses continued full bore, while Sumter and Moultrie exulted over a major technological development on September 24: That afternoon, "telegraphic communications" were established between them. This was an exciting event, prompting Capt. Joseph A. Yates, at Moultrie, to propose to Rhett, at Sumter, that an artillery salute be fired in honor of the accomplishment. Rhett agreed, and "the order to fire given at Fort Sumter was instantaneously sent over the wires to Fort Moultrie, and such was the effect that the reports of the two salutes were almost simultaneous," the *Mercury* reported.

Later that day, the blockader *Vandalia* eased in a bit too close and drew fire from both forts. "For a time she replied with spirit," the *Mercury* noted of the Union vessel, but the long-range duel came to nothing and she withdrew.[27]

The silhouettes of many more leviathans would soon darken the eastern horizon. On October 29, a Union armada churned out of Hampton Roads, Virginia, bound for the South Carolina coast. The seventy-nine vessels included warships, troop transports carrying some twelve thousand soldiers, supply vessels, and support craft, the most powerful American fleet ever assembled to that time. Led by now Commodore Du Pont, this strike force was on a supposedly secret mission that had been in the planning stages for months. Du Pont's target was Port Royal, South Carolina, a deepwater port between Charleston and Savannah which, if taken, would give the Union navy a great base for its blockading efforts along the southeastern coast. Du Pont's problem, however, was that Northern newspapers discovered and printed the fleet's destination—alerting the Confederates in the process—days before the fleet arrived off Port Royal. The Rebels had a bigger problem, since they were mostly creating a navy from scratch and had little to face the juggernaut bearing down on them.

The Union force was scattered by storms off North Carolina but reassembled near Port Royal on November 3–4. Facing them were a few hundred Rebels manning Forts Walker and Beauregard, which protected Port Royal Sound, and a ragtag Confederate naval squadron. Du Pont attacked on November 7, his ships blasting the enemy earthworks into submission after several hours. Assault troops went ashore to secure the captured forts, and Port Royal was in Union hands, giving the North a base to strengthen its blockade of the south Atlantic coast. Brig. Gen. Thomas W. Sherman, who commanded the army force in the expedition, would oversee the Federal troop buildup.[28]

On the same day as the Port Royal battle, a relatively obscure Confederate general was riding toward the action from the railroad stop at Coosawhatchie, South Carolina. Robert E. Lee, fifty-four, was the new commander of coastal defenses in South Carolina, Georgia, and eastern Florida, but this was long before he had earned his iconic reputation as the South's finest soldier. In fact, Lee was still seeking to prove himself in the conflict. He had been sent to western Virginia in July 1861—his first major assignment of the war—but command difficulties and awful weather had doomed his efforts there. Still, Jefferson Davis had enough faith in him to send Lee to the southeastern coast, an assignment that the Virginian apparently did not relish, despite the opportunity for redemption. "Another forlorn hope expedition. Worse than western Virginia," he wrote to his daughter, Mildred.[29]

Learning of Port Royal's fall, Lee established his headquarters at Coosawhatchie on the Charleston & Savannah Railroad, which connected the two most important cities and ports in the region. For the next four months, he would spend most of his time in those two cities, bolstering their defenses (including Fort Sumter) and making troop deployments. In the immediate wake of the Port Royal catastrophe, however, Lee realized his new command was in serious jeopardy: Hilton Head was occupied, a Union fleet was in Port Royal Sound, and his meager forces were scattered and ill-equipped. The C&S Railroad was key to his defense, a 115-mile stretch of track that cut through lush cypress swamps, pine woods, and snake-infested backwaters. It had been laid well inland for the most part, but the jagged configuration of South Carolina's coast closer to Charleston was a maze of serpentine rivers, inland creeks, bays, and inlets, all of which made the railroad vulnerable at some points to attack from Union gunboats or troops coming ashore from transports. The Confederates simply did not have the men, guns, or navy to protect all of these weak spots.

The Rebels who had escaped the Port Royal debacle had lost most of their arms, tents, and provisions in their exodus. "The enemy, having complete possession of the water and inland navigation, commands all the islands on this coast, and threatens both Savannah and Charleston," Lee wrote to Confederate Secretary of War Judah P. Benjamin on November 9. "We have no guns that can resist their batteries, and have no resource but to prepare to meet them in the field. . . . The garrisons of the forts at Charleston [including Fort Sumter] and Savannah and on the coast cannot be removed from the batteries while ignorant of the designs of the enemy." In other words, the 560 men of the 1st South Carolina Artillery under Alfred Rhett, posted at Sumter, and other garrison troops might have to be sent to danger points if and where the enemy launched a serious attack. With his manpower spread thin, Lee had no choice in the matter.[30]

Still, Charlestonians were generally confident in the ability of Lee and Ripley to defend the city. Should enemy gunboats appear, "they must pass between the tremendous batteries of Forts Moultrie and Sumter, which have splendidly drilled artillerists," the *Mercury* said on November 15. "The only danger here is the enemy attempting to run the gauntlet in large numbers in the day . . . or by sneaking in at night."

The first year of the war had indeed been a wild ride of emotions for the city and fort where it all began. "It was a time of varied sorrow and gladness," a Charlestonian later reflected. "Now the news of some victory, like that of Bull Run, would stir the whole heart of the city, and cause it to beat high with hope. Then some defeat, like that of Port Royal, would equally depress it. But, upon the whole, there was the most confident assurance in regard to the result."[31]

Affairs were not so settled at Sumter and Moultrie, however. Benjamin wrote to Lee on November 14 discussing reinforcements, new guns, and other equipment that were being sent to the latter. The secretary also had received a letter from John H. Robertson, who described himself as a Charlestonian and advised that the harbor forts "are in very incompetent hands." The officers mentioned were Rhett at Sumter and Maj. Thomas M. Wagner, also of the 1st South Carolina Artillery, at Moultrie. Robertson "speaks highly of Captain Rhett as a gentleman, but says he is totally without the experience necessary for so important a post," Benjamin stated. "Of . . . Wagner he speaks in very different terms, representing him to be not only incompetent, but neglectful and dissipated, never spending the night in his fort, but coming to town to indulge in excesses with the common prostitutes. Of course this is for your private information. . . . I know, however, your habitual vigilance, and this communication was perhaps needless."[32]

Possibly, Lee felt that the best way to rein in Wagner was to post him at Sumter, surrounded by water, a moat of sorts from Charleston's taverns and ladies of the evening. Perhaps Rhett needed some seasoning and a change of scenery after some seven months at the fort. Whatever the reason, Wagner replaced Rhett as Sumter's commander in late November 1861.

Wagner was a thirty-seven-year-old Charlestonian who had served several terms in the state legislature—both House and Senate—and was a prime mover in the construction of the new statehouse in Columbia. A rice planter before the war, he had been active in backing railroad construction across the South and instrumental in establishing the first company of the 1st South Carolina Artillery in December 1860. "Educated and at all times a reading man, his knowledge was large and varied," noted one contemporary account. "Since his connection with military matters, he had made himself adept in the science of gunnery, and his ability for business enhanced his value." As a lieutenant, he had served bravely and efficiently at Fort Moultrie during the bombardment of Anderson's garrison in Sumter, leading to his promotion to captain and command at Moultrie. Later described by the *Mercury* as "mild in spirit" and "firm in resolution" with a "single eye to the public cause," Wagner's other eye was apparently fixed on more earthly delights, but Lee gave him the benefit of the doubt. "I know nothing of Major Wagner," he said, responding to Benjamin on November 23 and telling him of Wagner's Sumter assignment. While at least one general in Charleston portrayed Wagner as "an efficient officer," Lee added that he "had no confidence . . . in his experience" and had placed Cmdr. Duncan Ingraham of the Confederate navy in charge of supervising the batteries in the city's defenses.[33]

Ransom Calhoun, Rhett, and Wagner had all been among the young officers who had played key roles in creating the 1st South Carolina Artillery. Calhoun and Wagner were especially good friends. The relationship between Calhoun and Rhett, however, was vastly different, dating to Sumter's opening bombardment. During the shelling, then-Captain Calhoun had received orders from Ripley for the Moultrie gunners under Rhett to shift their pattern of fire against Sumter. For whatever reason,

Calhoun relayed the order directly to the men, bypassing Rhett, who was angered by the apparent snub. Matters were aggravated in the excitement after the battle when Calhoun told Rhett and some of his men who were celebrating on Moultrie's walls to return to their posts. With Rhett's already hot blood burning to bad blood toward Calhoun, the feud worsened in the coming months.[34]

Wagner, meanwhile, was settling into his new post. The Confederates had been busy for several weeks laying a submerged telegraph cable, or "submarine telegraph cable," between Sumter and Moultrie to replace the connection made in September with cables on poles; this was completed on November 27. "When the bedding of the cable was completed, a salute was simultaneously fired in honor of the event from the two forts, the order having been transmitted from Fort Sumter over the wire. . . . The communication between the forts was perfect, and much to the satisfaction of the skillful operators concerned," the *Mercury* related.[35]

In early December, Lee reorganized the Carolina coast into five military districts, with Roswell Ripley assigned to command the Second District and headquartered in Charleston. The Fourth District was given to Brig. Gen. John C. Pemberton, who had recently been assigned to the area. Pemberton was a Pennsylvanian and, like Ripley, a Northerner who had cast his fate with the Confederacy. This common bond would do nothing to smooth issues between them during the coming months.

Lee himself was still largely an unknown at this time, yet had impressed the Carolinians not only with his calmness and military prowess, but also with his physical presence. Charlestonian Paul Hamilton Hayne, a writer and poet, was among several people enjoying a winter sunset view from Sumter's parapet when they were distracted by the voices and footsteps of an approaching cluster of officers, including Lee. Hayne recalled that "in the middle of the group, topping the tallest by half a head, was perhaps the most striking figure we had ever encountered." The officer appeared to be at least in his mid-fifties and was "erect as a poplar, yet lithe and graceful, with broad shoulders well thrown back, a fine, justly-proportioned head poised in unconscious dignity, clear, deep, thoughtful eyes and the quiet, dauntless step of one every inch the gentleman and soldier."[36]

By December 11, Charleston was crowded with refugees who had flooded the city from the sea islands to escape the Union occupation and

Prewar portrait of Confederate general Robert E. Lee.
AUTHOR'S COLLECTION

accompanying raids. That night, some slaves who had accompanied their master from an outlying plantation kindled a small cooking fire on the grounds of a factory at Hasell and East Bay streets. What followed would be one of the worst disasters not only of the war, but also in the city's long history. Just after 8:00 PM, the fire got out of hand and ignited the factory building. At first there was no reason for anyone to believe this was anything more than a routine blaze, but as the wind began to rise, the flames jumped to structures across Bay Street. The wind continued to strengthen, whipping sparks onto roofs on Market Street, and the conflagration worsened. Institute Hall, where the Ordinance of Secession had been signed, and the Circular Congregational Church next door, both on Meeting Street, were soon ablaze. Stores and houses on Pinckney and Hayne streets were consumed, and the gasworks on Church Street was smothered in flames, the gas feeding the fire's fierceness. Watching the spectacle from their defenses some seven miles from the city, Confederate soldier W. W. Stribling later described how he could see the faces of his comrades twenty yards distant due to the awesome glare. It was "one of the most powerful fires I have ever seen in my life," he wrote to his wife, Emily, the next day.

General Lee and several of his staff officers had completed a tour of inspection and were dining at the nearby Mills House when they heard the alarm bells clanging. They watched the inferno from the hotel roof before helping some women and children leave, Lee himself carrying a baby to safety. The general and his men escaped the fire uninjured, and the Mills House also survived due to wet blankets being hung from the windows and water poured on them. Yet the flames raged on for hours after midnight. There was a brief lull when the winds calmed and a light rain began to fall, but the relief was temporary; the rain stopped and the wind swirled to gale force, igniting more buildings. Ripley ordered fourteen houses blown up on Queen Street to save an orphanage and two hospitals, while structures on both sides of Broad Street, as well as buildings on Tradd, Council, New, Limehouse, Savage, and Greenhill Streets, were leveled or damaged. By sunrise the blaze had subsided, but proud Charleston had been devastated. Some 540 acres lay in smoking, charred ruin, and 575 homes had been destroyed.[37]

Even as Charleston tried to recover from the fire's ravages, another aspect of the Union blockade was falling into place just a few miles offshore. Since late summer, Federal authorities had been ready to proceed with another option to cork up Southern ports: They would sink derelict vessels in the mouths of the harbor channels, thus causing serious obstacles to enemy ships coming or going. These decrepit boats would be known as Stone Fleets, because they were weighted with rocks to make them sink quickly and be even more of a navigation hazard. A Stone Fleet composed of sixteen old whaling ships from Massachusetts was scuttled in a checkerboard pattern at the entrance to Charleston's main channel, between Sumter and Morris Island, on December 19–20, 1861. "A few stone ships in Charleston harbor will make Sumter and Moultrie valueless, and shut out the nest of treason from all commercial importance hereafter," the *New York Herald* boasted. The Federals were confident the sunken hulks would do the job, wrote another New York newspaperman, adding that "at least one cursed rathole has been closed."[38]

As the year waned, the 1st South Carolina Artillery Battalion was undergoing significant changes that would also affect Ransom Calhoun, Alfred Rhett, and Thomas Wagner. The battalion was being expanded into a regiment, increasing its strength to ten companies over the next few months. The three officers would be promoted when the new regiment was organized in the spring. Calhoun had yet to return from Virginia, staying with his battery there. Compared to the relative inactivity of the troops at Charleston, Calhoun was apparently caught up in the wartime hustle, bustle, and social life of Richmond. Mary Chesnut had encountered him and some of his Carolina comrades in the capital in August, describing them as "foolish, rash, harebrained Southern lads" who were "thrilling with fiery ardor."

Still, Calhoun's prolonged absence from Charleston and the organization of the new regiment had already rankled his friend Wagner, the friction resulting in neither communicating with the other for a time. Others accused Calhoun of being unpatriotic for remaining in Virginia. The problem had festered so much by early December that Calhoun sent a dispatch to Beauregard—bypassing his immediate superior, Ripley—to rule on his decision to stay with his battery. Beauregard supported Calhoun in the matter, but the embarrassed Ripley was now added to the list of those who disliked Calhoun.

With no vile enemy creeping toward The Battery, the Charleston Confederates were turning even more on themselves. Since November, Lee and Ripley had disagreed on some issues about defending the coastline, but Ripley's mood worsened in January 1862, when John Pemberton was promoted to major general over him. In the months after Sumter's surrender, while he oversaw the fort's rebuilding, Ripley had chafed over how long it took for him to be made brigadier. Now Pemberton, who had only been on the Carolina coast since early December, outranked him.[39]

There was also strong jealousy and resentment among other officers—many of them at Sumter—over preference and promotions at other levels, including an appointment for one of Beauregard's sons. "I regret to hear and to know of the unpleasant feeling amongst the officers under General Ripley," Governor Pickens wrote to Lee on December 31. "Appointments cannot be made to please all . . . besides I thought it would be very agreeable to all to appoint a son of General Beauregard. . . . Why these appointments should create such excitement among the junior officers in Fort Sumter I am at a loss to understand."

This was a relatively minor problem in Lee's realm of headaches that winter as he tried to gird a vast stretch of shoreline with not enough troops, guns, or warships. An iron hurricane was brewing, and no amount of flag waving, molten words, or whiskey-fueled oaths against the cursed Yankees would hold off the flood tide when it came. Thirty-plus years in the U.S. Army had shown him the will and the power that now was his foe, and he realized the daunting challenge faced by the tod-dling Confederacy. "Our enemy increases in strength faster than we do and is more enormous," he wrote from Coosawhatchie on Christmas Eve 1861. "Where he will strike I do not know, but the blow when it does fall will be hard."[40]

CHAPTER 2

Dueling Blue Bloods and Whispers of Mutiny—1862

The Federals were so confident that the Stone Fleet sunk off Charleston in December would plug the main channel that they immediately began organizing another group of hulks to clog up Maffitt's (Sullivan's Island) Channel. Maffitt's was the waterway between Sumter and Fort Moultrie, a pipeline for blockade runners due to the protection offered by the forts and the Sullivan's Island batteries. The second Stone Fleet appeared off Charleston on January 20, 1862, and, despite stormy weather, fourteen derelicts stocked with granite were sunk in an effort to close the channel. If the North believed in the Stone Fleets' effectiveness, they did not expect the international outrage over the sinkings. The British press widely vilified the action as a crime against humanity, and France joined in the criticism. The controversy was short-lived, however, as nature itself defeated the Stone Fleets. The weighted hulls soon disappeared into the sea mud, worms feasting on the ships' timbers. Strong tidal currents in the harbor also helped wash away portions of the hulks. As soon as five days after the sinking of the first fleet, Ripley reported, "From such observation as has been lately made the sunken fleet is gradually disappearing."[1]

While Sumter's garrison under Major Wagner was busy bolstering the defenses and drilling during this period, many of the men were chafing for combat. None was as impatient as Lt. John Mitchel, the Irish-born artillerist who had been one of the first Confederate officers to set foot in Sumter after Anderson's surrender. He "disliked garrison duty, and had too active and restless a spirit to brook with much patience the wearisome routine and confinement of a fort that was seagirt," said one account. "It reminded him too forcibly of a prison." Mitchel wanted to raise a company and form a light battery that could be sent to Virginia to aid in the fighting there—much as Calhoun had done—but his superiors nixed this plan and he was forced to stay on the Carolina coast.

On March 3, Robert E. Lee was ordered to report to Richmond to serve as a military adviser to Jefferson Davis, thus ending his short-lived, but difficult, command on the southeastern coast. He was replaced by John Pemberton, his second-in-command. Like Lee, Pemberton concentrated primarily on making Charleston and Savannah too strong for the enemy to capture. This month also saw a leadership change for the Federals; Thomas Sherman was succeeded by Maj. Gen. David Hunter in command of the newly created U.S. Department of the South. This department encompassed the coastal areas held by the Federals in South Carolina, Georgia, and Florida. Hunter had about seventeen thousand troops to cover this vast stretch, but more than twelve thousand of them were concentrated near Charleston.[2]

By late March, the 1st South Carolina Artillery Battalion was no more, having been expanded and reorganized to establish the 1st South Carolina Artillery Regiment. Its prodigal commander, Ransom Calhoun, had finally returned to Charleston a few weeks earlier. Calhoun was promoted to colonel, Wagner to lieutenant colonel, and Alfred Rhett to major of the new regiment, but the turmoil was as hot as ever, stoked by Calhoun's return. Governor Pickens alleged that Calhoun had offended Wagner, and possibly Ripley, the previous summer while in Virginia. When Calhoun returned to Charleston in early January, Ripley pursued charges against him for "writing an insulting letter either to or about" the general, Mary Chesnut wrote on January 11. Pickens noted that Ripley's action "generated wide-spread dissensions." The controversy would snowball in the coming months. With Calhoun immersed in drawn-out court-martial proceedings (which would come to nothing), he, Wagner, and Rhett would be involved in an irregular rotation of command at Sumter into the early summer.[3]

The most pressing and immediate concern for both Hunter and Pemberton was the Union buildup in the Georgia salt marshes and sand flats near Confederate-held Fort Pulaski at the mouth of the Savannah River. For weeks, the Federals had been constructing batteries and hauling big guns into place to bombard Pulaski, a brick bastion of similar design to Fort Sumter. Under the direction of engineer Capt. Quincy A. Gillmore, the Yankees had emplaced thirty-six pieces of heavy artillery by early April, including rifled cannon and mortars, to pound Pulaski. Rifled guns had never been tested against a masonry fort, and conventional wisdom among the military—including Lee, Pemberton, Thomas Sherman, and most of the Union brass—held that heavy artillery was ineffective against forts like Pulaski or Sumter at a range of more than eight hundred yards. Gillmore's closest guns were more than twice that distance from the fort's $7^{1}/_{2}$-foot-thick brick walls, but the Ohioan was convinced that rifled guns and mortars could pulverize it.

The bombardment began on the morning of April 10, the fort's cannoneers replying with vigor. Watching the artillery duel from a distance, Pemberton remarked that Pulaski was wasting its ammunition. After all, wasn't the fort impregnable? Pemberton was so confident of the outcome that he returned to his headquarters in Charleston that afternoon. But the Union rounds were causing massive damage, tearing huge gaps in the brick. The barrage lasted nine hours and, after intermittent shelling overnight, resumed early on the eleventh. By afternoon, Union projectiles were roaring through jagged openings in the walls, threatening to ignite the fort's magazine. With little choice, Pulaski's commander, Col. Charles H. Olmstead, surrendered. Gillmore had proven himself right, noting: "The effect of our fire upon the walls of the fort is interesting, as the first example, in actual warfare, of the breaching power of rifled ordnance at long range."[4]

In Charleston, the one-year observance of Sumter's capture was tempered by the bad news from Savannah. "The first anniversary of the surrender of Fort Sumter," Emma Holmes penned in her journal on Sunday, April 13. "We scarcely feel like celebrating it, when Pulaski has just fallen." April indeed would be a bad month for the Confederacy on all fronts. In addition to Pulaski, a major battle had been lost at Shiloh—also known as Pittsburg Landing—in southern Tennessee on April 6–7, and a Union naval squadron would take New Orleans on the twenty-fifth. Indeed, the U.S. Navy's development of ironclad warships, including the revolutionary USS *Monitor* and the differently designed—and ultimately much less effective—USS *Galena* encouraged many in the North that spring that Charleston would now be an easy target, standing no chance against these new dreadnoughts. The *New York Times* boasted there was a general patience about capturing the "traitor city" because "everybody knows we can take Charleston any moment we please. The *Monitor* and *Galena* can coolly steam into the harbor, past Sumter and up to the city, while all the shot the fort can rain on them fall off their mailed sides like the peas of a pop-gun."

Southern troops, many from rural areas, continued to be sent to Charleston and marveled not only at her charms but also at the rising food prices as a result of the blockade and other wartime shortages. Many, like sharpshooter S. M. Crawford, caught their first wondrous glimpse of the ocean, with Sumter perched on the horizon. "I have walked over Charleston it is a considerable sitty the bildings look like they have bin standing a grate while," he wrote to his family that April. In stores, molasses was selling for $1.25 a gallon, beef was 50 cents a pound, and the soldiers were grumbling about not getting enough to eat.[5]

The next tense chapter in the Calhoun–Rhett feud occurred on April 23, when the two squared off at Fort Sumter. Calhoun was critical of some actions the major had taken in his absence, and the issue became more heated. Finally they assembled six witnesses in the adjutant's office and exchanged accusations. When this was over, Rhett asked his witnesses to write letters supporting his view that the colonel was the aggressor in this encounter. Rhett's brother, Edmund, presented the letters to Calhoun, but he promptly returned them without comment. Nothing was settled, and the difficulties between the two continued to fester.

There was other excitement involving Sumter—locally and nationally—a few weeks later when a slave and harbor pilot named Robert Smalls steered the side-wheel steamer *Planter* out of Charleston Harbor in a daring attempt to reach the Union fleet. (Rhett commanded Sumter at the time of the *Planter* incident, but Calhoun was back at the fort by May 22.[6]) Smalls had planned the seizure of the Confederate vessel and early on the morning of May 13 got his chance. The *Planter's* captain, mate, and engineer had left the ship earlier, with Smalls in charge of the few black crewmen aboard. About 3:00 AM, the crew built up steam in the boiler and quietly eased away from the wharf. The steamer had become a common sight around Charleston—even serving as General Ripley's flagship—so Smalls was familiar with procedures and signals that would keep the Confederates from suspecting any problems that morning. He guided the *Planter* toward another wharf where his family awaited on a docked ship and brought them aboard. They then headed toward the harbor's throat and the dark mass of Fort Sumter. Nearing the fort, Smalls pulled the captain's familiar straw hat low on his head and stood on the bridge to try to deceive the lookouts. A sentinel on the walls alerted the officer of the day, but Smalls blew his whistle with the proper signal, and the *Planter* was allowed to pass. Once out of range of Sumter's guns, Smalls and his crew lowered her flag, ran up a white sheet, and steamed toward the nearest Union ship.

The incident was a source of embarrassment and anger for the Rebels, especially Pemberton, but Smalls became an instant hero in the North for his daring voyage to freedom. Adding salt to the Southerners' wounds was the fact that in addition to the *Planter*'s armament of two cannon, Smalls and his band escaped with four other guns on board, two of which had belonged to Anderson's garrison in 1861. Perhaps more importantly, Smalls informed the Federals that the Rebels had abandoned Coles Island, at the mouth of the Stono River, on the twelfth. Smalls would serve as a pilot for the Union navy, his popularity and bravery not waning after the war, when he climbed the political ladder from state representative to senator to U.S. Congressman.

The fragile and volatile command situation at Sumter, possibly aggravated by the tedium of garrison life and still no combat, was a perfect witch's brew for dissension within the ranks of the 1st South Carolina Artillery. Whispers about the reliability and loyalty of Calhoun's men were growing in volume and number. Charleston was unsettled by all of this; many people worried whether the suddenly shaky regiment could be relied upon to protect the Confederacy's most treasured prize, which also was the linchpin of their defenses. At the same time, the working relationship between Pemberton and Ripley continued to frazzle, intertwined with the problems at Sumter. The two generals had disagreed about Pemberton's decision to evacuate Coles Island and thus open James Island to possible attack. But the issue went much deeper: Ripley resented Pemberton's promotion over him in January. Beginning in late April, Ripley had made several requests to be transferred from Charleston to "service in the field."[7] Governor Pickens wrote to Lee in Richmond on May 12, describing the situation in Charleston. Lee also had received a telegram days earlier from three prominent Carolinians who requested that Ripley be given command authority independent of Pemberton, a concept Lee would not support. Lee responded to Pickens on the fifteenth, asking for suggestions in "remedying the evil." He made it clear, however, that he believed Ripley should be transferred, despite his skill, knowledge, and value to the Rebels, whenever the expected Union attack came. "As he seems to be dissatisfied . . . and not in harmony with those above and below him, it may be the best thing to gratify his wishes" for transfer, Lee wrote of Ripley. "One or the other [Pemberton] must be removed."

Sumter's issues garnered more attention on May 20 when James Chesnut Jr., chief of the state's Department of the Military, wrote to Pemberton from Columbia. Several "worthy and distinguished citizens" had told Chesnut and other officials that "disaffection prevails in a large portion of the garrison of Fort Sumter, extending to threats of mutiny and refusal to fire against the enemy if he should appear." Chesnut added that those who made the allegations, to his knowledge, were "ready to substantiate them." Fueling the mutiny fears was the fact that Confederate troops in some of New Orleans's defenses, mainly Fort Jackson, had revolted after the city fell, forcing their commanders to surrender.[8]

There would be a flurry of communications regarding Sumter on May 23. That day, Pickens replied to Lee's letter of the fifteenth and blew the top off the barrel. There was "great disorganization" at both Sumter and Fort Moultrie, but more so at the former. He described the problem between Ripley, Wagner, and Calhoun stemming from Calhoun's offending the others while still in Virginia and stated that Ripley "has lately had Calhoun out of the fort" apparently as part of his "protracted court martial." Wagner also was away from the fort much of the time, based on Ripley's orders. This left the fort in Rhett's command, with Pickens claiming that Rhett "is said to be a favorite of General Ripley." Additionally, the governor had heard that five soldiers from the fort had deserted, going out to the Union fleet, and that some of Sumter's guns had been spiked. Pickens repeated his claims about the desertions and damaged guns in a letter to Pemberton that day, adding, "I hear also that the division amongst the officers has produced the worst effects as to the strict organization" of the garrison. To both Lee and Pemberton, Pickens proposed that "two native-born artillery companies from Charleston" be sent to Sumter to guard against any unrest. He added to Lee that "after the Fort Jackson mutiny, let us not be placed in the same position at Fort Sumter." To Pemberton, he suggested the Charleston companies to be assigned at the fort should come from the Washington Artillery, Marion Artillery, or Palmetto Guard, saying, "These men would restore confidence, and it is all-important that this confidence should be restored."[9]

Pemberton had also heard the rumors—even before receiving Chesnut's letter of the twentieth—and had ordered Ripley to investigate the matter. Indeed, a private in the 1st South Carolina had been arrested and was awaiting court-martial proceedings for "making use of seditious language," Pemberton replied to Chesnut on the twenty-third. Pemberton also had received assurances from Calhoun and some of the fort's other officers regarding "confidence in the courage, patriotism, and discipline of the men"—the colonel's own words. "It may be that there are disaffected individuals among the rank and file of Fort Sumter, as there probably are disaffected individuals in most of the corps," the general told Chesnut, "but that this feeling extends to any considerable number I see no reason to believe."[10]

Still, the possibility of problems at Charleston was very much on Lee's mind in a May 29 dispatch to Pemberton. He said that not only must Pemberton pay attention to the armament and supplies of the harbor forts, but also he must see to the "condition and feeling of the garrisons. This is particularly important, as any disaffection might be attended by irreparable mischief." Because of the Fort Jackson incident, "we cannot be too particular in guarding against mutiny," Lee added. "Let it be distinctly understood . . . that Charleston and Savannah are to be defended to the last extremity. If the harbors are taken the cities are to be fought street by street and house by house as long as we have a foot of ground to stand upon." Lee wrote to Pickens that same day, stressing the importance of defending Charleston and adding that Ripley was being reassigned to help "remedy to some extent this evil" disrupting the Charleston officers and troops. Ripley was ordered to Virginia on May 24. After all the discord and his repeated requests for transfer, Sumter's first Confederate commander had finally gotten his wish to leave Charleston. He was assigned to the Army of Northern Virginia and would soon find himself leading a brigade in the Seven Days battles near

Richmond. Ripley "is an officer of great skill and energy," the *Mercury* said of his departure. "Whatever the loss to Charleston, it will be a gain to the army in Virginia."[11]

Pemberton answered Lee on the thirty-first, assuring him that he had looked into the matter of the forts and "arrived at the conclusion that there is no real cause for apprehension. The officers of the garrison express full confidence in the integrity, courage, and discipline of their men," he noted. "I presume that in all commands of several hundred men there are some few discontented, and perhaps in heart disloyal; but I see no reason to suspect the garrisons of Forts Sumter and Moultrie to be less trustworthy than others." Pemberton added that it would be difficult to replace the garrison of either fort because both were well drilled and "invaluable in their present position," but that he would do so if Lee felt it necessary.

Calhoun had by now reacted to the rumors about his men by having his company commanders write letters attesting to the loyalty of their troops. Capt. W. H. Peronneau of the 1st South Carolina's Company G exemplified the responses by the officers. "I have been much annoyed in the last few days by the expression of feeling of the people of Charleston against this regiment," he wrote on May 31. "They seem to have lost all confidence in us, and I have no doubt that it would be as agreeable to them as it would be certainly to me, and I think to many of the officers . . . that we should be removed to some other field of action." Capt. Joseph A. Yates of Company A agreed, telling Calhoun that the regiment should be sent without delay to a battle zone "where we will have an early opportunity of proving to the citizens of Charleston the wrong they have done us." Calhoun enclosed the letters in a June 12 dispatch to Pemberton. "The opinions of the company officers are the only guides I have in this matter," he wrote. "They are aware of the rumors and the seditious language held by one or two of the men, but still have confidence in the loyalty, courage and fidelity of their commands. . . . While all the officers of this garrison would feel sensibly the mortification of being removed from a post of so much importance at such a critical time, we would prefer to be placed immediately in front of the enemy, where an opportunity would be afforded to restore that confidence in our rank and file which has been shaken by rumors amongst an anxious and excited community." Notably missing from the letters was any message from Alfred Rhett,

Calhoun's second-in-command. Still, the letters seem to have quashed the controversy as quickly as it arose and reassured most Charlestonians that Sumter was well protected.[12]

By late May, Sumter had eighty-seven guns mounted, according to Pickens. "To garrison it for fighting night and day in a great engagement would require at least 800 men, as you yourself once observed to me," he wrote Lee on May 23. Pickens estimated about fifteen thousand men could be concentrated to defend the city in this period. "I speak what I believe is the deliberate feeling of the State when I say that we universally prefer it a city of ashes and the site defended to its being in possession of the enemy. . . . It is due to us and our cause that we should make it a slaughter-house rather than to retire, even if it is threatened to be over-powered. . . . We can afford to lose the city entirely, but not our honor."[13]

Despite the Sumter distractions, Pemberton had continued Lee's defensive plans for the coast, but war developments in Virginia and Tennessee caused the Confederate brass to siphon troops from his department during this time. Pemberton was forced to constrict his defenses due to this loss of manpower, and because of this one of the major worries for the Confederates in Charleston that late spring and early summer was the threat of a Union offensive across James Island, where their lines were weaker and undermanned. Indeed, the evacuation of Coles Island had helped open this door for the Federals. The Northerners were "virtually investing the city," the *New York Herald* reported on June 8, adding that "we confidently expect before the lapse of many days to report . . . the restoration of the flag to Fort Sumter, and the capture of the hotbed in which this great but hopeless rebellion was hatched." This optimism welled despite Federal forces also being shipped north from the Charleston sector to bolster Gen. George McClellan's Peninsula Campaign, the massive spring and early summer offensive to try to capture Richmond. Still, if the Federals could gain control of James Island, they could not only bypass Sumter and the other posts guarding the outer harbor, but also gain access to the inner harbor and be able to bombard Charleston itself.

Union forces indeed tried just that on June 16, 1862, but were repulsed after a bloodily sharp fight at Secessionville on James Island. This was the only time in the war that the Federals tried this avenue of attack on Charleston. Fort Sumter had not been engaged in this battle, but the two hundred or so Confederate casualties at Secessionville—compared to almost seven hundred Union—had an emotionally direct effect on the garrison. "Many of our finest men were killed, and all the friends or relations of some officers in the Fort," a Rebel officer wrote to a relative on June 18, "and a general gloom is spread over all here now." Days later, Alfred Rhett joined those who had lost a loved one or comrade when he learned that one of his brothers, Robert W. Rhett, was mortally wounded at Gaines's Mill near Richmond on June 27–28.[14]

From Sumter's walls, Ransom Calhoun watched the Union gunboat *Seneca* approach Morris Island on the afternoon of June 21 and briefly shell Confederate positions there. He retaliated with a warning shot, noting, "I do not deem it proper to waste the powder in this fort at extreme ranges for our heaviest guns." A few weeks shy of his thirty-fifth birthday, the colonel was an 1850 West Point graduate but resigned his commission in the 1st U.S. Dragoons within a few months due to the already simmering sectional troubles and returned to Charleston. He later served with the U.S. legation in France, his most conspicuous prewar post that of the American *chargé d'affaires* in Paris. By early 1861, he was back in Charleston and raised a company of cannoneers that would soon become part of the 1st South Carolina Artillery. Calhoun continued to command Sumter at various times through summer 1862, but suffered from bouts of bad health and was often on sick leave, recuperating in the city. This often left Rhett in command of the regiment as well as the fort.[15]

The sadness over comrades lost at Secessionville was temporarily forgotten on the night of the twenty-second when Sumter sprang into action against a phantom ship trying to slip past it. There already had been some excitement earlier that day when the *Seneca* steamed within range of the fort. That night the blockade runner *Memphis* approached the harbor, its crew showing a red light to signal Sumter and Fort Moultrie. Her sign returned, the steamer churned toward the city with her cargo of 112,000 pounds of gunpowder, but she grounded in the darkness. Not realizing this was the *Memphis*, Sumter's defenders opened fire on her, all of the shots missing before the vessel again showed a red lantern, which ended the firing. The steamer's ordeal was far from over, however, as she remained stuck on the morning of June 23. The Federals lobbed shells at the trapped ship all day as Confederate crews from Sullivan's Island worked to lighten her. It was tough, grim work since a direct hit would likely obliterate the *Memphis* and anyone on or near her. But the Yankee rounds were astray and by about 5:00 PM the blockade runner was pulled free and made it to safety.[16]

Charleston had long been branded as the serpents' nest of secession by the North, and during this time the *New York Herald* let it be known that this sentiment still boiled ever deeply: "In brief, we may truly say that in the work of concocting, arranging, precipitating and directing the elements of this terrible rebellion . . . , Charleston, among all the cities of the South, stands pre-eminent as Lucifer among his rebellious confederates of the infernal regions." This was volatile rhetoric, but the reality for the Union men at land and sea facing "Lucifer" was much harsher than printed words. Hunter had sent seven regiments to reinforce the Army of the Potomac by July, forcing him to temporarily abandon several sea islands near Charleston and weakening him for other offensive action in the wake of Secessionville.[17]

The roulette wheel of command at Sumter, meanwhile, continued to spin. Calhoun was there as of July 6, but Rhett was in charge by July 28, Pemberton personally advising him about some changes to the fort's defenses. Pemberton himself, however, had fallen out of favor with many of the most influential Carolinians that summer. His decision to evacuate Coles Island, which the Rebels were trying unsuccessfully to recover by July, plus the uproar among Charleston's troops, had damaged him. While he still had the confidence of most top Confederates in Richmond, his days were numbered on the coast, with Lee telling Jefferson Davis: "I hardly see how the removal of Pemberton can be avoided." Pemberton was informed in July that he was to be transferred, but a dearth of ranking—and healthy—replacements meant that it would be weeks before he would leave Charleston.[18]

There was shockingly bad news in mid-July when Thomas Wagner was mortally wounded in an artillery mishap. The freewheeling former commander at Sumter had been appointed chief of ordnance in the Department of South Carolina and Georgia in early June and performed admirably in the Secessionville fighting, temporarily leading the Rebel forces after his superiors were wounded. On July 16, however, he was severely injured at Moultrie when a gun burst during artillery practice. His death the next day "spread gloom over . . . Charleston; for few men in our midst could have been illy spared, and the causeless occasion of his death has added sensibly to the weight of the loss," the *Mercury* said on the nineteenth, the day after his funeral. "The State has lost a useful patriot. A true son has gone to his final rest. May the hand of the mother lie gently upon his head." Wagner would be immortalized when a strong new Confederate earthwork on Morris Island was renamed for him in November 1862.[19]

Beauregard was ordered back to Charleston in late August 1862 to take command of the Department of South Carolina and Georgia, finally replacing Pemberton, who was promoted and sent west. This was by no means a triumphant return for the bayou general; the thirteen months since the glory of First Bull Run had been an open Pandora's box to his career. Egos, miscommunication, and disagreement over strategic objectives led to clashes with Jefferson Davis and Secretary of War Benjamin, among others. These issues had previously led to Beauregard's reassignment from Virginia to the western theater. He had been second-in-command to Gen. Albert Sidney Johnston at Shiloh, and when Johnston was killed in the April 6 fighting, he assumed command of the Army of Tennessee. The Confederates had launched a stunning surprise attack that first day, but the tide turned with the arrival of Union reinforcements on the seventh, and Beauregard ordered his exhausted forces to retreat to Corinth, Mississippi.

This shocking reversal of fortune, plus Beauregard's further withdrawal south from Corinth a few weeks later, further fueled the animosity directed at him from Richmond. The fire grew hotter in mid-June when Beauregard took leave due to illness but did not go through the proper channels of authorization. Within days, an angry Davis relieved Beauregard of army command, replacing him with Braxton Bragg. If Davis was riled by the Creole's leave, Beauregard was infuriated by the president's decision. "If the country be satisfied to have me laid on the shelf by a man who is either demented or a traitor to his high trust—well, let it be so," he wrote to one of his staff officers in July 1862. "My consolation is, that the difference between 'that individual' and myself is that, if he were to die today, the whole country would rejoice at it, whereas, I believe, if the same thing were to happen to me, they would regret it."[20]

Returning to the Carolina coast, Beauregard spent September 16–24 inspecting the defenses and troop dispositions of his new department, primarily around Charleston and Savannah. On the eighteenth, he and Pemberton inspected Forts Moultrie and Sumter, "which were found to be in good order and condition" despite repair work still ongoing at the latter. Sumter bristled with seventy-nine guns of various calibers, from 10-inch Columbiads to 32-pounders, along with seven 10-inch mortars, and boasted a garrison of about 352 troops. The major repair work at that time consisted of the barracks' still being reduced in height. A small steam engine used for making fresh water was in a somewhat exposed position and ought to be moved or better protected, Beauregard noted. Because of the extensive tours and inspections needed to familiarize him with the defenses, Beauregard did not actually take departmental command until September 24. By this time, Sumter's garrison had been increased to five hundred artillerymen and one hundred infantry.[21]

Even as Beauregard was preparing to return to Charleston, the ill-tempered feud of honor between Calhoun and Rhett still shrouded Fort Sumter in an ever-darkening cloud. The deadly storm was about to break. On August 7, Alfred Rhett and his brother, Edmund, a captain in the 1st Battalion of South Carolina Sharpshooters, were drinking at the Charleston Club, a historic and popular gathering spot then located at the corner of Broad and Meeting Streets. With them was their friend, Arnoldus Vanderhorst, another Carolina blue blood whose grandfather and namesake had been governor in the late 1700s. The conversation drifted to the merits of West Point–trained officers (like Calhoun) compared to volunteers (like Rhett) and the discussion grew heated. Vanderhorst contended that Calhoun was a fine and well-qualified officer, but Alfred would have none of it, saying Calhoun was a "damned puppy," which in the vernacular of the time was the same as calling him a "son of a bitch." At least one other account states that he described Calhoun as "an unmentionable part of the female anatomy." Whatever the insult, Vanderhorst was incensed, and Alfred fueled the fire, telling him, "you may take it as you please." The slur cut so deeply that Vanderhorst published a notice the next day demanding an apology or satisfaction, the latter meaning a duel. Rhett refused to apologize, and he and Vanderhorst agreed to face off with pistols on August 9. Twice previously Rhett had been involved in challenges that were resolved before gore was spilled for honor. But he cherished his pistols and had been a second in an 1856 duel that resulted in a distant relative's death.

On the ninth, on a farm near the present-day site of The Citadel, he and Vanderhorst paced off the distance, turned, and fired, both missing. Rhett still was unapologetic, and they reloaded. On the second exchange, Vanderhorst pulled the trigger first, his ball zipping wide of Rhett. Under the dueling code, Rhett could have taken his time in aiming and shot Vanderhorst dead—but he didn't. Instead, he discharged his pistol into the air, the affair declared ended without satisfaction. Rhett "had no personal difference with V[anderhorst]," Charlestonian Emma Holmes later wrote in her diary, "but all his insolence and arrogance have been directed against Calhoun, about whom he has made many insulting speeches. This has been going on for two months."[22]

With the city abuzz over the daily-worsening rift, Calhoun, who also frequented the Charleston Club, was outraged over the insult and threatened to horsewhip Rhett after the war. On the thirteenth, he issued a written statement which opened, "In view of the probable serious termination of the difficulty between Major Rhett and myself." The "serious termination" meant that another duel was likely to be fought. Calhoun also claimed that he had first heard of Rhett's personal attacks on him the previous April but had not pressed the issue due to "patriotic reasons" although he intended to hold the major "to account for it." There was another twist on August 18, when Calhoun resigned his commission due to "health reasons" and was granted a leave of absence.[23]

The bitter words and feelings were beyond healing now, and Calhoun demanded satisfaction. Thus a Rhett or a Calhoun—whose families had both played such giant roles in leading the South to war—would shed blood not against Yankees but against the other. Emma Holmes noted that "the affair was to have been settled after the war. The first duel [with Vanderhorst], however, brought on the second. . . . Colonel Calhoun has known, as well as many others, for some time past, that Rhett has been practicing constantly with a pistol for the express purpose." Calhoun addressed Rhett directly on September 3, writing to him, "You have on many occasions assailed me with a view to injure my character, and under circumstances which give me a right to demand redress." They met at 5:00 PM on Friday, September 5, 1862, at the Charleston Oaks Club, then located on the Cooper River north of Magnolia Cemetery. "Every arrangement was made with most punctilious courtesy and military precision," stated one account, "and it was evident that all attempts to reconcile the former comrades in arms, were utterly futile." Two surgeons were there, along with the seconds, Col. O. M. Dantzler for Calhoun and Dr. J. K. Furham for Rhett. Calhoun was dressed in civilian clothing while Rhett was in full uniform.

Recalling that Rhett had fired into the air rather than shoot Vanderhorst, Calhoun apparently asked that such a ploy not be allowed in this affair. Now it was time. Each man stepped off ten paces—about thirty feet—before wheeling and triggering their smoothbore pistols. The seconds seemed to stop for a moment as the almost simultaneous shots echoed, and puffs of smoke from the weapons soiled the air. The eyes of those in attendance darted from one rival to the other to see if either had been hit. Rhett was unharmed, but Calhoun staggered and fell into the arms of his party. The three physicians could tell immediately that "the ball through the middle of his body" had mortally wounded the colonel. Calhoun was conveyed to the mansion of Charleston resident Mitchell King but died within an hour.[24]

The *Mercury* on Saturday did not mention the duel, but news of the bloodletting crackled through the parlors and sitting rooms of Charleston. "The Rhetts have been hitherto hated enough, now the name is almost execrated—the public are almost unanimous against him," Emma Holmes wrote in her diary the day after the duel. She added that "it is universally hoped that he will be arrested, court-martialed and broken of his commission. We hear that Pemberton has arrested all parties and that it will go very hard with them." The morning edition of the *Charleston Daily Courier* that day noted only that Calhoun's funeral would be held at 4:00 PM at St. Philip's Church. After the service, a procession headed toward Magnolia Cemetery, where Calhoun was buried. From the St. Philip's pulpit the next morning, a Sunday, the bishop based his sermon on the evils of dueling.[25]

A *Mobile Advertiser* correspondent who was in Charleston during the period wrote an account of the duel that was published in a number of papers. "The late fatal duel at Charleston, S.C. . . . did not obtain much publicity through the papers of that city," the *Richmond Daily Dispatch* said on October 24 before giving the Mobile reporter's description. "Duel at Charleston, S.C.—One of the Calhouns Killed by one of the Rhetts" said a headline in the November 19 *Sacramento Daily Union*, which printed the same account.[26]

The event further fueled outrage against dueling, especially during wartime and particularly after the battle butchery at Antietam. "While the blood of our countrymen is flowing like water . . . it is horrible that another conspicuous victim should be sacrificed to this savage and murderous custom," the *Southern Christian Advocate* in Augusta, Georgia, scolded on September 24. "The murder of Col. Calhoun was not the sin merely of the man who immediately took his life. It is the sin of the whole land. The whole people are involved in it." The paper went on to state that if dueling were outlawed, "Col. Calhoun would have still lived to serve his country."[27]

A coroner's inquest in the coming weeks came to the obvious conclusion that Rhett fired the fatal shot, and there was gossip in the streets that Dantzler, Dr. Furham, and everyone else present could face charges as accessories to a crime. With Charleston under martial law, it would be up to the military to dispense justice, since dueling was illegal under Confederate military law. Word of the incident soon spread to Richmond, and the government demanded action against Rhett. "Colonel Calhoun's death in a duel being announced in the papers, I desire to call your attention to the 25th and 26th Articles of War, and to request an immediate execution of them," Confederate secretary of war George W. Randolph wrote to Pemberton on September 22. The fact that Rhett had engaged in a duel while an officer in the Confederate army was among the most serious charges he faced. But the war rumbled on and leadership changes likely affected the way the case was handled. Beauregard replaced Pemberton on the twenty-fourth, and Randolph, a brigadier general, resigned his cabinet post in November to return to field duty. A military board of inquiry was soon convened in Charleston and would hear testimony for almost two months, but it would be early in 1863 before Rhett learned his fate.[28]

Despite the violent shock of the duel and fragile psyche of the garrison, much of the work begun in spring 1861 to make Sumter an invulnerable fortress was nearing completion by now. The large spaces left for firing embrasures in the upper casemates, which were unfinished at the time of the bombardment, were finished with brick masonry, but with only a small hole where the embrasure was to be. Three casemates at the salient were completed as originally designed. A large concrete-and-brick

Alfred M. Rhett, the volatile and controversial officer who rose through the ranks of the 1st South Carolina Artillery to command Sumter during the April 7, 1863, Union naval attack.

AUTHOR'S COLLECTION

traverse was erected at the east angle of the ramparts to protect the barbette guns of the right face from naval gunfire. A brick platform—or caponnière—mounting two howitzers, was built just east of the sally port to guard the quay and pier. The officers' quarters and enlisted men's barracks were rebuilt at a reduced height, with the roofs lower than the parapet. The telegraph system had been expanded, linking the fort and Charleston via James Island, and the hot shot furnaces were repaired. Sumter also was equipped with gasworks, a forge, a bakery, a shoe factory, a fire engine, and a machine to convert sea water into fresh water. The fort also had large cisterns, fed by a drainage pipe system, to collect and store rainwater. The fort's four magazines, located in pairs one atop the other, were at either end of the gorge and were bolstered by a fifteen-foot-high stone and masonry barrier outside the fort. A possible Achilles' heel, however, was that this barrier was only as high as the lower magazines and offered no protection to the upper ones.[29]

During this period, a floating boom also was being constructed across Maffitt's Channel between Fort Sumter and Sullivan's Island. The boom consisted of railroad iron linked by strong metal bands and was placed about four feet below the water's surface. It was held in place by timber floats and anchors. A quarter of the boom had already been constructed and tested successfully by running a loaded vessel towed by a steamboat against it. Work on the boom had begun in May—some immense chains for the obstacles were manufactured in Columbia and sent to Charleston—but the bulk of the construction had only begun in September, primarily due to material shortages. It would not be ready before early the next year. The Confederates were considering a second boom, to be located some one hundred yards behind this one, if sufficient chains, timber, and anchors could be found. "Preparations for explosive obstructions in the channels"—torpedoes—were underway but not yet completed. A rope obstruction also was on the drawing board and would be used to entangle propellers of enemy ships if they tried to run the gauntlet between Sumter and Moultrie. It was not yet in place because the rope would rot in the water over an extended time.

Sumter had forty-six heavy guns, not including 32-pounders, aimed at this crucial point in the channel, while Moultrie had nine. Additionally, four new sand batteries were being built on the west end of Sullivan's, soon to add their weight to the firepower protecting the channel. Beauregard, however, pinpointed some weaknesses—including the boom, which he considered "fragile and unreliable"—in the overall defenses and set about correcting them. He not only relied on his expertise as a military engineer, but also called in Lt. Col. David B. Harris, a top-notch engineer who had served with Beauregard in Virginia and in the western theater. One of Beauregard's prime concerns were the big guns, many of which were smoothbores. A number of these were hauled to foundries in Charleston, where they were banded and rifled to improve their accuracy and range.[30]

The Federals underwent a leadership change on September 17, when Maj. Gen. Ormsby M. Mitchel replaced sixty-year-old David Hunter as commander of the U.S. Department of the South. Hunter had experienced a rough few months since his forces captured Fort Pulaski in April. Always more of an abolitionist than a soldier, he had taken the bold step in early May to issue a decree freeing all slaves in Georgia, Florida, and South Carolina. He also had begun recruiting a regiment of black troops in the Port Royal area. Hunter's efforts were praised by the antislavery element, but many of his officers and men opposed these actions. Abraham Lincoln did as well, feeling that the timing was not yet right for such extreme measures that could swing the war for the Confederates. The failure of the James Island offensive in June, culminating in the Union repulse at Secessionville, was Hunter's last straw—at least temporarily.

Nicknamed "Old Stars" by his soldiers due to his passion for astronomy, Mitchel was a Kentuckian and an 1829 West Point classmate of Robert E. Lee. He had shown aggressiveness in operations and raids in northern Alabama earlier in the year, and the Federals hoped he could provide a spark to the army's seeming stagnation outside Charleston. Beauregard, however, did not hold his new adversary in very high regard, telling one of his officers, "Mitchel [is] more fussy than dangerous." Mitchel's troops were organized as the X Army Corps at this time.

The blockade, meanwhile, was ongoing and becoming more efficient, but it was tough, boring, and frustrating duty for many of the Union officers and sailors afloat. "I am kept pretty constantly upon blockade service, and hard and discouraging duty it is, off Charleston," a lieutenant on the gunboat USS *Huron* wrote to a fellow officer in September. "I do not believe it possible to blockade the place effectually [and] would be glad if I could only impress upon you some faint notion of how disgusting it is to us, after going through the anxieties of riding out a black, rainy, windy night . . . with our senses all on the alert for sound of paddles or sight of miscreant violator of our blockade and destroyer of our peace, when morning comes to behold him lying there placidly inside of Fort Sumter, as if his getting there was the most natural thing in the world and the easiest."[31]

There was an air of urgency and high alert in mid-October when the Confederates received word from the War Department that now-Rear Admiral Du Pont—promoted in July 1862—would likely attack Charleston within the next two weeks, with Sumter expected to be in the very center of the bull's-eye. There was no truth to the rumors, but the Southerners were confident they could greet the Yankee navy with hell on earth. The Federals were equally frisky in their anxiousness to punish the city for its lead role in the rebellion "As Boston was regarded as the cradle of American liberty, where the infancy of the Union was nurtured, so Charleston, in later days, came to be considered the nursery of disunion," a U.S. Navy officer related. "Therefore . . . no city in the South was so obnoxious to Union men as Charleston. Richmond was the objective point of our armies, as its capture was expected to end the war, but it excited little sentiment and little antipathy. It was to South Carolina, and especially to Charleston, that the strong feeling of dislike was directed, and the desire was general to punish that city by all the rigors of war." Indeed, Du Pont was under pressure from his superiors in the Navy Department to launch a quick strike against Charleston, but the admiral was waiting for the arrival of several of the navy's revolutionary new monitors before making the attempt. These would not be ready for several months. Foremost among those anxious for the squadron to go in was Gustavus V. Fox, now the assistant secretary of the navy since August 1861. Fox was still bitter and sensitive about his failure to resupply Anderson at Fort Sumter. For him, no chance to punish and humble the Confederates in Charleston could come too soon.[32]

Gen. Roswell Ripley returned to Charleston in mid-October, recuperating from a throat wound he sustained at Antietam on September 17. His performance with the Army of Northern Virginia had been lackluster, and Charleston beckoned again, his wife and family waiting. Ripley had butted heads with John Pemberton there, but with that general now out of the picture, he found a somewhat better working relationship with Beauregard—at least temporarily. In fact, some of Charleston's leading citizens had lobbied Beauregard to bring Ripley back, and Ripley himself during his recuperation had asked Beauregard to allow him to return. Ripley's engineering talents, combined with those of Beauregard, Harris, and their officers, contributed greatly to the defenses over the coming weeks, but he was always a magnet for trouble. It was just a matter of when it would arrive.[33]

Despite the ongoing work, by early October Beauregard still felt that he needed fifty-one more heavy guns to gird the inner harbor forts and batteries, especially since he was not overly confident in the boom between Sumter and Sullivan's Island. "I consider them [the requested guns] indispensable, for my reliance in the boom and other obstructions now being laid . . . is but very limited, except for their moral effect," he wrote to Governor Pickens on October 8. Pickens also had earlier—on September 29—expressed concern about the state of Sumter's garrison, based on the Calhoun–Rhett controversy and the disloyalty rumors, and Beauregard addressed this as well: "With regard to the condition of the

Union admiral
Samuel Du Pont.

HARPER'S WEEKLY (APRIL 25, 1863)

garrison . . . after the thorough investigation of the matter lately made by a military board, I can find no cause for fearing the disloyalty or evil designs of the men composing it. They appear to be well disciplined and zealous, but I agree with you in the necessity of having an able and old artillerist in command of the forts at the entrance of this harbor." Beauregard added that he had already made two applications for Ripley's services, "which have been promised me."[34]

For Ormsby Mitchel, however, the stars that had aligned for his impact on this new assignment quickly faded to blackness. He led a failed Union strike against the Charleston & Savannah in October but, stricken by yellow fever, he died at Beaufort near sundown on Thursday, October 30, after only about six weeks in command. Mitchel's replacement was Brig. Gen. John M. Brannan, a West Pointer and Mexican War hero who had temporarily led the department for twelve days in September before Mitchel took over.

With Mitchel in his death throes a few miles down the coast, the Confederates' board of inquiry about the Rhett–Calhoun duel was ongoing that day in Charleston, and Ripley testified on Rhett's behalf. Ripley said that he was aware of some differences between the officers dating to late summer 1861. The general also stated he had heard rumors that

Calhoun threatened Rhett while the former was visiting a "house of ill repute" in Richmond. He also knew that Rhett had considered leaving the regiment rather than serve under Calhoun. The board also addressed other rumors that Rhett had practiced constantly for the duel in front of a large mirror in his quarters at Sumter. Testimony showed this to be true, but that Calhoun had also practiced for the confrontation.[35]

Ripley had much more pleasant duties at the fort the day after his testimony. On a sunny and warm Friday, October 31, he reviewed the Sumter garrison, composed of the beleaguered 1st South Carolina Artillery. Despite the pesky blockaders, the war seemed to have taken a holiday as a bevy of ladies also ventured out from the city to watch the troops and be serenaded by the regiment's "excellent" band. "The general looked as fine as a fiddle, and performed his part with style and expedition," said a newspaper account. After the soldiers showed their drill sharpness on the parade ground, the guests watched an artillery demonstration. Ripley, Sumter's officers, and the civilians then enjoyed a luncheon before "the visitors retired in a state of decided gratification."[36]

In November, after almost two months of testimony, the board of inquiry into Calhoun's death adjourned, failing to render a verdict other than that the matter should undergo further investigation. Rhett could not be exonerated since he had violated the 25th Article of War in accepting a duel while an officer in the Confederate army. The controversy would drag on into 1863 and beyond.

Work on the boom continued, meanwhile, but Beauregard remained unconvinced of its worth, telling Confederate adjutant and inspector general Samuel Cooper on the twenty-sixth that it "is likely to prove a failure, which increases the necessity for [a] much larger number of heaviest guns." The threat of a Union strike against Wilmington, North Carolina, in mid-December caused Beauregard to send five thousand troops there from Charleston and Savannah as reinforcements. Just after Christmas, however, the War Department warned Beauregard that Charleston was to be attacked instead, and these forces were recalled on the twenty-eighth. Ripley was planning to establish his headquarters at Fort Sumter to help direct the defense of the harbor due to this menace and issued orders to the various forts and batteries regarding fields of fire. It was a false alarm—one of many over the coming months.[37]

Still, Charleston and her defenders knew they would soon be engulfed by the cyclone of war that had already swept across much of the South, leaving death, carnage, and soul-gutting grief in its wake. Only the day and time were unknown. But yet there was still time for gaiety, or at least some semblance of it, as the winter and the Yankees seemed to close in together. Hoist a toast and damn the enemy silhouetted on the ocean's horizon! To this end, Sumter had held another gala on December 8 with Beauregard and Ripley as the hosts. The generals left Charleston that Monday afternoon "with a large number of invited guests, including many ladies," the *Mercury* gossiped, on a "boat specially provided for the occasion." Among the notables was the captain of the French steamer *Milan*, which was anchored in the harbor. Beauregard reviewed the "battalion of regular artillery, constituting the garrison of the post," and the "superb precision of the men in every movement called forth universal admiration from the spectators." There was a tour of the fort's interior before everyone gathered in the officers' quarters for food, drinks, and dancing. "Excellent music and abundant refreshments had been provided by the hospitable officers, and for hours those grim walls echoed with the sounds of merriment," the paper said. By about 9:00 PM, the partygoers boarded the boat to return to Charleston, "leaving the garrison to its wonted rest, with no sign of life upon the dark outline of the fortress, save the sentinels pacing the bleak parapet, in their lonely rounds."[38] Such social pleasantries would soon be distant memories for Sumter's defenders, as if they drifted past in fitful, long-lost dreams.

CHAPTER 3

A Gathering of Leviathans—1863

The scandalous repercussions of the Rhett–Calhoun duel still scarred Charleston in the waning days of 1862 and into the new year. Despite the cloud lingering over Rhett, Beauregard believed that he was entitled to be promoted to lieutenant colonel upon Calhoun's death, because Calhoun's second-in-command, Thomas Wagner, was also dead. Secretary of War James A. Seddon agreed with this assessment in late December (although Beauregard referred to Rhett as "Colonel Rhett" in late November 1862), and Beauregard ordered Lieutenant Colonel Rhett to report for duty to Ripley on January 8, 1863. In short order, however, and with the threat of an enemy attack looming greater each day, Beauregard boldly went even further. He closed the court-martial proceedings, claiming that it would be unfair to oust Rhett from the service when no others had been punished for dueling. He did, however, order that any future dueling incidents would be subject to the Articles of War. The pardon paved the way for Rhett to be named colonel of the 1st South Carolina Artillery and return to command at Sumter, where the bulk of the regiment was still garrisoned. Thus Rhett had attained—with one well-aimed pistol ball—all to which he aspired: the colonelcy of his regiment, the fame of defending the Confederacy's most hallowed shrine, and the elimination of his loathed rival, all with no real consequences. The revelations stunned and infuriated Calhoun's family, friends, and other supporters, but again the Rhett-controlled *Mercury* hushed up the news. "To universal indignation, Alfred Rhett has been placed in command of Fort Sumter," Emma Holmes wrote in her diary on Tuesday, January 13, "the Board of Inquiry having decided it was inexpedient to try him now."[1]

A few miles away, the plotters and planners of Charleston's destruction cared little about this snooty fuss among the damned Southern chivalry. The greatest military technology man had yet created and assembled would soon smite these "Secesh" with doomsday fury. Du Pont was indeed organizing a naval attack force to strike Charleston, but he still needed more time to pull the pieces together. A number of the formidable monitors would be the centerpiece of the assault, but in January most of them were still being fitted and would not reach him until early spring. Du Pont by now did have one monitor, the USS *Montauk*, with Cmdr. John L. Worden at the helm. Worden already had made history by leading the original *Monitor* in its epic sea battle with the CSS *Virginia* on March 9, 1862, the world's first clash of ironclad vessels. With weeks to spare, Du Pont decided to see how his new weapon would fare against a land fort. Worden's target would be Fort McAllister, an earthwork at the mouth of the Ogeechee River south of Savannah. Escorted by four gunboats, the *Montauk* attacked McAllister on January 27. Confident of his armor, Worden closed to within 150 yards of the fort and a point-blank firefight ensued with little damage to either side. Worden attacked again on February 1, testing his marksmanship from a greater distance. The monitor's shells killed McAllister's commander and disabled a gun, but otherwise the destruction was repairable within a few hours. Du Pont was not at all impressed with this performance, writing to a friend, "If one ironclad cannot take eight guns, how are five to take 147 guns in Charleston harbor?"[2]

With the Union fleet still organizing, the greatest glory of the Rebel navy at Charleston to this point occurred on January 31, when the ironclads *Palmetto State* and *Chicora* steamed out to engage the Federals in a predawn sneak attack. They pounced on the wooden gunboats *Keystone State* and *Mercedita*, forcing them to surrender, but both Union vessels escaped amid the confused combat. The assault briefly left the Confederates in control of the harbor mouth, allowing Beauregard to proclaim that the blockade had been broken. Du Pont's ships, however, returned to their stations a few hours later, and the city was corked up again.[3]

Rumors of possible attacks against Charleston, Savannah, or Wilmington kept Confederate troops shuttling back and forth by railroad from Beauregard's command to North Carolina during the first weeks of the year. "Grand attack on Charleston to be made soon," the Louisianan wrote in a February 4 dispatch. "Yankee officers say they will soon test iron against bricks." This was another way of saying that the monitors were coming for Fort Sumter. Indeed, the many months of offensive inactivity by the Federals on the Carolina coast were beginning to chafe many Northerners who felt a great opportunity had been squandered when the forces that seized Port Royal had not soon thereafter been unleashed against Charleston or Savannah in 1861, before their defenses became so formidable. "But the Charleston of February, 1863, is not the Charleston of November, 1861," noted the *New York Herald* in calling for immediate action. "The intervening time has been appropriated by the rebels in the erection of a system of defensive works . . . which it will probably require a protracted siege, by land and water, to reduce."

Charleston also was steeling for the storm. "All information points to an early attack . . . by the water approach and by land," the *Mercury* said on February 12. "Charleston is bitterly hated, because of her early prominence in secession, and because of the victory of Fort Sumter, when the stars and stripes were first lowered to the Confederate arms." Beauregard on the eighth wrote, "Every indication is that Charleston or Savannah will soon be attacked by an overwhelming force." To face this menace, the Confederates had almost eleven thousand troops in and around Charleston and about 5,500 at Savannah.[4]

Any land offensive against Charleston would be led by Union major general David Hunter, who had returned to department command on January 20, replacing John Brannan. The untimely death of Ormsby Mitchel had given the controversial Hunter a second chance at department command some four months after being relieved. Hunter received about ten thousand troops as reinforcements in February's first week—doubling his force posted on the Carolina coast—and believed that the army and navy would cooperate in the coming attack. "We only await the readiness of the Navy, and with the additional iron-clads which have been ordered to report to . . . Du Pont there can be no doubt but that a glorious success will await our efforts," he wrote to Maj. Gen. Henry W. Halleck on February 17. This sounded good, but the Department of the

South was in turmoil. Maj. Gen. John G. Foster—the same Foster who had been an engineer in Robert Anderson's garrison—had brought the reinforcements from North Carolina. He and Hunter immediately clashed about the command hierarchy regarding the new troops, with Foster's subordinates drawn into the fray. Hot words and accusations flew before Foster abruptly left on a scouting mission. Hunter was fuming, accusing Foster of being disrespectful and insubordinate; if Foster returned, he would have him arrested. Hunter also was not impressed by the reinforcements, many of whom he claimed were undisciplined and demoralized. Nevertheless, Hunter expected to be involved in the operation against Charleston.[5]

By February 17, Beauregard was recalling all officers and soldiers on furlough, distributing provisions not already issued, and making last-minute defensive preparations, including strengthening Fort Sumter's southeast angle, which the Confederates expected to take a pounding since it was the closest point to the enemy advancing from the south. The Rebels were also concerned about rumors that Foster and Brig. Gen. Truman Seymour were with the Union forces being arrayed against Charleston or Savannah. Like Foster, Seymour had been with Anderson in the bombardment and knew Sumter's vulnerabilities. Beauregard also called on the state's planters to immediately send at least three thousand slaves to aid in completing the defenses. That same day, he issued a proclamation to the civilians and soldiers of Savannah and Charleston, detailing the "supreme trial" they all faced: "Carolinians and Georgians! [T]he hour is at hand to prove your devotion to your country's cause. Let all able-bodied men, from the seaboard to the mountains, rush to arms. Be not exacting in the choice of weapons; pikes and scythes will do for exterminating your enemies, spades and shovels for protecting your friends . . . Come to share with us our dangers, our brilliant success, or our glorious death."[6]

Beauregard had taken another seemingly drastic step a few weeks earlier to combat the dreaded monitors, ordering Ripley to organize six boarding parties that would try to destroy or cripple any ironclads that penetrated the harbor. The men would be armed with revolvers and given blankets to throw over apertures. They would also have iron wedges and sledges to keep the turrets from revolving. Bottles of "burning fluid" were to be thrown into the turrets and leather bags of gunpowder dropped down the smokestacks from long ladders. The assault boats would be equipped with muffled oars, watertight casks to increase their buoyancy if damaged, and a life preserver for each man. These attacks never made it past the planning stages.

Beauregard also recognized the daunting challenge faced by Sumter, not only from Du Pont's dreadnoughts but also from the big guns that had torn apart Fort Pulaski. "The introduction of heavy rifled guns and iron-clad steamers in the attack of masonry forts has greatly changed the conditions of the problem applicable to Fort Sumter when it was built, and we must now use the few imperfect means at our command to increase its defensive features," he wrote to Ripley on February 8. Amid this drama, the *Montauk* was still operating against Fort McAllister on February 28 when she shelled and destroyed the grounded blockade runner *Rattlesnake* in the Ogeechee. The monitor did not escape unhurt, however, hitting a submerged mine that tore a ten-foot gash in her side. She was towed to Port Royal and repaired within days, but her action against McAllister was done.[7]

"Charleston or Savannah, or both, are now awaiting . . . the onslaught of the greatest war fleet ever seen in our hemisphere," the *Richmond Enquirer* said. "The crisis is upon them. Many a beating heart longs and burns to be with the envied defenders of those cities, under command of the heroic and devoted Beauregard." But the *Montauk*'s ineffectiveness against McAllister, especially the monitor's slow rate of fire, was cause for much concern for Du Pont. On the flip side, it showed the Confederates that the ironclads might not be as fearsome as imagined. Another Richmond scribe suggested that the "coveted city" of Charleston was a greater trophy for the Yankees than the Confederate capital. "But the Charleston grapes still hang in tempting clusters, and the grudge they owe South Carolina is older and more venomous than that towards Virginia," said the *Richmond Dispatch*. "With Beauregard at the head of [the] Carolina chivalry, there will be such an entertainment ready for the Yankees at Charleston which will satisfy their appetites for invasion for years to come."[8]

Still, the Union concentration of a formidable naval and land force at Port Royal, Hilton Head, and Edisto Island was a strong signal that an offensive against the city was likely imminent. Both sides knew that it was only been a matter of time before the boiling point arrived, and the

Rebels seemed ready to face the expected onslaught of the armada arrayed to destroy them. And the longer the Yankees delayed, the stronger they became.

Charleston's land defenses "were as perfect as the engineering skill and the resources of the Confederacy could make them," one Southerner noted, and consisted of three lines, each a "circle of fire." Masterminded by Beauregard and Ripley, with contributions by Pemberton and Lee, the fortifications commanded the ship channels with crossfire artillery, which was only one aspect of their formidability. Fort Sumter—with Rhett and his garrison—anchored the center of the first line, which continued south to Batteries Gregg and Wagner on Morris Island. Gregg was a strong earthwork located at Cummings Point, only three-fourths of a mile from Fort Sumter. Wagner was an even larger earthwork with bombproofs and a well-built magazine, situated about a mile and a half from Sumter. To Sumter's north, Sullivan's Island bristled with Batteries Bee, Marion, Rutledge, and Marshall, as well as four smaller, detached batteries, all works of well-sodded sand. Fort Moultrie, a brick bastion built in 1811, was the key to Sullivan's; Robert Anderson's force had been posted there before evacuating to Sumter in December 1860.

If enemy ships managed to slip past this line, they would encounter the second circle, composed of Fort Johnson, Batteries Cheves, Wampler, and Glover, and some minor works southeast of Charleston on James Island. The second line also boasted Castle Pinckney, a small brick fort on Shute's Folly Island; the wood-palisaded Fort Ripley, in the Folly Island channel; two batteries at Mount Pleasant on the north side of the inner harbor; and a battery on Hog Island. The third line was fortifications in and near the city itself. A swarm of submerged torpedoes awaited in the main channel and other principal waterways, including the entrances to the Cooper and Ashley Rivers, which formed the peninsula on which Charleston lay. The floating boom (much maligned by Beauregard) was finally in place in two sections—one between Cummings Point and Fort Sumter and the other from Sumter to Sullivan's. It had openings for the passage of blockade runners and Confederate navy vessels. Earlier in the year, it had been augmented with floating mines as well.[9]

"Now more than ever the eyes of the Confederacy are centered on that bulwark of our eastern defenses, Fort Sumter," Lt. Col. Alfred Roman of Beauregard's staff wrote after inspecting the post on January 28. "It is the first historical monument of this war, and as it opened our struggle for independence so it will likely close it with equal glory to our national honor." Roman was quite effusive in his praise of Rhett and the garrison—no doubt supporting Beauregard's views at least in part—but his report offered a rare and vivid description of Sumter during this time. "The gallant colonel" Rhett commanded the garrison, which was composed of seven companies of the 1st South Carolina Artillery, with 437 men present for duty. Joseph Yates, recently promoted to lieutenant colonel, and Major Ormsby Blanding were his senior officers. "The troops present quite a remarkable appearance on inspection. I doubt whether any corps in the old United States Army ever looked as well," Roman noted. "The uniforms, arms, and accouterments were in a perfect condition as regards cleanliness," although some muskets needed work and "many uniforms want repairing." Their knapsacks were another issue, made of poor material so that "it is almost impossible to give them regular form and to wear them properly." The Carolinians had no haversacks and were short of canteens, the latter becoming "indispensible during action to prevent the men from leaving their posts to get water," Roman said. He found their quarters to be neatly kept but crowded and not well ventilated due to recent changes at the fort. The kitchen and mess rooms were clean, the "cooking apparently well attended to." Every company received wheat bread once a week and corn bread on the other days. The garrison also got a daily ration of beef. "The allowance of bread is rather short, but it is good, well baked, and I believe perfectly wholesome," he stated. The hospital, under the direction of surgeon M. S. Moore, needed more ventilation, the lack of which caused Roman to recommend "more care be given to the cleanliness of both the room and bedding."[10]

With an attack expected at any time, Sumter had a six-month supply of provisions, including 27,550 pounds of bacon, 32,900 pounds of pork, 446 barrels of flour, and a plentiful supply of rice and meal. Bad weather prevailed on the day of Roman's inspection, preventing him from having the troops drilled, but he had seen them enough on other occasions to be quite impressed with their martial sharpness: "The regularity and mechanical precision of their manual at arms is remarkable; their five hundred muskets, their thousand hands, move as if one musket only and one pair of hands were put in motion. In that respect and in many others regarding important details of the service the . . . companies of the First South Carolina Artillery now at Fort Sumter have no rivals."[11]

A few miles across the water, Du Pont had more monitors to join the *Montauk* by now and in early March sent three of them—*Passaic, Patapsco,* and *Nahant*—to again test the ironclads' efficiency against Fort McAllister. All of these ships were of the *Passaic* class, essentially improved versions of the original *Monitor,* and would see more action than any of the forthcoming class of monitors; these leviathans bristled with a pair of smoothbore Dahlgren guns in their turrets. The strike against McAllister would be a final trial run before Du Pont took on Sumter and the rest of Charleston's defenses. It would also provide combat experience for his sailors, most of whom had spent little time aboard the newfangled iron contraptions.

The monitors slammed McAllister for some seven hours on March 3, and Union mortar boats continued the shellacking through the night. All of this flying iron resulted in three Southerners wounded, the death of the garrison cat, and minor damage to the earthwork. Still, the monitors withstood numerous hits from enemy rounds, a fact that impressed Du Pont, although he still had doubts about their slow rate of fire. These ironclads soon steamed north to join the admiral's fleet for the coming blow to retake Charleston. The Confederates in that city well recognized the curious and history-changing marvel the coming battle would offer. "The fight in the harbor between our batteries and the ironclad gunboats is going to be an experiment, concerning which we and the world have no experience from the past," the *Mercury* said. "Although very hopeful of the result, we should prepare to fight the city itself in defence." Additionally, the Union blockaders were continuing to tighten their noose on Charleston, with ten vessels stationed off the port in early March, another three in the nearby Stono River, and twelve or so being repaired or provisioned or coaling at Port Royal.[12]

Du Pont's victory at Port Royal and in regaining possession of vast stretches of the southern coast won him the thanks of Congress, his rear admiralship, and a high degree of confidence from the Navy Department. "He had not only its confidence, but also to an extraordinary degree that of the commanding officers under him," noted C. R. P. Rodgers, the admiral's chief of staff and later an admiral himself. Almost sixty years old, Du Pont was a native of New Jersey whose uncle was the

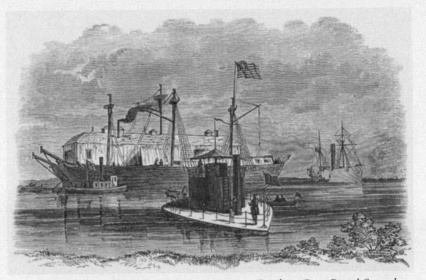

The Union navy's machine shop at Station Creek in Port Royal Sound, South Carolina. FAMOUS LEADERS AND BATTLE SCENES OF THE CIVIL WAR

founder of one of America's top business conglomerates. One of his monitor captains, Cmdr. Daniel Ammen, described the admiral as "distinguished, over six feet in height, admirably proportioned, graceful and urbane, with an intelligent expression and action." Ammen added that "no officer in our navy within the past half century was gifted with a more distinguished appearance or exalted character." Du Pont was thorough, able, and brave. His naval career was long and proud, beginning as a twelve-year-old midshipman in 1815 and including stations around the world and action in the Mexican War. Promoted to captain in 1855, he contributed to the planning of the Union's naval operations in the war's first months and was given command of the blockading squadron in September 1861. "Few commanders in chief have had the good fortune to inspire the same admiration, affection, and trust that the officers who came in contact with Admiral Du Pont felt for him," said Rodgers.[13]

In late March, Charleston's defenders noticed a new and strikingly different addition to Du Pont's fleet. The double-turreted monitor *Keokuk* had joined the blockaders after being commissioned about a month earlier. Cmdr. Alexander C. Rhind's 677-ton ironclad boasted a 100-man crew, but her pride were her twin towers (the other monitors had one turret and were basically identical to the original USS *Monitor*) and her experimental "sandwich armor," composed of rows of iron and wood extending almost four feet below the waterline. Her main armament were two smoothbore Dahlgren cannon, weighing almost eight tons each. Rhind was a brave, smart, and experienced skipper who had almost sixteen years of naval service under his belt. With this new, formidable weapon in his hands, Du Pont had gathered the most powerful and lethal armada in history as wooden ships sailed deeper into a bygone age. Now he could make final preparations to assail Fort Sumter.[14]

This attack could not be soon enough for Gustavus Fox, who had been pushing Du Pont to take the offensive since late 1861. Secretary of the Navy Gideon Welles also wanted action from the admiral, but it was Fox in particular who wanted Sumter and Charleston to feel the terrible power of the ironclads. He had complete confidence in the monitors' ability to steam into Charleston Harbor and force the city to surrender. There was more: Fox also was so pro-navy that he strongly advocated that the attack be made by Du Pont's squadron alone with no army involvement. The assistant secretary's views placed the admiral in quite a bind. He did not share Fox's overwhelming confidence in the ironclads and was quite aware of the strong defenses ringing the harbor.

Du Pont also believed that a joint operation between the navy and army was essential to success. In a visit to Washington in fall 1862, he proposed that an army force of at least twenty-five thousand men should attack James Island simultaneously with the naval assault. He was told that no such force could be spared. Now the leadership uproar in Hunter's department, combined with the desire of Welles and Fox for the navy to attack on its own, meant Du Pont's warships would conquer Sumter or fall short, either way without army support. Hunter, however, was preparing as if his troops would be a part of the offensive. Du Pont had confided in him his reservations about the monitors in their Fort McAllister attacks, and Hunter had taken it upon himself to inform Halleck of these concerns in mid-March. Based on what the admiral told him, Hunter said the assaults had "demonstrated certain defects grave enough in the opinion of the admiral to call for a postponement of active operations until they shall have been remedied." To the Navy Department, the attack had already been delayed for too long. By March 27, Hunter was reporting that "all of the troops destined to take part in the expedition are in complete readiness to move whenever the necessary repairs and additions to the iron-clads shall have been made." He added that within a few days "the joint expedition will be under way."[15]

Might was about to meet might. By early April, Sumter was at the height of its power as a Confederate stronghold, boasting eighty-five guns, seven mortars, and a garrison of about 550 men—seven companies (B, C, D, E, F, G, and I) of Rhett's 1st South Carolina Artillery. With months to prepare and under Rhett's harsh tutelage, the Carolinians had been honed to bayonet sharpness, the past controversies seemingly forgotten. "Under strict discipline, with constant drill and practice, the garrison had attained the highest degree of excellence," an officer wrote. Sumter remained a popular attraction for civilians out for a pleasant day excursion that spring. "An afternoon trip down the harbor to see the dress parade and hear the band playing at Fort Sumter was held by the Charlestonians to be an indispensable custom—a tribute due both to the war spirit of the time and to the merit of a fine command," a Confederate noted. The artillerists enjoyed "a spirit of emulation" with their comrades across the ship channel, the 1st South Carolina Regular Infantry who garrisoned Fort Moultrie. "The people of the state and city were proud of the two regiments."[16]

Rhett's subordinates, Lieutenant Colonel Yates and Major Blanding, assisted him in overseeing the gunners, Yates in charge of the forty-five barbette guns and Blanding the forty in the casemate batteries. Yates had only returned to duty at Sumter the first week of April, but was widely respected for his soldierly skills. Described by Beauregard as "this excellent officer," Yates had been instrumental in planning and carrying out the ambush and capture of the U.S. gunboat *Isaac Smith* on the Stono River in January when hidden field artillery had pounded the vessel into submission. He also had been outspoken in defending the regiment's honor amid the mutiny furor the previous May. Sumter's chief engineer, Lt. John Johnson, had literally watched the fort built from the ground up. As a boy growing up in the Charleston area in the 1840s, he was friendly with the U.S. Army Corps of Engineers captain in charge of the project and visited the construction site frequently. The walls had not been erected then, and the structure was only a few feet above the high-water mark. Those carefree days long gone, the thirty-one-year-old Johnson would now spend a year and three months of his life at Sumter in 1863–64, praying to get home alive.

There was more pressure heaped on Du Pont from Welles and Fox on April 2. Both sent dispatches to the admiral, in essence with the same message: Monitors were needed for naval operations to regain control of the Mississippi River, and Du Pont was to send all but two of his ironclads to Union-held New Orleans as soon as the assault at Charleston was finished. General Hunter, meanwhile, was moving about ten thousand troops by transports from Hilton Head north toward Charleston to participate in the "joint attack," as he described it, on April 3. "I have seen Admiral Du Pont this afternoon, and find that he is merely awaiting fine weather, all his preparations being complete," he noted. Most of Hunter's soldiers would see little, if any, combat in the coming days.[17]

Du Pont issued final instructions to his skippers on April 4. His order of attack would be the *Weehawken, Passaic, Montauk, Patapsco, New Ironsides* (the massive ironclad frigate that served as the admiral's flagship), *Catskill, Nantucket, Nahant,* and *Keokuk.* The ships were to pass the Morris Island batteries without returning fire unless ordered to do so. They were then to "open fire on Fort Sumter when within easy range," taking positions north and west of the fort and at a distance of six hundred to eight hundred yards. The gunners were to fire low; the commanders were to "instruct their officers and men to carefully avoid wasting a shot, and will enjoin upon them the necessity of precision rather than rapidity of fire." Each ship was to be prepared to "render every assistance possible to vessels that may require it." Finally, the ironclads should be ready for more action after Sumter was silenced. "After a reduction of Fort Sumter it is probable that the next point of attack will be the batteries on Morris Island," Du Pont stated. A reserve force, led by Capt. J. F. Green, would be stationed outside the bar, ready to support the monitors if and when they assailed Morris Island. The reserve consisted of the *Canandaigua, Housatonic, Unadilla, Wissahickon,* and *Huron.*

Commanding the monitors and *New Ironsides* were some of the most talented and bravest officers in the navy, entrusted with the most terrible weapons ever to weigh anchor. "It would have been difficult to find in the navy men of higher reputation for skill and courage, of better nerve, or more fully possessing the confidence of the service," one of Du Pont's staff wrote of John Worden, John Rodgers, Percival Drayton, Daniel Ammen, Thomas Turner, George W. Rodgers, Donald M. Fairfax, John Downes, and Alexander Rhind.[18]

On the morning of Sunday, April 5, the "abolition ironclad fleet," as Rhett described it, appeared in sight. The nine enemy vessels, including the *New Ironsides* and the eight monitors, crossed the bar and anchored in the main channel later that day. It was about noon when "the first intelligence was flashed to the city from Fort Sumter, that the turrets of the far-famed Monitor gunboats were looming up against the southeastern horizon," the *Mercury* reported. From his vantage point, Rhett counted a total of twenty-seven Union ships offshore, including support vessels. "The enemy are mustering," Ripley wrote from Sumter that day to Brig. Gen. J. H. Trapier, commanding the Confederate troops on Sullivan's Island. "Have everything in readiness and keep a sharp lookout to-day and to-night. I am going to hoist all the flags and fire a broadside to show that I am ready."

The appearance of the enemy behemoths and reports of Federal troop transports on the Stono were the last straws for some civilians, who hastily packed some possessions and jammed the last trains out of Charleston on Sunday. But like most of the Confederates, the *Mercury* was also seething for a fight. "Let Them Come!" blared a headline on Monday, the sixth. "The long delayed hour seems at last to have arrived," the paper said. "The attack on our city . . . is now imminent. Whatever careful preparation, unlimited resources, all the instruments and agents of modern warfare, undisguised hate and the bitterest feelings of revenge can suggest, have been arrayed against the 'Nest of the Rebellion' for the avowed purpose of wiping out the insult to their flag" made when Sumter fell.[19]

Du Pont wanted to attack on the sixth and massed his ships near the north end of Edisto Island, but hazy conditions limited the visibility of his pilots in recognizing landmarks, so the assault was delayed until the next day. On the *Nahant*, seamen peered across the waves at a "row of black dots on the water" between Moultrie and Sumter, realizing they were looking at the dreaded rope and timber obstructions the Rebels had placed there. "This iron-clad fleet had been expected by us for some time," recalled Claudine Rhett, a Charleston belle and a sister of Sumter's commander, "as they had been loudly vaunted by the Northern press for months before they arrived . . . and we received the New York papers constantly from the 'blockade runners,' and knew therefore, that they were supposed to be invulnerable, and that they believed they could 'take Charleston' without the least difficulty." Another Charlestonian, W. F. G.

Peck, agreed: "The dread of the monitors . . . was very general throughout the city. None had seen one except at a great distance, but every one
had heard the most fabulous accounts of their formidableness and
power." Most of the Union tars also reflected this confidence in their
leviathans: "The opinion before the attack was general . . . that whatever
might be the loss in men and vessels . . . at all events Fort Sumter would
be reduced to a pile of ruins before the sun went down," related Commander Ammen of the *Pataspco*.[20]

CHAPTER 4

Du Pont's Attack— "A Grand and Imposing Spectacle"

Tuesday, April 7 was a magnificent spring day in Charleston with clear skies, mirrored seas, and a lazy northeast wind. Much like April two years earlier, this one was scented with azaleas, gunpowder, and rebellion, the current drama at Sumter even more emphatic, urgent, and kinetic than the nation-shattering act when Anderson lowered his flag.

Everyone realized this could be the day of reckoning, and hundreds of people lined The Battery and the rest of the harborfront or found vantage points on roofs or upper-floor windows and church steeples. British illustrator and correspondent Frank Vizetelly was trying to reach Sumter in a small boat and passed the crowded Battery. He made a quick sketch of the scene and noted that "the ladies of Charleston had no undue fear for the result of the attack, which, if successful, would place their homes at the mercy of an exasperated foe."

The hours seemed like days to the monitor crews waiting for the attack to begin. Many of the men who were stationed in the bowels of the ironclads took the opportunity to go topside and savor the spectacular conditions. "During this long wait I was glad to spend as much time as possible in the open air," wrote Alvah Hunter, a sixteen-year-old New Hampshire sailor on the *Nahant*. "The weather was mild and spring-like, and the gentle sea breeze . . . made it a delight to be out in the open." In preparation for combat, the galley stovepipe had been taken down, meaning the crew could not cook, but they had prepared a meal in advance, including baked bread and ham. Hunter and his buddies made hot coffee by heating it over shovelfuls of coals from the boilers. Each of the monitors had been thoroughly smeared with grease to help deflect projectiles, and their smokestacks were painted various colors so that they could be identified during the battle.

Finally, Du Pont signaled for the assault to begin at 12:30 PM. "In every direction there seemed to be nothing but batteries and guns, while Fort Sumter's walls were crowded with pieces of every description," related Edgar Holden, a crewman on the *Passaic*. The *Weehawken*, skippered by Cmdr. John Rodgers, was pushing a mine-clearing raft called a "devil" to help dislodge any submerged torpedoes and almost immediately ran into trouble, her anchor chain entangling with the raft. This delayed the attack for about an hour before the *Weehawken* could free itself, the rest of the assault force waiting quietly and motionless. Finally, Rodgers signaled the "all clear" about 1:15 PM, and the attack resumed. "Slowly we steamed along in single file, and gradually there settled down a solemn hush almost death-like," Holden recalled. "The moments seemed to lengthen to hours; and not a sound save the splash of the propeller broke the terrible silence." Aboard the *Nahant*, an officer scanned the enemy batteries with his telescope and muttered, "This isn't going to be any such picnic as we had at Fort McAllister."[1]

Rhett watched from the fort's southeast angle, the closest point to the squadron, as the monitors—or "doughty ironclad dogs of war," as one journalist described them—proceeded. The ironclads had such low profiles that very little of them was visible above water other than their turrets and smokestacks, their hulls a mere black line on the sea. As the Union vessels neared Cummings Point, inching closer to within range, drummers beat the long roll at Sumter about 2:30 PM. The Carolinians, itching to fight, turned out in their dress parade uniforms in their excitement to finally meet the enemy. "The whole garrison knew that the hour of trial was at hand, and the greatest enthusiasm and alacrity prevailed," the *Mercury* said. "The men rushed to their guns with shouting and yells of exultation." Due to the monitors' slow advance, the defenders had had time to eat a pre-battle meal before 2:55 PM, when the blue-and-white state flag and the black-and-white regimental banner were raised; the garrison's Confederate flag already flew defiantly. The hoisting of the other banners was accompanied by a thirteen-gun salute as the regiment's band played "national airs," including "Dixie," from the rampart. "Every heart beat high. Every face was flushed with calm excitement," the *Mercury* said. From the fort's second tier of casemates, a company of sharpshooters from the Charleston Battalion peered out, awaiting targets.[2]

Five minutes later, a cannoneer at Fort Moultrie yanked a lanyard, sending a round whistling toward the monitors to open the dance. The *Weehawken*, still in the lead, did not immediately reply, steaming to within 1,400 yards of Sumter before answering with blasts from her 15- and 11-inch guns. Both shrieked harmlessly over the fort. Rhett's gunners then went to work, targeting the lead monitor with battery fire. The action soon became general as Du Pont's ironclads churned in closer to join the fight, as did the Rebel artillery on Sullivan's and Morris Islands. Sumter's defenders soon switched to firing by individual gun, which improved their accuracy. The regiment's musicians by now had dropped their instruments and joined their batteries to aid in the defense. One of Du Pont's staff officers recalled that "When the Confederate guns . . . were turned upon the ironclads, the sight was one that no one who witnessed it will ever forget; sublime, infernal, it seemed as if the fires of hell were turned upon the Union fleet." Holden, on the *Passaic*, wrote that "like the crash of thunder, every battery opened, and for a few long moments the roar of guns, the hiss and scream of shells, the quivering of the ship, and the tremendous explosions from our own heavy pieces drowned the loud voices of command." The billows of gun smoke obscured the vision of cannoneers on both sides for a minute or so before clearing enough for them to resume their work "with redoubled fury."[3]

The *Weehawken* was nearing the line of obstructions when there was an explosion near her bow. Believing that she had hit a torpedo, Rodgers steered away from the obstructions, not wishing to strike any others. This movement held up and momentarily confused the monitors coming up behind her. Aboard the *New Ironsides*, Du Pont was dealing with other problems. The crew was having difficulty controlling the vessel, forcing it to anchor; the admiral ordered the trailing monitors to move on and attack Sumter's northeast face. Again the *New Ironsides* tried to resume the assault, but her pilot could not negotiate the channel, and she again halted. The flagship was out of the battle, getting no closer than 1,700 yards to Sumter, according to Rhett; the ship's surgeon added that the *Ironsides* "was of no more use than if she had been at the Philadelphia navy yard."

"Through the thunder of artillery ran the heavy thud of the huge shells as they pounded the brick walls of Sumter and the metallic ring and crash of the shot and shells as they struck the iron turrets . . . of the monitors, tearing away the iron plates, crashing through the sides and decks, or shivering into fragments," a Southern officer wrote. The engineer Johnson recalled the giant shells fired by the monitors and the earthquake-like effect when they impacted with Sumter, all the rounds larger than anything the Confederates had to answer. "All in the garrison . . . will remember the prodigious size of those black spheres, fifteen inches in diameter, as they bounded in full view from the ports of the turrets to the walls of the fort," he related. "The powerful shocks given by these projectiles to the solid masonry of the fort was something new and could never be forgotten. The massive walls, piers and arches seemed to tremble to their foundations." A Union officer in the fleet also was transfixed by the terrible missiles cutting across the cobalt sky: "The air seemed full of heavy shot, and as they flew they could be seen as plainly as a baseball in one of our games." Through all of this Sumter's artillerists labored, their red-and-gray uniforms often obscured by gun smoke while men scurried up and down the fort's spiral staircases.[4]

On the *Nahant*, Capt. John Downes shouted commands to his crewmen as shells clanged against his armor. One big round smashed into the turret, dislodging a bolt and nut and sending their fragments ricocheting across the interior of the pilothouse with deadly velocity. At the helm, Quartermaster Edward Cobb crumpled, mortally wounded, a chunk torn out of his skull. Pilot Isaac Sofield also slumped to the deck with a bloody slash to his back, and Downes was hit on the foot, causing a painful injury. "My quartermaster is killed! Pass him down and send up another!" Downes roared over the battle din. Noting that the rounds from his 15-inch gun had all gone astray, the incensed skipper yelled to the ensign in charge of the piece: "Mr. Clarke, you haven't hit anything yet!"

"We ain't near enough, Captain Downes," Clarke replied.

This only riled Downes more: "Not near enough! God damn it, I'll put you near enough! Starboard your helm, quartermaster!"

The *Nahant* by this time had toiled to within five hundred yards of Sumter, the closest any Union vessel had gotten to that point, but she did not have the firepower to stay there long. Her steering mangled by the deadly shell, she nevertheless was able to withdraw.[5]

With the monitors in front of her heavily engaged, and with Du Pont's line of attack further muddled by the *New Ironsides'* halt, the newly minted *Keokuk* barreled into the melee. It would be her first—and last—combat. Rhind, her veteran commander, tried to keep from fouling or colliding with any of the other ironclads, but the maneuvering brought the *Keokuk* within a few hundred yards of Sumter's southeast walls, the most serious penetration of the attackers all day. Rhett's artillerists had been waiting a long time for this chance to display their gunnery prowess and took full advantage of it. They plastered the *Keokuk* with shell and shot, soon disabling her forward gun. Ninety projectiles crashed into her, including at least nineteen at or just below the waterline. Rhind later reported that "The turrets were pierced in many places, one of the forward port shutters shot away; in short, the vessel was completely riddled." After a half hour of this punishment, in which fifteen of his seamen were wounded, Rhind, slightly injured himself, pulled his stricken vessel out of the line about 4:00 PM. "Finding it impossible to keep her afloat many minutes more under such an extraordinary fire, during which rifled projectiles of every species and the largest caliber, [and] also hot shot, were poured into us, I reluctantly withdrew," he later noted. She managed to limp to safety, but she was doomed.

Inside the turrets of the other monitors, the nuts securing the armor plates flew about wildly with each direct hit, injuring, unnerving, and distracting the gunners. In Charleston the crowds were enthralled by the distant cannon blasts and the violent drama before them, everyone squinting to see what was happening as gun-smoke clouds stained the sky. "From every point of view in the city, the eyes of the many thousands of spectators [were] riveted on the grand and imposing spectacle," a Virginian wrote. "The church steeples, roofs, windows and piazzas of houses on the 'Battery' were crowded with eager, breathless witnesses." Described as "a radiant and confident spectator," Beauregard watched the battle from the East Bay battery promenade with his staff officers.[6]

With the *Keokuk* gone, his other vessels getting pummeled, and no chance of punching past Sumter and the other forts, Du Pont ordered a withdrawal about 5:30 PM. The two-and-a-half-hour fight was over, the *Weehawken*, *Passaic*, and *Nahant* also severely battered.

*This Currier & Ives engraving depicts the intense combat of Admiral
Du Pont's ill-fated naval assault against Sumter and surrounding
Confederate defenses at Charleston on April 7, 1863.
The* New Ironsides *is in the foreground.* LIBRARY OF CONGRESS

The Union vessels had been completely outgunned from the outset,
the Confederates having almost three times as many artillery pieces in
action (almost seventy to twenty-three) with a more rapid rate of fire.
Forty-two of Sumter's guns—just over half of its armament—were
engaged in the battle and fired 810 shots. A total of more than 2,200
rounds had been hurled at the Federal fleet, the majority from Moultrie
and the Sullivan's Island batteries. The *Weehawken* had fired twenty-six
shots while being hit fifty-three times and heavily damaged. The *Passaic*
also had been beaten up, thirty-five Rebel rounds disabling one of her
guns and jamming her turret, while *Nahant* likewise was "badly mauled,"
as a Union officer put it, struck thirty-six times. *Patapsco* had been plastered by forty-six rounds and one of her guns put out of action, while
Nantucket weathered fifty-one hits. *Catskill* and *Montauk* were banged up
but not seriously hurt.

Sumter had certainly borne the brunt of the attack. The assault force
had aimed all but twenty or so shots at the fort; the others, out of 139
rounds total, were directed at Morris and Sullivan's islands. While the
Confederates respected the bravery of the Union crews, Rhett was not

impressed by the aim of Du Pont's gunners. "The enemy's fire was mostly ricochet, and not very accurate," he reported. "Most of their shot passed over the fort, and several to the right and left. He added that the bulk of the incoming rounds "were from 1,300 to 1,400 yards distant, which appeared to be the extent of their effective range; some shots were from a greater distance, and did not reach the fort at all."[7]

Conversely, C. R. P. Rodgers, Du Pont's chief of staff, felt that the buoys the Confederates had moored to give them accurate ranges contributed greatly to the "perfect precision and tremendous effect" of their fire. "Each ship was only about forty-five minutes under the heavy fire, and they encountered only the outer line of defense, but their battered armor, their crippled turrets, and their disabled guns proved the power of the forts and the coolness and skill of the Southern gunners," he noted. Despite the pounding they suffered, the ironclads sustained minimal losses—only one killed and twenty-one wounded—but the emotional toll was shocking. "The result of the attack was mortifying to all the officers and men engaged in it," recalled Commander Ammen of the *Patapsco*. "The damage inflicted on the vessels shows that they were incapable of enduring heavy blows sufficiently long to effect the destruction of Sumter." The teen sailor Alvah Hunter on the *Nahant* agreed, lamenting that "a feeling of disappointment and chagrin at our failure settled down upon us."[8]

Five men were wounded at Sumter, but Rhett initially reported no bloodshed, instead describing shrapnel tears to the fort's flags. But its armament had not escaped damage. An old 8-inch Columbiad had exploded and two other guns had been disabled, the latter repaired and back in service within a few hours. The Columbiad crew added a touch of levity to the proceedings just after the battle. Capt. Charles Inglesby, the fort's officer of the day, was making his inspection when one of the artillerists asked him in a serious tone, "Mr. Officer of the Day, have you seen an eight-inch Columbiad running around anywhere that you have been?" When Inglesby replied sharply for the man to explain himself, the gunner pointed to his empty gun carriage and answered, "We fired our gun just now, but when we started to sponge her for a new load we saw that she had gone!" Part of the fractured cannon had plummeted outside the fort while the rest had fallen some sixty feet onto the parade ground. The joke went that it would have been almost as difficult to lose a church steeple as it would a gun the size and weight of the Columbiad. The Rebs also got a chuckle about the detonation of a big Yankee shell that sent a giant plume of water cascading over the east wall. The water drenched Adjutant S. Cordes Boylston and his new uniform, filling the top of his scarlet cap "like an overflowing saucer."9

On a more serious note, Sumter itself sustained structural damage that was severe in some places, engineer Johnson said. At one point on the eastern (seafront) wall, two shells, an 11-inch and a 15-inch round, had struck nearly together, completely breaching the upper casemate and leaving a six-by-eight-foot crater in the exterior wall. At a different spot, the parapet was loosened for twenty-five feet in length, some bricks falling away and exposing a gun carriage. All four of the fort's magazines were unscathed, but the lack of protection for the upper magazines was a constant concern for the defenders, especially now that the Yanks had gotten down to business. "The damage to Fort Sumter could be plainly seen, and numerous immense holes showed the power of 15-inch shell," noted Edgar Holden on the *Passaic*. Ripley toured the fort later in the day, noting that Rhett, Yates, and Blanding were already leading repair efforts where the "walls [had been] badly shaken in two or three places." He also requested that Charlestonians send "their petticoats and pillow-cases—at once" to be used as sandbags. "Some of the enemy have been badly hurt," he said. "The *Keokuk* is probably for sale. Whether the attack will be renewed or not I cannot judge. . . . I don't think we had better say it is over, but will let you know in the morning."10

The sound repulse could have been even costlier to the Federals. Confederate engineers had developed a massive underwater mine containing two thousand to three thousand pounds of gunpowder and designed to sink an enemy ship. The mine was placed outside the harbor and a cable run from it to a position onshore. Relying on directions from the Signal Corps, engineer Capt. Langdon Cheves was set to electrically detonate the mine if an enemy vessel got reasonably close to it. Incredibly, Du Pont and the *New Ironsides* floated almost directly over the mine when the ship anchored the second time. The big ship had not taken part in much of the battle but had taken about fifty hits, none of which penetrated, due to the thick armor. Now, however, the Rebels had a huge opportunity to possibly blow her out of the water. Excitedly, lookouts flagged the news of the vessel's location to Cheves, who flicked the switch—no explosion! Cheves quickly checked his connections and tried again and again, without result. The *New Ironsides* still floated defiantly on the waves as the admiral supervised his assault. After about ten minutes, the flagship steamed away, everyone aboard unaware of the volcanic blast they had escaped. In the following days, the frustrated Confederates blamed each other for this botched opportunity. Reasons for the failure varied from the cable being too long to detonate the mine to the line being cut when a wagon ran over it on the beach. "The big torpedo did not explode; I do not know why," Ripley reported later that day.[11]

Despite the failure to destroy the flagship, the Southerners had won a solid victory, and Rhett complimented his garrison: "Officers and men were alike animated with the same spirit, and I can not speak in too high terms of their coolness and gallantry throughout the action; all acted as though they were engaged in practice, and the minutest particulars of drill and military etiquette were preserved." That night, however, Sumter's Confederates prepared for the monitors to renew the attack the next morning. Working parties from the 46th Georgia were shipped in to assist the garrison in its repairs while stores also were replenished. Including the Sumter casualties, the Confederates defending the harbor suffered three dead and eleven wounded. Across the dark waves, the *Keokuk*'s tars struggled through the night to plug the many rips in her hide, but sunrise on Wednesday, April 8, brought wind-whipped swells that would spell her end. Rhind hoisted a distress signal flag about 7:30 AM, and the tug *Dandelion* was soon alongside to bring off the crew. "The stoppage of the leaks . . . proved altogether ineffectual when the sea got up," Rhind noted. "So large and ragged were the apertures that it was impossible to keep anything our means supplied in the holes." Obviously, her sandwich armor had been a colossal failure.[12]

The monitor sank upright about 8:30 AM in shallows about 1,300 yards off the south end of Morris Island, the Confederates marking her location by her smokestack and turrets, visible at low tide. Beauregard basked in his victory and the *Keokuk*'s end. "This successful repulse and first destruction of the dreaded iron monster of the deep must add new laurels to the fadeless wreath he already wears," the *Mercury* noted of the general on April 8, later adding that the monitor's sinking was "glorious news." Beauregard, in one of his many reports about this battle, described how the monitor was mortally wounded: "The *Keokuk*, having meantime approached . . . Fort Sumter, was quickly riddled, her guns silenced, and she was withdrawn from the fight, vitally crippled."

Still, the Confederates believed the enemy fleet was not yet licked, the presence of the Union troop transports adding to their consternation. "Doubtless the Yankee generals intend, before venturing upon a land attack, to await the issue of the struggle between their ships and our batteries," the *Mercury* said on the eighth. The monitors had been hit hard, but a civilian crew of mechanics from the Port Royal base labored overnight to get them back into fighting trim. This proved to be a remarkable feat, and Du Pont's tritons were ready for action again that Wednesday morning. The Union sailors watched the Rebels at Sumter mount new guns and stack sandbags to patch some of the destruction to the north wall, bracing for the assault to be continued.[13]

It would not. Du Pont met with his ironclad commanders shortly after the battle. They assessed the vessels' damage and each officer gave his account of the fighting. As a body they expressed doubt that the attack could be resumed with any reasonable chance of success. The admiral slept on his decision before announcing on the morning of the eighth that the offensive was over, believing that to renew the strike would turn a "failure into a disaster." No matter that his decision had unanimous support from his senior commanders, Du Pont's order frustrated and angered many of the rank and file in the squadron. "Murmurs, dissatisfaction, and hard names were frequently heard among the officers and crew, who naturally could not and would not see any reason for not going in again," stated the *Passaic*'s Holden.[14]

Du Pont was honestly blunt in his assessment of the operation in writing to General Hunter on the eighth. "I attempted to take the bull by the horns, but he was too much for us," he wrote. "These monitors are miserable failures where forts are concerned." He added that the longest one of the ironclads had withstood fire was an hour, while it was forty-five minutes for the others, and "five of the eight . . . [were] wholly or partially disabled." In another dispatch to the general that day, he said he was convinced Charleston could not be taken by the navy alone and that another assault on the harbor would likely "end in disaster, and might cause us to leave some of our iron-clads in the hands of the enemy, which would render it difficult for us to hold those parts of the coast which are now in our possession."

Hunter had watched the attack from afar but did not know the result when he congratulated the admiral that same day "for the magnificent manner in which the vessels . . . were fought." The general added that he had prayed for the strike force that had "sailed so calmly and fearlessly into and under and through a concentric fire which has never heretofore had a parallel in the history of warfare. . . . No country can ever fail that has men capable of facing what your iron-clads had yesterday to endure." Appreciative of the compliments, Du Pont replied to Hunter later in the day, saying that he would have the general's letter read to the all of his monitor crews. In a note to Hunter on the ninth, he confided some relief regarding the attack: "I feel very comfortable, general, for the reason that a merciful Providence permitted me to have a failure instead of a disaster."[15]

In Washington on the ninth, Lincoln, Welles, and everyone else were anxious for news from Charleston, scanning Richmond papers from the previous day for anything about Du Pont's actions. By the tenth, a picture was beginning to emerge that was not at all promising. It appeared the admiral had indeed attacked and had been repulsed, the *Keokuk* lost in the process. Gustavus Fox, however, had to be the most wildly hopeful man in the capital, discounting the early dispatches, especially since the assault was reported to have occurred in the afternoon. "The real attack would be made in the morning, so as to have all day for the work," he wrote on the tenth. "The next affair will decide the matter and will be made after preparations found necessary from the experience . . . of Tuesday." The Union vessels still inside the Charleston bar were likely supply ships with coal and ammunition, Du Pont's "depot," the assistant secretary claimed, "and if the obstructions in the harbor render the reduction of Sumter necessary the admiral may have to go back to his base several times before finishing his work." Fox reiterated his thoughts that day in a telegram to Postmaster General Montgomery Blair: The afternoon foray was a reconnaissance in preparation for the main attack, he reassured. "The damage upon Sumter can not be repaired. The only question is, Can the ironclads stand the work? I believe the monitors can. . . . I see no reason whatever to be the least discouraged. On the contrary, my faith in the vessels and the officers is strengthened by these rebel accounts."[16]

His faith was not shared among Du Pont's squadron, where gloom was deepening by the hour that same day. Despite the decision to not renew the assault, the attack force did not retreat immediately, aggravating the morale and misery of the tars aboard the monitors. Holden recalled: "For five days we lay thus, our discomfort growing almost unbearable . . . and the sea constantly breaking the decks, a constant stream of water was poured underneath it upon the blower belts and our supply of air, added to this, the hatches were necessarily kept down, and the tracking of grease down below, the darkness, the intensely foul air from the congregation of eighty men into so narrow a space, and the rolling of the ship, could not fail to enervate and sicken the healthiest crew." Indeed, the monitors remained inside the bar until April 12 before they withdrew. Their presence so close to the defenses during that time tempered the Southerners' jubilation about their victory, since it appeared the ironclads might make another attempt. "Let us render thanks to the Lord of Hosts that the result, thus far, has been one of proud triumph to our country," the *Mercury* stated cautiously the day after the battle. "As yet, however, we have but entered upon the ordeal. It will be for the next few days to tell the tale of our sad disaster or complete success." When the monitors disappeared over the bar, however, Sumter's garrison was turned out for a dress parade, flags were raised, and a thirteen-gun salute fired in celebration. The enemy's departure negated Beauregard's plans for a naval strike on the squadron that night.[17]

The setback was a jolt to the Northern public, which had expected great tidings from Du Pont's fleet. "The repulse of the ironclads from the gateway of Charleston . . . may be classed among our most discouraging military disasters," the *New York Herald* said on April 14. "After many months of preparation, and with the enormous means and forces at the command of the government," the attackers had been simply outgunned by Sumter and the rest of Charleston's sturdy defenses. Still, there was great hope since the monitors had displayed "splendid fighting qualities" and might have actually "passed directly up to Charleston but for those obstructions which were stretched across the channel" between Sumter and Fort Moultrie. Nevertheless, this was quite a step back for the *Herald*, which had proclaimed on the seventh, even as the ironclads were preparing to attack, that "The fort cannot make a very good fight against such vessels as those of the Monitor pattern."[18]

Lincoln himself wanted Du Pont to remain aggressive but stopped short of ordering him to resume the assault. He wanted the navy to hold its position inside the bar and prevent the enemy from building or strengthening defenses on Morris Island. "I do not herein order you to renew the general attack," he wrote Du Pont on the thirteenth, well after the ironclads' retreat. "That is to depend on your own discretion or a further order." Lincoln followed up on the fourteenth with a joint dispatch to Du Pont and Hunter, stating: "We still hope that by cordial and judicious co-operation you can take the [islands] batteries . . . and Fort Sumter" but the effort was to be "a real one (though not a desperate one) if it affords any considerable chance of success." In other words, the monitors should not be sacrificed in a daringly hopeless foray against Charleston's guns when they were still likely to be sent for operations on the Mississippi. Remaining in a threatening posture would also likely prevent more of Beauregard's men from being transferred to Virginia. Most of Hunter's troops, other than those left to hold the sea islands near Charleston, had returned to Port Royal by the fifteenth, Hunter believing that the army would still be involved in a joint strike when Du Pont regrouped his vessels. His soldiers were "in good spirits, regarding the postponement of the expedition as merely a brief delay while certain necessary alterations and repairs of the iron-clads are being made," he wrote to Halleck that day. Within weeks there were wild reports in the Northern press that Sumter had been on the brink of collapse when the monitors withdrew. The *Herald* reported that the navy's rounds had so damaged the fort that a "portion of the garrison mutinied" during the assault and "a company of sharpshooters from the city was ordered out to quell the disturbance."[19]

Beauregard, meanwhile, was also unimpressed by the monitors and by what he described as "exaggerated" reports of damage to Sumter. "The east wall was pretty badly struck in two or three places, but the fort will soon be as strong as ever—no doubt much more so and much sooner than the enemy's ironclads can be repaired," he wrote to Francis Pickens on April 18. "Upon the whole, I think the Abolitionists will come to the conclusion . . . that their monitors are great humbugs; more terrible in imagination than in reality. Forts McAllister and Sumter have been terrible blows to them, and they will become the laughing-stock of Europe." He added that he needed rest but "All that I ask for the present is that my health should hold out to the end of the struggle." Beauregard also would later criticize Du Pont's decision not to launch a night attack on

Sumter, claiming that Rhett's gunners would have had a tough time targeting the low-profile monitors in the darkness. Beauregard contended
that the defenders could not have kept up with repairing damages if the
assault was sustained over several nights "and I am confident now . . .
that Fort Sumter, if thus attacked, must have been disabled and silenced
in a few days. Such a result at that time would have been necessarily followed by the evacuation of Morris and Sullivan's Islands, and, soon after,
of Charleston itself."[20]

Despite her demise, neither side was yet done with the *Keokuk*'s
corpse. In the days after her sinking, Union divers examined the wreck
and reported to Du Pont that she could not be raised. The admiral's chief
engineer, Edward D. Robie, balked at the idea of trying to blow up the
ironclad, apparently since she lay so close to Rebel-held Morris Island.
The Confederates had their own agenda: Army and navy officers visited
the hulk to examine the effects of their artillery fire on the monitor's
armor plating. Their discussions soon turned to the seemingly remote
possibility of salvaging the ship's two Dahlgren guns for use by the
Southerners. Some officers dismissed the notion but others, primarily
Beauregard's trusted engineer David Harris, convinced him to make the
effort. The man to make the attempt was Adolphus W. LaCoste, a civilian engineer employed in the Charleston district Ordnance Department.
A rigger by trade, LaCoste was experienced in moving huge guns, and
Beauregard chose him to oversee the project. LaCoste's brother, James,
and a handpicked group of workmen—including some Fort Sumter soldiers who had the needed skills based on peacetime jobs—and civilians
composed the recovery team. Additionally, Rhett provided a cover force,
consisting nightly of an officer and a detachment of troops in boats, to
protect the salvagers, if necessary. The covering squads were from the garrison's 1st South Carolina Artillery and on most of the nights were led by
Lt. S. Cordes Boylston, although he was occasionally relieved by Lt.
Julius M. Rhett, a relative of Sumter's commander, and others. The
Keokuk rested in only eighteen feet of water at high tide, but the men
had to work at low tide when the turrets were exposed, the night shield-
ing them from discovery by Union naval patrols. This meant that they
had less than three hours a night for their labors. The sea had to be calm
as well so the men wouldn't slip off the turrets. The Rebel ironclads
Chicora and *Palmetto State* provided additional protection.[21]

The salvagers came under fire from a Union vessel on one of the first nights of the operation, the *Chicora* trading a few rounds with the enemy ship with no harm done to either side. Amazingly, all through the three weeks of the recovery effort, Du Pont's force was unaware of the work occurring at the wreck. Struggling night after night in cold, waist-deep water, the Southerners used hammers, chisels, crowbars, and other hardware to cut through the top of one of the turrets. More men were added to the workforce as the chances of success increased. When the hole in the turret was large enough to accommodate the thirteen-foot-long gun, an old lightship, converted into a construction hulk equipped with a derrick, blocks, and tackles, was brought alongside to raise the cannon. Some 1,500 sandbags were placed in the hulk's bow to counterbalance the Dahlgren's 15,700 pounds. The giant gun was slowly winched upward, the breech appearing from the turret—but the gun stopped there. Frantically, the crew shifted the sandbags, but this did not help lift the cannon, and with dawn approaching, it appeared the operation would finally be unveiled to the fleet. Suddenly, the Rebels' frustration and exhaustion were washed away as a big wave rolled in, lifting the cannon and the construction hulk so that the gun swung free in its hoist. Quickly securing their prize, the salvagers got underway, basking in the cheers of soldiers at Sumter and the other batteries as they headed toward Charleston.

The work of prying open the other turret and recovering the second cannon went much more smoothly and rapidly, despite the absence of Adolphus LaCoste, who fell ill due to exposure. James LaCoste supervised this work, and by May 5 both cannon had reached the city. That day, Beauregard wrote to Secretary of War James Seddon, complimenting the LaCostes and the other salvagers, including the Fort Sumter contingent. "Too much praise cannot be bestowed on their zeal and energy," he said. The Charleston papers, not wanting to reveal the salvage project to the enemy, remained silent until after the second gun had been retrieved. The Dahlgrens would "soon be mounted for our defense—valuable acquisitions, no less than handsome trophies of the Battle," the *Mercury* boasted on May 6. In about two weeks, the *Keokuk* twins were indeed incorporated into the harbor defenses. One of the guns was mounted at Sumter at the eastern angle of the barbette battery. The other was hauled to Sullivan's Island and emplaced at Battery Bee. Both instantly became the pride of the Charleston defenses, the heaviest pieces in the harbor other than two British-made Blakeleys, which were unreliable due to the inferiority of their ammunition.[22]

Because he did not renew his offensive, Du Pont almost immediately came under withering criticism from the Navy Department and the Northern press. The surprising loss of the *Keokuk* guns only aggravated the festering situation. This went on for several weeks, but Du Pont himself was sinking fast. His reluctance to continue the assault, though likely a logical and correct decision, would essentially scuttle his career. "Admiral Du Pont never showed greater courage or patriotism than when he saved his ships and men, and sacrificed himself to the clamor and disappointment evoked by his defeat," Rodgers, his chief of staff noted. General Hunter also had become frustrated waiting for Du Pont to resume the supposed joint operation and took direct aim at the admiral in a May 22 dispatch to President Lincoln. Hunter claimed that his troops were in position to seize Morris Island on April 8—the day Du Pont aborted the naval assault—but did not risk it because Du Pont refused to offer supporting artillery fire. Hunter contended that if the lightly defended island had been occupied that day, Union guns could already be emplaced at Cummings Point and "the fall of Sumter would have been as certain as the demonstration of a problem in mathematics," as he and Gillmore had proven against Fort Pulaski. In the ensuing six weeks, however, the Confederates had strengthened their Morris Island defenses, making it a much more difficult task to take the island. "I fear Admiral Du Pont distrusts the iron-clads so much that he has resolved to do nothing with them this summer," he told Lincoln, asking to be released from orders to cooperate with the navy, "which now tie me down to share the admiral's inactivity." Hunter wanted to break loose on a rapier thrust through Georgia, a column of ten thousand soldiers freeing slaves, arming them with pikes, and generally wreaking hell and havoc on railroads and supply stores.[23]

The general's boldly creative plan met a dead end, but his contentions likely added a log to the fire already charring the admiral's hot seat. Secretary Welles relieved Du Pont on June 3, replacing him with Rear Adm. Andrew H. Foote, a reliable and combat-savvy veteran who had some four decades of service in the navy. Du Pont knew Foote well as an aggressive fighter, describing him as a "splendid navy officer, sort of a Northern Stonewall Jackson, without his intellect and judgement." Despite Welles's decision, the coming weeks would herald major changes before Du Pont's replacement finally reached the Carolina shore.

The Union blockade, meanwhile, continued to gnaw away at Charleston's maritime commerce, but the port was not bottled up by any means. In April and May, fifteen vessels reached the city while twenty-one cleared the harbor, the latter with more than ten thousand bales of cotton in their holds. The Confederates were still being weakened by numbers of men transferred elsewhere, with troop trains leaving Charleston for Virginia and Mississippi. The entire Confederacy had been cheered by Lee's dazzling victory at Chancellorsville on May 1–3, but it was a dearly bought triumph with the loss of Lt. Gen. Thomas J. "Stonewall" Jackson and Capt. George B. Cuthbert, a soldier who had a starring role in the drama of Sumter's 1861 bombardment. (His Palmetto Guard had shelled the fort and was honored to be among the first troops to occupy Sumter on the night of Anderson's surrender.) Mistakenly shot by his own men, Jackson lingered until May 10, when he died in a Virginia farmhouse. A short distance away that same day, Cuthbert also succumbed to wounds sustained at Chancellorsville. As Cuthbert struggled through his last hours, it had been almost exactly two years earlier—May 9, 1861—that he and his Palmettos had grandly marched through the Charleston streets to board a train for Virginia. Now many of these Carolinians were gone, claimed by sickness or combat on distant fields.[24]

By early June, Sumter had been repaired so that it bore few scars of the naval shelling some eight weeks earlier. A British dignitary, Sir Arthur J. L. Fremantle of the Coldstream Guards, was in Charleston at this time as part of a three-month tour of the Confederacy, and Ripley took him on an inspection of the fort. Fremantle was shown around "the now celebrated fort," as he called it, and was Rhett's guest for lunch in one of the casemates. Sumter's commander was "a handsome and agreeable man, besides being a zealous officer," Fremantle noted, a description that might have surprised some of Rhett's enemies other than the Yankees. The Englishman was impressed by the military bearing of the garrison and was especially interested in Sumter's armament, including "the best gun in the fort," one of the *Keokuk* twins. There was a deep hole in the parade ground where dirt had been removed to strengthen some casemates, and Fremantle was shown some of the 425 pounds of enemy shells that had plowed into the fort. During one part of his tour, the Englishman saw the wreck of the *Keokuk* and also a shell-pocked target made to roughly resemble the monitor. "In one of these [coastal creeks] I saw the shattered remains of the sham *Keokuk*, which was a wooden imitation of its equally short-lived original, and had been used as a floating target by the different forts," he recorded.[25]

From the parapet, Fremantle surveyed Charleston's wartime panorama, including thirteen blockaders outside the bar more than five miles to sea. The defenses, including Sumter, Moultrie, Fort Johnson, and the other batteries, were formidable. "In fact, both sides of the harbor for several miles appear to bristle with forts mounting heavy guns," Fremantle wrote. A few days later Fremantle had a long meeting with Beauregard. The general expressed complete confidence in the ability of land forts to defeat ironclads, as Sumter had, and added a novel idea that was being considered for the fort's protection. Sumter was "to be covered by degrees with the long green moss which in this country hangs down from the trees," Fremantle said of Beauregard's plan. The Spanish moss would be pressed into place, the Confederates believing it would help absorb enemy rounds and prove inflammable.

It was about this time that a soldier who would rival Beauregard as a leading player in the Fort Sumter saga would arrive on the Charleston coast. Union brigadier general Quincy A. Gillmore, of Fort Pulaski fame, assumed command of the U.S. Department of the South on June 12, 1863, succeeding David Hunter. Gillmore, a thirty-eight-year-old Ohioan and West Pointer, was a man on a mission. He had been summoned to Washington, D.C., in late May and met with top military and political brass regarding a new army–navy offensive against Charleston. Confident in his big guns and the lessons learned at Pulaski, Gillmore told them that he believed Sumter could be reduced or its offensive capability destroyed. "I have . . . expressed the opinion that the forts in Charleston Harbor could be reduced by the means (naval and military combined) now available in the Department of the South, increased by a suitable number of the best heavy rifled guns," he wrote to another officer on May 23. "I have also said that I am willing to risk my own reputation upon the attempt, as I did at Pulaski." The keys were establishing a strong Union

Union brigadier general
Quincy A. Gillmore.
HARPER'S WEEKLY (MAY 10, 1862)

foothold on Morris Island, so that he could bring his heavy artillery into range of the fort, and a good working relationship with the navy.

The conferences included Admiral Foote and Rear Adm. John A. Dahlgren. As Du Pont's star faded that summer, there had been discussions in the Navy Department about a joint command of the squadron by Foote and Dahlgren, who were both longtime veterans and good friends. Dahlgren had wanted sole command, but Foote was Welles's choice, despite still being bothered by a leg wound he suffered in the fighting at Fort Donelson in February 1862.

Other than overwhelming Sumter, the bigger question bandied about in the meetings was how would the fort's reduction influence the capture of Charleston itself? Gillmore had only about eleven thousand troops in the immediate area (he had approximately seventeen thousand in the department) to accomplish this with the navy. If Sumter could be silenced, it would be up to the fleet to blast in past the other harbor defenses and seize the city. Gillmore also proposed to knife the Charleston & Savannah Railroad so that reinforcements could be prevented from reaching Charleston once the attack was begun. The Federals had made halfhearted thrusts to accomplish this earlier but with no success. The brass agreed to Gillmore's plan, and by July's second week, the Yanks ashore were ready for action.[26]

The Union navy off Charleston, however, was in a much different situation—shockingly so. After his intense involvement in planning the Charleston offensive, Foote was en route to join his squadron when he fell ill from a worsening infection of his wound and died suddenly on June 26. With little time to mourn his comrade, fifty-three-year-old John Dahlgren took the squadron's helm and headed south to the most important assignment of his career. The new commander—best known as the inventor of the Dahlgren rifled guns—was a tall, slender officer with thinning hair and a dour demeanor better suited to a fire-and-brimstone preacher than an admiral. Born in Philadelphia in November 1809, Dahlgren was the son of the Swedish consul in that city. Appointed midshipman in the navy in 1826, he was commissioned lieutenant in 1837 and served in the Mediterranean Squadron for a time. From 1847 to 1857, he was an ordnance officer; during this period he developed what would become the Dahlgrens. There were several types of these heavy smoothbore guns and howitzers, used mainly by the navy and characterized by their "soda-water bottle" design. Later serving at the Washington Navy Yard in 1860–61, Dahlgren was appointed commandant of that installation after war broke out. Commissioned captain in July 1862, he shortly afterward became chief of the navy's Ordnance Bureau. Dahlgren was promoted to rear admiral in February 1863, and was about to embark on the first combat assignment of his mostly desk-bound career. Ironically, he had never seen nor heard one of his artillery creations at war and would be on the wrong end of two of them—the *Keokuk* guns—if he ventured too close to Charleston.

Two weeks after Du Pont's failed April attack, Dahlgren had met with Secretary Welles, who was not satisfied with the effort and felt Du Pont "gave up too soon." Based on Dahlgren's account, he had defended Du Pont. "I reminded him [Welles] that Dupont [*sic*] was a judicious and brave officer and that the Captains of the ironclads, who were chosen officers, concurred with Dupont" in calling off the assault. Dahlgren arrived off the Carolina coast on July 4 and had a cordial meeting with Du Pont before going ashore to confer with Gillmore, who was in the final stages of planning his attack on Morris Island. The two of them firmed up the operation the next day, and Dahlgren formally relieved Du Pont on the sixth. Dahlgren was certainly not in the dark about the army's plans, since he, Foote, and Gillmore had been in the discussions

Union rear admiral John A. Dahlgren. LIBRARY OF CONGRESS

about Charleston in Washington. But having just arrived, he was forced to play catch-up.[27]

As the dispirited, frustrated, and depressed Du Pont headed north, now it was the army's turn. Early on the morning of July 10, 1863, troops of the X Corps crossed Lighthouse Inlet from Folly Island and, after a brisk fight, occupied a large portion of Morris Island. The blue infantry at some points came under fire from Brooke rifles mounted on Sumter's barbette. Some Yanks were killed by this solid shot, and one round kicked up enough sand to temporarily bury some officers of the 3rd New Hampshire, wounding its lieutenant colonel. But the outnumbered Confederates were steadily pushed north, back to Battery Wagner, as the Federals' artillery was joined by ground-rattling blasts from the monitors. After receiving reinforcements, the Union troops made two assaults on Wagner, but were repulsed with heavy losses, ending the major combat that day. The Federals launched another attack against the battery the next morning but were repelled, despite some bluecoats fighting their way onto the parapet. From Sumter's walls, Alfred Rhett watched the bluecoats fanning out on Morris Island and realized he and his post would soon be in desperate trouble. "Gillmore will silence us, but I will fight the fort low down," he is said to have remarked.[28]

In July 13 orders complimenting his forces for their "brilliant victory" on the tenth, Gillmore wrote that the action had moved them three miles closer to "the rebel stronghold, Sumter, the first among all our country's defenses against foreign foes, that felt the polluting tread of traitors." He continued, "Our labors, however, are not over; they are just begun; and while the spires of the rebel city still loom up in the dim distance, hardships and privations must be endured before our hopes and expectations can find their full fruition in victory." Gillmore also exhorted his soldiers to "emulate the heroic deeds of our brothers in arms at Gettysburg and Vicksburg." On a negative note, the Federals' strike against the Charleston & Savannah Railroad had failed, as had a simultaneous diversionary move up the Stono River toward James Island. The Northern press, however, was confident that all of Morris would soon be in Union hands and that the end for Fort Sumter and Charleston was near. Once Gillmore captured Wagner and posted his big guns there and at Cummings Point, "Fort Sumter cannot stand twenty-four hours," the New York Herald said during this period. "Forty-eight hours will suffice to reduce it to a pile of ruins. We may reasonably look for this work to be accomplished before the middle of August and then the gates to . . . Charleston will be open to the navy."[29]

With the Union savoring signature victories elsewhere that amazing July, Gillmore was on the verge of joining the warrior elite in Yankee blue if he could destroy Sumter. "Fancy a fine, wholesome-looking, solid six-footer, with big head, broad, good-humored face, and a high forehead, faintly elongated by a suspicion of baldness, curly brown hair and beard, and a frank, open face, and you have him," New York journalist Whitelaw Reid wrote of the general. "A quick-speaking, quick-moving, soldierly man he is," said Reid, adding that Gillmore "is among the handsomest officers of the army." It had been an improbable journey for Gillmore to reach this point in his life. Born into a farm family in Lorain County, Ohio, he was a schoolteacher before being appointed to West Point in 1845 at age twenty. He graduated at the head of his class four years later and was assigned to the Corps of Engineers. Before the war his main duties had been constructing forts guarding Hampton Roads, Virginia, instructing at the Military Academy, and serving in New York City. Gillmore had been chief engineer on the Port Royal expedition in 1861–62 before his eye-opening conquest of Fort Pulaski brought his promotion to brigadier.[30]

Like Rhett, Beauregard was quick to recognize that the enemy foothold on Morris Island would, in all likelihood, lead to Sumter's eventual fall. On July 11 he sent orders to Rhett to prepare for bombardment. The defenders were to bolster the gorge wall with sand and other material. The sally port was to be closed and a new entrance constructed on the western face, safely away from Morris. The garrison also was to prepare for the removal of most of Sumter's heavy guns so they could be used elsewhere in the defenses and not fall into enemy hands. The fort had sixty artillery pieces at the time, about fifteen of which, including mortars, could be used to sting the ever-advancing enemy on Morris. Beauregard would later contend that the enemy's successful landing there was due to so many of his troops having been sent west to assist in the defense of Vicksburg, despite his protests.[31]

Beauregard called a conference on July 12 to discuss the crisis and how best to defend not just Morris Island but Charleston as well. The meeting was attended by Ripley and other generals along with South Carolina governor Milledge L. Bonham and Confederate congressman William Porcher Miles, among others. There was talk of making a counterattack to push the Federals off Morris, but that plan was nixed due to a lack of vessels for the operation. All realized that Sumter would soon be assailed by land-based batteries and could no longer be considered the linchpin of the city's defenses. With that being said, the men also agreed that Wagner had to be held as long as possible so that the inner harbor defenses, primarily Fort Johnson and the works on Sullivan's Island, could be strengthened. Most of Sumter's guns would be sent to these locations; Rhett's force would keep only a few pieces with which to defend the fort. Beauregard and the others reasoned that Sumter's ability to repel the Union navy would soon be blasted away. Thus any of the fort's bigger guns that could soon be removed could be emplaced elsewhere and escape destruction or capture when the expected avalanche of Union shells engulfed Sumter. The brass at the meeting also knew that the brick pancake at the harbor mouth was the Confederacy's most treasured icon. Even if blown to bits, it had to be held at any cost.

Aware of the approaching storm, Beauregard sent orders to Ripley about Sumter's artillery: The fort should have several guns always loaded and trained at night on the creeks near Wagner and other batteries on the islands. "Should events oblige us to abandon Fort Sumter, not one heavy gun must be left in serviceable condition, to be turned against our own works," Ripley was told on July 16. The commanders at Wagner and Gregg were to be given the same instructions.[32]

Sumter's "traitors," as Gillmore called them, got the first taste of Yankee heavy metal on the evening of the seventeenth. Steamboats with supplies arrived at the gorge wharf about 6:30 PM and were rudely greeted by at least one artillery round from a Union gun on Morris. "This is the first shot fired from land in the direction of this fort," Rhett noted. Sumter answered with four percussion shells that exploded on the island. It already had been an exhausting day for the garrison. The long roll had been beaten at 2:00 AM, the defenders scrambling to their posts to contest a possible attack. With no Yankees to be seen, the recall was sounded thirty minutes later. At 6:00 AM, a 10-inch seacoast mortar, with its bed and almost three hundred shells, was shipped to Sullivan's Island. The disarmament of Sumter had begun, as Beauregard ordered. Later in the morning, a 32-pounder rifle was shifted from the northwest casemate to the gorge battery. Rhett was also preparing for the worst to come: Some of the lower casemates in the western face were being converted into a hospital, and the officers' quarters in the southern wall were to be filled with cotton bales and sand. That night one hundred black laborers arrived at the fort.

Gillmore tried another attack against Wagner on July 18, one that would be especially historic because of some of the men involved. The navy and the land batteries spent some eleven hours slamming the bastion with a merciless barrage, trying to soften it up before the troops went in at twilight. The ranks of blue infantry squeezed into a narrow beach approach to Wagner as Confederate guns, including some at Sumter, began to bloody them. Undaunted, the Yankees bulled through a storm of musketry and shellfire, the body count rising at every step. Some bluecoats fought their way inside the fort but couldn't maintain the foothold, and the assault faded out in the night with heavy Union losses. The 54th Massachusetts regiment of U.S. Colored Troops charged into American legend that night, but its gallantry and determination weren't enough to take Wagner. "During the fight we assisted with such a fire as old Sumter was able to give . . . , " one of the fort's officers wrote in a letter home, "and now and then gave their monitors a turn." For the day, Sumter's gunners loosed 125 rounds at the enemy.[33]

Despite this setback, the Federals' trenches were edging ever closer to Wagner and Gregg, the ingenuity and determination of the bluecoats not lost on at least one Confederate at Sumter. "Evidently the object of the enemy is now to endeavor to take Wagner by gradual approaches," he wrote, "and ours seems to be to dispute every inch of ground. . . . The enemy are far ahead of us in skill and energy. In a [*sic*] open field fight I believe we can whip them . . . but when you come to regular operations requiring engineering skill, we can't compare to them. But the want of energy in this department, on our side, has surely been unpardonable." Both sides were tormented by temperatures exceeding 100 degrees by late July. And despite their vigor, the Yankees' work was often interrupted by fire from Wagner and James Island. Sumter added to this menace, its 7-inch Brooke rifles mounted on the barbette able to throw shells the length of Morris, some reaching the Federal camps.[34]

On the afternoon of July 20, the fort came under fire from enemy batteries, the shelling lasting until dark. One Union projectile hit cotton bales piled on the parapet for defensive purposes and set them afire; the only Rebel casualty was a drummer boy, John Graham, who was seriously wounded. Rhett's cannoneers replied with fewer than twenty rounds aimed at the Federals ashore and a few thrown at the *New Ironsides*. Over the next week or so, Sumter was periodically shelled and in turn aided in pounding the Federal positions. Despite the incoming rounds, the partial disarmament of the fort's artillery was underway; a 10-inch Columbiad was dismounted during the night and hauled to the wharf for shipment on July 24. This was the first big gun sent out since the mortar on the seventeenth, due to a lack of "proper implements," Rhett noted, but the equipment apparently was now in place and the cannon would be leaving with regularity in the coming days and weeks. The new sally port was also nearing completion.

By the end of July, more than twenty guns and mortars had been removed from the fort and sent to the inner harbor defenses or to batteries on James Island. Still, Sumter had plenty of bite left. A mortar set up on the end of the old wharf blasted away at the Federals menacing Wagner, as did a few other pieces. Some of Rhett's men also manned barges carrying provisions and ordnance to the beleaguered Rebels on Morris after a supply vessel was driven off by Yankee fire overnight on August 2–3. Through all of this, Ripley advised caution in removing so many of Sumter's big guns. If Morris fell, "Sumter becomes the salient point of our defense, and, as it must hold out and repulse the enemy, too great a reduction of its offensive armament is deemed unadvisable," he wrote on the second, adding that another "reason why the heavy and reliable guns ought not to be taken from Sumter too indiscriminately is the moral effect on the garrison, which is expected to do the hardest work of the struggle, if continued."

Beauregard saw matters a bit differently in orders to Ripley on August 3. Sumter and Sullivan's Island were to be furnished with ammunition and provisions "that may be required for their prolonged defense, for, should the north end of Morris Island fall . . . little, if any intercourse by water could be kept up with those posts." For the same reason, there was an "immediate necessity of transporting to Sullivan's Island all the guns and ammunition which can be spared from Fort Sumter. These matters cannot be attended to with too much expedition."[35]

Dahlgren's squadron, meanwhile, had been active throughout this phase of operations, blasting away at enemy positions in support of the army. The hellish summer had been especially tough on his monitor crews baking in their iron boxes, the *Nantucket* recording a high of 141 degrees in her engine room during this time. The admiral had gotten quite an initiation during his first two weeks in command. This was salted by news on July 20 that one of his sons, Capt. Ulric Dahlgren, whom he called "Ully," had been wounded in combat in Gettysburg's aftermath. "My mind is with my poor boy," the caring father wrote in his journal two days later. "I do wish to know how it fares with him. Oh, that he may escape any permanent injury!"[36]

CHAPTER 5

"He May Knock
Fort Sumter to Pieces"

After the failed July 18 attack, Gillmore reasoned that while Wagner would be tough to subdue, he had heavy guns capable of firing over it and reaching Sumter. If the latter could be subdued, the navy might be able to enter the harbor, isolating Morris Island and possibly allowing the Federals to take Wagner and Gregg without more tough combat and casualties. Thus the Union plans were modified: Instead of trying to seize Wagner and then shelling Sumter into oblivion, the Federals would bombard Sumter from ground already in their possession. "The demolition of Fort Sumter was the object in view as preliminary to the entrance of the iron-clads," Gillmore would later say. "Neither Fort Wagner nor Battery Gregg possessed any special importance as a defense against the passage of the iron-clad fleet. They were simple outposts of Fort Sumter. Fort Wagner was specially designed to prevent the erection of breaching batteries against that work, and was valueless to the enemy if it failed to accomplish that end."

In the face of this looming danger, Sumter's defenders already were strengthening the walls believed to be most vulnerable to Union guns on Morris. Most of the work was done by parties of slaves shipped in from Charleston, laboring day and night in relays of three to four hundred men. The soldiers also were subjected to the backbreaking efforts, all under supervision of the fort's engineers. By early August, all casemates on the sides facing the island were crammed with bales of compressed cotton soaked in salt water and packed in sand. Because the old sally port and wharf might soon be exposed to even more Union artillery, work continued rapidly on the new entrance and dock being built on the left flank. Traverses were erected at vital points and hundreds of sandbags were piled outside the gorge, sealing up the old sally port and extending along the original wharf. Much of the sand was dug from the three-acre parade ground. The Rebels had been worried about the vulnerability of Sumter's upper magazines even prior to Du Pont's April attack, but the Federals' steady progress on Morris Island caused them to take decisive action during this time. The upper magazines were abandoned and emptied shortly before the anticipated bombardment. Both were partially filled with sand to protect the lower magazines directly beneath them. Since Du Pont's assault, the four magazines had become increasingly more at risk as the east wall was knocked down to a level where the monitor crews could look into the arches of the west casemates.[1]

While all of the best guns had been removed from the fort by now, their positions filled by "dummies, or sham-guns," other pieces had been shifted to better, more protected, posts in the fort. "The rebels . . . are beginning to sniff their danger in Gillmore's occupation of Morris Island," the New York Herald said on July 22. "They know that this occupation gives him a foothold from which he may knock Fort Sumter to pieces, after the fashion of Fort Pulaski; and so they are already beginning to talk of resisting his entry into the city street by street." The song was much the same five days later, the paper telling its readers: "It now appears that upon the success or failure of our efforts to take Fort Wagner the fate of Charleston hangs. It is the key to the entire position. With it in our hands, Fort Sumter would of necessity fall, and then Charleston would have to surrender." By August 7, the Confederates had positioned two mortars, including the one that had been operating on the old wharf, on new platforms on Sumter's parade ground, where they continued the fire on the enemy. The gate for the new sally port had been hung the previous day. The Rebels also were trying to raise another mortar that had fallen overboard while it was shipped from the fort, but their efforts had failed to this point. The Confederates were still sending guns away from Sumter into August's second week, the weight of these pieces already damaging the new wharf as they lay on it, awaiting shipment. And thousands of sandbags were being brought in, four steamers arriving on the night of August 9 with such cargo.[2]

While the Confederates bolstered Sumter structurally and Wagner tried to survive almost daily naval shelling and ever-nearer Union parallels, Gillmore set about establishing twelve breaching batteries to pound Sumter from Morris Island or to provide covering fire against the expected return fire from Wagner and Gregg. The armament for these batteries would be the most powerful in the Union arsenal, but getting many of these giant cannon into position in a combat zone on a sand island in the teeth of a South Carolina summer would be a herculean task to say the least, requiring hundreds of soldiers. The forty-three guns to be used were rifles (Parrott and Whitworth) and mortars (seacoast, Coehorn, and siege) varying in weight from 9,700 to 27,500 pounds each. They were shipped to Morris Island from the Union base at Hilton Head. The vessels transporting the guns could only enter Lighthouse Inlet at high tide due to their cargo's bulk. Hauled ashore, the cannon were loaded onto sling carts, huge wheels connected by an axle from which the gun was suspended. As many as a hundred men were needed to pull these titans about two miles to the batteries at night, often under enemy fire. Another five hundred or so Federals composed the guard for these details. Capt. Alfred Mordecai of the Ordnance Department and Lt. James E. Wilson of the 5th U.S. Artillery were given the lion's share of credit for erecting the batteries, primarily constructed with sandbags, timbers, and earthworks. Twenty artillery pieces in nine batteries would be aimed at Sumter while twenty-three would deal with Wagner and Gregg. The guns were located at much greater distances—3,330 to 4,240 yards—from Sumter than were the Federal batteries that blasted Fort Pulaski into submission more than a year earlier.

News of the powerful weapons being emplaced fueled optimism among some Northerners that Sumter would soon have to submit or be obliterated. "It is said that Fort Wagner might have been taken by General Gillmore before now, only that it would be untenable while Fort Sumter was in the hands of the enemy," the *New York Herald* exaggerated on August 8. "To disable Sumter, therefore, is of paramount importance. It is reported that the batteries being erected . . . are of such calibre that Fort Sumter cannot stand before them an hour and a half after the fire is opened."

The experiences and trials of mounting big guns in the marshes near Pulaski aided the Federals in building their works amid the sand and sucking marsh mud on and around Morris Island.[3] Named for Union officers and fallen heroes, Gillmore's batteries were Brown, Rosecrans, Meade, Kearny, Reynolds, Weed, Hays, Reno, Stevens, Kirby, Strong, and the Naval Battery, the latter manned by a detachment of Union sailors from the frigate *Wabash* under Cmdr. Foxhall A. Parker. Battery Strong was especially significant to the Yanks here since it honored Brig. Gen. George C. Strong, mortally wounded in the July 18 assault on Wagner. At least nine of the batteries had artillerists who had sharpened their skills in battering Fort Pulaski into submission, including the 3rd Rhode Island Heavy Artillery and the 7th Connecticut Volunteer Infantry. Construction of the batteries was begun on July 24 and most of the work, including the mounting of the guns, was done at night to keep from drawing Rebel fire. Amazingly, it would take only eighteen days for the bulk of the construction to be done, all with "unusual rapidity and without serious loss." The primary function of Batteries Weed, Reynolds, and Kearny would be to suppress return fire from Wagner and Gregg. Battery Hays also would aid in this mission with seven of its guns, but had one Parrott that would participate in bombarding Sumter.

Dahlgren, meanwhile, was gearing his fleet for its role in the offensive, despite myriad mechanical problems and the physical breakdown of his crews in the stifling throes of a Dixie August. "Increase of debility and disease alarming; many have to go home," he wrote on the ninth, adding the next day: "Equatorial weather. Much of this will not leave many men." Dahlgren also had finally received word about Ulric's fate, almost two weeks after learning that his son had been wounded. "News from Ully," he related in his August 4 journal entry. "Poor child! He had to lose his foot to save his life. . . . I feared the result, and have been kept in extreme anxiety since I heard of his wound." On a positive note, Ully had been promoted to colonel a few weeks after his injury.[4]

Despite the limited comforts afforded by their ranks, Dahlgren and Gillmore both were feeling the strains, wear, and tear of tough campaigning in southern climes and were weak due to the stress and heat. Watching the batteries take shape, Gillmore spent his limited spare time reading novels and magazines, sometimes with enemy rounds "bursting in inconvenient proximity," said one account. He was confident about Sumter's doom, but unsure about what would follow. "After that is done, the monitors must take the lead, in accordance with the project which was discussed and informally adopted when I left Washington," he wrote to Halleck on August 10. "I therefore beg the department not to lose sight of the fact, that after the gate is open to the monitors and ironclads by the reduction of Fort Sumter, the army here, so long as it remains greatly inferior in numbers to the enemy, must remain defensively upon these sea islands."

Gillmore's troops also were suffering in the summer sun. "Our men are wearing out as well from their arduous and exhaustive labors," a correspondent wrote. "The lists of sickness have increased considerably," most due to exposure and exhaustion. He added, however, that a sea breeze tempered the blazing sun somewhat and kept the mosquitoes away, but that windblown sand made life miserable. It "blows hither and dither at all hours, covering everything with its gritty particles, and insinuating itself into our eyes, ears and mouth, until one heartily wishes himself a thousand miles away." The same reporter also had heard rumors that Sumter was to be blown up by its garrison if Wagner was captured. "When Fort Sumter is captured it will be taken through hard knocks, and hard knocks alone," he wrote. Another worry for Gillmore during this time was a defective supply of cannon powder, which had to be replenished by the navy.[5]

On the night of August 11, Ripley went to Sumter; a *Mobile Tribune* reporter was among the party who accompanied him. They found the members of the garrison stacking sandbags against the interior walls. "The men seemed to be in the best of spirits and from the jolly mirth that prevailed, one would have supposed that they were enjoying a frolic," the correspondent noted. Rhett hosted Ripley and the others in his quarters and "expressed every confidence of it [Sumter] being able to stand any assault. . . . The quarters of the officers are very comfortable and well vented." A much more violent and less comfortable "venting" of Sumter would be coming within a few hours. It was also about this time that Fitzgerald Ross, a British captain of hussars in the Austrian army, visited Sumter. Ross was impressed by the stoutness of the fort's walls and watched one of the parade ground mortars blasting away at enemy outposts on Morris. Rhett told him that this firing spoiled the garrison's ability to bake bread because it shook the foundation so much that the yeast wouldn't rise.[6]

Even though not all of them were completed, the breaching batteries began testing Sumter on the morning of Wednesday, August 12. This was as much a military experiment as anything else, only one or two guns firing at the same time so that Union observers could measure the effects of the projectiles if and when they hit the fort's walls. During the morning, the *Hibben*, a small steamer anchored at Sumter's wharf, was gutted by a Parrott shell that burst the boiler, scalding several men. Another round tore into the bakehouse, demolishing an oven, and the western barracks were damaged by three hits, but there were no other casualties. By this time the garrison had transferred the commissary stores to the northeast angle where they would be safer. "An immense uprising of brick and mortar followed the terrific blows of these ponderous projectiles," a Northern journalist wrote that day, "and wide, deep holes . . . are plainly visible from our batteries." Sumter did not answer, and the correspondent watched with glee as some of the Confederates could be seen reacting to the shelling. "It was amusing to see the inmates of the fort cautiously creep to the edge of the parapet and gaze down with some appearance of anxiety at the work of a single shot, while another group ventured out of the covered portcullis and peered upward with equal wonder and astonishment," he wrote.

Capt. A. W. Colwell of the 3rd Rhode Island Heavy Artillery and his men, posted at Battery Reno, took credit for eviscerating the *Hibben* and damaging the fort from two-and-a-half miles distant. "That is what we call fine shooting," Colwell wrote that day of his guns, which the cannoneers had named "Baby Waker," "Brick Driver," and "Whistling Dick."[7]

At Sumter, Lt. Iredell Jones of the 1st South Carolina Regulars had started a letter to his family that morning, but the mini-barrage and his duties prevented him from finishing it until that night. From such long range, "I venture to say the world never witnessed better shooting," he wrote of the Union artillerymen. "It is a rare thing [when] they miss the fort. We have not replied today, owing to the Brooke gun being slightly out of order. Tomorrow we will feel them a little." The defenders had a busy night, answering with occasional fire from their pair of 10-inch mortars, which apparently had little or no effect on the out-of-range enemy works. Laborers also dismounted an 8-inch Columbiad from the east face and prepared it for shipment to James Island. Another Columbiad was shifted to the east face. Overnight work also was underway on two traverses, and sometime on the twelfth a small boat was sent to Fort Johnson to bring in a supply of fresh beef for the garrison. Rhett reported that seventeen 200-pounder Parrott rounds hit the fort "during the entire day." Ominously, the Confederates noted that one of these projectiles ripped five feet into the brick of the gorge wall, leaving an entry crater some three feet in diameter.[8]

Col. Charles H. Olmstead of the 1st Volunteer Regiment of Georgia had arrived in Charleston from Savannah on July 10 with a mixed force of about 460 troops and was sent to Wagner, where he would witness Sumter's August bombardment. Olmstead had as much experience with Gillmore and the effects of the Union rifled guns as anyone in the Confederacy. He had commanded Fort Pulaski in April 1862 when Gillmore's forces besieged the stronghold. Pulaski was very similar to Sumter, with the same basic design and brick construction, but a two-day battering by enemy artillery, including the rifles, had forced Olmstead to surrender on April 11, the shelling having exposed his magazine. Olmstead met with Gillmore during the surrender proceedings and spent months in Union prisoner of war camps before being exchanged. Thus in summer 1863, Olmstead found himself again facing Gillmore and his guns. "The power of rifled guns against masonry had been conclusively demonstrated . . . at Fort Pulaski," Olmstead recalled after the war. The major difference, however, was that the artillery arrayed against Pulaski was only about a mile distant, while the land batteries targeting Sumter were at more than twice that range. Among the Confederates, "there were few who could believe that . . . Sumter was seriously endangered," Olmstead wrote. "It had been thought that the grand old fort was safe so long as Wagner held out." He vividly recalled the first day that the Union big guns opened on Sumter as he and his comrades watched from Wagner. "The shot and shell went high above our heads, and were hurled with irresistible power against the wall of Sumter. Great masses of masonry from the outer wall fell as each shot struck."[9]

Thursday, August 13, 1863

The steamer *Mary Francis* docked at 6:00 AM with ammunition and other supplies for the fort and was unmolested by the Federals, whose fire was infrequent on August 13. Four of Dahlgren's gunboats did come up and throw a few shells in, but a day of only ten rounds striking Sumter was nothing of great importance, especially since none of the garrison was injured. One of the mortars, however, was temporarily disabled by a round which burst under its platform. Undaunted, the Rebels again replied with deliberate fire that night from their other mortar.

The big excitement before sunrise on the fourteenth was the grounding of a schooner off the fort's northeast face. The vessel was loaded with sand for the fort but dragged its anchor and wrecked; two men aboard were rescued. The bluecoats launched only two shots that morning, but one of them cut the top of the flagstaff near the fort's southeast angle. By now, however, the Confederates were strengthening the fort as rapidly as possible, realizing that a devastating storm of iron could soon be expected. A force of almost five hundred laborers and mechanics was engaged in two shifts—night and day—in bolstering Sumter's defenses. Two sandbag traverses on the east face were completed by the fourteenth and the arches of the western magazine were covered, Rhett reported. Some 3,000 sandbags were brought in overnight, 2,500 of which were piled high on the exterior of the gorge wall.

Gillmore wanted to start the wholesale bombardment on the fourteenth, but told Dahlgren on the night of the thirteenth that he was not feeling well enough for it. Thus only six shots hit the fort on the fourteenth—one of which was from a gunboat—resulting in no bloodshed.[10]

In New York City on the fourteenth, the *Times* told its readers that Gillmore was preparing his "grand assault" and that great success should ensue. The article was based on an August 10 dispatch from the Carolina coast that had arrived in New York aboard the transport steamer *Arago* on the thirteenth. "The greatest confidence is felt as to the result," the writer claimed. "The fall of Forts Sumter, Wagner and Cummings Point is regarded as certain to take place in from two to six hours after the ball opens." A deserter from Wagner had revealed that two-thirds of Sumter's guns had been removed and that the fort's demise "is regarded by the rebels as a certainty, the damage done by the Monitors in April last rendering the possibility of the rebels holding it not to be thought of," the dispatch noted. The deserter also said that Sumter "was on the point of surrendering" during the April 7 attack, "when fortunately for the rebels, the Monitors withdrew." The *New York Herald* was also on the bandwagon: "But a few days can elapse before the fire of our batteries will be loosened like a whirlwind of destruction," one of its correspondents, Galen H. Osborne, wrote from Morris Island on August 15. "Our heaviest guns are in position; our ammunition is at the front; our artillerists are ready. Only the details of the majestic programme remain to be arranged and perfected." Osborne also described the nightly artillery exchanges between the rival armies: "It is interesting to watch the monster shells as they go grandly up from [C]olumbiads and mortars, curving and twinkling through the midnight air, and spitefully flashing their lurid light over the scene as they explode." They reminded him of July 4 fireworks, although on the night of August 10 there was a meteor shower that greatly enhanced the spectacle: "As if to put to shame the efforts of the opposing artillerists, Dame Nature brought out an extraordinary number of aerolites, lending additional beauty and majesty to the scene, and additional confusion to those who at first mistook them for the hostile missiles of the enemy," he penned.[11]

Dahlgren issued orders to his skippers on the fourteenth for the joint operation with the army to begin in the next few days. When the offensive opened, *Passaic* and *Patapsco* would take position some two thousand yards from Sumter, the *Passaic* serving as the admiral's flagship. The other monitors, *Weehawken, Catskill, Montauk,* and *Nahant,* would close with Wagner and try to overpower that fort and Gregg. The *New Ironsides* would assist as needed, with further support from the squadron's gunboats and mortar boats. The ship commanders were to keep a vigilant eye on the *Passaic* so that if the admiral displayed a red flag, "every effort is to be directed by all upon Sumter." The squadron's marine battalion, equipped with boats and howitzers, was to be ready to land if signaled, apparently at Sumter.

The two mortars on Sumter's parade kept up a slow fire overnight on August 14–15 while workmen mounted a 10-inch Columbiad on the salient. A mortar and an 8-inch Columbiad also were readied for shipment from the fort. The morning of the fifteenth was quiet and the afternoon was interrupted by only two shots from the "Abolition land batteries," as Rhett called them. Both missed. Almost three thousand additional sandbags had been stacked outside the gorge, reaching the level of the tops of the second-story windows with a two-bag thickness. By the night of the fifteenth, the bags would be up to the crest of the parapet along the gorge's western half.[12]

The English officer Fitzgerald Ross was still in Charleston when the bombardment began and he watched some of it from Fort Johnson. He marveled at the artillery might on display and quickly realized that

Sumter was in trouble. "It was an entirely novel feature of war; but it soon became evident that they would have the best [of] it," he wrote of the Federals, "and that the brick walls of Sumter would not be able to stand the pounding . . . from that extraordinary distance." Dahlgren went ashore on the fifteenth to confer with Gillmore and found the general resting in bed, still weak. The general was concerned about the quality of his gunpowder and asked Dahlgren for an additional supply, the admiral complying. In his journal that day, Dahlgren, who was not well himself, noted that "Nothing but the will has kept me up."[13]

Beauregard that day ordered one of the fort's three mortars sent to Battery Gregg, adding, "It will be prudent to see that every gun, not actually required for the defense of . . . Sumter, and the new relations of that work to the general defense of the harbor, shall be removed without loss of time." Sumter's pair of mortars on the parade resumed sporadic fire overnight with no reply from the Yankees. Forty-eight rounds were launched at Sumter on the afternoon of August 16 as Gillmore neared completion of his fine tuning. Two of these shots damaged the parapet and one soldier was slightly wounded. The hundreds of workmen continued their exhaustive labors, piling another 2,300 sandbags outside the gorge wall. Overnight on August 16–17, a Columbiad carriage and chassis were shipped from the fort. Work also was underway to cover the second floor of the eastern magazine with four feet of sand and the same floor of the western magazine with sixteen inches. Sandbags had been placed to protect the post hospital.[14]

For four days the Federals had tested Sumter, but now the preliminary barrage was over and Gillmore was apparently feeling better. On the sixteenth he reminded his troops, "especially those to whom he has this day assigned the posts of honor and of danger, that the eyes of a beneficent country are fixed upon them, with not only the ardent hope, but the confident expectation, of success. The nation is indeed waiting to crown you the victors of Sumter. We need not, and must not, fail." At 5:00 AM on Monday, August 17, he raised the curtain on what became known as the First Great Bombardment, as an 8-inch round from Battery Brown arced through the silver light toward the fort. Soon afterward, ten other guns thundered, hurling more than three thousand pounds of metal at Sumter at ranges varying from three to four thousand yards. Later in the day, they were joined by five of Dahlgren's vessels, including an ironclad and four gunboats.[15]

When the day began, Sumter still had plenty of firepower to defend itself—thirty-eight guns of various makes and calibers and the two 10-inch mortars—but nothing with the accuracy and range capable of retaliating against these huge pieces. By 9:00 AM, more than three hundred shots had been aimed at Sumter—some two hundred finding their mark—"the practice being astonishingly accurate and the effects severe," noted engineer Johnson. Most of the rounds targeted the left flank and face, taking the latter in reverse. "The inside of the fort buildings has been much torn," Rhett wrote at this time, "The damage to outside has not yet been ascertained. The firing is still going on." The garrison's chief blacksmith was killed and five other soldiers wounded, including some bruised by flying or falling bricks. Two guns had also been slightly disabled, but hell's kitchen was just opening for business.[16]

After the bombardment opened, Dahlgren put his monitors into motion about 6:00 AM. The navy's primary mission was to suppress return fire from Wagner and Gregg and prevent them from interfering with the army batteries focused on Sumter. The naval gunfire opened some forty-five minutes later and soon overwhelmed those strongpoints, some of the squadron's wooden gunboats joining in the shelling. "The most serious attack yet attempted," Beauregard wrote to Adjutant General Cooper at 9:30 AM. "Sumter fiercely assailed with heavy rifled ordnance." He added that the enemy had launched more than a thousand rounds at the various Confederate positions in a two-hour period.

The *New Ironsides*, which would fire more than four hundred rounds this day, turned her guns on Sumter about 10:15 AM, but they splashed short; the gunners were unable to elevate their pieces high enough. In late morning, *Passaic* and *Patapsco* churned toward Sumter, trading punches with Moultrie, Gregg, and Wagner. Sumter also took some hits from these monitors, but its artillery reply, beginning about 11:15 AM, was feeble, the garrison apparently bewildered by the worst shellacking any soldiers had endured to that point in history. *Patapsco* and *Passaic* withdrew just after noon to give their crews a meal break, but soon returned to join other Union vessels in plastering Wagner and Gregg.

The bombardment was halted for a few hours during the middle of the day when the heat was most intense, and then continued until dusk. By 11:00 PM, Sumter's defenders had counted 919 projectiles thrown at the fort, 663 of which had found the target. "The firing during the day

was very rapid," Rhett reported. "Sumter still in reliable fighting condition," Beauregard wired Cooper at 9:30 PM, giving an assessment of the
overall damage to the city's defenses. He added, "This is the thirty-ninth
day of the siege. We have cause to be satisfied with the result." His math
dated from the July 10 Yankee landing on Morris Island.

The Federals continued the barrage overnight with one shot every
fifteen minutes to prevent repair work, he added. Watching the shelling,
a Yank in the 52nd Pennsylvania Infantry described how at the end of
the first full day of bombardment, "Sumter had the appearance of a bad
case of smallpox." He also marveled at the work of the batteries: "Every
puff of smoke from these ungainly piles of sand, over which these Parrotts loomed long and black, was followed by a little cloud from
Sumter," he wrote, "the great bolts hissing quietly, but unerringly"
toward their objective. "For any sign of life we saw or heard, every man
within the battered walls might have been killed," a Massachusetts officer
added of the fort's early-morning inactivity. "The only moving thing was
the fluttering flag that still waved on its staff."[17]

For the day, the Confederates had sustained casualties of one dead
and seventeen wounded. The lone fatality was the blacksmith, Pvt.
William Barringer, of Company K, 1st South Carolina Artillery, who was
killed by a Parrott shell that burst on the parade ground some one hundred yards from him. The unfortunate Barringer was standing under
cover of the gorge near the southeast angle when the round exploded, its
base flying off and striking him. Another projectile ripped into the third
floor of the east barracks, wounding six men. The most serious of the
injured was a sergeant who had four fingers cut from his left hand. Battery Wagner also had been decimated, with several men killed and all but
one gun disabled.

Dahlgren's vessels had escaped in good shape, with only two killed, a
few minor injuries to crewmen, and scant damage to three monitors, but
one of the dead was a major loss. Capt. George W. Rodgers, the
squadron's fleet captain, and another officer died instantly when a shot
struck the *Catskill*'s pilothouse, and two others were slightly wounded.
News of Rodgers's loss had circulated among the squadron by about 1:00
PM, the ships all half-masting their colors in mourning and tribute. The
New Ironsides, meanwhile, had been hit more than thirty times, with little effect.

Sumter itself had managed to get off only sixty-four rounds, fired at long range against the monitors before they withdrew in the early afternoon. Ironically, the first shot had been hurled by the *Keokuk* gun, but the fort's barrage had been harmless to the enemy.[18] Seven of Sumter's guns had been damaged, six of them on the northwest face. This left the defenders with only two pieces—an 8-inch Columbiad and a 42-pounder—serviceable on that wall. During the night, two disabled 42-pounders were removed from the parapet to the parade so they could be shipped out. With the shelling dying down, engineer Johnson was already endeavoring to repair damage done to the western magazine. Col. David Harris, the department's chief engineer, reached the fort about 9:00 PM, joining Rhett and Johnson on an inspection of the carnage. "The damage done to the gorge face . . . is considerable," Rhett wrote overnight. Also during the night, "a large quantity of ammunition and stores" was removed from the fort and taken to Sullivan's Island, Johnson related.

"We have been pretty severely pelted and shelled today," Lt. Iredell Jones wrote to his father from Sumter that night. "The enemy opened at daybreak . . . with their monitors and land batteries on Wagner and Sumter, and the bombardment continued with unabated fury until dark." Even as he wrote, the barrage was ongoing, but at a much slower pace. "For some reason our fort did not reply this morning until 11:30 . . . , when we opened a brisk fire on the monitors and gunboats, and in the course of an hour succeeded in driving all of them off. The . . . batteries, however, we could not silence, and they have given us bricks all day long. . . .The fort is badly used up—four guns dismounted, though all unimportant. . . . We expect a renewal of the attack to-morrow."[19]

A few miles away in Charleston, Beauregard also sat down to put his thoughts on paper, writing to his friend, John Slidell, a Confederate commissioner in Paris. "The enemy . . . has not yet accomplished much," he said of operations since the Union landing on Morris Island. "He has not yet, however, put forward all his strength. Whether we will again be able to defeat him is still a mystery. He has immense advantages over us in the way of numbers, ordnance means, and materials, but the race is not always to the swiftest and victory to the strongest."

Also writing that Monday was Emma Holmes, who watched the bricks and sand fly up from direct hits on the fort and felt the concussion of shells rattle the windows of Charleston. The loss of her family's home in the city during the December 1861 fire had eventually forced them to relocate inland, but Emma was visiting at the time of the bombardment. "Sumter is so identified with us and our cause that it will be like tearing out our heart-strings should it fall," she scrawled in her diary. "Each day that I stay in Charleston makes me love and cling to it yet more fondly. But all we can do is to hope and trust in the mercy of a righteous God."[20]

Tuesday, August 18

At 5:00 AM, fourteen Union guns in the breaching batteries—three more guns than the previous day and all in Battery Reno—began the second day of battering Sumter in rapid succession. "The fire was resumed this morning and is now in progress," Gillmore informed Halleck. "I am satisfied with the results thus far." He added that all the breaching batteries would be completed on the eighteenth and would "enable me to increase the intensity of my fire fully one-third." Gillmore also had observed that the Confederates had spent the night "piling up immense quantities of sand-bags against the gorge wall" and that two monitors, as well as the *New Ironsides*, were still assisting in the bombardment. The latter vessel, along with *Passaic* and *Weehawken*, were in action early, steaming near Wagner about 5:15 AM to prevent any reinforcements from being sent from there to Sumter.

Within the walls, a frustrated Rhett was stymied in his efforts to ship out any of his artillery due to the rubble already accumulating from the ongoing enemy shelling. "It is impossible to get out a gun today," he telegraphed at 10:15 AM. "The sally port and the way to it [are] covered with rubbish and shells [are] continually bursting near." The pair of damaged 42-pounders taken from the northwest parapet overnight could not be sent off because debris prevented them from being transported to the wharf. "It is simply impossible to dismount or remove one disabled gun today," Rhett said in another dispatch about an hour later.[21]

As morning turned past noon, hundreds of shot and shells had rocketed over Morris Island to either plow into Sumter or send tall geysers of water skyward in the harbor. The weather soon came into play as well. A heavy northeaster blanketed the coast early in the afternoon, soaking soldiers on both sides. An army reporter for the *Philadelphia North American* said, "we experienced a terrible storm of rain, wind and drifting sand. The tents blew around in a terrible manner, and the sand filling one's eyes was anything but agreeable." Combined with high tides, the intense rain submerged the Union trenches in front of Battery Wagner and "seriously interfered with the accuracy" of the fire against Sumter. But the ferocious barrage and the continuing carnage being wrought by the rain of big projectiles prevented the defenders from replying. "No firing took place from this fort," Rhett noted in the fort's journal.[22]

The garrison flag was twice shot away, but this was the least of the mayhem this day, as the fort's armament suffered a devastating blow. All but two guns on the gorge face were damaged, and both pieces on the west face were put out of action, as were the remaining guns on the northwest face. Two 10-inch Columbiads were rendered unserviceable, and the Brooke gun had part of its carriage blown away but was remounted that night.

Two Rebel deserters reached the Federal lines on Morris Island that Tuesday and gave Gillmore a reasonably accurate description of the work being done at Sumter. The deserters said they were crewmen from a boat that regularly traveled between Cummings Point and the fort. They told the Yankees that all of Sumter's casemates and the officers' quarters on the gorge wall had been filled with cotton bales and sandbags to a depth of about twenty feet. The deserters also said all of the guns on the gorge wall had been removed to James Island and replaced with fake, or "Quaker guns." Gillmore relayed this information to Halleck that day, believing it to be correct.

By the time the shelling stopped at 7:00 PM, Sumter had been targeted by almost 900 shots (Rhett and Johnson said 876 while Jones counted 895). Of these, 696, according to Rhett, struck the fort either inside or outside. The lull in the bombardment was, needless to say, a welcome respite for the Rebels since it was the first halt in the pounding since the morning of the seventeenth. Again, despite the tons of airborne iron, Confederate casualties were amazingly light; only three men were wounded, one severely.[23]

The eastern lower magazine had been in the line of fire from the enemy batteries, but its walls and the exterior stone barrier held up under the blasting, giving the Confederates time to decide if and when its ammunition and powder should be removed. Engineer Johnson checked the magazines almost hourly. He recalled how his small lantern cast "fantastic shadows on the piled-up kegs of cannon powder." Then he would hold his ear close to the wall and await the crash of the next incoming shell "to hear how much it shook the fort than the last, and to estimate its . . . penetration." At night when the firing eased, Johnson would go outside the fort with a rod and measuring tape to inspect the damage. The Confederates were living "on the crater of a volcano that is rumbling and threatening to make an eruption at any instant," a Charlestonian wrote of the threat to the magazine.

Dahlgren, meanwhile, boarded the *Passaic* that evening and went in for a closer look at the carnage wrought by the shelling. "Pretty well used up, but not breached," he wrote in his journal. Overnight the Confederates tried to prepare one of the broken 10-inch Columbiads for shipment "but it was found to be impossible," Rhett wrote. Still, other work was done to bolster the defenses. The traverse on the southeast pan coupe was raised another two feet; the floors of both upper magazines were covered with four feet of sand; and the revetment of sandbags protecting the western magazine was increased by two feet.[24]

Wednesday, August 19

The gale still raged, but the Federals resumed the bombardment about 4:30 AM with fifteen big guns, one more than on Tuesday. The *Philadelphia North American* correspondent awoke to at least an inch of sand layering his army cot, an angry tide washing away the beach three feet from his shelter, and half of Gillmore's staff tents torn down by the snarling wind. Across the roiling waves, he saw Union vessels "tossing about in a terrible style" and the transport *New Jersey* aground, possibly wrecked.

The real storm, however, was breaking over Sumter. By just after 9:00 AM, 245 pieces of flying metal had been launched at it, only twenty-eight sailing overhead and not adding to the fort's breakdown. Already the casualty list was higher than the previous day—one man dead and four wounded. The foul weather was no match for the man-made turbulence swirling over Sumter that morning. "We need all the garrison we have to hold the fort and are short of officers," Rhett telegraphed to Charleston at 9:50 AM. "The firing . . . is the heaviest yet and the walls are seriously damaged. . . . All gorge guns useless." About 10:20 AM, a projectile crashed completely through the gorge wall, exiting out of an area the soldiers called "General Ripley's room," Ripley's quarters when he stayed at the fort. The round had torn through the brick and masonry after striking under an arch where there was little sand to reinforce the wall, landing in the parade.[25]

Late morning saw the steamer *Sumter* dock at the fort's new wharf on the city side of the fort. This was considered the least vulnerable area to the enemy shelling, and the *Sumter* was subsequently loaded with 190 barrels of gunpowder to be shipped out. A stray or lucky shot to her innards likely would have ignited a sizeable explosion with untold damage to Sumter, not to mention obliterating the ship and her crew. Near noon, the vessel slipped her ropes and left the wharf, unscathed by the shelling, and headed back into the inner harbor. Rhett noted that he would try to ship the rest of the fort's powder that night on the steamer *Etiwan*. Minutes after the *Sumter's* departure, a twenty-foot-wide section of the gorge wall collapsed, and Rhett dispatched that daylight was showing through three or four of the gorge wall casemates. The battery fire slackened amid the midday heat and then regained its intensity through the afternoon until 7:00 PM when the bulk of the bombardment was halted. The navy had also gotten into the act late in the afternoon, Dahlgren "going up to feel Sumter with the monitors." The bluecoats ashore fired 780 rounds, 649 of which hit the fort while 131 passed overhead. The Federals' fire for the night was reduced to one round every thirty minutes.

Amazingly, all of the five casualties this day occurred before 9:00 AM.[26] The shellacking, however, had been horrific. About half of the gorge wall had been knocked down, exposing the interior arches and the sand and sandbags packed in the rooms. A large portion of the remaining gorge wall would soon collapse, the defenders expected. On the northwest face, seven casemates in the upper and lower tiers were badly damaged, as was the terreplein. The remaining 10-inch mortar on the parade was hit and dismounted, its bed splintered. Fortunately for the Confederates, the magazine was still safe and, despite the shelling, a partial traverse was erected to protect the hospital. More carnage had been averted after three fires broke out in the fort during the day due to the bombardment. Each of them had been quickly extinguished, and Sgt. Theodore Schaeffer, Company H, 1st South Carolina Artillery, earned mention in reports for his bravery. Schaeffer, the garrison's acting provost sergeant, repeatedly went "directly in the line of fire from the enemy" to douse the blazes, the fort's journal noted.

With rounds whistling or splashing nearby, Ripley arrived at Sumter about 5:00 PM, and soon afterward Dahlgren's ironclads moved up, as if to make some noise of their own. The Confederates greeted them with four long-range shots from the *Keokuk* gun. The warships withdrew shortly without replying, but hurled several rounds at Morris as they retreated. Ripley spent some time examining the condition of the fort. "He found the garrison still maintaining the admirable discipline for which it has always been remarkable," the *Charleston Mercury* stated on the twentieth. "Guards were turned out, and the usual etiquette observed as strictly as if nothing was going on without. This, under such trying circumstances, as those through which the garrison are passing . . . is a most convincing proof of its high tone and soldierly fortitude."[27]

"My dear Father—The bombardment still continues hot and heavy, and we are holding out as well as possible under the circumstances," Iredell Jones penned that night. "It is useless any longer to conceal the fact—the fort is terribly knocked to pieces. Though there is no reason at present to abandon it, its fall is only a question of time. Many guns have been dismounted, and all the guns on the gorge face are unserviceable on account of the parapet's being knocked away. The enemy throw 200-pound Parrotts at us at the rate of one thousand per day." Jones also expressed frustration that Sumter had done little to fight back since the first day of the cannonading. "I cannot imagine the reason, and the policy is condemned by every officer of the garrison," he wrote. "It may not, it would not, alter the state of affairs to open fire, but the honor of our country, the honor of ourselves, and the reputation of the gallant old fort demands it. I trust we will remain and fight the fort to the very last extremity. If she falls, let her and her devoted defenders fall together and gloriously." Even as the lieutenant scrawled those words near midnight, Gillmore's bluecoats were toiling, Jones adding, "the shells are bursting all over us and the bricks are flying wildly." At some point that day, Jones offered his black servant, George, the option of leaving Sumter. "George behaves like a man," Jones told his father in the letter. "I gave him his choice to go to town or not, as he wished. He replied that he would not leave me."

In the Union lines, the men were saddened by the mortal wounding of Lt. Henry Holbrook of the 3rd Rhode Island Heavy Artillery. Holbrook was commanding Battery Meade that day when he was struck down by a shell fragment, one of his superiors describing him as an "energetic, zealous, and brave soldier."

By 9:10 PM, Dahlgren had returned from his probing of Sumter and told Gillmore of his findings, especially regarding the gorge wall. "It is very much pierced over its whole extent by ragged holes, large and deep," he wired the general. "There seems to be some debris at the foot, but the wall is not breached. . . . It has been well pommeled, but will endure more."[28]

Thursday, August 20

The fourth day of the bombardment was marked by the addition of three more Union big guns, including a 10-inch Parrott rifle (300-pounder) to the "battering engines"—as one Confederate labeled them—pounding Sumter. This meant the Yankees now had a total of eighteen rifles—100-, 200-, and the 300-pounder—aimed at the fort. "Indeed, it may be said that Sumter for the last three days has probably withstood a heavier fire than any fort of its class ever sustained before," the *Mercury* noted that day, unaware of what ravages the new dawn had brought. The 10-inch Parrott, emplaced at Battery Strong, would be the most powerful gun used in the bombardment, and it had taken a monumental effort by the Yanks to get it in position. The Federals had hauled the 26,000-pound gun more than a mile from the dock, most of it through deep sand and "semi-marsh" that was flooded at high tide. Three sling carts were broken down in the grinding, inch-by-inch move that took about a week and was done at night. During the day, the piece was covered with brush and weeds to conceal it from the Rebels while it was transported to Strong. The Parrott was fired only once every eight to ten minutes and was soon "tearing away stone and bricks where both had not been already beaten into dust," a Union officer recalled. At a distance of more than 4,300 yards from Sumter and with a charge of twenty-five pounds of powder, it took a round some eighteen seconds to reach the fort once it cleared the muzzle, but its penetrating power was terrific.[29]

The pulverizing began at 5:00 AM Thursday, and over the next four hours the bluecoats in the batteries threw 244 projectiles at Sumter, only 39 missing, Rhett reported. One piece, a rifled 42-pounder on the east face, was put out of action, but there were no casualties during this period. "The firing this morning has been exceedingly heavy, more destructive than it has ever been," Rhett wrote in a 12:40 PM telegram to Charleston.

It had already been a predawn day of herculean labor at the beleaguered fort. The steamers *Etiwan* and the lucky *Sumter* had docked at the wharf overnight, and workmen had filled them with twenty-five thousand pounds of powder, almost three hundred shells and other artillery projectiles, and various war materiel. The vessels were loaded and away by 3:00 AM.

The garrison flag was shot away about 12:15 PM. It was quickly replaced by the Confederates, but the Union batteries were intensifying their lethal work. "The enemy kept up a heavy and continuous fire during the whole day," Rhett noted, "but increasing perceptibly toward the afternoon."[30] The screech of shells across the harbor mouth and its environs was constant and deafening as the *New Ironsides* and four gunboats spent the day blasting Confederate positions on Morris. Meanwhile, the three Rebel batteries on James Island—Simkins, Cheves, and Haskell— were shelling Union entrenchments on Morris, adding to the awesome cacophony of Sumter's punishment.

As more of the gorge wall caved in, he and his Carolinians trying to elude death from above, Rhett had another major worry—would he have enough troops to hold Sumter if they all survived this day? Hunkered in his headquarters, his arithmetic suggested otherwise. On the nineteenth, fifteen artillerymen of the 1st South Carolina's Company E who had been on detached service at Battery Wagner were sent to Castle Pinckney for a rest. Now two of his other companies—F and K—were to be transferred elsewhere in Charleston's defenses. The loss of these soldiers "will leave us but 200 men for duty," he telegraphed his superiors that afternoon, "out of these to be taken magazine men, police, cooks, old guard, and new guard. I do not think it would be advisable to send volunteers among our garrison at this time; think it would have a bad effect." Despite his opinions, Company K was readied to move out that night.

The Confederates counted 879 shots launched at Sumter that day, including 408 that hit outside, 296 that struck inside, and 175 that passed over. All of this flying metal accounted for only three slight casualties, but further broke down the fort. The barrage ended around dark and the Rebels tallied the damage. The greater part of the gorge wall was now down, and most of the northwest terreplein had collapsed, the latter caused by reverse fire—rounds that hit this area from the rear. The northwest wall also had several large holes, clean breaches by the enemy cannon. Two 42-pounder guns were disabled. By now, much of the lower portion of the fort was inundated with heaps of debris from the upper levels. All of the powder was removed from the east magazine and a crack was found in its west corner. Work parties immediately began repairs and improvements in the few hours of darkness they had for cover. They packed four rooms east of the gorge with sand, completed a traverse for the hospital, bolstered the western magazine's revetment, and began another traverse.[31]

"Night and day the air was filled with shrieking shell and whizzing shot," Charlestonian W. F. G. Peck recalled about this period. "Standing on the Battery promenade in the darkness . . . I have counted no less than eight bombs in the air at one time." He added that the "thunder of artillery would be so great that every house in the lower part of the city trembled to its base." For Iredell Jones, the Federals' "incessant fire" over the past four days was a bleak harbinger of Sumter's fate, although his frustration over the fort's lack of biting back at the Yanks had calmed somewhat. "We have been forced to shrink our shoulders and take all this iron hail without the gratification of replying," he wrote his mother that Thursday. "But, however humiliating this may appear, it is probably the wisest policy. We have but one battery left, and we had best not expose [it]. The fact is, we all know now, what we all thought before, that the fort can't stand against land batteries. . . . That the fort may, and is likely to be abandoned, I think very probable . . . but that time has not arrived. . . . It is true that one-half . . . is laid in ruins." Still, Jones put on a brave face, telling his mother that two of the fort's faces were largely unscathed and that he and his comrades remained defiantly awaiting the expected naval assault. "We will rest quiet until the ironclads come in, when I trust we will be able again to reflect credit on the glorious old fortification," he penned.[32]

Jones also contended that Sumter's devastation had at least one positive result: The falling bricks accumulating on the sand outside the shattered gorge had "built up of themselves a complete breastwork, behind which we can take refuge." Still, there was no masking the awe he—and likely most of the garrison—felt about the terrible power arrayed against them. "No one that has not been here to witness the effect of the enemy's ordnance can have the least conception of what has been done in four days," he wrote. "Who, on Sunday last, would have thought that even the weakest face of this fort could have been knocked down by guns at distances ranging between two miles and three miles? I expected them to knock it down when Wagner fell, but I admit my surprise when I saw them open on us from such distances." The Federals were intent on leveling or capturing Sumter, "and we may expect all their hatred to be raised to its highest pitch towards us until they accomplish their object."

The day's casualties amounted to several of the black workmen who were slightly injured and a captain who sustained a minor ankle wound. Sumter's defenders, meanwhile, clung to their morale—and sense of humor—despite the pounding. "As yet we are all in fine spirits," Jones wrote that same day. "Like others under similar circumstances, we have become accustomed to the shelling, and there is always someone to crack a joke. We slip in any corner that we can find—every one for himself" to avoid bricks and brick fragments (which often became missiles when shells landed) as well as the rounds themselves. "Nearly every officer has been struck, more or less," Jones said. "I have been struck several times— once on the arm with a [shell] fragment . . . which stung me slightly, but did not even break the skin. On one occasion I was so unlucky as to get a brick side my head, though some say it was in my hat."[33]

As Sumter was pasted that afternoon, Gillmore was rowed out to the flagship USS *Philadelphia* to confer with Dahlgren about the state of the campaign. The commanders agreed on their satisfaction with the overall progress against Wagner and Sumter. Dahlgren felt that the success was largely due to not only the bombardment but also the element of surprise. "No doubt the Confederates thought we would wait for fine fall weather," he wrote. Fortunately for the Confederates, the giant Parrott at Battery Strong was disabled by a premature explosion of a shell near its muzzle soon after opening fire, blowing off about eighteen inches of its length. The gun was not destroyed, however, and Capt. Sylvester H. Gray of the 7th Connecticut Volunteer Infantry, the battery commander, assembled a detail of machinists and handymen from the ranks to try to salvage the piece. Working with chisels, files, and other tools, the New Englanders incredibly had the now-shortened Parrott ready for action in less than forty-eight hours. Rightly proud of this accomplishment, one of

Gray's bluecoats quipped, "The American Eagle is a fine bird, but he cannot beat the Ten Inch Parrott." The joke was soon making the rounds in the Union camps.[34]

Overnight on August 20–21, a detachment from Sumter was involved in a daring attempt to destroy the *New Ironsides*. The Confederates had converted a small steamer into a ram equipped with a torpedo spar. The *Torch*, as she was named, was leaky, unarmored, and commanded by Capt. James Carlin, who also was the skipper of a blockade runner. That night, Carlin guided the *Torch* out of the harbor. At Sumter, he brought aboard eleven soldiers, led by Lt. Eldred S. Fickling, to guard against enemy boarders. Near midnight, the *New Ironsides* was sighted anchored off Morris Island with several monitors nearby. Carlin silently proceeded toward her, lowering the torpedo to ram into her side. When she was about fifty yards away, a Union ensign on lookout spotted the suspicious craft astern and hailed her twice. Carlin shouted back that she was the steamer *Live Yankee*.

Within forty yards, Carlin ordered the engine stopped, but quickly realized he would drift past the huge ship and be unable to torpedo her. By now, the *Torch* was so close that Fickling's soldiers could see the faces of Yankee seamen looking out the portholes. The *Torch* limped away, her engine sputtering, as the *New Ironsides'* rounds ripped fountains in the water around her. Fickling and his men made it back to Sumter shaken but unharmed. "They all have frightful stories to relate about the drums beating to quarters, seeing men rush on deck and to their guns, and seeing guns run in battery," wrote Iredell Jones. "But . . . they succeeded in getting off safe, though making a hair-breadth escape."[35]

An assortment of artillery shells and equipment, along with nine hundred pounds of powder, were shipped from the fort that night. Despite the deadly rigors of that Thursday, Sumter's defenders had kept an eye on a new enemy gun emplacement being built on the mud flats between Morris and Black Islands. "The battery in [the] marsh . . . appears to be built of sand," Rhett stated in a telegram that night to Charleston. Within a few days, the massive gun located there would become one of the most famous in American history.[36]

CHAPTER 6

"I Could Scarcely Restrain My Tears"

Friday, August 21

"The slow but steady bombardment of Sumter has continued without intermission night and day," the *Mercury* related on Friday, August 21. "Grimly and in silence the grand old fort receives the terrible fire of the enemy. But still her flag floats defiantly from the ramparts. The end is not yet." At sunup, the Union cannonade resumed like Swiss clockwork, but the direction of fire was now focused on the eastern half of the fort. The enfilade shelling was so effective and intense that by 7:40 AM, a 10-inch Columbiad on the east face and a rifled gun in Harleston's battery on the northeast face had been knocked out. The fort's flag was twice shot away that morning; another shell crushed a desk in the adjutant's office—that officer had the good fortune to be out at the time. "The fire of the enemy is very heavy on the east battery," Rhett said in a 10:55 AM telegraph message, "and should the fleet come up, I do not think the men could stay at the guns." Rhett sent another dispatch at 11:45 AM, stating that he had only nine effective pieces *en barbette*, "and the probabilities are that this afternoon most of them will be disabled."[1]

The fourteen hours of daylight from 5:00 AM to 7:00 PM were a time of almost continuous shelling, which slackened somewhat around the dinner hour. If Sumter's defenders were getting hammered, the boys in blue were suffering mightily too in the seething summer heat. Toiling in their batteries under a scorching sun and handling the heavy projectiles for the guns was a hellish task. And every movement was tough, since the Union camps were on the south end of Morris Island, almost a mile from the position of the breaching batteries and over ground within range of the Confederate guns on James Island.

The Yanks would have gotten no sympathy from the men in the fort, black or white. On this Friday, as on any other day, there were never enough sandbags to fill the jagged gaps, and the work of filling them with dirt from the potholed parade ground was a round-the-clock struggle. Repairs in the shattered casemates were torturous since there was scant ventilation and the temperature burned to 120 degrees. Weary men who earned a few hours of fitful sleep staggered to their feet to wring the sweat out of their clothing as if they had been washed.

Still, the day was deadlier for the Federals. The tars in Cmdr. Foxhall Parker's Naval Battery had been quite active since the seventeenth, serving their two Parrotts and two Whitworths from daylight to dusk. "Although shot and shell were constantly passing over and around us, through the mercy of God they harmed us not," Parker reported two days later. But on the twenty-first the bloody carnage that visited the battery came from within. With one of the Whitworths out of action, the seamen were still firing the other despite shot continually jamming in the barrel. Tragedy struck when a charge prematurely exploded in the gun as a round was rammed home, the blast killing four sailors. The gun was still serviceable, but Parker understandably halted its further use.[2]

"The firing continued all day . . . with unabated fury," Iredell Jones wrote his mother, "no less than 1,000 shots being thrown at us." About 6:30 PM, the *New Ironsides* churned in for a brief tussle. Five 11-inch rounds from the *Keokuk* gun were sent her way before she retired. Jones was a bit high in his shot total—the fort's journal showed 724 out of 943 rounds hit Sumter, with 219 projectiles missing the mark—but four more of Rhett's guns were now silent. The flagstaff had been snapped, and the fort's flag had been shot away—and replaced—four times. Most critically, the eastern face had been badly battered and twelve casemates in the northwest scarp wall had been punished as well. The obliteration of the remaining gorge rampart continued and the east barracks sustained serious damage. Seven men, including two slaves, were wounded, and by day's end, Sumter had only seven guns still operational on the parapet.

Near sundown, Beauregard arrived at the fort to assess the situation. He was accompanied by Cols. Jeremy F. Gilmer and David Harris, his top-ranking engineers. Beauregard, despite appearing "pleased and confident, could not help displaying a silent wonder and amazement at the ruined and dilapidated Fort," Jones penned. "He says it must be held for one month yet." General Ripley made his own inspection, arriving with his staff about 10:00 PM. Overnight, 9,700 pounds of gunpowder, along with twelve bags of sugar and a laundry list of artillery equipment, was shipped from the fort. Rhett had another problem to deal with as Sumter seemingly toppled around him: The workforce was physically worn down, unable to sleep due to the shelling during the day and the exhausting labors at night. A requisition was made around this time for fresh laborers.

The night of the twenty-first also saw a foray by Dahlgren's monitors to "batter Sumter," as the admiral put it. The ironclads slid by Battery Wagner and were approaching the fort, but the *Passaic* ran aground about a half-mile from their objective, apparently due to an uncooperative civilian pilot. It took so long for her to float free on the tide that the attack was aborted.[3]

Saturday, August 22

About 1:30 AM on Saturday, August 22, lookouts at Sumter heard the boom of a giant gun and watched in wonder as a shell streaked across the heavens from Morris Island. The Sumter defenders were calloused to being bombarded, but the sound and direction of this trajectory was much different. The round seemed to scar the night sky forever before falling into Charleston itself, the dull sound of its explosion rolling across the water. This was the debut of the "Swamp Angel," as the Federals called her, firing from the marsh battery the Confederates had been keeping an eye on for a few days. This 200-pounder (8-inch) Parrott rifle blasted away that morning from a range of 7,900 yards, hurling a number of 150-pound incendiary shells into the city.

Gillmore had received word on the twenty-first that the 16,500-pound Parrott was ready for action. By way of Battery Wagner, he sent an ultimatum to Beauregard that day, demanding the immediate evacuation of Morris and Sumter; otherwise the city would be fired upon. "The present condition of Fort Sumter, and the rapid and progressive destruction which it is undergoing from my batteries, seem to render its complete demolition within a few hours a matter of certainty," Gillmore wrote. "All my heaviest guns have not yet opened." He added that his forces had "batteries already established within easy and effective range of the heart of the city."[4]

The note reached Beauregard's headquarters at 10:45 PM on the twenty-first, but the general was out. And because Gillmore had not signed the message—an apparent oversight—it could not be verified as legitimate. Thus, the Confederates took no other action, and Charleston was left unaware of the threat. When Gillmore received no reply by midnight, he ordered the marsh battery to begin firing. Aiming the Angel based on compass readings taken on the St. Michael's Church steeple, the bluecoats launched fifteen shells into Charleston before dawn Saturday. The Angel's rounds, twelve of them filled with an incendiary known as Greek fire, caused some blazes and spotty damage, along with panic and excitement throughout the city. "Pandemonium reigned, and everyone cursed General Gillmore," one witness recalled. The Angel was done for the day, needing repairs after the sixteenth shot, but there would be more to come from her.

Now it was Sumter's turn again. For the sixth straight day, Gillmore's breaching guns saluted sunrise with their lethal thunder, beginning at 6:00 AM. Over the first three hours, 266 rounds sliced the sky, 161 of which rocked the fort, wounding one man. The Confederates had worked through the night to repair a previously disabled rifled 42-pounder gun on the northeast face. But that piece, along with the Brooke gun, was knocked out of action early on Saturday, leaving Sumter with only seven working guns on its ramparts. For the day, shot and shell totaling 604 rained on the fort, 419 finding the target while 185 missed. All of the barbette pieces had been silenced by now, other than the *Keokuk* Dahlgren and a 10-inch Columbiad on the east face. The east parapet had been pummeled and weakened and huge craters were everywhere in the fort.

"Today the firing has been unusually heavy, and . . . has resulted in considerable injury to us, in the way of dismounting guns," Lieutenant Jones wrote to his mother that night. "We have now only four guns fit for immediate service, though these are well protected by sand traverses and probably will not be hurt at all." He added that several other pieces were temporarily out of action and would likely be repaired during the night after the shelling ceased. "One company [K] was sent out of the Fort last night, (the 21st) and tonight another goes," Jones wrote. "This will leave three to keep the old machine going. . . . Our men act splendidly. No troops probably ever stood with so little concern and for so long a time such a terrific and constant shelling, and the more honor is due to them for such behavior when it is recollected that they do it without being allowed to reply. They have to sit quiet and take it the livelong day. . . . You have no idea what a relief it is at night when the enemy stops pelting us," he continued, "the feeling is delightful; we feel refreshed and rejoiced, and seem to breathe more freely an air that seems purer."

Sumter's eastern face was still not seriously damaged, Jones claimed, "and the Fort is still tenable, though no one expects it to be held any length of time." The Confederates were trying to buy time to remove the rest of the fort's powder, which was done "as rapidly as possible," and also for construction or completion of batteries on James Island. The lieutenant was pessimistic that the artillery still at Sumter could be saved "when we evacuate" and probably would have to be blown up. "The Fort is so torn to pieces, and there is so much rubble in it, that it would be a difficult job to get them (the guns) out, and would require too much energy."[5]

Few, if any, of Sumter's officers yet knew about Gillmore's surrender demand and the ongoing correspondence between the rival commanders that Saturday. Charleston was still abuzz over the Swamp Angel when Gillmore's ultimatum, now signed, was received by Beauregard about 9:00 AM. With the booming of Union cannon as a backdrop, the Creole general replied promptly in scathing fashion. He accused Gillmore of "inexcusable barbarity" by bombarding a city of unsuspecting civilians who had not had enough time to be withdrawn. He added that if Charleston was shelled again before the noncombatants could be evacuated, "I shall feel impelled to employ such stringent means of retaliation as may be available." In closing, Beauregard rejected the surrender demand. Gillmore answered about 9:00 PM Saturday, claiming that the steady progress of his advance should have given Charleston ample "notice of her danger" and blaming Beauregard for not evacuating the civilians sooner. Still, Gillmore agreed to stop the shelling of Charleston until 11:00 PM on August 23, thus giving more time for the civilians to leave. His decision was influenced by protests, similar to Beauregard's, by foreign consuls in Charleston. Gillmore also knew that the Swamp Angel wasn't yet operational again and likely wouldn't be ready until later in the day on the twenty-third.[6]

Even as Gillmore crafted his verbal retort, Sumter's defenders tried to recover from the day's bombardment and were reacting to news that was a few days old. The garrison had been stung by criticism that had reached it from Charleston regarding the fort's fate, and Iredell Jones did not mince words in thrashing the naysayers. "It has come to our ears that the croakers have already opened their terrific battery that never ceases firing," he wrote that night. "Every gun must be saved, say they, and the Fort must be defended . . . brick by brick! Build a bomb-proof, and get in it . . . and never give it up! I wish some of these boys would come down and give us a lift. . . . I venture to say that if one of these same boys were to come down here and sit with us six hours, his battery would be completely silenced, and he would never open again." In the same train of thought, Jones described how "one of Ripley's fancy aids-de-camp came down the other night with orders to Colonel Rhett to hold the Fort at all hazards." Circumstances forced the officer to stay at Sumter overnight and into the next day, "but he left . . . as soon as possible, the most disagreeably scared man you ever saw in your life, and I venture a prediction that he won't come back to this place any more."[7]

As the garrison tried to find some respite that night, a greater menace than any Charleston "naysayer" was moving closer by the minute. Dahlgren was again launching a night attack against the fort with five monitors. Earlier in the day, he had sent a dispatch to Secretary of the Navy Gideon Welles, updating him about the condition of the squadron, especially his seven ironclads. "The shore batteries have so ravaged Sumter that if I had seven complete monitors the work on it would be over in two or three days," he told Welles. "But the cooperative measures that were required to bring this about have so drawn on my means that I can not attain the purpose." One of his "turrets" was stationed off Savannah to guard against the big ironclad there—the CSS *Savannah*—and the *Catskill* was undergoing repairs at Port Royal. Of the five at Charleston, the *Montauk* had a gun disabled, the *Patapsco*'s 8-inch rifle was cracked at the muzzle, and mechanical issues plagued the *Nahant*. Only the *Weehawken* and *Passaic* were at full strength.

Dahlgren mentioned the failed assault the previous night and described his futility: "Now I am hesitating between an open attack by daylight or renewing the night affair. The difficulty by day is that most of the guns of Sumter have been sent to Moultrie, and in approaching Sumter, you are about the same distance from Moultrie, so that there are as many if not more guns now bearing than in April. Still, I would try it with even five complete monitors, and probably will, as it is." The admiral added that the army's "calls from shore tax me heavily, for the trenches can not be advanced nor even the guns kept in play, unless the ironclads keep down Wagner, and yet in doing so the power of the ironclads is abated proportionally." He closed by asking Welles for more monitors "if you have them."

Dahlgren also earlier that day had aired his concerns to Gillmore after the general requested naval suppressing fire on Wagner. The admiral replied that he would be glad to do so, but "this course is likely to expend the force of the ironclads so much as to render other . . . operations on my part impossible; so that I shall not be able to operate after Sumter and Wagner are reduced." The sailors were exhausted by round-the-clock duty, the monitors' armor was battered, and their guns were wearing out and becoming dangerous. "I desire now to begin directly on Sumter, but can not do so if the ironclads are to be otherwise employed. So that it remains to choose between this as well as further operations toward Charleston when Sumter falls, or to expend power daily on Wagner." Thus Dahlgren suggested that he and Gillmore had to "agree definitely, which choice shall be made; for, after Sumter is taken, further progress will be arrested if the monitors are used up either in armament or otherwise."[8]

Having unburdened himself to Welles and Gillmore, the admiral stepped aboard the *Weehawken* about 11:00 PM on Saturday, and his strike force, also consisting of the *Montauk, Nahant, Passaic,* and *Patapsco,* rode a strong tide up the channel toward darkened Fort Sumter.

Sunday, August 23

Overnight work to shore up the fort was negligible on August 22–23; there were too many distractions. Another attempt to drop a 10-inch Columbiad off the northwest wall so that it could be shipped had failed. Minor improvements were made to some of the traverses and two hundred shells were sent away, but the progress was delayed by the much-needed relief of the black laborers. A fresh group of 112 men arrived at Sumter, relieving 216, engineer Johnson noted. This left the workforce at 220 men. All of this activity ended when Dahlgren's iron-clads—appearing like phantoms out of the thick morning fog—steamed to within eight hundred yards of the fort about 3:00 AM, "its great walls looming over us in the obscurity of the night," he noted, and began a deliberate fire. Not wanting a repeat of the damage Sumter's gunners had inflicted on April 7, the monitor crews had piled sandbags around the turrets and at other vulnerable places on the vessels, giving them an even stranger appearance than normal.[9]

The first round from the monitors mortally wounded a sentinel atop the west wall. "His piercing screams were remarkable, and must have been heard by the enemy," Johnson stated. "As heard by those in the fort, the sound they made, breaking upon the stillness of the night, was longer to be remembered than the loud artillery." The fort had only two work-ing guns by now—the 11-inch *Keokuk* gun and a 10-inch Columbiad—and the defenders managed to reply with only six shots at the monitors. The fog hindered the vision of both sides, and some of the monitors ceased firing, although others kept blasting away based on the position of the stars. Moultrie joined the party about 4:00 AM, as did other batteries, taking shots at the ships when they could be seen through the drifting mist. Even at this close range, the monitors' fire resulted in insignificant new damage to Sumter, but three shells landed near the western maga-zine, making the Confederates extremely jittery about the possibility of a direct hit and titanic explosion. Desperately, about a hundred men were detailed to roll three hundred loaded shells—which were stored in a room near the magazine—into the water to keep them from being hit by the monitors.

With the fog still clinging, Dahlgren ordered his ships to withdraw about 5:30 AM. The *Weehawken* had launched thirty-three shots, nearly half of the sixty to seventy total expended by the five monitors, leaving the admiral frustrated about a lack of initiative among his skippers. Still, the blue tars managed to punch two 15-inch shell holes in Sumter's east parapet. Two other naval rounds had plunged dangerously close to the magazine. Overall, some forty projectiles from the fleet added to the fort's demolition, only seventeen going astray, the Confederates recorded.[10]

As the eastern horizon brightened over the ocean, another considera-tion for the navy to pull away from Sumter was that the barrage from the

Federals' breaching batteries resumed at daybreak on Sunday. God rested on the seventh day, but Gillmore had no intention of doing so. "Their ponderous missiles, thrown with great precision, had wellnigh done their work of destroying the strong artillery post," John Johnson wrote during this time. He went on to describe how the Confederates "could watch the shot and shell rising from little clouds of white smoke far away among the low hills of Morris Island. Sometimes two or three in sight at once, they would come rushing on their way, and as they neared the fort would be hissing and tearing through the air straight to their mark—at one moment to bury themselves far within the solid masonry; at another to crush the mass to fragments, sending up clouds of dust or scattering the debris to the winds and waves." Some of the guns were so distant that the firing and the blast upon reaching the fort were almost simultaneous.

From his post at Wagner, Charles Olmstead marveled at the destructive harvest Sumter had reaped and at the continuing evolution of warfare he witnessed. Fort Pulaski's epitaph had been taken to another level with Sumter's pummeling and "in that time a first-class masonry fort was reduced to a shapeless ruin from batteries located at points far beyond the remotest distance at which any engineer had ever dreamed of danger," he related.

About 2:00 PM, a round penetrated the floor of the upper tier, sending debris crashing into some lower rooms in the eastern barracks. Rhett and four other officers had just sat down for a meal when the blast destroyed their table, slightly wounding all of the men—along with an orderly—and "filling the case mate with a blinding blast of powder, and a shower of bricks and mortar." Others rushed to their aid, including Rhett's black servant, Dick, who was relieved that Rhett was unharmed other than a cut to the hand sustained when his dinner knife was broken. Almost immediately, Dick took "a very practical view of the situation, looking with profound disgust and melancholy" at the ruined meal and the damage the round had inflicted. "All the dinner is gone," he remarked, shaking his head sadly, "and God only knows where we are to find any more."

The barrage ended about 6:30 PM. For the day, 633 enemy rounds were fired, 492 hitting the fort and 141 missing. The casualties were two men seriously wounded and a handful with slight injuries.[11] The east wall had taken a pounding, some of the damage attributed to the monitors, and the last 10-inch Columbiad had been put out of action. Thus, as the sun dipped that Sunday, Sumter had only one functioning gun left; ironically, it was the *Keokuk* Dahlgren, located on the east face. No one knew it then, but Fort Sumter's artillery had fired its last rounds in anger replying to Dahlgren's tars that morning. The fort's flagstaff, relocated to the crest of the gorge that day, had been snapped twice and "had been previously deprived of its colors seven times," Johnson said.

That night the Confederates frantically went to work to fortify the interior barriers of the western magazine, which had earlier proven vulnerable to the shelling from the monitors. No one knew if the enemy ships would come again before the next sunrise. "This was felt to be a critical place and a critical time," Johnson wrote. The entire garrison— soldiers and slaves—labored all night. About eleven thousand pounds of powder were transferred from the lower east magazine to the safer lower west magazine. Even though the former remained relatively intact and the west magazine had sustained some recent near misses, the severity of the damage to the east wall made it unstable and even more dangerous to store munitions there. In truth, there were few reasonably safe spots in the fort at this point. Some fifteen thousand pounds of powder already kept in the west magazine was readied for shipment, as were more artillery rounds and equipage.

"My dear Father: You will have heard, before this reaches you, of the fight with the enemy's monitors this morning," Iredell Jones wrote that night. "We had but one solitary gun amid the ruins, the remnant of thirty-five splendid barbette guns, with which to contend against them. . . . I could scarcely restrain my tears at our helpless situation. It was a sad reflection indeed to think that all our guns were disabled . . . and that we only had one with which to fight the sneaking sea-devils. . . . I need not speak of the injury that we sustained, for we could scarcely be injured more than we already were. We have endured another day's shelling and pelting. It is now just after dark, and not a sound salutes the ear. The whole harbor seems at rest and quiet; whether they are or not, I cannot tell. We look for the monitors to come up again in the morning. How I wish we had something with which to fight them!"[12]

Incredibly, there were few casualties among the garrison during these days, but there had been numerous close calls. Lt. James S. Heyward was sitting at a table, writing a letter to his mother, but needed to refill his pipe. He rose from his chair and walked across his quarters to retrieve some tobacco from the mantelpiece. Before he could do so, a huge projectile smashed into the room, obliterating the table and chair which he had left seconds earlier. Unfazed, Heyward picked through the debris, found his letter, and added a postscript: "A 300 pound shell has torn off the last page of my letter, so you'll have to imagine what I wrote, as I have not time to re-write it." Another officer, John Middleton, had been on duty overnight and when relieved in the morning went to his quarters, fell into bed, and was soon asleep. He placed his personal belongings, including his watch, on a chair beside him. Suddenly, an enemy projectile roared into the room, destroying nearly everything and hurling Middleton out of his splintered bed. As soon as he regained consciousness, the lieutenant, uninjured, located his watch and held it to his ear to see if it still worked. Later he jokingly lamented to comrades that the shell had split his hairbrush.

Rhett himself escaped death or maiming by a matter of inches on at least one other occasion. One morning just after sunrise, he mounted the parapet with his field glass to check the progress of the Union works on Morris Island. Dressed in his white uniform and with dark piles of sandbags on either side of him, he apparently presented an inviting target for deadeye Federal gunners. There was a distant boom, and Rhett soon saw a man-made meteor hurtling toward him. The bluecoats' aim was so accurate that he had to dive onto some of the sandbags to avoid possibly being cut in two. The round exploded on Sumter's parade ground and, moments later, Rhett was back on his feet, calmly continuing to inspect the enemy lines with his glass. Indeed, Rhett, by this point, had earned the respect of his men despite his dueling notoriety. "Colonel Rhett has fully equalled our expectations, as regards being a cool, collected, brave man, and he has certainly acted well in this affair," Iredell Jones noted.[13]

Sumter had already been so perforated by projectiles that gaseous smoke from them was seen slowly wafting out of shell holes long after the rounds struck "as from the crater of a volcano." Johnson noted that the "peculiar odor" of the powder used in the enemy fuse plugs in the shells "so pervaded everything that the air in the fort seemed to be entirely composed of it." Iredell Jones, meanwhile, guessed that Beauregard wanted to hold Sumter until more fortifications were completed on James and Sullivan's Islands. He expected that his unit eventually would be sent to the latter, but he and the rest of the garrison were ready for any trial until then. "I don't think the enemy will make [a small-boat] assault," he wrote that night. "If they do, however, they will find it an ugly little job. Our men are in good spirits, though considerably chafed and worried in consequence of the tremendous bombardment that they have been under for seven days. If it is the wish of our generals that we should remain here and suffer for the good of our country, I hope we will be equal to any danger or hardship that we may be required to endure."[14]

Among those who watched the continued dismantling of Sumter from Morris Island that day was Oscar Sawyer of the *New York Herald*. "Grim old Fort Sumter still stands and frowns upon the harbor. But it is not the Fort Sumter of a week ago," he wrote in a dispatch that would appear in his paper five days later. "In fact, it is certain that no serious offensive powers are left to the rebels in Fort Sumter, and the passage of the fort by our iron-clads is entirely practicable, without much danger from its fire. At all events, we have inflicted enough damage . . . to justify us in regarding it as practically reduced, and incapable of inflicting serious harm upon a fleet. If the navy cannot now pass the work, we may as well regard that arm of the service as of little value. The long looked for moment will soon arrive when a second attempt to pass it by our iron-clads will be made."

As if to punctuate an incredible day for the enemies, the Swamp Angel returned to the stage for a short-lived curtain call that Sunday night. It had been silent while repairs were made on the night of the twenty-second, the battery under fire from Confederate mortars. The gray gunners had been generally accurate, but their rounds plunged into the deep mud, bursting harmlessly. With the passing of Gillmore's surrender deadline, the Angel banged away at Charleston again, nineteen shells arcing into the city. But the big gun still was in bad shape, either from defective rounds or heavier-than-usual powder charges. On its twentieth discharge, it burst and careened off its carriage. The Angel had unleashed a total of thirty-six rounds toward the "cradle of secession," eventually earning its place in Civil War legend. But by early Monday morning, it was merely a huge and useless chunk of sizzling iron.[15]

That Sunday night, Col. John W. Turner, Gillmore's chief of artillery, sat down to give his evaluation of the seven days of destruction in which 5,009 projectiles had been hurled at the fort, about half finding their mark. With surgical precision, Turner described the "almost complete mass of ruins" that had been Sumter's gorge wall and the overall widespread carnage the big guns had wrought. "In fine, the destruction of the fort is so far complete that it is today of no avail in the defense of . . . Charleston," he informed Gillmore. "By a longer fire, it can be made more completely a ruin and a mass of broken masonry, but could scarcely be more powerless for the defense of the harbor." Turner added that, in his opinion, "a continuation of our fire is no longer necessary, as giving us no ends adequate for the consumption of our resources."

After a solid week of punishment, the initial period of the first bombardment was over, but it had exacted a human toll on the Federals as well. Despite working in shifts, the cannoneers were exhausted after serving the big guns for such a long period; casualties were the lamented Lt. Holbrook, three men killed, and twelve others wounded. Gillmore would later claim that prompt action by Dahlgren that Sunday might have led to Charleston's capture: "The failure of the fleet to enter immediately after the 23d of August, whether unavoidable or otherwise, gave the enemy an opportunity, doubtless much needed, to improve their interior defences."[16]

Monday, August 24

"I have the honor to report the practical demolition of Fort Sumter as the result of our seven days' bombardment of that work," Gillmore wrote Halleck on the twenty-fourth. The destruction would have been worse if not for the two days when the "powerful northeasterly storm most seriously diminished the accuracy and effect of our fire. Fort Sumter is today a shapeless and harmless mass of ruins." Since all but one of Sumter's guns had been knocked out of action, it would be hard for anyone to question his claim. Gillmore told Halleck that his batteries remained "as efficient as ever" but that "I deem it unnecessary at present to continue their fire upon the ruins." He also informed Halleck about the shelling of Charleston itself and the Confederates' reaction: "I have also, at great labor, and under a heavy fire from James Island, established batteries on my left, within effective range of the heart of Charleston City, and have opened with them, after giving General Beauregard due notice of my intention to do so. . . . The projectiles from my batteries entered the city and General Beauregard himself designates them as 'the most destructive missiles ever used in war.'" Gillmore included a sketch of Sumter, drawn the previous day, with his report to his superior.[17]

Despite telling Halleck that he had discontinued blasting Sumter, some of Gillmore's pieces resumed fire about 6:30 AM, but it was much lighter than the previous week. Rhett reported 150 rounds aimed at Sumter that day, with only twenty-four misses and no casualties. With the barrage slackening, he was able to count seventeen enemy ships off the bar that morning, including the *New Ironsides* and four monitors, while work was ongoing behind the shattered mounds of bricks. In addition to relocating the hundreds of powder kegs, the fort's laborers had spent the overnight of August 23–24 piling sandbags into damaged embrasures on the southeast and east walls, bolstering the western magazines, and repairing the east barbette traverses.

Beauregard, meanwhile, needed to know how badly Sumter had been mauled and if it could still be held. That Monday, he ordered his chief engineers, Gilmer and Harris, to again go to the fort and confer with the garrison's officers about Sumter's defense "and the advisability of abandoning the work." The engineers were to meet with Rhett and his most trusted officers, Maj. Ormsby Blanding and Capt. F. H. Harleston of the 1st South Carolina Artillery, and engineer Johnson. Despite being warned by Beauregard not to make the trip "if too dangerous," Gilmer and Harris reached the fort by the afternoon and discussed the situation with Rhett and the others. Johnson reported that the fort had only one piece—the *Keokuk* Dahlgren—capable of offensive action; the others had been dismounted or destroyed. Two 10-inch Columbiads were in good condition, but needed timber platforms and sandbag épaulements— work that would take time, especially if the laborers were under enemy fire. Other guns already had been removed to prevent their loss.[18]

The officers then discussed whether Sumter could be held against a barge attack and how many defenders would be needed. All felt the fort could repel an enemy landing if it had a force of 250–500 troops. The talk then shifted to the question of how long Sumter could hold out against assaults in its present condition. Johnson and Harleston estimated thirty-six hours if it were a joint attack by the Union fleet's Parrott guns and land-based mortars, while Blanding was less optimistic: twelve hours. Rhett was greatly concerned about the heavily damaged east wall, which had been riddled by the April 7 shelling and further weakened by the bombardment. Two casemates there had been rebuilt and sandbags had been piled, but Rhett believed two or three hours of shelling by the monitors might bring down the entire wall. He also was worried about the upper west magazine, which was exposed to reverse (rear) fire from the Yankee fleet. Still, there was a general concurrence that Sumter was not yet untenable if the garrison could be supplied with material and labor to bolster these weakened points. Beauregard, meanwhile, knew that if Sumter was to be held, he would have to rely on Flag Officer J. R. Tucker's Confederate navy squadron now more than ever. "The condition of Fort Sumter—its inability to offer further substantial reply, with heavy ordnance, to the enemy's fleet, makes it in place for me to acquaint you formally with the fact," the general wrote to Tucker that day. He asked Tucker to station his ironclads between Sumter and the Sullivan's Island batteries, not only to protect the fort but also to prevent Dahlgren's ships from passing into the harbor.[19]

Iredell Jones received a letter from his mother that evening about the time that he was reading the Charleston newspapers' accounts of Gillmore's surrender demand and the threat of the city being shelled. Having seen the Swamp Angel's shells coursing across the sky on Saturday morning, his pen boiled with vitriol as he replied to his mother about the "vile, brutal, uncivilized demand of the wretch who commands the Yankee forces," and who was now waging war on innocent civilians, as Jones viewed it. Writing the next day, Jones said the "atrocious demand . . . had the effect to increase, if that were possible, the deep feeling of disgust and revenge that I already harbored in my breast, from witnessing on Saturday morning the unprecedented act that he [Gillmore] threatened, actually performed. And now, before God, I vow that if such an act is repeated, and I am ever placed in a situation to take revenge, I shall neither give nor ask quarter, but slaughter every wretch that comes within my power. . . . Such an act forewarns us what we may expect at the hands of . . . Gilmore [*sic*]. . . . Beauregard's reply everybody considers excellent. The general can write if he can't fight."

The Northern public, meanwhile, was learning of Sumter's punishment of the previous week by steamers that had arrived in New York and Philadelphia on the twenty-third. The *New York Herald* on the twenty-fourth described how the bombardment had "fearfully damaged" the fort, "its walls scarred, broken up and breached in several places, and the safety of . . . Charleston placed in imminent peril. . . . It is evident that Sumter is prepared to make a desperate defence, and will hold out to the last," the account continued. "So with the other defences of Charleston. Although the fight has been valiantly begun, and the result can hardly be doubtful, yet there is much severe work to be done by our . . . forces before we can call Charleston our own."[20]

Tuesday, August 25

By Tuesday, August 25, Gilmer and Harris had returned to Charleston and sent a detailed report to Beauregard about the fort's condition. The engineers agreed that "in our opinion, it is not advisable to abandon the fort at this time. On the contrary, we think it should be held to the last extremity. How long it may hold out is now only a matter of conjecture; but there are many elements of defence within the fort, in its present shattered condition, which, if properly used, may enable a resolute garrison to hold it for many days." The engineers added that any question of abandoning Sumter should be Beauregard's, "and not left to the discretion of the Commander of the fort."

The engineers' report helped Beauregard decide not to evacuate Sumter. The bastion had been pummeled to the point that it could no longer function as an artillery post; many of the cannoneers of the 1st South Carolina Artillery had already been sent elsewhere in the Charleston defenses. It was time for the infantry to take over. Sumter's cannoneers had accomplished their task "and it now devolved upon the infantry . . . aided by labor, 'the pick, spade, and shovel,' to perform the part required of them, until, if possible, other heavy guns could be mounted, under cover, amid the ruins that still bade defiance to . . . the land and naval forces of the enemy," wrote Col. Alfred Roman of Beauregard's staff.

Indeed, Companies C and F of the 1st South Carolina Artillery had left Sumter that morning, reassigned to Fort Johnson. The troops had departed on the steamer *Spaulding*, which also had been loaded with twelve thousand pounds of powder, fifty damaged muskets, a few hundred artillery shells of various sizes, and other hardware. The Carolinians were immediately replaced by 150 men of the 28th Georgia Volunteer

Infantry, led by Capt. George W. Warthen, part of Brig. Gen. Alfred H. Colquitt's brigade. These Georgians were veterans, some of whom had seen action in the Peninsula Campaign and at the battle of Antietam. The exit of the artillerists and the arrival of Warthen's men was the first step in the transition of the fort.[21]

Most of the garrison had again toiled the entire night to not only ship the small mountain of powder kegs and ordnance but also shore up the fort. The western magazine was secured from reverse fire, a traverse was begun on the parade to protect the hospital, and the telegraph office underwent repairs. Traverses on the east barbette were restored and embrasures on the northwest and northeast faces were started to be bricked up. It had been a stormy overnight into Tuesday morning, with gusty winds and the rain sometimes falling in torrents, but the work went on anyway.

The Union shelling, meanwhile, started early on Tuesday and continued all day, but not at the rapid rate of the previous few days: Only 175 total rounds were thrown at Sumter, 98 of which found their mark. Their damage was done mainly to the fort's exterior wall and to the interior of the northeast casemates. One shell, however, ripped through the gorge ramparts over the east magazine and exploded, causing concern among the defenders that it had cracked the archway between the inner and outer doors of the upper magazine. The Rebels were relieved to find that no smoke had filtered into the magazine itself, meaning the chamber had not been penetrated. "The shock of the 10-inch Parrott shells is very great," the fort's journal noted on the twenty-fifth. Indeed, the huge Parrott at Battery Strong had returned to action possibly as early as August 23, having been repaired by Captain Gray and his Connecticut mechanics.

The carnage wrought even by the slow fire of the big gun greatly concerned Sumter's defenders since it had taken three or four days of pounding by the enemy's 100- and 200-pounder rifles to accomplish the same amount of destruction the week prior. In one day alone, this gun would hurl fifteen thousand pounds of metal at Sumter, primarily targeting the right flank and the interior of the right face. With its shortened tube, the gun threw 375 more rounds at Sumter in the coming days, "without any appreciable difference in the range or accuracy being noticed," Colonel Turner related. The continued premature explosions of shells, however—

a perpetual problem for Gillmore's cannoneers—soon permanently disabled the Parrott.[22]

The Confederates also continued to keep watch on the Federals' Marsh Battery, not yet realizing the Swamp Angel was out of action and not positive about where it was situated. "There seems to be some mystery in regard to the location" of this "obnoxious battery," the *Mercury* said on the twenty-fifth. Some even believed the gun was in a floating battery run up at night in the inland creeks. "It is hoped that the mystery will soon be solved and the battery silenced," the *Mercury* said. No one in Sumter's garrison believed the enemy gun could do much damage to Charleston from some five miles away. "We cannot imagine any other object that General Gilmore [*sic*] could have had, save malicious spite," Iredell Jones wrote to his mother that night. "He is chagrined that he cannot, with his all-powerful combined force, make two poor little batteries [Wagner and Gregg] crumble before him; that Sumter, though knocked to pieces, still continued to show fight; and that he has expended on the latter alone 100,000 pounds of powder and 1,000,000 pounds of wrought iron. But, though he cannot boast of having whipped us at all . . . he cannot injure us much more than he has already."

Jones also had heard ugly scuttlebutt about the decision to either hold or evacuate Sumter, backing Rhett's stance: "The Generals tried to make him [Rhett] shoulder the responsibility of abandoning the fort . . . by inducing him to say the fort was untenable; to which he replied that he intended to hold the fort until he received orders, and that if they refused, on his applying, to give him any, he would then not sacrifice his garrison, but leave when he thought fit."[23]

As Jones and other defenders stewed, three contrabands approached the Union lines on Morris Island that Tuesday after making their way from Fort Johnson with information of great interest to the Federal brass. The men said they were servants to officers at the fort and, from conversation picked up from the Rebels, had learned that the destruction inflicted at Sumter was much greater than just the gorge wall. The north and northwest faces were just as severely damaged, and Sumter had no serviceable guns, the men claimed. Gillmore found the information credible enough to send to Halleck the next day. By the twenty-fifth, however, the Confederates had tripled their artillery, repairing two pieces to join the one gun still in service at Sumter. The defenders would man them despite the parapet having been obliterated in front of both. Also, the grueling and hazardous task of removing other guns from the fort had begun. It was "slow and difficult work" that could only be done at night.

Beauregard, meanwhile, informed Richmond of the decision to defend Sumter. "Sumter received no additional injury today," he dispatched Adjutant General Cooper that day. "Conference of engineers in Sumter decided it could be held, even in ruins. It will be done." Beauregard's optimism was not shared by all of his officers, however. Major J. T. Trezevant, in charge of the Charleston arsenal, was worried about all of his valuable machinery "in the event of the reduction of Fort Sumter." Trezevant sent word to Beauregard's headquarters, stating that he would not dismantle and ship his machinery "unless the general shall think it best for me to do so, under all the circumstances."[24]

Wednesday, August 26

The Union land batteries greeted Sumter with a few shots beginning at 6:00 AM Wednesday, but the day's shelling was "slack and inexact; damage not very perceptible," the fort's journal noted. If the Confederates indeed had three working guns, contrary to the contrabands' report on Tuesday, Gillmore still had no evidence of them. "No guns have been mounted on Fort Sumter, as far as I can judge from appearances," he noted on Wednesday. Sometime that day, however, the fort did launch one round at the Yankees' advance trenches on Morris Island, the general noted in a later report. "Last night two of our companies were relieved from here and sent to the batteries on James Island," Iredell Jones wrote. "Their place was supplied by two picked Georgia companies. There are now only two of our own companies in the Fort—Captain Harleston's [Company D] and Captain [David G.] Fleming's [Company B]."

Despite being so ill that he could barely rise from a chair and walk across his cabin, Dahlgren was planning an attack for that night to operate against the harbor obstructions. The operation would include the monitors, two gunboats, and a tug, the latter provided with "tackles, straps, fishhooks, and smart seamen; also with saws, augers, cold chisels, hammers, and mechanics to use them," among other equipment. Dahlgren also had made an earlier request of the marine battalion stationed with the Naval Battery for a detachment of one to two hundred men for a boat landing on Sumter. "The operation is the most important yet undertaken here, and I rely on the energy and zeal of all who participate to spare no effort," the admiral wrote in his orders that Wednesday.

Gillmore, meanwhile, was planning to use at least one calcium light to illuminate the water off Morris Island. He hoped that this powerful searchlight would, with the navy's assistance, prevent the Rebels on the island from getting supplies and disrupt their communications. One of these lights had been used with great success during the siege of Battery Wagner. The general planned to use the light that night but decided otherwise after learning of the navy's plans. "Tonight I shall need all the darkness I can get," Dahlgren wrote to Gillmore. "If you light up, you will ruin me." The admiral did request army fire on Sumter that afternoon and Gillmore complied, his gunners sending a slow barrage at the fort. For the day, Sumter recorded 130 shot and shell aimed at it, only 40 missing.[25]

The night of the twenty-sixth was exceedingly dark and foggy, allowing the Union naval force to churn in near Sumter before it was discovered. The "detested monitors came sneaking close up to the fort," Jones wrote, "and it would have made the blood boil in the coldest-hearted coward to have seen the men rush to battery to man their disabled guns." Before the Confederates could see well enough to open fire, "they sneaked out again and left us to surmise, as usual, as to their object." Dahlgren indeed had called off the attack about 2:30 AM on the twenty-seventh, the effort burdened by delays, worsening weather, and an incoming tide.

During the night, the *Etiwan* docked with a supply of sandbags. She left Sumter with a large quantity of mortar shells, the garrison toiling the entire night. Beauregard, meanwhile, apparently was convinced he had made the right decision not to evacuate the fort. "Everything practicable, with our means, has been done to protect Sumter," he wrote that Wednesday to Confederate president Jefferson Davis. "[I]t shall be held, if necessary, with musket and bayonet." In another dispatch that day, Beauregard again noted his confidence in Gilmer and Harris, reiterating that Sumter "must be held to the last extremity, i.e., not surrendered until it becomes impossible to hold it longer without an unnecessary sacrifice of human life."

Charleston's populace also was beginning to learn of the reality of Sumter's changing role. "Sumter is no longer a double-tiered battery for the defence of the water approach," the *Mercury* said that day. "As a great artillery fortress its proud proportions are reduced to ruins. But the ground is sacred to Southern independence" and "with even the rifle and bayonet only, it may be held still from the hands of our foes." Hundreds of miles to the north, the *New York Herald* took a slightly different tone: "The news which we publish this morning from Charleston will fill every loyal breast with rejoicing. Fort Sumter is in ruins, and the proud little city itself, which first raised the standard of revolt, is being bombarded, and will be laid in ashes unless its defenders eat humble pie and capitulate."[26]

CHAPTER 7

"Hold the Fort to the Last"

Thursday, August 27

Only four shots were thrown at the fort on Thursday the twenty-seventh, the Confederates guessing that all were aimed at Sumter's flag, based on their trajectory, and all missing. On the same day, Beauregard sent orders to General Ripley, commander of the First Military District, regarding the changes to be made at the fort. Ripley was to reduce Sumter's garrison to one artillery company and two full infantry companies—the force not to exceed three hundred or fall below two hundred men. "Of course you will select the companies, which must be of the best in your command of both arms," Brig. Gen. Thomas Jordan, Beauregard's chief of staff, stated in the order. Through Jordan, Beauregard recommended Harleston's gunners "would be suitable," adding, "The infantry should be carefully selected, and might be relieved once a week."

Because the garrison was to be so much reduced, Beauregard offered Rhett the option of retaining command at Sumter or transferring his regimental headquarters, since most of the 1st South Carolina Artillery already had been posted elsewhere. If Rhett chose the latter, he would be placed in command of "Fort Johnson and adjacent batteries" (where most of Rhett's men had been sent), and Maj. Stephen Elliott Jr., another Carolinian, would take over at Sumter. In his grandiose style, Beauregard, through Jordan, also offered high praise for Rhett and the 1st South Carolina for their stout service and fortitude during the historic bombardment: "The Commanding General has witnessed with genuine pride and gratification the defence made of Fort Sumter by Colonel Rhett, his officers and men . . . noble fruits of the discipline, the application to their duty, and [their] soldierly bearing . . . and of the organization of the regiment. In the annals of war no stouter defence was ever made, and no work ever before encountered as formidable a bombardment as that under which Fort Sumter has been successfully held."[1]

This much-deserved tribute would be read to Rhett's remaining cannoneers and the rest of the garrison at dress parade, but another dispatch from Beauregard to Ripley on the twenty-seventh returned to the hard reality of war and Sumter's possible fate. The fort "shall be held and defended to the last extremity, and not surrendered until it cannot be longer held without an unnecessary sacrifice of life. It will only be evacuated under explicit orders from these headquarters."

Ripley also was told to remove all of Sumter's powder other than a few hundred pounds to supply the three guns which, it was hoped, could be kept in action. As many shells as possible, "of the most valuable sort" also were to be shipped out and the workforce was to be reduced to the minimal number of laborers needed to hold the fort. Ripley also was ordered to stock up on a four-week supply of provisions for the soldiers and workers. This was especially ominous, since it implied the defenders, now with little artillery, might be cut off and have to fend for themselves for a long time if the Yankees got really nasty.

Dahlgren was feeling well enough to make another thrust at the harbor obstacles on the night of the twenty-seventh. Again the monitors congregated, but like the previous evening this assault was doomed. At the last minute, the admiral learned that the only steam tug he had available to assist in maneuvering the ironclads had been sent outside the bar. The strike was canceled, the exertion and frustration aggravating Dahlgren's condition such that he could barely sit up the next day. Charlestonian Emma Holmes, meanwhile, celebrated the stand by the men in the shattered fort in the harbor. "Hurrah for glorious old Sumter—her brave defenders have made her well worthy of the proud name she bears," she wrote in her diary that Thursday.[2]

Friday, August 28

Only six shots were fired at the fort; three hit outside and three missed. With no additional damage to repair, the overnight work parties were able to complete a traverse at the entrance to the west magazine and the hospital, located at the southwest angle, as well as strengthen and improve the east barbette battery. The laborers also loaded the steamer *Etiwan* with a 10-inch Columbiad, four hundred mortar shells, and a variety of other projectiles, fuses, fuse extractors, and various other artillery equipment. "The garrison worked day and night," the fort's journal noted of the twenty-eighth. "No casualties." Actually, there was one major loss: A 9-inch Dahlgren, which had been located on the southwest face, was thrown over the parapet and disabled in the fall.[3]

In New York City that day, readers of the *Herald* were assured that Sumter had been mostly destroyed. "Fort Sumter is finally reduced to a heap of ruins. . . . Much stress is laid upon the fact that the fort has not yet surrendered; but, since its guns are now harmless to prevent the operations of our fleet in the harbor, General Gillmore has accomplished the object with which he opened fire upon it, and the surrender of its garrison is merely a question of pride. If they can content themselves with permission to dodge behind a ruined wall whenever a shell comes toward it, and can find any triumph in that exercise, they ought to be welcome to it. Otherwise the operations progress satisfactorily, and we may look forward with confidence to the complete reduction of the place."[4]

Saturday, August 29

Saturday was a rare day of little or no shelling, but there were fireworks anyway at Sumter. By the twenty-ninth, Rhett had received the report containing the opinions of Gilmer and Harris about Sumter's condition and the question of how the fort should be defended. Always with a hair trigger regarding a personal slight—real or perceived—Rhett reacted angrily to the notion that he would even consider surrendering Sumter without a death fight and that he had to be ordered to do so. He penned a bristling reply to General Jordan, Beauregard's chief of staff, stating that he already was under orders to "hold the fort to the last" and had informed Gilmer and Harris of this. Further, he had not asked for a consultation with the engineer officers and never recommended or "contemplated for one instant" that Sumter be evacuated. "Fort Sumter will not be surrendered by me until in my opinion it becomes 'impossible to hold it longer without an unnecessary sacrifice of human life.' The commanding general is kept informed by reports as to the condition of the fort, and alone must determine as to the evacuation or not. . . . Should emergencies arise requiring, in my opinion, the surrender of the fort, the responsibility will rest with me."[5]

While Rhett fumed, the lack of shelling since the twenty-fifth was puzzling to the fort's defenders, although certainly welcomed. "I am happy to inform you that we have been spared the disagreeable whiz of 200- and 300-pound Parrotts for the past few days," Iredell Jones wrote his mother that night. "Some say they are out of ammunition; others that they have accomplished all they expected of their land batteries, and others, still, that they are only waiting to get their mortars in position." Jones believed the Yankees were running low on ammo because it had taken longer than expected to flatten the fort. He also believed the next blow would be made with "redoubled fury" and would be a combined attack by the monitors and the land batteries. "As to ourselves in the poor old fort, I hope we will give them the best we have got."

That night, Frank Harleston's Company D of the 1st South Carolina Artillery left for Charleston while a fifty-man detachment of the 27th Georgia Volunteers, led by Capt. Hezekiah Bussey, replaced them at the fort. This left only David Fleming's Company B as the last of the 1st South Carolina at Sumter. Jones watched Harleston's men depart, "so that our company is the only one of the regiment now left here to guard the honor of the fallen fortress." Bussey's men also belonged to Colquitt's brigade and were no strangers to combat, having been in action at Antietam and Chancellorsville, among other battles.

Sumter still had three barbette guns to fight, Jones claimed, but one had a cracked trunnion and the other two were exposed, the parapet in front of them blown away. The progress of the bombardment led the *New York Herald* that day to proclaim Gillmore the greatest engineer officer the war had yet produced: "That reputation has heretofore been pretty generally assigned to Beauregard. But the little Creole has found more than his match in the man who commands the forces now operating against Charleston."[6]

Near evening, the *New Ironsides* and two mortar boats came close enough to pummel Wagner in conjunction with the land batteries. Their heavy fire was answered by Confederate guns on James Island and possibly Sumter itself. This clash was a prelude to an attack Dahlgren was planning for that night, but the minor retaliation from Sumter caused the admiral to have second thoughts. By 9:00 PM, he informed Gillmore that the assault had been postponed since "Sumter has fired several shots," and "operations were based on the supposition that Sumter was silenced." He added that his chief pilot reported that the obstructions had been strengthened between Sumter and Moultrie and asked if the army could "keep up a fire tomorrow on Sumter, in order to completely dismantle her." Gillmore was surprised by this claim. "Sumter has not fired a shot today," he answered less than an hour later. "My lookout, who has been on the watch all day, is positive on this point. His attention was specially directed to this matter."

The next couple of hours brought a stream of telegrams between the commanders regarding whether Sumter still had artillery capable of harming the fleet and what should be done about it. Dahlgren supported his chief pilot's claim that the fort still had guns and had fired that day. "Your lookout may be correct, but if he is in error it would be fatal to my plans," he wired Gillmore at 11:00 PM. If Sumter still had functioning cannon, it would be tough for his monitors to shield crews trying to cut through the obstacles if they were subjected to fire from both Sumter and Moultrie. "I can cover my men while working . . . from one side, but not from both," he said, adding a request that the army batteries resume the bombardment the next day "with full vigor . . . as a proper precaution." Gillmore responded that other lookouts also had not seen any action from Sumter, but he agreed to resume the shelling despite the wear on his guns. He asked the admiral for some rounds for his 200-pounders, saying, "My supply is very low. A constant fire on Sumter is more than my guns can stand very long."[7]

Sunday, August 30

"A bright Sunday morning . . . I had hoped we would enjoy in peace," Jones penned on the thirtieth, "but the scoundrels are giving us bricks in reality as I write." Gillmore had reopened the heavy barrage of Sumter about 5:00 AM based on Dahlgren's request. Whether the information about the presence of the fort's artillery was accurate or not, it "prevented the monitors from operating as they intended to do," the general wrote to Halleck that day. "It is not at all improbable that guns may have been remounted on Sumter during the night time within the past week. I admit my inability to prevent it without a constant bombardment and enormous expenditure of guns and ammunition." Gillmore contended that no cannon had been fired from the fort for the past five days—other than perhaps one round on the twenty-sixth—and his lookouts had not observed any active guns there. Still, he vowed that if Sumter had working artillery, it would be soon be destroyed. "Fort Sumter was thoroughly silenced on the 24th instant," he told Halleck, "and can be again." For all of Sunday, a total of 634 enemy shots were thrown at Sumter, 490 of which smacked the fort, either inside or outside, the Confederates recorded; five men were wounded.

While the human toll was minimal, the fort and its weapons continued to be torn apart. "Damage . . . most apparent inside," stated the garrison journal that day. In the east barbette battery, two 10-inch Columbiads that had been in action until that day had their carriages smashed while another Columbiad was dismounted, its muzzle shot off. Sumter's artillery threat was done. "Parapet all shaky and partially demolished," the journal related, "traverses badly cut up. Three arches with ramparts, on northeast front, cut away and tumbled in, burying some commissary stores." The east scarp, near the southeast pan coupe, also had been slammed, large blocks knocked from the face of the second-tier casemates.[8]

Iredell Jones had weathered the flying metal while completing the letter to his mother, but even he confessed it had been an unnerving process: "You must not judge from the tremendous blot or smear that I have just made that I am scared, though, if you should think so, probably you will not be very far wrong," he scrawled. "How I would like to enjoy now some of the cool water, delicious breezes and butter-milk, with which you in one of your late letters were placed to taunt me!"

"The fire was heavier than Sumter has received for a week past," the *Mercury* reported later that Sunday. The paper went on to say that the brief assault by the five monitors on the morning of Sunday, August 23, had been more devastating than originally revealed. The damage from that shelling had not been that great, but added to the ongoing and relentless breakdown of the fort at the time, the blasts of shells near the magazine could have spelled Sumter's end. The *Mercury* claimed that when the ironclads retreated that morning they left the fort in "a very precarious condition. If the fleet had then pushed the bombardment with vigor, or if they had renewed it with determination, after a brief interval, they would have penetrated the magazine, and doubtless, have blown up the fort or compelled the garrison to surrender. As it happily turned out, the monitors withdrew before the destruction was complete." The paper went on to claim that in the week since, the powder in the magazine had been taken care of and the fort strengthened with sandbags.[9]

With Sumter subdued, the last week of August was a highly anxious time for Charleston's Confederates, who hourly awaited the monitors to slip past the fort and begin lobbing shells into the city itself. "I am unable to understand why Admiral Dahlgren did not . . . avail himself of the opening thus offered and push with his iron-clads for the inner harbor," the Georgian Charles Olmstead wrote. "We certainly looked for such a dash. . . . Whether or not such a course would have been successful is problematical. There can be no doubt, though, that it would have added grave complications to the Confederate military position, to say the least."

Overnight on August 30–31, the fort's working party, now reduced to about 110 laborers, concentrated on shoring up the east barbette, repairing the traverses and patching the riddled parapet. They also prepared sandbag cushions on the berm for the two 10-inch Columbiads, which were thrown over the ramparts in preparation to be sent elsewhere.[10]

Monday, August 31

During the predawn hours of Monday, some of Sumter's defenders were called on to help save lives rather than trying to take them. The transport steamer *Sumter* had been sent to Morris Island with troops to relieve some of those in the Confederate strongholds there. It was a foggy night, but the *Sumter* had anchored at Cummings Point, unloaded the replacements, and, after boarding the soldiers being relieved, headed back toward Sullivan's Island by the main channel between Fort Sumter and Sullivan's Island. The *Sumter*'s skipper had been forced to change to this alternate route due to the troops boarding late, causing him to have to deal with the shallows of an ebbing tide. The approximately six hundred troops aboard belonged to the 20th South Carolina Volunteers, the 23rd Georgia Volunteers, and an artillery company.

The Sullivan's Island batteries were on alert for a possible strike by the monitors that night and had not been notified of the *Sumter*'s return via the main channel. Lookouts at Fort Moultrie mistook the side-wheeler for an enemy ship, and the Confederate gunners opened fire on her about 2:30 AM. In minutes, the vessel was hit four times as soldiers and crew frantically tried to signal the batteries to stop the cannonade. She grounded on a shoal near Fort Sumter before the mistake was realized and everyone ceased fire. Casualty reports ranged from two to twenty-five on the *Sumter* killed or drowned while an untold number were wounded. Despite the fact that the mishap occurred near low tide and many of the soldiers could stand on the shoal in about two feet of water, small boats from the *Palmetto State* and *Chicora*—as well as volunteers from Fort Sumter led by Iredell Jones and Lt. Henry M. Stuart—joined in the rescue effort. The rescued soldiers were brought to the fort. A few hours after she was abandoned, the severely damaged *Sumter* capsized.

The Rebel batteries had been on alert for good reason, since Dahlgren had indeed planned to assail Fort Sumter and try to enter the harbor overnight. The foggy conditions, however, caused him to delay his assault until the weather cleared. It would be the night of September 1 before he was ready to strike.[11] Jones, meanwhile, had finished his letter to his mother shortly before the rescue operation, reassuring his parents that he had no intention of being wounded—or worse. "Banish any such idea from your mind, for, I assure you, you never were more mistaken. I am as well and as happy as possible."

During the day on the thirty-first, only fifty-six Union projectiles were hurled at the fort, thirty-nine finding the target and seventeen going astray. There were no casualties. The "night force" as Rhett called it, was occupied in bolstering parts of the upper west magazine and casemate arches over the hospital. A detail of soldiers was employed repairing one of the east upper casemates, essentially replenishing its supply of sand. The steamer *Etiwan* also returned to Sumter overnight, again leaving with an assortment of ordnance and artillery parts along with other military stores.

About 8:00 PM on Monday, the men who had been rescued from the ill-fated *Sumter* boarded the steamer *Chesterfield* after recuperating from their ordeal for most of the day. They were taken to Sullivan's Island, along with a cargo of about a hundred incendiary rounds.[12]

Tuesday, September 1

Sumter's pounding had exacted a toll on Gillmore's iron titans, but the navy continued to want more artillery support against the fort for its operations. This was a big problem for the army. Six Parrotts—five 8-inch rifles and one 100-pounder—were out of action, along with two Whitworths. The wear and tear of the long bombardment had been too much, and a number of the guns still active were considered unsafe by now. Gillmore had been forced to borrow three 8-inch and three 100-pounder Parrotts from Dahlgren's vessels for his breaching batteries. Some already were in position by September 1, while the others would be by the next night.

The admiral had asked the army to bombard Sumter again on the first, and Gillmore had reluctantly agreed to the request. The navy, despite Dahlgren's lingering illness, was attempting to go on the offensive again that night.[13] Still, the situation of Gillmore's batteries was so dire that only four guns had been working the previous day; he had five pieces to aid the navy on September 1. These were all that he had "available for that purpose," he dispatched Halleck that day. Sumter had not fired a cannon shot in anger since the lone shot on August 26, he noted, other than an occasional "sunset gun" to mark the end of the day. The tons of iron already thrown at the fort continued to offer results, with the Federals now able to see portions of the casemate arches of the southeast face. In a postscript to Halleck, Gillmore revealed his true feelings: "I must add that, in my judgment, the bombardment of Sumter, now in progress, is entirely unnecessary."

The general was much more diplomatic in conversing with Dahlgren during the day. "All my heavy guns will operate on Sumter," Gillmore wrote to the admiral at 2:00 PM. "Many of them are not considered safe, and will have to be fired with a slow match. My lookout reports the firing this morning as remarkably accurate." Dahlgren answered at 5:00 PM: "I am glad to learn of the accuracy of your fire. . . . I shall go up with the monitors tonight." By early evening, Gillmore felt that his artillerists had completed the job. "Three guns on Sumter have been knocked out of sight today and another was cocked up in the air and pointed toward Morris Island," he informed Dahlgren at 6:40 PM. "If there was a serviceable gun on Sumter this morning there is not one now." The army batteries had thrown 382 projectiles at the fort on the day, only 121 missing, prompting a Massachusetts officer's wry observation that the pummeling "was making the place very uncomfortable for a peaceful resident."

The six monitors, meanwhile, assembled about 9:30 PM on September 1, based on the admiral's orders. With the *Weehawken* leading, they would proceed up the channel in tight formation and anchor to drill the fort at close range. While Gillmore believed Sumter did not have any artillery left that could fire, Dahlgren was still concerned about the fort's ability to damage his vessels. By now, the fort's garrison still contained only Fleming's Company B of the 1st South Carolina's gunners, the rest of Sumter's contingent composed of infantry detachments from the 27th and 28th Georgia.[14]

The monitors churned quietly into the channel and by about 11:30 PM were within five hundred yards of Sumter's ominous shape. It was an especially dark night, which likely prevented the Union behemoths from being sighted sooner, but suddenly the Southern batteries on Sullivan's Island came alive. The blackness was rent by big shells tearing over the water amid the white glare of muzzle blasts as the monitors retaliated. Most of the Confederate rounds targeted the *Weehawken*, but the gray cannoneers were not especially accurate, apparently due to the darkness. In their iron turrets, the bluejackets quickly realized that no guns—or possibly just one—were firing from Fort Sumter. By now, the monitors had been joined by the *New Ironsides*, and all steamed even closer to the bastion, booming away at it point blank with 11- and 15-inch guns.

The massive uproar lasted some five hours, awakening Charleston; many residents gathered at White Point Garden on The Battery to see what was happening. The firefight at the harbor mouth was terrific, as the Confederate outposts other than Sumter continued to engage the intruders and "the whole horizon at times seemed to be on fire," when the *New Ironsides* unleashed her broadsides, one observer wrote. "Sumter received the fire in steadfast silence," the *Mercury* reported, the harbor "filled with one grand diapason of artillery." When rounds struck the monitors, "the shot against their mailed sides produced sounds like the deep thud of distant cannon through a heavy atmosphere. Sparks of fire, visible even in the city, were elicited by every blow which they received."[15]

With the tide against him, Dahlgren, aboard the *Weehawken*, ordered a withdrawal near dawn on the second; the monitors *Passaic* and *Lehigh* collided during the pullout but without serious consequence. The attack force had taken 71 hits with minimal damage while firing 245 shells from their heavy guns. Amazingly, the human bloodshed was even less. The worst injury on the Union side occurred when a Rebel round shot hit near the turret base of *Weehawken*, driving in an iron fragment that broke the leg of Fleet Captain Oscar C. Badger.

At Sumter, Rhett had narrowly escaped serious injury or death by an exploding shell that slightly wounded his orderly sergeant as they crossed the parade ground. Two other soldiers at Sumter had minor injuries to complete the fort's casualty list, and two additional Confederates were killed by an exploding shell on Sullivan's Island. Still, the monitors' shelling caused more severe damage to the east wall, some rounds passing entirely through and striking the west wall. Three shells had exploded dangerously close to the west magazine. The blast of two of these rounds actually penetrated down a stairway to the magazine's outer door, which was—fortunately for the garrison—closed at the time. Two other shells had burst in the commissary store. "The damage to Sumter was considerable, the monitors having fired with good accuracy," the *Mercury* said.[16]

By far, this was the heaviest naval assault Sumter had yet endured, much worse than the April 7 attack; Rhett noted: "Damage very great by day and night fire. . . . Since monitor fire last night, every casemate, upper and lower, has been more or less breached, in most of them exposing sand-bags." The garrison counted 185 shots thrown at Sumter by the navy until 5:00 AM, only 34 passing over. Having just gotten to bed about 7:45 AM, Dahlgren was resting when he received a message from Gillmore asking, "Will you want the fire of my batteries on Sumter today?" The weary admiral replied, "I think your fire on Sumter may be remitted today. . . . Do not know how much damage our fire did Sumter." Dahlgren was especially bothered by Badger's having been wounded, since he had now lost three fleet captains in about two months: Capt. George Rodgers was killed in action aboard the *Catskill* on August 17 and Capt. William R. Taylor left due to sickness. "I shall feel greatly the loss of Captain Badger's services at this time," he wrote to Gideon Welles later on the second.[17]

Gillmore's artillery subjected the fort to little more than harassing fire that day, throwing only thirty-eight rounds, of which seventeen missed. Both the garrison and the labor force worked all day, however, trying to plug the gaping wounds previously slashed by the Union blows. Laborers strengthened the west magazine and made repairs necessitated by Dahlgren's shelling. They also opened an embrasure on the northwest face so that the gun there could be removed when necessary. The workforce was relieved that night. The soldiers, meanwhile, spent the day stuffing sandbags into the casemates on the eastern face.

Also on the second, Lt. John Johnson, the fort's chief engineer since April 7, 1863, was relieved from duty due to the aggravation of a wound he sustained on August 17. Lt. F. Marion Hall took over his responsibilities for a few days before the arrival of engineer Capt. John T. Champneys. Before Champneys assumed his duties, William Mathewes, a civilian engineer, came to Sumter to assist Hall, while a relative, J. Fraser Mathewes, arrived on the night of September 1–2 to remove some guns that had been dropped over the wall onto the berm. This effort was thwarted by rough waters, but the fort's *Keokuk* gun was shipped from Sumter that night. The piece, which had done great service at Sumter for several months, was brought back to Charleston and emplaced in Battery Ramsay at White Point Garden, where it remained until the war's end.

Dahlgren, meanwhile, was quite impressed with the destruction wrought by the army and praised Gillmore in a dispatch that day to Secretary Welles. "It was a new illustration art," he wrote of Sumter's ruined walls, "and will always be deemed a great triumph for General Gillmore; without regard to further results, I think he has already handsomely earned his next step in rank." The admiral also recognized the still daunting task to be faced. "Having thus rendered Sumter useless to the Confederate system of defenses . . . it still remains to turn the acquisition fully to account," he said. "A glance at the map and at the means at disposal will show that the entire advantage can not yet be realized to ourselves, because we cannot occupy the fort. The army is unable to do it unless possession of Fort Wagner is had, nor the navy without forcing the defenses by water, in the shape of obstructions protected by Fort Moultrie and under its full range, even to Sumter." With Gillmore actively engaged in trying to seize Wagner, Dahlgren had committed his forces to assisting the army. "This necessarily compels me to forego an immediate move on the obstructions," he told Welles.

With the Federal batteries quiet toward Sumter on the third, the fort's soldiers and laborers worked day and night in reliefs to make it more defensible. Hall and William Mathewes focused on building bombproofs in the fort's interior and hacking openings in the upper-tier casemates so that two 42-pounder rifled guns could be thrown outside the fort for shipment. On the night of the third, two disabled guns were shoved over the parapet, landing without further damage. The Confederates believed there were still twenty-seven guns buried in the fort's ever-mounting rubble.[18]

There was little or no firing by the Union land batteries on September 4, the first bombardment finally coming to an end. But the damage had been significant, possibly making it untenable to hold Sumter. "I consider it impracticable to either mount or use guns on any part of the parapet, and I deem the fort in its present condition unserviceable for offensive purposes," Rhett wrote that day. "What the engineers may effect by rebuilding or remodeling, I am unable to say." Had Sumter finally been pummeled into submission? Charleston and the rest of the Confederacy wondered if Gillmore had added their most precious gem to his collection, along with Fort Pulaski.

Unknown to most, wholesale changes were on the way for the fort. That night—the fourth—Rhett left Sumter, reassigned to command Charleston's inner ring of fortifications. While his posting to Sumter had come under controversial and violent circumstances, he had led the defenders and performed exceptionally under some of the harshest conditions soldiers could endure over months at a time. Rhett's replacement was Maj. Stephen Elliott Jr., a thirty-two-year-old Carolinian who had seen considerable action along the coast. Elliott was born in Beaufort, his father the first bishop of the Episcopal diocese of Georgia, and attended Harvard for a time before graduating South Carolina College in 1850. He became a planter on the South Carolina coast and enjoyed his renown not only as a state legislator but also as a fine yachtsman and fisherman. Prior to secession, which he personally opposed, Elliott also was captain of the Beaufort Volunteer Artillery, a militia company that would later enter Confederate service. To this point in the war, he had served solely in his native state. He participated in the defense of Port Royal in November 1861 and was wounded in the leg there. Through the intermingled bloodlines of the Carolina chivalry, he and Alfred Rhett were distant relatives.[19]

Knowing Elliott's record and talents, Beauregard had personally interviewed the major in late August, wanting him to fully realize what a

*Confederate brigadier general
Stephen Elliott.*
LIBRARY OF CONGRESS

tough—and possibly suicidal—assignment he was considering. The Carolinian's popularity and public service also had to figure in to his choice as Sumter's commander. Beauregard told Elliott that he was to be sent to a fort "deprived of all offensive capacity" and with only one small cannon to salute its flag in the morning and evening. "But that fort is Fort Sumter, the key to the entrance of this harbor. It must be held to the bitter end; not with artillery, as heretofore, but with infantry alone; and there can be no hope of reinforcements. Are you willing to take the command upon such terms?" Before Elliott could reply, Beauregard said he should think about it for twenty-four hours, during which time he should examine the fort and make his decision. Surprisingly, Elliott returned to Beauregard's headquarters only a few hours later. He had been to Sumter, conferred with Rhett, and didn't need any more time. "Issue the order, general; I will obey it," he told Beauregard. Elliott arrived about 10 PM on the fourth.

The fort also completed its transition from artillery to infantry post during this time with the arrival of the Charleston Battalion to relieve the garrison. These 320 or so veterans who made up six infantry companies cut across all levels of the city's social strata; they had been bloodied at Secessionville and on Morris Island in the horrific and ongoing struggle for Battery Wagner. The battalion was temporarily led by Maj. Julius A.

Blake because its commander, Lt. Col. Peter C. Gaillard, was recovering from the loss of his left hand in the Wagner combat a few days earlier. The Carolinians replaced Fleming's cannoneers and the 27th and 28th Georgia.[20]

All of these incoming Southerners were about to face a situation even graver than the officers and troops they relieved. By now the Union siege lines on Morris were almost within spitting distance of Wagner, the Rebel bastion torn apart by Union guns. There likely was no more desperate and literally last-ditch defense of any place in the war than the one made in the sandy hell of Wagner, but the Federals were too many in number and had overwhelming firepower by land and sea. On the night of September 6–7, the Confederates abandoned Wagner and Battery Gregg, evacuating Morris Island entirely.

Some of Wagner's troops were temporarily brought to Sumter so that the few vessels involved in the operation could return to Cummings Point relatively quickly and load more men. This helped expedite the withdrawal, but the loss of Wagner and Morris Island were twin blows to the Confederates, and the blasted appearance of Sumter made it look as if the fort would be the next chess piece blown off the board. The fort would be in even greater danger now since it would be only a matter of days or weeks before the Yankees fortified the entire island, paying special attention to Cummings Point, the northernmost tip that was so close to Sumter. Once again the fort would be the nearest to the enemy of all of Charleston's defenses.

"By transforming Fort Sumter into ruins, at the unprecedented distance of four thousand yards, he [Gillmore] has accomplished a task the like of which was never performed, and earned for himself a reputation such as few men have lived to acquire," a *New York Herald* correspondent penned from Morris Island on the sixth. "Now Sumter is a thing of the past, no longer to be considered in the contest. Charleston has been fired, our shells in the stillness of the night dropping into the inhabited portion of the town, distant from our batteries, as the crow flies, not less than five miles."[21]

From the captured earthworks of Battery Gregg, Union soldiers peered across the harbor entrance at the wreck of Fort Sumter less than a mile away, its Confederate flag still fluttering insolently in the sea breeze. Dahlgren and Gillmore both recognized that now was possibly the most opportune time to try to seize Sumter while the Rebels regrouped elsewhere. And the commander who accomplished this feat would be one of the Republic's greatest heroes since George Washington or John Paul Jones. Now more than ever, the stronghold appeared ripe for the taking, its walls reduced to just mounds of jumbled brick, sand, and other debris. The rubble even looked to have formed a ramp leading into the fort. Capturing Sumter would allow the Federals to possibly clear some of the major channel obstacles barring their vessels from entering the harbor and inching closer to Charleston itself. But Gillmore and Dahlgren were no longer working in tandem. The tough, long, and bloody campaign for Morris Island—plus the unrelenting heat and their own personal ills— had frazzled their relationship to the point that cooperation between the army and navy was minimal. Yet admiral and general both had immediate designs on Sumter to be played out in the coming hours.

In the city, many people were apprehensive that Charleston could continue to hold out. The Yanks would soon be swarming like blue hornets down Bay Street. The disheartening fall of Vicksburg and the heart-wrenching defeat of Lee's army at Gettysburg in July still stung greatly, contributing to the grim mood. But Beauregard's decision to hold Sumter was met by widespread enthusiasm as word spread, first by Charlestonians, then the rest of the state and across the Confederacy. "Brave officers, who had watched it [Sumter] day by day crumbling under the heavy fire and losing all its fair proportions, grew disheartened at the sight," John Johnson recalled, "and gave it as their candid military opinion that the holding of it any longer would be impossible or would amount to a mere sacrifice of the garrison. But this was little in accord with the mind and purpose of General Beauregard. . . . The defense assumed from this time greater importance than ever. Pride and sentiment were enlisted in it. The military spirit of the troops around Charleston was stirred and stimulated. The fort was henceforth regarded as the post of honor." Georgia's *Augusta Constitutionalist* exemplified the defiance rekindled in the Southerners. "The Sumter of the old time is a demolished fortress," it said. "But the old spirit haunts the spot; the blood of the brave in their winding sheets cries aloud to the brave in life, and is nobly answered."

With uncharacteristic aggression, Dahlgren wasted little time in trying to build on the momentum of Wagner's fall. About 8:00 AM on the seventh, a small boat from the fleet, bearing a truce flag, approached the Confederate lines and was received by an officer from the ironclad *Palmetto State*. Shortly afterward, Elliott was reading an ultimatum from Dahlgren demanding Sumter's surrender. Elliott already knew his answer to the admiral, but he had to go through the proper channels and have his superiors make it official. He wired news of the demand to Beauregard's headquarters, adding, "I presume I shall refuse." The reply was not long in coming from General Jordan, Beauregard's chief of staff: "Inform Admiral Dahlgren that he may have Fort Sumter when he can take and hold it." Knowing this would be the likely response, the admiral had earlier signaled Gillmore that if his summons was not met he intended to "move up with all the iron-clads and engage it [Sumter]."

The squadron had other designs underway as well.[22] Earlier that morning—about daylight—Dahlgren had dispatched *Weehawken* to probe Rebel obstacles between Sumter and the inner harbor defenses; the Southerners in late August and early September had sown a number of floating torpedoes in the waterways. The monitor, skippered by Cmdr. Edmund R. Colhoun, was to head into the shallow and dangerous channel between Sumter and Cummings Point, marking its path with buoys. The blue tars knew at this point that Sumter no longer had artillery to punish the ironclads, much less any other ship in the squadron. Thus the *Weehawken* entered the channel, dropping markers, and anchored between Sumter and Cummings Point, waiting for high tide to proceed farther. About 10:00 AM, however, Dahlgren had second thoughts about sending the *Weehawken* on such a hazardous foray and recalled her. But as the monitor withdrew, her crew's unfamiliarity with the waters, difficulty in steering, and an ebb tide all contributed to her soon running hard aground in eleven feet of water. High tide that afternoon failed to free her.

All of this was ongoing while Dahlgren's surrender demand was being addressed. As if the admiral did not have a full-enough plate on the seventh, the removal of channel obstacles, including the variety of mines, seeded by the Rebels, remained very much on his mind. He met with one of Gillmore's engineers, Col. Edward W. Serrell—who had supervised construction of the "Swamp Angel" battery—to discuss this issue. If Sumter no longer had big guns to fight off the Union warships, the infantry still there were a cause of some concern for this operation. "I learned from Colonel Serrell, and subsequently from the admiral himself, that the musketry fire that might be delivered from the ruins of . . . Sumter was considered a serious obstacle in the way of removing the channel obstructions," Gillmore wrote.[23]

At Sumter, Elliott and others were puzzled by the *Weehawken's* bold daylight advance, seeing her anchor and then retreat before halting again. They were also frustrated in their inability to blow her apart, since she was within easy range if they had any guns remotely big enough for the job. The Sullivan's Island batteries also were eyeing the ironclad, holding fire because of the extreme range and the monitor's thick armor. Amazingly, no Confederates—especially the officers and lookouts at Sumter, who were closest to the monitor—realized the *Weehawken* was in trouble at this point. Dahlgren, however, saw Colhoun's predicament and ordered an immediate diversionary attack in the afternoon against the enemy forts on Sullivan's. By about 6:00 PM, the *New Ironsides* and five monitors cruised into range and engaged these batteries. This quickly heightened into a sharp duel waged with huge chunks of metal shrieking back and forth before darkness ended the cannonading with little damage to either side. *Weehawken*, meanwhile, was still immovable.[24]

From the fort's parapet, Elliott had been able to do little more than watch the firefight and report on the number of hits on the enemy ships. Equally galling were the blue masses that had suddenly cropped up on the Morris Island dunes—Yankee soldiers watching to see how the *Weehawken* drama played out. Dahlgren's vessels withdrew for the night, but the work continued to free the *Weehawken*. Tugs were sent in and the monitor's ammunition removed to lighten her, but still she remained stuck. Colhoun's men toiled futilely through the night, and as fog carpeted the outer harbor near daybreak on the eighth, the skipper told his exhausted crew to get breakfast and some rest. They would need it for whatever they would face when the fog burned off.

Elliott reported hearing hammering overnight—but still didn't realize the *Weehawken* was snagged. Finally, about 7:00 AM, he confirmed the monitor's dilemma, possibly due to the fact that she was listing heavily and still in the same channel position. He signaled this information to nearby Confederate outposts, and when the haze lifted around 8:30 AM, the *Weehawken* was in the bulls-eye. Guns at Fort Johnson, Battery Simkins, and the Sullivan's Island positions opened a methodical pounding of the stricken monster. Due to a lack of ammo, the gunners aimed even more deliberately, trying to hit the *Weehawken*'s hull, which was partially exposed due to her list.

Dahlgren again tried to save her, sending the *New Ironsides*, along with the *Patapsco, Lehigh, Nahant, Montauk,* and *Passaic,* to assail Sullivan's and try to draw fire away from the *Weehawken.* Colhoun's tars also retaliated, and the second shot from the monitor's 15-inch gun found its mark. The round glanced off a Columbiad at Fort Moultrie and crashed into some ammunition boxes that detonated, killing sixteen Confederates and wounding twelve. The Rebel positions also were slammed by Dahlgren's attack force, which anchored and fired at ranges from 900 to 1,400 yards, but the gray artillerists, while firing more slowly, were making their shots count as well. Sumter's defenders had to find cover due to some of the *Weehawken*'s rounds directed at the fort. The punch and counterpunch of screeching metal lasted some five hours before the Federal vessels turned seaward about 1:00 PM, their ammunition spent.

The *Weehawken* finally floated free on the afternoon tide about 4:00 PM. She was battered by twenty-four hits, but had suffered only three casualties during the ordeal, and as she staggered back out to the fleet she was cheered by crews on the other Union vessels. Despite one Confederate's assertion that this was "probably the severest naval engagement in American history up to that time" and "by far the heaviest cannonade heard from the naval force off Charleston," the Rebels sustained minor damage to their works—two guns dismounted, nineteen killed and twenty-seven wounded, none at Sumter. To Elliott's soldiers it appeared the Federals had gotten the best of the fight, since the *Weehawken* had escaped and the Confederate guns appeared to have been silenced more than once by the enemy's blows. The Southerners also grudgingly admired the tenacity and bravery of the *Weehawken*'s Colhoun, described by one Rebel as a "doughty officer" who "made a very gallant fight under all his disadvantages."[25]

The September 8 combat also resulted in two of the most dramatic photographs to be taken during the war. George S. Cook, a Charleston photographer, reached Sumter by rowboat overnight on September 7–8 and prepared for the action on the eighth. Cook was no stranger to the fort, having pulled off somewhat of a coup in February 1861 when he was granted permission to go to Sumter and photograph Anderson and his officers. With the battle roaring on the eighth, he hauled his camera

*Amazing image captured by Charleston photographer George Cook of a
shell from the monitor Weehawken exploding inside the fort on
September 8, 1863.* LIBRARY OF CONGRESS

to the top of the smashed parapet and set up in full view of three of the
monitors. At the time, the Union gunners were concentrating their fire
on Moultrie, but this could change at any moment, and Cook was suddenly the most exposed man at Sumter. While he was under the camera's
black hood, he saw through the lens a shell passing a few feet from him.
Moments later, another round knocked one of his plate holders off the
parapet and into a rainwater cistern. Cook paid a soldier five dollars to
retrieve it for him while he worked to get his precious image. Finally getting his picture, Cook was ordered off the parapet since he was drawing
fire on the fort from Morris Island. The "most daring photograph ever
taken during the Civil War," as it was later described, shows the three
monitors in battle less than two miles from Cook's camera, the first photo
of ironclads in combat.

What had just become an incredible day for the photographer was
soon to become even more amazing. After being chased off the parapet,
Cook settled in to get some pictures of Sumter's interior. His luck continued when his lens immortalized the explosion of a shell from the *Weehawken* on the fort's parade ground. Photos of bursting rounds were rare
during the war, and Cook apparently captured his as he was exposing his
plates, accounting for the picture's poor quality. It shows a view north

across the parade ground and the colossal destruction wrought during the weeks of bombardment. Also visible in the upper right corner is the garrison's Confederate flag next to a brick traverse. Another picture, taken after the explosion photo, depicts two Confederates standing on one of Sumter's bake ovens in the same vicinity. The flag is no longer visible beside the traverse, and at least two barbette guns atop the now-blasted upper casement are gone.[26]

CHAPTER 8

"I Will Assault Sumter Tonight"

As the adrenaline rush over the *Weehawken* firefight subsided, the Confederates were already sensing something else was afoot. "From the repeated demands made for the surrender of this fort, I conclude that the enemy desires to possess it before it is demolished," Elliott wrote on the afternoon of September 7. "I would suggest that our batteries be directed to have their guns manned at night and trained with the axis of their pieces perfectly horizontal, as this fire keeps the projectiles always near the surface of the water. . . . In addition to the rockets, a blue light will be displayed on the threatened face. . . . All the appliances for resisting assaults should be furnished me. Greek-fire, hand-grenades, and turpentine should be sent down. The west face of the wreck should be mined." Beauregard also believed a Federal thrust at Sumter was imminent and issued orders for batteries on the nearest islands to take daily gunnery practice on the edges of the fort's debris to determine exact ranges. The cannoneers were to mark the settings on the gun carriages and traverse circles to try to ensure accurate fire during a night assault.

At this point, Elliott's garrison consisted solely of the three hundred or so men of Julius Blake's Charleston Battalion, which was part of the 27th South Carolina in Brig. Gen. Johnson Hagood's brigade. Their only armament larger than a musket was the 32-pounder cannon used to salute the flag every morning and evening. Engineer Champneys and his work gangs had been busy for a few days hauling sand and sandbags to various danger points. Even the post hospital had been turned into something of a trap, the Confederates driving stakes into the floor and bulwarking the embrasure shutters to prevent entry.[1]

The Confederates were right about the enemy's designs. Dahlgren and Gillmore both had plans to attack the fort overnight on September 8–9. Unfortunately for them, they did not see fit to inform each other about their intentions, much less coordinate the strike. The commanders earlier had discussed the possibility of a joint operation, but had not set a timetable. Both knew that Sumter's capture would immortalize one of them, and neither was eager to share that spotlight with the other in the national glory that beckoned.

Dahlgren announced his plans on the eighth, issuing orders to his fleet for the organization of "a force of sailors for special service." The men were to come from the various ships of the squadron, with volunteers preferred, but their objective was not revealed. Even as the *Weehawken* drama unfolded, Dahlgren was planning the amphibious assault on Sumter to be launched that night. "I am organizing an expedition for to-night," he wrote Gillmore in an 11:45 AM dispatch which did not mention his target. "It is reported that the enemy are mounting guns on Sumter which will soon open on the *Weehawken*, now aground. Will you please open with a full fire of your batteries on Sumter to stop their work?" Dahlgren also asked Gillmore to loan him some small boats, including some navy launches being used by the army, but the general said he had none to spare.[2]

Gillmore was making his own plans to seize Sumter, detailing the 10th Connecticut and the 24th Massachusetts Volunteers of Brig. Gen. Thomas G. Stevenson's brigade to make the assault. One hundred other men, from the 7th Connecticut and the 104th Pennsylvania, were detailed to serve as oarsmen, the force to be led by the 24th's Col. Francis A. Osborn. The units were to assemble and embark shortly after sunset on the eighth. The army was so confident of success that Union brigadier general Alfred H. Terry, one of Gillmore's division commanders, wrote, "After the capture of the fort, the force will return at once, leaving 100 men as a garrison." The soldiers were to burn a red signal light from Sumter's parapet when the fort was secured, and the new garrison would be supplied on the night of September 9–10. The watchword for the Yanks would be "Detroit" to recognize each other in the darkness.

Gillmore later stated that his operation was ordered "before the admiral's intentions were known to me," but the army had some idea that the navy was up to something similar since Terry wrote on the eighth that "A red light burned on the fleet prior to the arrival of Colonel Osborn's party, will indicate that a similar attack has been successfully made by the navy."[3]

"I will assault Sumter tonight," Dahlgren told Gillmore in a 1:00 PM message, finally revealing his intent. The Federals apparently communicated better with the Confederates than they did among themselves, albeit unknowingly, since the Southerners had broken the Yanks' signal code. About 2:00 PM, Lt. Clarence L. Stanton was officer of the deck on the Rebel ironclad *Chicora*, a signal officer named Daniels standing near him as they watched signaling from Dahlgren's flagship, the *Philadelphia*. Daniels turned suddenly to Stanton and said, "Fort Sumter will be attacked tonight."

"How do you know?" Stanton replied.

"I have just read a message from the flag-ship for a boat from each ship, commanded by a lieutenant, to assemble at the flag-ship at 10 o'clock for such an attack," Daniels answered. The Rebels would be ready.[4]

Dahlgren chose Cmdr. Thomas H. Stevens and Lt. Cmdr. Francis M. Bunce, both from the monitor USS *Patapsco*, and Lt. Moreau Forrest of the admiral's staff to lead the strike. Incredibly, Stevens did not learn of the mission at all until he was lighting his pipe after supper that night, his contentment interrupted by an officer summoning him to the flagship. The enemy he was to engage, meanwhile, already had several hours to prepare for him, thanks to the intercepted messages. Stevens had been engaged in heavy fighting much of the day aboard the *Patapsco* and was perplexed when the officer, Flag Lt. Samuel W. Preston, told him that a boat attack on Sumter was planned and that he was to lead it. By now, barges of men from the various warships already were gathering around the *Philadelphia*, assembling for the assault.

Meeting with Dahlgren, Stevens raised his objections to the plan and asked to be allowed to decline command of the operation. Stevens recalled: "My judgment opposed the movement on the grounds that we were without reliable knowledge . . . of the fort, and of the practicability of scaling the walls, for which no provision had been made; that sufficient time had not been allowed for the proper organization of a force for service of so desperate a character; that the enemy had been fully notified that some demonstration was to be made by the gathering of boats around the flagship, in open daylight; that they would naturally conclude Sumter to be the objective point and would defend it to the last extremity." Based on Stevens's account, he also told Dahlgren that even if the fort was taken, it could not be held for long. At some point during the conversation, the admiral said, "You have only to go and take possession. You will find nothing but a corporal's guard to oppose you," Stevens related.

Leaving Dahlgren, Stevens still was mulling over his decision when he learned of Gillmore's effort, Preston telling him, "If you do not go, the naval demonstration will fall through and the army will reap all the glory." Stevens reluctantly decided to head the attack. The force of about four hundred sailors and Marines was divided into five divisions, headed by Lt. Cmdr. E. P. Williams, Lt. G. C. Remey, Lieutenant Preston, Lt. F. J. Higginson, and Ensign C. H. Craven. The seamen were primarily armed with revolvers and cutlasses while the Marines carried carbines. The force was composed of men from the *Powhatan, New Ironsides, Patapsco, Housatonic, Wissahickon, Mahaska, Lodona, Memphis, Canandaigua, Racer,* and *Dan Smith,* as well as the Marine battalion camp on Morris.[5]

Gillmore responded to Dahlgren's 1:00 PM message at 7:00 PM, informing the admiral of his own plans. He also made a very unpopular offer—at least to Dahlgren—that the forces should act in concert and be led by General Stevenson. "In an operation of this kind there should be but one commander to insure success and prevent mistakes," the general wrote. "Will your party join the two regiments that I have designated and let the whole be under command of the senior officer, or will the two parties confer and act in concert? The former method is, I think, to be preferred."

Dahlgren answered at 8:10 PM, wanting no part of a joint attack: "I have assembled 500 men and I can not consent that the commander shall be other than a naval officer," he wrote. "Will you be kind enough to let me know at what time you will move and what the watchword will be, to prevent collision." Gillmore bristled in his reply shortly thereafter: "You decline to act in concert with me or allow the senior officer to command the assault on Sumter, but insist that a naval officer must command the party. Why this should be so in assaulting a fortification, I can not see. I am so fearful that some accident will take place between our parties that I would recall my own if it were not too late. . . . We must trust to chance and hope for the best. No matter who gets the fort if we place our flag over it."

Dahlgren and Gillmore traded terse dispatches over the next two hours or so. "I have found it impossible to communicate with you," the general wrote in a 9:30 PM telegram, blaming "an incompetent signal officer" on the admiral's flagship for the snafu. Dahlgren huffed at 10:00 PM, "Will you please name the hour [of the army's attack]. I am waiting."[6]

While the brass bickered, Stevens's expedition, about twenty-five boats in all, got underway from the *Philadelphia* about 10:00 PM towed in two lines by the steam tug *Daffodil*. On the way, Stevens halted the force twice to communicate with the monitors *Lehigh* and *Montauk*, which were on picket, giving orders for them to move in to support the assault. The *New Ironsides* also was to cover the attack. Even as the navy headed toward Sumter, Osborn's soldiers embarked from Morris at about the same time. Osborn had orders to withdraw if he found Dahlgren's tars going in. If not, Osborn was to attack and burn a red light from the ramparts if he was successful. The army barges had not gone far, however, when lookouts spied boats filled with bluejackets in the distance. "According to order, the army withdrew and allowed the navy the glory of putting the colors on a fort which they had done nothing to subdue," wrote a newsman attached to Gillmore's headquarters. Frustrated by his lack of communications with Gillmore, Dahlgren sent Preston ashore about 10:40 PM to confer with the general, but this did nothing to clear up the disarray, even as the seamen inched toward their objective.[7]

"We moved slowly on our way to the fort," Stevens recalled. "It was a calm, clear, starlit night. The only sound was the steady thumping of the tug's propeller, and nothing was seen ahead but the grim, half-defined outline of the fort." Across the water, Stevens saw another group of boats, apparently Osborn's troops. He reported that "we hailed them and directed them to pull in, but as no sign of a movement was made by them, then,—or, indeed, during the whole affair—we concluded that it was the army force awaiting the result of our demonstration." About eight hundred yards from the fort, the navy boats were stopped again while final instructions and the watchword were circulated. Higginson's division would serve as a diversion and move against Sumter's northwest wall. The four other divisions were ordered to close up for a strike at the fort's southeast, or gorge, face "which, being now a sloping mass of bricks and rubbish, seemed to afford the most inviting opportunity for the assault," the *Charleston Mercury* later stated.[8]

The *Daffodil*, meanwhile, cast off its lines and steamed away, the men to row in the rest of the way. Almost immediately confusion spread among the launches, the darkness and a strong tide worsening the disorder. A contingent of Marines under Lt. J. C. Harris in Craven's division had sat for several hours in their boat in the dark before joining others in tow and were unaware the tug had orders to cast off from them. Compounding their problems, the painter, or rope from a trailing barge, snared on a buoy, almost capsizing Harris's boat and the one behind, since they were attached. These Marines also did not hear the order to pull for Sumter that officers were passing among the boats. "We were completely at a loss what to do," the lieutenant wrote. The boats of a party of about one hundred Marines commanded by Capt. C. G. McCawley could not stay together due to the currents and amid the "great confusion," the captain reported. Stevens intended to let Higginson's diversion take full effect on the garrison before making the main strike, but upon seeing Higginson's barges heading in, men in other boats began the attack prematurely. Stevens reported that "mistaking his [Higginson's] movement, doubtless as intended for a general one, and in that spirit of gallantry and emulation which characterizes the service, many of the other boats dashed on; finding it too late to restrain them, the order was then given to advance."[9]

Inside the fort, Elliott and other Confederates watched the Federals approaching. It was about 1:00 AM, and Elliott ordered three companies of Carolinians to the danger point, their instructions to hold their fire until the enemy started to land. As the Union boats neared the silent work's southeast face, a sentry hailed them loudly, but the attackers did not reply. In seconds, a red signal rocket streaked into the sky from Sumter, and the night suddenly turned into an ear-splitting storm of noise and streaking shells. "Almost as it [the rocket] exploded the air was filled with hissing, shrieking missiles," Stevens related, adding that Confederate batteries on James and Sullivan's Islands "seemed alive with fire." The *Chicora*, anchored in the main harbor channel just north of the fort and only a few hundred yards away, added the weight of her guns to the thunder, the attackers inundated by grape, canister, and larger ordnance. "It was an understanding between the Confederate commanders that they should not spring the trap until the mice had walked into it," a Rebel sailor later recalled.

The fire from the ironclad and nearby batteries basically "encircled the work and effectually assisted to prevent any re-enforcement coming up," Elliott stated. "All these things were evidences of the enemy's fore-knowledge of our purpose and complete preparation to frustrate it," Stevens later wrote. "The 'corporal's guard' that we were to have encoun-tered proved to exceed our own numbers." Several boats, including two from the *Powhatan* in Williams's division, however, were close enough to land before the fire intensified, their men clambering out onto the bro-ken terrain. They were quickly forced to duck for cover. "The parapets and crown of Sumter were filled with men pouring a murderous fire down on our defenseless party, and heavy missiles and hand grenades helped on the work of destruction," Stevens recalled.[10]

The Confederates also blasted away with muskets and lighted shells, even hurling dislodged chunks of brick and mortar down on the intrud-ers; Stevens described the landing zone as "a vortex of the fire." He later added that the Yanks were "in the midst of a cyclone, where the air was blazing with bursting shells, and the ear deafened with the roar of can-non, the rattle of musketry, the whistling of grape and the explosion of hand-grenades!" Bunce was in one of the lead launches and described the predicament, in addition to the rain of iron, faced by the Federals. "We pushed in till the boat grounded, and it became perfectly apparent that there was no footing for the men, nor any means of scaling the high walls," he reported to Dahlgren. Williams, meanwhile, landed and led a handful of men onto the little beach. "I at once jumped from my boat, followed by the men, and started up the walls," not making much head-way, he reported. Additionally, Williams and his sailors were peppered by bullets from other Yankees in the incoming boats.

In one of the *Powhatan* launches were 1st Lt. P. C. Pope and twenty Marines, who followed Williams ashore. They tried to gain a foothold but were soon overwhelmed by the fire and driven back to their boat, los-ing eleven men. Pope related that his squad was "under a very much heavier fire and longer exposed than any others in the expedition,"

The Union boat attack on Sumter on the night of September 8–9, 1863.
THE SIEGE OF CHARLESTON, 1861–1865

adding that he was unsupported after landing. From their boats, McCawley's Marines returned fire, aiming at the flashes from enemy marksmen on the parapet and those shooting from loopholes. McCawley had orders to provide cover fire for the landing and then go in with the bayonet. "It was very dark near the fort, and there was great confusion," he recalled. Elliott noted that the first Yankees ashore "sought refuge from the galling fire under the projecting masses of the wall, whence grenades and fire-balls soon dislodged them." Among these Federals were Williams and his survivors, who, unable to scale the walls, had sought cover in shell holes. "The enemy sunk or disabled all the boats by shot and brick thrown from the wall," he stated. Clinging to hope that reinforcements would arrive, Williams saw a group of Union prisoners whom the Confederates above were directing to a portal leading inside the fort. He ordered these men to take cover under the walls and wait for more boats to land.[11]

The launch with Lieutenant Harris and his Marines, meanwhile, reached the fight after a roundabout trip. Earlier uncertain about orders, Harris steered back toward the *Philadelphia*, which had churned in closer to Sumter. The lieutenant briefly met with Dahlgren before—guided by the musket fire—he and his men pulled excitedly toward the battle. "We closed in rapidly among the other boats and got into the thick of the fight," Harris reported. It would be a brief battle for his leathernecks. "Every boat left us," Harris wrote, "the call all around was, 'Cease firing' and 'Draw off,' and, disgusted anew, we did so." McCawley and his men also heard the shouts to cease fire, the captain presuming that the order was due to the landing of sailors in the advance boats and the threat of them being hit by their comrades. In minutes these Marines were caught up in the rush of boats rowing away from the fort, McCawley reporting, "I called to the boats to cease firing and land, but to my surprise saw them all immediately turn and pull away after the crowd of others which were going out." Stevens ordered the retreat, later stating that "the evidences of preparation were so apparent, and the impossibility of effecting a general landing, or scaling the walls, so certain, that orders were given to withdraw."

Sailors in a boat commanded by acting Ensign William Knapp in Remey's division grounded near the fort's south angle and banged away with their revolvers before heeding the call to retreat. As the tars shoved off, they discovered other men in the water, pulling nine aboard, including a badly wounded Marine. Higginson and his men had reached the fort's north side unseen and tried to land but found themselves on a "narrow ledge of sharp rocks, in which no foothold could be obtained." Higginson made several attempts to ground, but with his boats in danger of cracking up against the rocks, was forced to withdraw. He decided to join the force assailing the southeast face. By the time his division reached the action, the boats there already were in retreat, and Higginson followed suit.[12]

Dahlgren, meanwhile, had embarked from the *Philadelphia* on his launch about 1:30 AM, intent on following his bluejackets in and sharing in the victory. The volume of Rebel fire, however, prompted him to board the monitor *Lehigh* and try to determine the results of this shelling. Shortly thereafter, barges withdrawing from the combat drew alongside, and officers informed the admiral of heavy losses. Ten minutes after stepping aboard the *Lehigh*, Dahlgren was being rowed back to his flagship. The dispirited Lieutenant Harris and his men pulled away from Sumter but remained full of fight. Their pluck was quickly dampened.

"After we got out a little, I reconnoitered our position and found the stampede was increasing and no boats on the ground; so, with the heavy, loaded down launch, we slowly made our way back to the flagship, where many boats were, and more were arriving," Harris related.

From the fort, the Carolinians began scooping up prisoners amid the surviving Federals left behind. "The enemy—with some of his boats disabled by hand-grenades and masses of masonry (convenient weapons to the ready hands of our garrison), and overwhelmed by our own and the fire of our supports—called for quarters," Elliott reported. Seeing that further resistance was futile, Williams consulted with his officers and decided to surrender. He and his men were taken inside the fort and "were courteously treated by Major Elliott," including the wounded. "All the officers and men who landed behaved gallantly and only surrendered when there was no hope of a relief and it was found to be impossible to close with the enemy," Williams recalled. The twenty-minute battle was over.

On Morris Island, soldiers squinted into the blackness to see if Osborn was successful, unaware that the army boats had turned back. They mistook the Confederates' red flares for Osborn's victory signal. A *Philadelphia North American* correspondent at the scene wrote on the ninth that "we, poor, over-confident mortals at headquarters, thought the coveted ruins was ours. Pop went the corks, though wakened at midnight, and high in the goblets flowed the sparkling Catawba. This morning told the story; the rebel flag still flaunted from the gorge wall and the navy were ingloriously whipped."[13]

The Southerners captured five barges and five colors, including a flag that prisoners said was the banner Major Anderson bore from the fort when it was surrendered in 1861. Some small arms were also taken, but the Federals dumped most of them overboard before retreating or surrendering. "The action was brief and decisive, as they found us prepared, and were themselves surprised at meeting more than a nominal resistance," Elliott reported on September 12. "The Charleston Battalion fully sustained its well-earned reputation by cheerfully enduring the hardships of their position and moving forward with energy in the moment of danger." Confederate naval historian John Thomas Scharf wrote that next to the second attempt to take Battery Wagner by storm, the amphibious attack on Fort Sumter "was the most mortifying defeat which the Federals suffered in Charleston waters."

For such a fiasco, the Federal losses were surprisingly light, although they constituted more than a quarter of the force involved. Stevens listed Union casualties as 124 killed, wounded, and taken prisoner. Chief among the dead was Lt. C. H. Bradford of the Marines. Elliott broke down the Yankee losses as 6 dead, 15 wounded, and 106 captured, of whom 11 were officers. There were no Rebel casualties. Elliott claimed that only 104 of his men were engaged—80 riflemen and 24 other soldiers "detached for service of the grenades and fire-balls. The remainder of the garrison were ready for action and remained in position."

The bulk of the fighting was done by Capt. J. W. Hopkins's Company D, Sumter Guards, and Lt. J. O. Harris's Company G, which had been organized less than a month earlier. Blake's boys earned the nickname the "Brickbat Battalion" for their heavy-handed defense of the fort. About fifty of the Northern prisoners were Marines from the *Powhatan*, the *Mercury* reported. The paper also printed orders from Dahlgren that were taken from the captured officers and which detailed the organization of the attack force.[14]

Dahlgren sent first word of the defeat to Secretary of the Navy Welles in a brief dispatch on the ninth. "I regret to say that an attempt to assault Sumter last night was unsuccessful," he wrote. "Our column was repulsed with loss." The admiral later reported to Welles that the coordination with the army was hindered "due to the want of competent signal officers." Beauregard sent a congratulatory note to Elliott on the ninth, calling the repulse "a brilliant success" and stating that he would attempt to have the captured Yankees removed from the fort that day or the next. He added, "Should, meanwhile, the enemy bombard Sumter, and you have not enough cover for your command, you will expose the prisoners, instead of your troops, to the enemy fire."

Under a truce flag, several boxes were delivered from the squadron to the Union prisoners, and the baggage of the officers also was allowed to be sent in. The *Mercury* noted that Dahlgren's force had been so sure of success that one of the boxes was addressed to Williams, "Commanding Fort Sumter." Some of the boxes "contained a great many delicacies, and were probably intended to grace a festival in honor of the capture of the fort," the newspaper stated. The Federal dead that fell into the hands of the Confederates were promptly shipped back to the fleet. A few days after the clash, the crew of the *Powhatan* contributed $216 to the wife of Marine private John Haviland, who had been "shot through the body."[15]

Gillmore reported that the navy met with "considerable loss" in the attack and tried to explain his lack of communications and coordination with Dahlgren: "Before I was informed by the admiral of his intentions to storm the work, I had made arrangements to do the same thing, but the force assembled . . . was detained by low tide at its rendezvous in the creek west of Morris Island, until after the naval attack had failed. The project was then abandoned. The only arrangements for concert of action . . . that were finally made were intended simply to prevent accident or collision between them. Each party was deemed in itself sufficiently strong for the object in view." The general continued his explanations after the war, stating, "No assistance from the land forces was expected or desired. In point of fact, it was declined. Each party was organized without any expectation of aid from the other."[16]

The failed assault made the front page of the *New York Times* for four days straight beginning on September 13, as brief dispatches filtered north. One correspondent saw little to gain in more efforts to seize the fort: "I understand that a combined attack is to be made on Sumter before long, but it can be of little use, so far as I can see, except that it is rather annoying day after day to see the rebel ensign floating from Sumter, riddled and knocked down as it is by our balls." As more details emerged, however, the *Times* warmed up its criticism, especially in a September 14 editorial titled "Zeal Without Wisdom." It stated: "The ill luck of the boat expedition to Fort Sumter . . . shows with what tenacity the rebels held on to the famous work which was knocked into a brick pile about a month ago, and whose defence will go into history as, perhaps, the most obstinate on record. The expedition seems to have been very badly planned and very incautiously executed. Indeed, the story of the affair reads like a skylark of a set of boys. . . . It was surely unwise of Admiral Dahlgren to have sanctioned so senseless an enterprise. . . . The navy meanwhile, can find legitimate employment enough without undertaking any such foolish and foolhardy schemes."

The *New York Herald* also attributed the debacle to poor preparations: "The failure appears to be attributable to a mistake as to the condition of the debris, as the fort was observed through glasses from the fleet and shore. The gorge wall, instead of sloping gradually from the parapet to the water's edge, as was supposed, was found to slope only from the parapet to the top of the sandbag barricade, which the rebels piled up to protect the wall against our breaching batteries. This wall of sandbags was at least twelve feet high, and without the aid of scaling ladders, no one could possibly reach its top."[17]

In Richmond, the Confederate victory and the seizure of the so-called "Anderson flag" were a wellspring of giddiness for *Charleston Mercury* correspondent Hermes, among many others in the capital. "Much glee and not a little fun is made over the capture of the Anderson flag," he wrote. "Dahlgren intended to bring in old Gen. [Winfield] Scott—in fact he is now hidden away in the strongest monitor—for the express purpose of wrapping him in that identical flag and seating him on the ruins of Sumter, like Marius at Carthage, with a slight variation. Calico sold at auction yesterday for six or seven dollars, and you will oblige me by speaking in advance to General Beauregard for that flag. I want it for shirts and pantaloons next winter."

The *Richmond Enquirer* was even more sarcastic, comparing the Northern repulse to a bad night at the theater: "The midnight attack upon the ruined fort, in thirty barges, with muffled oars—and the rebel batteries all lying asleep—the surprise, the escalade, and then the thunder of one final grand salute, as the sacred stars and stripes mounted victoriously into the midnight sky, announcing to all the ends of the earth that the grand American drama was finished; all this would certainly have been a triumph of scenic effect. But one single circumstance spoiled all— our batteries were not asleep; and so . . . the gray of morning dawned upon the crippled and shattered remnant of that barge flotilla crawling back to their ships, filled with mangled and groaning wretches." The *Enquirer* went on to state that, "The utter and disastrous failure of their enterprise will certainly make them more cautious for the future, in undertaking any dashing attack; and they will go back to their sage and cowardly system of warfare, with long range guns."[18]

On September 22, Beauregard sent the "Anderson flag" to South Carolina governor Bonham along with a set of photographs showing Sumter's condition at the time of the attack. "Among the colors taken was an old garrison flag, weather-worn, stained, and tattered," Beauregard wrote, adding that some prisoners claimed this was the banner Anderson had lowered when the fort was surrendered in 1861. "The appearance of this flag, and the circumstances under which it was found, satisfy me that really it is the same one that . . . Anderson was permitted to remove, and which our adversary hoped to replace [it] above the shattered walls of that fortress as a dramatic surcease to his humiliation." Union authorities denied that the captured banner was Anderson's historic flag.

The fallout from the botched assault remained heavy more than a year later when Commander Williams, who had been exchanged by this time, filed a report about the attack. He was especially critical of the boats led by Remey and Preston: "I know of no reason why they should not have followed their commanding officers," he wrote. "The small loss sustained in the boats which landed shows how easy it would have been for all to land."[19]

Despite the debacle, Dahlgren survived in command, but his working relationship with Gillmore had been further strained, if that was possible. While both still coveted the glory of capturing Fort Sumter, this continuing obstinacy hurt the chances of further large-scale cooperation between them. The monitors badly needed repairs and overhauls, and Dahlgren sent them to Port Royal to have this done. He also was hopeful that he was soon to receive reinforcements in the form of new ironclads, but there was no definite timeline for this. Still, Dahlgren had another wrinkle up his sleeve: He wanted to use a side-wheeler steamer to ram through the obstructions between Sumter and Moultrie. The vessel he had in mind was the army transport *Ben De Ford*, and he had requested its service from Gillmore by September 10, despite the difficulties between them. "That the risk is great there is no doubt, but if successful, it should pay," the admiral told Gillmore, promising to return the transport the day after the operation if possible.

As a backup plan, that same day he sent a request to Welles asking for a "large, powerful steamer, of high speed" and drafting less than sixteen feet. He wanted a side-wheeler due to the greater threat of a propeller-driven ship possibly becoming entangled in the rope obstacles. A few days later the admiral told Welles that felt he needed at least ten monitors to enter the harbor after the steamer had broken through the defenses but that he only had seven "and do not know whether the Department may be prepared to send me any more." Before the month was over, nothing had been accomplished in this forlorn project, the *Ben De Ford* deemed too slow and no other steamer assigned by Welles. And Dahlgren would have a long wait for more ironclads.[20]

While the navy recovered from its Sumter repulse and the monitors were repaired, Gillmore was so justifiably proud of the capture of Morris Island and the achievements of his troops over the past weeks that he issued congratulatory general orders on September 15. "Fort Sumter is destroyed," he wrote. "The scene where our country's flag suffered its first dishonor you have made the theater of one of its proudest triumphs. The fort has been in possession of the enemy for more than two years, has been his pride and boast, has been strengthened by every appliance known to military science, and has defied the assaults of the most power-ful and gallant fleet the world ever saw," he continued. "But it has yielded to your courage and patient labor. Its walls are now crumbled to ruins, its formidable batteries are silenced, and though a hostile flag still floats over it, the fort is a harmless and helpless wreck." Gillmore praised the men for taking batteries Wagner and Gregg, then added, "You now hold . . . the whole of Morris Island, and the city and harbor of Charleston lie at the mercy of your artillery from the very spot where the first shot was fired at your country's flag, and the rebellion itself was inaugurated."[21]

For the next nineteen days after the failed amphibious assault, Sumter was unmolested by the enemy, although there still was much work to be done in the fort. The Federals also were busy, repairing Wag-ner and Gregg and mounting guns there, ominously close to Elliott and his garrison. "Fort Sumter was already silenced," a Rhode Island can-noneer wrote about this period. "Nothing, however, would satisfy us but the complete destruction of the work that had so proudly defied us." When not on duty, the bluecoats supplemented their basic army rations with oysters and fish, along with local fruits and vegetables. In the bivouac of the 7th Connecticut Infantry, soldiers held prayer meetings almost every night around a large campfire, a number of officers always in attendance. Overnight on September 17–18, the Yankees again used their powerful calcium light, set up at Cummings Point and first employed during the campaign to capture Wagner. Now it was playing on Sumter and its approaches.

The veterans of the Charleston Battalion were relieved from duty at Sumter on the night of September 19 after adding to their reputation for combat toughness. Their replacements were some 250 men of the 11th South Carolina Volunteers, commanded by Capt. J. J. Gooding. Another development was an inspection of Sumter on the evening of the twenty-second to judge the feasibility of mounting three or four guns in the northeast face of the fort. Maj. Gen. Jeremy Gilmer—Beauregard's second-in-command—along with the engineer Colonel Harris, surveyed the defenses and recommended the artillery additions.[22]

By September 23, high winds over the past three or four days had prevented J. Fraser Mathewes, the civilian engineer, and his crew from loading and shipping two cannon from Sumter. The pieces were on the fort's berm, but better conditions were needed before they could be safely handled. Other than these two, there were now only eleven guns left within Sumter's walls—four Columbiads, two 42-pounder rifled guns (one with its band burst and the other buried in the rubble), one 8-inch shell gun, and four 32-pounders, including the evening gun.

Dahlgren had a brief meeting with Gillmore that day, but no definite plan of action was brought to the table. In his journal, the admiral wrote that Gillmore claimed the army and navy together were out of position and weaker than the enemy, and that Dahlgren would lose half of any strike force he sent into the harbor.

The next two days were occupied by Sumter's officers and lookouts in watching and reporting Union activity. Battery Wagner continued to be an anthill of work parties, their labors periodically interrupted by barrages from Confederate batteries Cheves, Haskell, and Simkins, as well as Sullivan's Island. The Southerners also fired a "national salute" on September 24 in honor of the Confederates' triumph at the battle of Chickamauga. The defenders had been startled early that morning by explosions outside the fort. These turned out to be six of Elliott's "sub-terra torpedoes," which had been placed to guard against another Federal boat landing and had ignited when the rising tide rolled debris upon them.[23]

Gillmore was promoted to major general during this period, ranking from his successful assault against Morris Island on July 10. There were artillery salutes, bands playing, speeches, and a review of the island's troops on September 24 to mark his achievement; a private presented the general with an eagle he had captured from a nest on the island. "It was a proud day for the Commander and his war-worn, victorious, honored army," a Rhode Islander wrote of the occasion. Amid the festivities, the eagle was unimpressed, some soldiers quipping that it was, after all, a southern species. The "noble bird stood on the edge of a full water-bucket devouring chickens and fish, oblivious of its own heroic nature," a Massachusetts officer observed. Dahlgren, meanwhile, noted Gillmore's promotion in his journal and also that by late September the general had moved his headquarters from Morris well behind the front lines to Folly Island. "Promotion is a sedative," the admiral sniffed about his rival.

Despite their already rocky relationship, Dahlgren called on Gillmore on the twenty-sixth to resume the heavy bombardment of Sumter, this time from the much-closer guns at Cummings Point. "I have no doubt I could do this with the ironclads, but so much of their power has already been expended, and so much will be required after passing . . . Sumter that it will be highly important to spare them as much as possible," he told the general. "With Sumter in our possession," the navy could remove obstructions between that fort and Moultrie "with no great trouble and little risk, and I should advance upon the next series of defenses with the least possible expenditure of means, and with the ironclads in the best condition." He concluded by asking Gillmore when he could open on Sumter and "whether I may depend on your driving the enemy out of it," adding that he would gladly contribute cannon to aid in the shelling. Dahlgren was also very concerned that the guns removed from Sumter had been used to greatly strengthen the other enemy forts in the harbor and couldn't guarantee success if he tried a naval assault. "I could offer no assurance, therefore, that an attack with seven monitors would yield, with certainty, such a result as the Department might deem desirable," he wrote to Welles about this time.[24]

Gillmore responded promptly the next day, stating that he would open against Sumter on the twenty-eighth if the admiral desired. But the rest of his dispatch was critical of Dahlgren's strategy and salted with frustration since Sumter's artillery—indeed the fort itself—had already been basically blown to hell. Gillmore did not agree that the fort had to be taken in order for the obstacles to be removed, especially since Sumter had only one known gun—the 32-pounder evening gun—and its defenders had only small arms. The 32-pounder wasn't even emplaced to guard the obstructions, but certainly the Rebs could have mounted more cannon since the end of the First Great Bombardment some three weeks earlier. The more severe fire would come from the Sullivan's Island artillery. To seize and hold the fort, however, could be more costly in casualties, the general stated. Obviously the navy's amphibious assault showed how tough it would be to attack and overwhelm the defenders. And if Sumter was overrun, the Yanks who tried to hold it would then be under fire from many of the other Confederate batteries girding the harbor.

For Gillmore, "the question is, shall we attempt to carry Sumter by assault and hold it under a concentric fire upon all its faces from batteries within easy range . . . or shall we remove the channel obstructions abreast of Sumter while the latter is held by the enemy? It is easy to see which of these operations is attended with the greatest degree of peril and the least prospect of success," he told Dahlgren. Then Gillmore aimed at the admiral himself in stinging fashion, essentially saying that the army would tackle the defenses if the navy couldn't do it: "I am myself willing to attempt the removal or destruction of the . . . obstructions rather than sacrifice men in carrying a work that possesses no power to harm an iron-clad fleet; that has already repulsed one naval assault from small boats, and would be held with difficulty . . . if we possessed it, and which must fall into our hands whenever the naval part of the programme before Charleston is carried out."

Dahlgren returned the salvo on September 29, writing of the "strange misapprehension" in the general's dispatch. The admiral said he was unaware of Sumter's artillery strength, if any, but that it was "capable of severe musketry fire, which will prevent me from using boats to cut away rope obstructions and compel me to risk the fouling of the propeller. If this fire did not exist, it might be possible to cover [shield] the boats" from Moultrie's fire. If the army gunners on Morris could silence Sumter's riflemen, "it will relieve the monitors of the work; and this is very desirable to do, because they have already expended nearly two-thirds of the endurance of their cannon and sustained a loss of six weeks in repairing" due to the two months the ironclads aided in capturing Wagner. Dahlgren added that he was not contemplating another amphibious attack on Sumter, nor asking the army to do so. "No assault is in question. If the cannon will not do it, the remainder will be on my hands, though I may say that even an assault was not so remote from your calculations at one time," he wrote, referring to Gillmore's aborted operation on September 8–9. The admiral went on to say that he was not asking for army help in removing the obstacles: "There is nothing in my letter to warrant the idea, and your offer to do this—my proper work— sounds to me very much as mine would have sounded to you if I had proposed to work the trenches when you asked me to keep down the enemy's fire."[25]

Gillmore was quick to reply, his tone much softer now. He knew that he and Dahlgren had no choice but to work together despite their differences, but stressed that it was time for the navy to take the lead. "I certainly did misinterpret the meaning of certain portions of your letter" of the twenty-sixth, he told the admiral on September 30, adding that Dahlgren's second dispatch had cleared things up for him: "I am expected to do what I have made and am making preparations to do—open a heavy fire on Sumter whenever the monitors are ready to move. . . . I believe I can prevent any anoyance [*sic*] from Sumter to parties operating against the outer obstructions, and may be able to accomplish much more, even to the occupation of the work." Gillmore also acknowledged the great efforts of the monitors, adding, however, that they were now on center stage. "I most cheerfully accredit to the ironclads much valuable cooperation in my operations here; but these operations have all had direct reference to the immediate end in view, the passage of these ironclads into the inner harbor," he wrote. While the army had led the way in "executing the first part of the programme," the general said, "It now is my time to play a subordinate part, and all the means under my control are at your disposal for that purpose." His closing line must have twisted his own stomach as he dictated it just as much as Dahlgren's when he read it: "What I stipulate for is a continuance of that cordial, open, and sincere interchange of views that has characterized our efforts thus far."

Elliott's Confederates knew nothing about this little dustup between the Union bigwigs and were just thankful that they weren't being blasted by airborne iron. As they did every morning, weather permitting, Sumter's lookouts counted and described the vessels in the U.S. naval squadron. On the morning of the twenty-eighth, thirty-three ships rode at anchor inside the harbor bar, including the most lethal—the *New Ironsides*—along with four monitors and four gunboats. Overnight on September 27–28, some of Sumter's troops were relieved, although under controversial circumstances. A company of the 25th South Carolina Volunteers, led by Capt. James M. Carson, debarked at Sumter to replace Company D of the 11th South Carolina. The captain of Company D had been the senior officer under Elliott but "was reported incompetent to command the fort in case of accident to Major Elliott," Beauregard's headquarters journal noted. Carson "is now the senior line officer, and is believed to be fully competent to command in an emergency." The garrison was now composed of Carson's soldiers along with Companies H, I, and K of the 11th South Carolina, a total of 267 men.[26]

Also on the twenty-eighth, Elliott reported the completion of a "covered way" between Battery Gregg and the Morris Island sandhills. He also complained to Beauregard that the garrison was low on fresh water, most of which was supplied by a vessel that had to elude Union patrol boats to reach the fort. Elliott was unhappy with this arrangement, calling the water boat's skipper "an arrant coward" and adding "if the boat is not seized and placed under military control, the garrison may suffer from want of water, as was the case last night." These matters were forgotten amid a scramble for cover about 1:45 PM as the Federals' land batteries again began shelling Sumter. One hundred rounds were launched at the fort that day, almost half nailing the bulls-eye. The barrage was concentrated on the southwest angle near the flagpole but caused minimal damage. The lone casualty was a laborer who had been slow to seek shelter.

"The enemy has at last broken his long silence," the *Mercury* said on September 29. "Those who watched . . . say that the Yankees threw their shot with considerable general accuracy." The newspaper two days later noted the continued shelling but also lamented the stifling effects of the blockade: "It is melancholy to see the perfect quiet of the harbor. . . . But the quiet is anything but the quiet of peace." This minor bombardment of Sumter would last until October 3; some 567 rounds were thrown at the fort, resulting in a total of one dead and one wounded.[27]

Beauregard, meanwhile, was still waging his own war of words with Gillmore. After reading his rival's accounts of the capture of Morris Island and Battery Wagner, he claimed Gillmore had exaggerated the strength of Wagner's fortifications and manpower, thus embellishing his accomplishments and reputation in finally securing the island only after the Southerners withdrew. He made these points in a September 30 dispatch to Adj. Gen. Samuel Cooper. In this report, Beauregard compared the timeline of how long it had taken Gillmore to take Morris Island—July 10 to September 7—with what had occurred at Fort Sumter during the same period. A total of 6,202 projectiles, varying in weight from thirty to three hundred pounds, had been thrown at Sumter over that time, killing only eight men and wounding forty-nine. "Indeed, the hand of the Almighty would seem to have protected the heroic garrison of that now historic work."

The *Mercury* on the twenty-ninth also ran an account it claimed was taken from "a late [but unidentified] Yankee paper" regarding the reduction of Sumter and prisoners of war. According to the *Mercury*, the account stated that if Gillmore was to destroy Sumter's walls he would also have to silence Confederate guns on James Island. The problem was that some Union sailors captured in the failed amphibious attack against Sumter were being held there. Thus, the Northern writer reasoned, "By the usages and customs of civilized nations, the rebels should remove the prisoners to a place of safety. If they fail to do so, would not Admiral Dahlgren be fully justified in covering the decks of his monitors with rebel prisoners, and sail past the forts to Charleston?"[28]

As always, Elliott kept a careful watch on the Yankees' activities. "Appearances on Morris Island suggest permanent occupation rather than immediate operations," he noted on October 2. "All of the enemy's movements by land and water show caution and fear of surprise." Seventy-four rounds were thrown at Sumter that day, but after the third, there was minimal firing on the fort until October 26, when the Second Great Bombardment began. The defenders also continued to ship out any guns that could be salvaged from the ruins. Two damaged pieces were thrown over the wall on the night of September 30, some of the garrison employed in patching together "cushions" placed on the berm below to soften their landing.

The most excitement during this period came on the night of October 5, when the Confederates made another attempt to destroy the *New Ironsides*. A small torpedo boat, the *David*, with navy lieutenant W. T. Glassell and three crewmen aboard, made its way out to the Union blockaders and took aim at the big warship. Incredibly, the little vessel managed to ram the Union Goliath, its spar torpedo detonating against the larger ship's side, causing significant damage. Glassell and one of his sailors were captured, but the other two crewmen were able to get the *David* safely back to Charleston. The event prompted Dahlgren to implement precautionary measures to prevent other such assaults and invigorated the Confederates to build more—and better—attack craft and torpedoes.

Sumter's defenders were preparing their own unpleasant surprise for the Yankee squadron. A five-man detachment led by Sgt. S. E. Barnwell of the Beaufort Artillery had prepared four torpedoes to be floated toward the fleet and possibly sink or damage an enemy vessel, a forlorn hope at best. Still, the devices were sent out on the waves overnight on October 10–11 and the Rebels heard a "heavy explosion," but there were no apparent results the next morning when the ships could be seen. Stephen Elliott was quite familiar with the building and use of torpedoes. He dabbled in their construction, including some of his own design, and had positioned a number of these devices in the Savannah River in 1862, after the fall of Fort Pulaski. And in late August 1863, a few days before assuming command at Sumter, he wrote to his close friend and colleague, Lt. James A. Hamilton, about a torpedo-making project. "I consider the blowing up of the [New] Ironsides of so much importance that it overcomes my scruples," he told Hamilton.[29]

Dahlgren, meanwhile, was coming under increasing criticism from the Northern press and was convinced that Gillmore was feeding negative information about him to the correspondents based with the army. "I am not pleased with General Gillmore's doings," he wrote in his October 11 journal entry. The attacks continued and the admiral's anger mounted until he confronted the general about it when they met eight days later. According to Dahlgren, Gillmore "very good-naturedly disclaimed any idea of disagreement" between them. This settled things, at least temporarily, although Dahlgren remained suspicious.

The Rebels at Sumter took advantage of the October letup in shelling to strengthen their defenses. A large bombproof with quarters for a hundred men was constructed on the interior of the gorge wall. By the fourteenth, the defenders had mounted three heavy guns—two 10-inch Columbiads and a rifled 42-pounder—in the lower-tier channel casemates on the northeastern front, or right face, as suggested by Gilmer and Harris. To protect this "three-gun battery," as the Confederates described it, work was soon underway to build a barrier of palmetto logs outside the wall to shield it from naval gunfire. At some point, Elliott also had masses of timber floated down from Charleston at night and cobblestones pried from city streets brought in to bulwark the defenses.

By the third week of October, the Federals were close to completing work on their batteries on Morris Island. Wagner had been renamed Fort

Putnam while Battery Gregg was now Battery Strong, in memory of the late general. Between these former Confederate strongholds, the Yankees had constructed Battery Chatfield, and near the southern end of the island Fort Shaw had been erected. Besides Strong, the others honored Union colonels killed in the July 18 attack on Wagner: Robert Gould Shaw, John L. Chatfield, and Haldimand S. Putnam.

At Sumter, a frustrated Elliott had watched the enemy buildup for weeks, unable to do anything about it other than harassing sniper fire. His fort had no guns bearing on Morris, and other Confederate batteries that might have bedeviled the Yanks were quiet for the most part due to the extreme range for the Rebel smoothbores and a lack of ammunition. "Their [Union] working parties suffer greatly from the want of being shelled," an obviously dismayed Elliott wrote.[30]

To this point, few—if any—mortars had been used against Sumter, but this was about to change. Putnam, Strong, and Chatfield had sixteen mortars in place—two 13-inch pieces and the others 10-inch—well within range of the fort. Added to this were twelve Parrott rifles (100-, 200-, and 300-pounders), as well as a 10-inch Columbiad, meaning these Union works had twenty-nine big guns aimed at Elliott and his garrison, along with a number of smaller rifles. A Pennsylvania officer wrote that he and other bluecoats were so close to Charleston now that they could see people walking on the streets, the time of clocks in church steeples, and laborers working on a new ironclad—either the *Charleston* or the *Columbia*—at the wharf.

Dahlgren, meanwhile, was apparently restless for action and called an October 22 war council of his officers to discuss an attack on Charleston in mid-November when his seven monitors returned from being repaired and refitted. The majority of the officers, including his most senior commanders, recommended waiting for reinforcements, which were scheduled to arrive in December. "Monitors not ready yet, and no reinforcements," he confided in his journal on October 24. "The worst of it is, that the public is kept in ignorance of my being *unable* to move, and I am abused because I do not move. At the same time the Government continues to express its full confidence in me."[31]

The *New York Herald* illustrated the admiral's point on Monday, October 26, with an article about the working relationship between

Union mortars and crews target Fort Sumter from Morris Island.
LIBRARY OF CONGRESS

Gillmore and Dahlgren and the Charleston stalemate. The paper claimed there was no friction between the two: "petty squabbles are foreign to the nature of both; but it is useless to deny that a question of grave import is at issue between them—namely: who is responsible for the long pause in our offensive operations against Charleston." The army's main mission had been completed by taking Morris Island; it had been the navy's turn since then and everyone was still waiting, the *Herald* said.

Nearly sixty days have passed . . . and men have waited patiently for the second act of the drama; but the curtain is slow to rise. The Monitors swing idly to their anchors . . . while precious moments are slipping away. . . . No one can believe that this state of things will be allowed to exist without severe censure being incurred by one or both commanders; indeed it is highly probable that, justly or unjustly, both will be made to sustain a share of the odium. . . . If then Admiral Dahlgren finds the task . . . too arduous to be attempted, or the means at his disposal inadequate, it is clearly his duty to make this known to the proper authorities, that no time be lost in abandoning an impracticable scheme. We, the people, must swallow our chagrin at the disappointment of our cherished hopes as best we may.

As the *Herald* was getting ready to hit the streets that Monday, the Union forces at Charleston were preparing a nasty surprise for Sumter. The Federals had received word "from refugees and deserters" about Sumter's defenders remounting guns in the northeast wall. To quell this threat, Gillmore ordered artillery barrages—totaling about two hundred rounds—against the fort from Strong and Putnam on the twenty-sixth. The shelling would be concentrated on the right flank—or seawall— which, if significantly breached, would possibly allow the Yankees to blast these three guns from the rear of their casemate. "The firing is progressing today with satisfactory effect," he wrote on the twenty-seventh, oddly referring to these strongholds as "Wagner and Gregg" rather than their new names honoring Union heroes.[32]

CHAPTER 9

"Sumter . . . Laughs at Her Enemy"

The rounds tearing at Sumter on October 26–27 marked the genesis of the Second Great Bombardment. It would last without intermission, day or night, for forty-one days, until December 5, 1863. This artillery onslaught would be vastly different from the First Great Bombardment due to the much closer range of the Union guns and the addition of the mortars. From the Cummings Point batteries, the range was less than a mile to the fort—the result being much heavier destruction. "The bricks on Fort Sumter flew in clouds and the fire upon Moultrie and Johnson had the desired effect, the rebels there replying feebly and inaccurately," the *Herald* said of the Monday, October 26, shelling.

On Tuesday, the "Parrotts belched out as loudly as ever," tearing big chunks of masonry from the fort. "The battle blast was resumed at sunrise," a Rhode Island gunner noted on the twenty-seventh. "Charleston harbor and vicinity, rolled and rocked under the awful and most deafening thunders." That morning, several of the monitors ran in close to Fort Putnam and added the might of their guns to the pounding of Sumter. By late afternoon, more than seven hundred rounds had been hurled at Sumter, causing severe damage to the gorge and the southeast and southwest angles. A Georgia lieutenant was killed—or seriously wounded, based on conflicting reports—by an explosion and falling brick. As the Confederates dodged for cover, it was disheartening for them to see large numbers of Union soldiers congregating on the sand dunes and along the beach on Morris to watch the bombardment. Many of the defenders huddled in the shelter of two bombproofs near the old sally port, the "only safe place in the fort now," engineer Champneys noted. "Our batteries were occasionally heard through the day, but faintly, and the enemy did not pay much attention to their shots." Amid the whistling shells and cartwheeling debris, a few snipers burrowed into the parapet mounds to try to needle the bluecoat cannoneers from long range.

The firing continued overnight and—as if the enemy's iron wasn't enough—the fort's post boat was mistakenly shelled by one of the Confederate ironclads while making its way from the city to Sumter. After a deuce of monitors hammered the fort all day on October 28, Dahlgren boarded the side-wheel gunboat *Sonoma* to get a better look at the result. He was wary of what he saw, despite an additional eight hundred or so projectiles being delivered by the army. "There is immense endurance in such a mass of masonry, and the ruins may serve as shelter to many men," he penned in his journal. Monitors *Lehigh* and *Patapsco* joined the island batteries in blasting Sumter the next day.[1]

The Confederates reported 779 shots fired at Sumter on the twenty-ninth, killing one man, wounding six, and continuing to cut down the sea face. That wall and the gorge were "perfectly accessible from the outside," Elliott noted, meaning that this ravaged sector was quite vulnerable to another enemy landing. Despite the storm of projectiles falling around him, Elliott was also annoyed that some officers of the 12th Georgia Battalion of Artillery assigned to the garrison were not at the fort. Four captains were away—two on sick leave, another on court-martial duty, and the fourth at Fort Johnson, based on a certificate issued by the officer's brother, a surgeon, but without Elliott's consent. "I have good reason to believe that none of these three who are reported sick are unfit for duty," he wrote on the twenty-ninth. "Unless I have my company commanders, I cannot be responsible for the result of a night attack."

Dahlgren, aboard *Catskill* and accompanied by *Lehigh* and *Patapsco*, again ventured toward the fort in the early afternoon, all three monitors adding a few rounds to the uproar before withdrawing in less than an hour. Expecting an assault overnight, Elliott kept a "strong guard" on the parapet and the "main body within a few yards, in readiness to move immediately," but again the enemy didn't appear.[2]

Four days into the cannonading, Gillmore was quite pleased with the carnage his artillery had wrought, especially against Sumter's southeast wall. "That face is now more completely a ruin than the gorge wall," he wrote to Halleck on Friday, October 30. Most of the arches in the southeast face had crumbled or were in the process of doing so, and there were no signs of any enemy guns that had been earlier reported. "Sumter replies with harmless musketry fire only," Gillmore told Halleck, adding that he would continue firing for at least twenty-four hours and then possibly make an assault, "although I have not yet fully determined upon it." Several of the monitors, including three that day, also had joined in the bombardment "and have done good execution." The batteries on Sullivan's and James Islands had retaliated, but their slow fire had been harmless to the Yankees. Occasionally, the Yanks would catch a glimpse of Sumter's defenders. "A few men were . . . seen on the outside, dodging behind the channel face when our guns fired, and keeping a sharp lookout for stray missiles and flying brickbats," the *Herald* correspondent noted. By the afternoon of the thirtieth, Sumter "resembled, at a distance, the ruins of some old Moorish castle, which the busy fingers of time had gradually leveled to the earth, leaving here and there its bastions to tower aloft, only to show how imposing and magnificent must have been the original structure," the newspaperman continued. "It had changed to a mass of ruins, with the tattered, dirty rebel flag floating from a shattered rammer staff . . . without a gun beneath it to utter a defiance or repel a foe."[3]

On the thirtieth, Union gunners, both army and navy, sent 955 rounds at Sumter, almost 900 hitting the fort. "Bombardment of Sumter from enemy's land and naval batteries has been incessant, night and day," Beauregard wired Richmond at 7:00 AM that day. "Casualties very few in Sumter." The bombardment continued that night, though at a much slower rate, and the twenty-four-hour period saw more than a thousand projectiles hurled at the bastion. "Neither day nor night passed without the enemy sending their compliments to Major Elliott and his brave garrison in the shape of shot and shell," wrote Maj. John G. Pressley of the 25th South Carolina Volunteers.

The Confederates also were expecting an imminent small-boat attack on the fort after the softening-up process by the big guns. With

that in mind, Beauregard also sent orders that day to the various commanders for all batteries bearing on Sumter to be "held ready at night to
sweep its exterior faces at a concerted signal from Major Elliott, or when-
soever the approach of hostile boats shall be evident." Also that Friday,
Elliott requested that two guard boats be posted—one between Sumter
and Morris Island and the other more to seaward—to help watch for
enemy barges. "I recognize the perilous nature of this service; but is not
the holding of this post worth some little risk?" he wrote. Elliott also
wanted a gunboat stationed between Sumter and Fort Johnson, saying
that the absence of this added firepower was critical since "the success of
an assault will be determined in a very few minutes."[4]

The relentless artillery pounding not only was incredibly dangerous
to those in Sumter but also required seemingly endless, back-breaking
work to hold the fort together. The soldiers generally were spared from
this "fatigue duty," or the manual labor associated with keeping the fort
repaired, unloading supplies, and so forth. The garrison had to be rested
for vigilance and possible action at night, and thus most of the men tried
to catch some sleep during the day. The "working force," composed of
slaves and possibly some black freemen, labored mainly overnight, finishing their shift at daybreak. In late 1863, this contingent numbered
about a hundred African Americans and ten mechanics organized under
the direction of the fort's chief engineer. The workers were relieved every
fortnight and, according to engineer Johnson, were as securely sheltered
as possible.

Still, official reports from Sumter's commanders throughout the war
are peppered with brief remarks of these men being killed or wounded.
The nature of their work often placed them in areas where they were vulnerable to enemy fire. Johnson admitted as much but was quick to add
that the soldiers were just as much or more in harm's way: "Necessarily
more exposed than the garrison, though never unduly so, they [the labor-
ers] suffered casualties in proportion when at work, but never in quarters,
as the garrison more frequently did." The latter assertion became painful
reality when Sumter—and Charleston itself—suffered an especially
heavy blow on Saturday, October 31. Among the garrison was the Washington Light Infantry, one of the city's oldest and proudest military units.
These Charlestonians were assigned to the 25th South Carolina Volunteers in Johnson Hagood's brigade.[5] Company A of the Washington

Light Infantry was led by James Carson, the popular and respected young captain who had been Elliott's second-in-command since late September. Carson was known to visit lookouts at the most dangerous points of the fort, offering encouragement and cheerful small talk despite shells whistling by or bursting all around.

That Halloween morning, some of these soldiers were posted on the first floor of the east barracks, still standing by the sea face. They were ready to climb topside if needed to repel a boat attack and were ordered to sleep with their arms and equipment. The two upper stories of this building had been seriously damaged, and there was an accumulation of debris on the second level, but the engineers believed all was safe due to the brick arches and thick iron girders bulwarking the second floor.

About 3:00 AM on the morning of the thirty-first, Company A was sleeping near the northern end of the building, an area thought to be relatively safe. Amid the round-the-clock bombardment, a Parrott shell smashed a girder, causing the overloaded floor above the soldiers to cave in. In an instant, eleven soldiers of the Washington Light Infantry were buried in the rubble, as were a private in the 12th Georgia Battalion and one of the ever-present Mathewes brothers, who was serving as a supervisor of the laborers. (Sources are unclear on whether Carson was in the casemate, but either way he was unhurt.) Others tried desperately to save the soldiers, digging and clawing at the mound in vain. "When the ruins were removed . . . , they were found exactly in the position in which they went to sleep," one of their officers recalled.

This sudden loss of so many local boys shook and shocked Charleston's society. Some of the dead "will be recognized as those of well known and much esteemed young men of this city," the *Mercury* reported on November 2, listing the deceased, many of whom were neighbors on Tradd Street. "The painful news reached the city at an early hour Saturday morning, and created a general feeling of sadness and depression in the community," the *Charleston Courier* stated. The bodies were brought into Charleston later that day, and funerals were held one after the other on Sunday afternoon, "being attended by a large number of sympathizing friends and citizens," the *Mercury* said. "The scene in Tradd Street, where the funeral processions followed in succession, was peculiar and painful to witness," added the *Courier*. "The bereaved families lived side by side."

Within hours of the tragedy, Beauregard ordered that all of Sumter's walls threatening to fall and injure more defenders be "pulled down or shot down, for which purpose an iron field piece can be sent there if desired."[6] It is unclear when Beauregard first learned of the incident, but at 7:30 AM Saturday, he dispatched a brief message to Richmond detailing the "terrible bombardment" of the previous day, adding, "Major Elliott and garrison are in good spirits."

The Federals were not immediately aware of their lethal blow, the shelling continuing on the thirty-first in its routine established over the previous few days. Two monitors, *Lehigh* and *Patapsco*, steamed in and added their weight to the punishment from the Morris Island positions as enemy rounds clanged against their armor. "The rebel shots glanced from them as pebbles from an alligator's back," a Yank cannoneer wrote that day. Dahlgren was now making almost daily trips in to see the destructive effects of the guns. That Saturday, he saw Sumter's flagpole shot down twice, he penned in his journal. As the admiral watched on one of these occasions, a Confederate "got out on the wall and put it [the fallen flagpole] up." Sumter's flag had indeed fallen twice on the thirty-first; both times it was raised again by men of the 12th Georgia Battalion of Artillery. If the Federals had looked closely, they might have noticed that the second time the banner went up, it was not the usual Confederate standard: The garrison flagstaff was so cut up by flying metal that the Georgians had to use their own battle flag to wave over the ramparts. This standard was known to the battalion as the "Pinkie Evans," nicknamed for the pretty belle who had presented it to them in 1862.

Casualties were especially heavy on the thirty-first. In addition to the cave-in fatalities, two other privates in the 12th Georgia were killed by a mortar shell, and four other soldiers were wounded by mortar rounds. The Confederates noted that the Federals cut their mortar fuses to explode a second or two after impact.[7]

Despite the day of combat, Dahlgren was seething over Gillmore's supposed collaboration with the press to scuttle his career. The general "has a whole corps of correspondents about him, and lets them abuse me," he wrote. By the next day, however, Gillmore was complaining to Dahlgren that his guns were wearing out. But that had not stopped the Union artillerists from sending about seventy projectiles at Sumter overnight on October 31–November 1.

The pummeling picked up "with the same fury" again after sunup on Sunday, the bulk of the Union rounds targeting the southwest angle, as they had for the previous few days. The monitors also churned in again, their blasts damaging the wall near the new sally port. After another 740 or so shot and shell were sent toward Sumter on the first— most of which targeted the southwest angle[8]—Elliott reported 5,565 enemy rounds since the bombardment began on the twenty-sixth, of which more than 4,700 hit the fort.

There may have been at least one brief incident of some harmony between the enemies during this time. The 12th Georgia Battalion had a fine band, and at sundown one day it ascended to the top of the sea face parapet. Despite the incoming shells, the musicians played the "Bonnie Blue Flag" with "as much spirit as if on dress parade," one of its officers related years later. Minutes later the guns at Cummings Point fell silent, and a Union band marched out on the beach, striking up "The Star-Spangled Banner." Despite the artillery roar from other sectors, the Rebels at Sumter could distinctly hear the cheers of sailors on the monitors and bluecoats on Morris Island.

The shaken survivors of Carson's company were relieved on the night of November 1, but there were command problems in getting relief troops for Sumter, which rankled Elliott. In a dispatch to Beauregard, he noted that "for the second time the movement to relieve a portion of the garrison failed" and that "some remedy be applied." He also told Beauregard that "the non-fulfillment of official promises is to be regretted, as it shows a want of confidence on the part of the troops." Beauregard responded that "very stringent orders relative to relief for Sumter" would be issued.

Charleston itself was still reeling from the Washington Light Infantry tragedy when Confederate president Jefferson Davis arrived there on Monday, November 2, 1863. Traveling by special train, Davis had left Richmond on October 6 and inspected Braxton Bragg's Army of Tennessee near Chattanooga. The chief executive also had made stops in Meridian, Mississippi; Mobile, Montgomery, and Selma, Alabama; and Atlanta, Macon, and Augusta, Georgia, before coming to Charleston after a two-night stay in Savannah. Despite an enthusiastic reception by the populace, Davis likely was not in the best mood upon reaching the city. His visit to Bragg's army had been contentious, with many of Bragg's senior officers almost mutinous in their opinion that Bragg was incompetent to command after not following up on the Confederate victory at Chickamauga in September. After their defeat, the Union forces had withdrawn into Chattanooga, where Bragg's army had besieged them, trying to starve them out. While in Savannah on Sunday, Davis received word that the Federals had been able to open a new supply line to relieve Chattanooga.

Beauregard and other dignitaries met the president at the Charleston & Savannah depot, although the relationship between Davis and Beauregard remained icy hot. This fact was quite evident later in the day when the president gave a speech at City Hall but did not praise—or even mention—Beauregard or any of the other generals who had played major roles in Charleston's defense. In fact, the only officer Davis *did* compliment was Stephen Elliott, Sumter's guardian, who had no time for fanfare that Monday. The president also lauded the fort's defenders, comparing them to the Spartan warriors who made the epic stand at Thermopylae. "Though crumbling in her ruins, she yet stands, and everyone looks with the anxious hope that the Yankee flag will never float over it," Davis said of Sumter. "Nobly has the little heroic garrison that now holds it responded to every expectation. . . . Whatever may be in the future, which is in the hands of the Supreme Being, we have written a proud page in our country's history."9

It would have been a perilous and unnecessary adventure for Davis to visit Sumter, since the fort was being lambasted by land and sea at the time. When the president arrived in Charleston, he likely at some point heard the thunderclaps of artillery at the harbor's mouth, punctuating the cheers of the crowds in the streets. Three monitors—*Catskill, Patapsco*, and *Lehigh*—poured 140 shots into the fort that Monday, coupled with 250 rifled rounds from Morris Island, 55 of which missed. The Yanks' mortars were also active, delivering 345 projectiles at Sumter, 135 of which went astray. The mortars killed one Georgia private, the only casualty that day, and left Elliott to be generally optimistic overall about the day's developments. "I consider the damage done to the fort . . . is, perhaps, less today than on any day of the bombardment," he reported to his superiors, adding that his men needed fresh beef. While the crest of the southwest angle had been shattered, "the disjoined masses have assumed a favorable position for the defense of the lower casemates," he wrote.

The monitors had steamed in close by noon, giving the heavy guns on Morris some relief and blasting away at Sumter. A seaman on the *Patapsco* was instantly killed late in the day when there was a premature explosion of the ironclad's rifled gun. Four others were slightly injured from the shock. The monitors withdrew after dark, but as Davis slept in Charleston that night he had to hear at least some of the almost one hundred rounds hurled at Elliott's men across the black water by the shore batteries.[10]

By that time, the fort's defenders had already dealt with another threat. Just after dark—based on Elliott's account—a small boat with four Union scouts landed undetected near the southeast angle. After a brief reconnaissance, the Federals shoved off. Rebel sentinels hailed the withdrawing craft; they knew that a picket boat was assigned to the fort and did not expect a lone enemy boat, allowing the Yanks to escape with only a smattering of musketry.

That night also saw a massive turnover of the garrison. Coming in were two officers and forty men each from the 6th, 19th, 23rd, 27th, and 28th Georgia regiments, as well as a total of ninety-six troops from two companies—C and D—of the 25th South Carolina. Elliott sent a request to Beauregard's headquarters on November 3 asking for the promise of a ten-day furlough for the garrison if his men repulsed a heavy assault. "It would contribute more powerfully to the success of the defense than any measure I can think of," he wrote. Beauregard wasted little time in approving the request, making the furlough fifteen days.

Still the guns continued, some 660 rounds targeting the fort that day and night from land and sea, but "on the whole the damage was not great," Elliott said, although several men were wounded by a mortar shell explosion in the three-gun battery. Another 500 or so rounds shrieked across the harbor waters on November 4, the fort's southwest angle being the primary target. The bombardment was ongoing, and Dahlgren gave his assessment of Sumter on November 5 after another day of demolition by his ironclads and the army's artillerists: "The work is very much cut up," he stated. "The only original feature left is the northeast face; the rest is a pile of rubbish." More than 500 projectiles were launched on the fifth, most aimed at the southwest angle while the monitors concentrated on the east angle. One Rebel was wounded.[11]

The flagstaff was shot down again on the sixth, two men from the 25th South Carolina replacing it. Again some five hundred rounds were thrown at the fort that day from the monitors and army cannoneers. All of this deadly fire killed two privates in the 28th Georgia and wounded twelve other men, most from the same regiment. In the Union encampments, much of the credit for the hawk-eyed sharpshooting in repeatedly bringing down the "rebel rag" during these days went to Cpl. C. M. Corey and Sgt. W. H. Manchester, both of the 3rd Rhode Island Volunteer Artillery. Both were recognized for accomplishing the deed twice, they and their comrades vowing to continue their "patriotic addresses" to Sumter's banner.

The fort's defenders had certainly come to respect the aim of their foe. Sgt. William Izlar of the 25th South Carolina was in charge of the sentinels one night during this period and found himself having to post one of his own brothers in a very exposed position outside the crumbled walls as shells streaked around them. "On leaving him, after reaching his post, I told him good-bye, never again expecting to see him alive," Izlar recalled. Two hours later the sergeant returned and was relieved to see his brother unhurt "but perfectly willing for the next man to take his place." Izlar and other Rebs were already much impressed by the pinpoint accuracy of the Union gunners, some of whom frequently cut the halyards on Sumter's flag when it was lowered at sunset. "The Yankee artillerists at this time had become very expert and I have seen some remarkable shots. . . . Such occurrences were too often to be mere accident."[12]

The engineer Capt. John Johnson returned to Sumter on the night of November 6–7 after recovering from his wound. He replaced Capt. John Champneys, who had served as the engineer in charge since September 3. By now, the defenders had been able to resume a minuscule amount of offensive power with the addition of four excellent Whitworth sharpshooter rifles with telescopic sights that had been brought in by a blockade runner. After some practice, the fort's best marksmen found they could be reasonably effective in peppering Union cannoneers at Cummings Point, some 1,300 yards distant. Johnson noted that "the sharpshooting with . . . these rifles was quite satisfactory and the effects on the enemy's detachments evident." With grim understatement, he contrasted the occasional long-range bullet sent from Sumter to the iron tempest lambasting the fort: "The disparity in weight of metal was prodigious."

Night and day, Gillmore's gunners kept up their steady fire on the "ruins of Fort Sumter," as he described them. The mortars were used most in daylight, blasting at low angles to try to "search" the casemates on the channel front. After dark, the Federals switched to lighter rifles whose fire was aimed at the various breaches to keep the Rebels from taking defensive measures in these weak points. Dahlgren's monitors still were occasionally engaged in the bombardment, Gillmore noted, adding, "The enemy do not reply, except sometimes with small arms."

Hundreds of miles to the north, there was brief excitement in Philadelphia on the seventh when the steamer *Salvor* arrived from Hilton Head with claims that Fort Sumter had fallen five or six days earlier and already had been occupied by two regiments of Pennsylvania troops. The report was quickly discredited, but not before being printed in the New York papers.[13]

The monitors took the day off on the seventh, and the army's fire slackened also to about 350 rounds aimed at the fort, wounding three soldiers and damaging a howitzer. The trend continued at about the same rate the next day (five laborers were injured by a mortar round blast) and with about 450 on Monday, November 9. Since the previous Monday when Davis had arrived in Charleston, Sumter had been the bulls-eye for more than 9,300 projectiles, of which 7,700 found their mark. Only one man was slightly wounded on the ninth, but the post's boat somehow broke loose from its mooring and drifted away. More importantly, a shell sliced the fort's telegraph cable about fifty feet outside the walls, temporarily knocking out its communications.

Overnight the Confederates noticed a change in the scale of the bombardment. For the first time since the onslaught began, the Federals used their mortars after dark. Also, the fire of the rifled guns was more intense than during the day, but from lighter pieces. "The heavy guns . . . have ceased their fire to a great extent," Elliott noted. "The rifle practice is conducted almost exclusively from light pieces. Day firing has in like manner given way to night." Trying to figure out why the Yanks had altered their shelling, Elliott reasoned, "This may indicate that their heavy ammunition has been much reduced and their heavy guns endangered." He was more concerned, however, that the night barrage meant the Federals would launch another amphibious attack within the next few days. The overnight shelling was possibly practice for the "means of covering an assault, which I think will probably be attempted within the present week," he wrote later that day. He requested that a section of howitzers be assigned to the post. No sandbags were brought to Sumter overnight, but the workforce of 160–70 hands was busy repairing a traverse, working on the mangled southwest angle, and placing chevaux-de-frise on the whole eastern slope.[14]

The tenth saw only some 160 rounds thrown at Sumter, including 30 from the monitors, but with no major damage or casualties. In a telegram that morning, Beauregard informed Adjutant General Cooper that 9,306 shots had been launched at the fort since the bombardment began on October 26, but added, "Fort is still in a defensible condition." The defenders' highlight that Tuesday was the arrival of 110 officers and men of the 17th South Carolina Volunteers under Capt. E. A. Crawford to relieve a similar number of troops from the 6th, 19th, and 28th Georgia. There was a brief scare that night, however, when the report of an unidentified blue light caused an already jumpy garrison expecting a night attack to scramble to their defensive positions. It proved to be a false alarm, but Elliott closely supervised the performance and readiness of his soldiers. "The men got upon the ramparts in fair time, with only a moderate amount of skulking," he wrote.

From his flagship *Philadelphia* anchored off Morris on the tenth, Dahlgren updated Navy Secretary Welles about the squadron's condition on the southern coast as he eagerly awaited the arrival of four new monitors. The army's batteries were continuing to smash away at Sumter and, he noted, "the monitors have assisted, until the indications of wear in the rifled cannon rendered them unsafe, and now it is necessary to replace them." The repaired *Montauk* had returned from Port Royal with a new gun, and the *Passaic* was also back in service after going in for maintenance; both ironclads had an improved top speed of about six knots. The *Weehawken*, meanwhile, had also gone to Port Royal to have some work done.[15]

The Union shelling totaled 373 on November 11, and the fort's flagstaff again was shot down, two men of the 28th Georgia replacing it. It was also during this period that Gillmore decided to finally use his calcium searchlight against Fort Sumter, positioning it at Battery Strong on the eleventh and illuminating the channel between Morris Island and the fort. The light was yet another new weapon in the Federal arsenal and featured a luminescence the likes of which few humans had experienced to that time. "It was not so bright as the full moon," John Johnson recalled, but from three-quarters of a mile distant, it was strong enough for him to read the largest type in a newspaper at the fort. "Our sentinels on the wall were dazzled and annoyed by it." Still, the technology offered a brilliance that the engineer appreciated: "The appearance of this light, thrown upon the battered walls and arches . . . was always striking and beautiful." Elliott added that the beam was turned on about 8:00 PM for "the apparent purpose of illuminating our works and preventing the location of obstruction[s] upon the slopes."

A forty-five-man company of the 1st South Carolina Artillery arrived by steamer later that night, but with mortar and rifle rounds sizzling and splashing around Sumter and the big spotlight still playing across the water, the ship's captain refused to dock at the wharf. Much to Elliott's irritation, the troop transfer had to be completed by small boats, which took some time. The incoming Carolinians, Company D led by Capt. Frank H. Harleston, relieved another company of the 1st South Carolina.[16]

It was during this time that Fitzgerald Ross, the British captain who was still touring the Confederacy, returned to Charleston and made another trip to Sumter. On a November night, Ross boarded the quartermaster boat bound for the fort and had to climb into a rowboat for the final approach to Sumter due to the calcium light. Still, the intense beam swept over the little vessel, and Ross and his Confederate companions quickly found themselves under fire from Morris Island. They made it safely to Sumter and ducked into one of the well-made bombproofs. "This night they [the Federals] were firing chiefly with mortar shells, which look magnificent as they soar majestically up in the air to a great height then slowly descend," Ross wrote. "If you are anywhere near, and look up, they appear as if they were coming straight towards you, and must inevitably hit the very spot where you are standing." On this visit, the Brit also noted that some of the Rebels gathered brass fragments from exploded shells and were making "little fortunes" selling them for a dollar a pound.[17]

The Federals ashore again flexed their artillery muscle on Thursday, November 12, sending almost eight hundred rounds at Sumter. The ironclads contributed two shots that day and were now essentially out of the picture as far as the bombardment; for the remainder it would be almost exclusively an army operation. The barrage killed two Confederates and seriously wounded another. One projectile zipped through the garrison flag. Still, Elliott did not report any additional major damage.

The garrison was able to complete a shift change of laborers using small boats without any other losses, despite being under heavy fire and the "strong light" again beaming for "a greater part of the night," Elliott said.

As his cannoneers toiled that Thursday, Gillmore remained confident that Sumter could be taken by an amphibious attack, but had not made any concrete plans to this effect. He also felt that Dahlgren could remove the channel obstacles, despite the presence of Sumter's defenders, with fewer losses than if the army stormed the fort and had to hold it. "Of the practicability of carrying the place by assault, I entertain but little doubt," Gillmore wrote to Halleck on the twelfth, "but I have never seen any necessity for doing so, while its sole power of doing harm consists in the protection which its infantry garrison affords to the channel obstructions. I am convinced that those obstructions can be removed while Sumter is occupied by the enemy with less sacrifice of life than we would have to make to occupy and hold the place. Should anything occur to convince me that there would be any advantage in holding the place, I shall not hesitate to make the attempt."[18]

Gillmore also chafed about his perceived lack of direction from his army superiors in Washington regarding how the Charleston campaign should proceed. Aggravating his annoyance, he had met with Dahlgren on the eleventh, and the Navy Department had supplied the admiral with dispatches containing its "views" on the Charleston operations. Gillmore claimed that he had been acting without direction "ever since I assumed command of this department. I do not shrink from responsibility, but I am convinced that the best interests of the service require that I should be intrusted [sic] with the views of the War Department in reference to matters here. Otherwise, I might take some step involving the Government in embarrassment," he penned Halleck. One "embarrassment" that Gillmore faced would be to send his troops against Sumter—no matter his great confidence in success—and fail to seize the fort. The navy had learned such a painful lesson with its small-boat attack in September, and Gillmore was not about to repeat this mistake based on his own initiative.

Amid this huffing and puffing, the real war raged unabated in and around Charleston, the storm of artillery streaking the sky night and day becoming as routine as breathing and sleeping. The only routine at Sumter, however, was the relentless and mind-numbing danger of being killed or maimed at any second and at any location in the fort. From November 13 to 16, more than five hundred projectiles rained on Sumter each day; the net result was a handful of wounded. Overnight on November 16–17, a private in the 27th South Carolina Volunteers, serving as acting coxswain on the quartermaster's boat, was killed by a shell fragment as the vessel neared the fort.[19]

There also was a nasty little tussle on November 16 involving the monitor *Lehigh*, which grounded overnight some 2,300 yards from Fort Moultrie. The Confederates noticed her plight that morning and began punishing her mercilessly with fire from nine batteries. Three other monitors moved up to aid her, and there was a firefight as the *Nahant* tried to tow her to safety. She finally succeeded, but not before the *Lehigh* absorbed hits that would put her out of action for more than ten days while she was repaired at Port Royal.

Despite the shelling, engineer Johnson was his usual energetic self, directing work to strengthen Sumter. The three-gun battery was his main focus, its traverse being repaired and a barricade with loopholes for infantry built at its north end. The center bombproof also was being remodeled for better defense by riflemen and, as always, the barriers against enemy landings were patched up, emplaced on the walls at night, and taken in before sunrise. Defending the fort against amphibious assault had assumed a much different dimension now than at the time of Dahlgren's failed attempt in September. Obviously, portions of the walls had been beaten down greatly since then, making it easier for attackers to ascend the slopes of debris and fight their way inside. To guard against this new threat, the Confederates had anchored a boom of logs and iron chains some thirty yards off the most likely points to be assailed. Wire entanglements were placed along the bases of the most vulnerable slopes, and an array of fraises, or sharpened wooden pikes set in frames, was set up atop the crest.

Even as the naval action unfolded on the sixteenth, the constant wear and tear was decimating Dahlgren's ironclads, the worsening winter weather only aggravating the situation. Seven of his monitors were undergoing some degree of refitting or repairs. "Our shore batteries continue to work at Sumter, but are now using mortars largely," the admiral wrote to Welles on the fifteenth, the day after his fifty-fourth birthday. "It looks as if a storming party must be resorted to eventually to obtain possession."[20]

Gillmore's bluecoats, meanwhile, refocused their attention to bombarding Charleston itself. No rounds had been launched at the city in September and only three in October, but this changed in mid-November when regular shelling was resumed. The cannoneers initially used the steeple of St. Michael's Church as a target; they would use other church steeples in the city as they shifted their aim to assorted parts of town in the coming months.

The *Richmond Enquirer* on November 13, meanwhile, had some macabre fun with the math associated with Sumter's bombardment. The paper estimated that from August 17, when the First Great Bombardment began, until November's first week, more than 15,500 projectiles had been hurled at the fort. The writer calculated that based on the number of Sumter's relatively few (27) garrison fatalities, the 200-pound average weight of the rounds, and the amount of gunpowder expended, the Federals used 115,439 pounds of iron and 3,657 pounds of powder for each Confederate killed. "Sumter, in ruins, laughs at her enemy, who still fear to pass her battered walls," the *Enquirer* boasted. "Charleston will have a valuable iron mine in the ruins of Sumter, and even now, when iron is scarce and sells high, industry, at very little risk, might make a fortune." The iron vein had gotten immensely richer since that dispatch: During the week ending on Monday, November 16, more than 3,000 shots had been thrown at Sumter.[21]

The Yankees also were probing the fort with small-boat patrols, and the artillery storm swelled to nearly eight hundred rounds on November 17—almost half of which were mortar shells—apparently in preparation for a minor reconnaissance that night. After dark, a sentinel at the northeast angle spied a boat approaching. He hailed it several times before he was answered with an oath. The sentry fired his musket, prompting the craft to pull away, but shortly afterward small-arms fire peppered the fort, apparently from bluecoats in boats between Sumter and Gregg. Near daybreak on the eighteenth, two other craft came within four hundred yards of the northeast angle but were driven off by a spray of bullets.

The Yankee gunners spent the eighteenth pounding Sumter with more than 570 shells, following that up with some 500 more on the nineteenth, as a prelude to a much stronger thrust that night. Gillmore ordered a "simulated attack," wanting to "compel the garrison to show its strength." Commanded by Maj. John B. Conyngham of the 52nd

Pennsylvania Volunteers, a force of about 250 soldiers proceeded toward Sumter in several barges but was driven off by a pelting of musketry and artillery, with two or three Federals wounded in the process. Union general Terry, commanding on Morris Island, wrote Gillmore on the twentieth that the "reconnaissance was as ordered. The boats met a heavy fire." Indeed, Elliott had been suspicious of such an assault and had his men ready, the rattle of their muskets augmented by battery fire from Sullivan's and Fort Johnson. "An assault was not to be made upon the fort unless it was evident that it could be easily taken," a Union officer wrote. "The garrison appeared to have been on the watch."[22]

The Federal was right. Knowing the moon was down and the weather was favorable, Elliott sensed he would be attacked. He and Captain Harleston had the entire garrison under arms by about 2:30 AM on the twentieth. The enemy barges appeared half an hour later and were driven off, but Elliott was quite unhappy with the conduct of some of his men. Despite orders, many "commenced a random fire into the air" while others triggered their muskets at the too-distant barges. Most alarmingly, however, some troops posted in the center bombproof on the parade refused to ascend the parapet. Elliott was especially incensed at the conduct of two lieutenants—J. A. F. Coleman of the 17th South Carolina Volunteers and J. D. James of the 6th Georgia—"who did not behave well," he reported later that day. "I have not evidence enough to convict them, but do not want them here longer. I have taken measures which I trust may insure better conduct in the future." The major also requested that the officers in question be relieved immediately. From the volume of musketry faced, Conyngham and other officers estimated the number of Sumter's defenders at about two hundred, intelligence that Gillmore included in a report to Halleck on November 26.[23]

The Confederates quickly realized the intent of these forays. "The enemy is evidently contemplating an early assault upon Sumter" and "has been making efforts to find out the strength of the garrison," the *Mercury* said on November 21. Indeed, by about mid-November, Beauregard and his commanders were considering a new defensive stance for Sumter with the fort's bombproofs as the key to repelling assaults by landing troops. Because portions of the walls had been blown away since Dahlgren's failed September landing and attack, the Confederates believed such a strike was a very real possibility and had a much greater chance of success. Engineer Harris had come up with the plan of using the bombproofs "so as to command all points within the works by musketry fire." Mines and torpedoes would be buried in the parade, and all cover not needed by the garrison would be destroyed—or mined also. Surrounding Confederate batteries would be prepared to shell Sumter itself to repulse or destroy enemy forces battling their way into the post.

Harris believed the plan could be "resorted to with good prospect of success" if the fort could not be defended from the parapets, but others, including Alfred Rhett and Maj. Gen. Jeremy Gilmer, had some reservations. Rhett maintained that the torpedoes and mines were unreliable and unpredictable, just as much a hazard to Reb as to Yank. Gilmer, agreeing with Rhett, stressed that Sumter's defenders would "abandon the great moral advantage of meeting the enemy at a moment when more or less confusion is inevitable with him; that is, when the approach is made to the broken walls in boats, and the men are being transferred to the unstable and unknown footing of broken bricks, stone and other material, and this under a plunging fire from our own troops on the top of the wall. If the enemy be allowed to pass this critical moment of debarkation unmolested, he will be much encouraged and even stimulated to renewed efforts." Gilmer added that the Federals must be met "at the threshold" and "on his first approach." Rhett concluded that the interior defense could be "a most brilliant exploit," but that there was a "great risk of not being able again to dislodge an enemy, who, from his devices and resources is more to be dreaded when he has once gained a foothold than in a hand-to-hand conflict." The defensive improvements proceeded as planned.[24]

Amid the excitement caused by the Yanks' barge patrols, a relief force of 103 troops reached the fort overnight on November 18–19 to replace the same number. This was an all-Georgia operation, with elements of the 6th, 19th, 23rd, and 27th Georgia relieving men from the 6th, 27th, and 28th Georgia. Sumter's 120 laborers, meanwhile, concentrated on repairing the heavily damaged southwest angle, building a howitzer position near the sally port, and strengthening the southeast magazine, among myriad other projects. "I keep up a slow shell fire on the ruins of Sumter to prevent any work being done inside," Gillmore dispatched Halleck on Friday the twentieth. The day brought another 520 projectiles hurled by the bluecoats, killing a Georgian and wounding three other soldiers.

From Charleston newspapers, the Federals learned that bombproofs and traverses had been built at Sumter in the period between the first and second bombardments. Gillmore also expressed pessimism that new monitors expected to join Dahlgren's squadron in mid-December would make much of a difference in the Charleston stalemate. "I have always entertained serious doubts that we would become relatively stronger by waiting for these new vessels," he confided to Halleck. "For every gun they will bring into action, the enemy will have had time to establish a dozen."

The Confederates, meanwhile, were noticing more reliance by the Yankees on their mortars rather than the rifled guns, the punishment from the mortars being quite severe that Friday morning. "Enemy shelling us more heavily . . . than usual, with mortars," Elliott recorded at 9:45 AM. That night the two lieutenants whose conduct had angered the major during the barge reconnaissance were replaced by other officers from these regiments, Elliott writing that the departing officers "were removed at my request."[25]

As the sun dipped that Friday, Sumter's engineers were focused on trying to haul down a dangerously unstable remnant of a terreplein arch near the center of the gorge wall. The Rebels had used ropes to try to pull down the arch before dark, but nothing had worked. An enemy Parrott shell completed the task about 5:30 AM the next morning with tragic results. The arch tumbled inward onto the parade ground below, burying ten members of a work party. Two slaves were killed, and eight other men, black and white, were injured, three severely. The fort had no time to recover from this blow as Saturday the twenty-first brought another 410 death messengers sent by the Federals. There were no other casualties or any serious damage that day, but the lone Parrott shell had exacted its toll.

As always, the shelling invaded the night, and there was another false alarm about 3:00 AM on Sunday when a light was seen at the entrance of nearby Vincent's Creek. "The parapet was handsomely manned by the garrison," Elliott reported, but no enemy was seen. For the day, the twenty-second, the Confederates recorded only 241 shots launched at Sumter. Overnight on November 22–23, a contingent of troops from the 27th South Carolina Volunteers relieved 111 men of the 17th South Carolina.

The mortars were again Sumter's main tormentors during the day of the twenty-third, with Gillmore's rifles taking over after dark. All told, 369 rounds were fired at the fort, but no casualties or significant damage were noted. In the Sullivan's Island defenses, sharpshooter S. M. Crawford wrote to his wife on the twenty-first: "The yankeys is still shelling Fort Sumpter [*sic*] but I hardly think they will take it but if they doo wee will have to give up Sullivan's Island there is some of the heaviest canonading [*sic*] here that I ever herd."[26]

The early hours of November 24, however, would bring more melancholy to the garrison with the loss of another popular officer. Capt. Frank Harleston's tour of duty at Sumter supposedly expired on the twenty-first, and he and his company were to be relieved. Harleston, twenty-three, also had been granted a well-deserved furlough, and was preparing to leave Sumter that day bound for Columbia for a long-awaited reunion with his family. "I will be with you tonight," he had written in a note to his mother. Before his departure, however, Elliott, relying on Harleston's leadership and bravery, asked if he would remain at the fort a few days more, since the Yankees were possibly preparing for another landing and attack. Elliott also had written to his superiors regarding this valued officer: "His removal just at this time will be a great misfortune for me, as I am greatly dependent on his watchfulness and ability." As was his nature, Harleston didn't hesitate in agreeing to stay.

About 4:00 AM on Tuesday the twenty-fourth, a sentry reported to the captain that some obstacles placed outside the fort to protect it from an enemy landing had been washed away by the tide. Shortly afterward, Harleston and engineer John H. Houston went to inspect these barriers. Suddenly a shell passed between them and burst nearby, mangling Harleston horribly across both thighs and an arm. Other soldiers carried him back into the fort, but there was nothing to be done for him before the end mercifully came some five hours later.

"Thus has fallen one of the most promising officers that our state has given to the cause," the *Mercury* lamented on the twenty-fifth. One period account stated that "he was laid to rest in his uniform, his frame having been too much shattered for his friends to attempt to touch him even after death." John Johnson described Harleston as combining "the best qualities of a spirited sagacious soldier with those of a true and gentle friend."[27]

Emma Holmes was becoming jaded by all of the bad news she was recording in her diary. "I sometimes think my journal will be merely a catalogue of deaths, for almost every day brings us intelligence of the loss of someone in whom we feel interested for their own or their family's sake," she penned on the twenty-fifth, after learning of Harleston's death in the evening newspaper. She described him as "another brave young hero, alike beloved and lamented by all who knew him," and said his loss was a blow "to his state and city, as well as friends. . . . He was a young man of fine talents as well as character & bore off the highest honors."

The shell that hit Harleston was one of 283 launched by the Yankees that day; another one killed a slave, while fragments from a Parrott round tore off the leg of another laborer.

As Harleston lay dying, the U.S. steamer *Massachusetts* joined the Union fleet about 8:00 AM on the twenty-fourth, bringing mail, supplies, and a special passenger for Dahlgren. To the admiral's "surprise and pleasure," his son, Ully, was aboard, still hobbled and recuperating from his severe wound, but bonding in a happy reunion with his father. A whirlpool of emotions overwhelmed Dahlgren: joy and pride for Ully's accomplishments and safe return meshed with the sobering, shocking sight of a son missing a limb lost in combat. "Poor fellow! With but one leg," the admiral confided in his journal that night. "I wish I could have borne the loss for him. But a colonel at twenty-one!" The admiral later recalled his first reaction upon seeing his maimed son come aboard the flagship on his crutches: "It almost killed me; but I smiled pleasantly and welcomed him as the dearest thing on earth."[28]

Dahlgren received a note from Gillmore the next day, asking if he still wanted to renew the slow shelling of Sumter and adding that he wasn't feeling well. The Confederates reported 263 rounds thrown at the fort on November 25, the shelling overnight on November 24–25 wounding a captain in the 23rd Georgia and killing one laborer and seriously wounding another.

Gillmore appeared to be becoming increasingly bored with the state of affairs on the Carolina coast as winter crept in. "I have nothing of special importance to report," he told Halleck on the twenty-sixth. "I fire but slowly at Sumter . . . while the navy are getting ready. I fire into Charleston at irregular intervals day and night." From the city's newspapers, Gillmore learned that "nine-tenths of all the missiles" entered

Charleston itself and that most "of the business offices are being removed beyond range." He also wanted to curtail the shelling of Sumter. "The slow bombardment of Sumter requires considerable ammunition, and I propose to stop it, or at least greatly diminish it, unless you think there is great advantage in keeping it up," he wrote to Dahlgren that day. "The only object for the last two weeks has been to prevent the enemy doing any work inside while you are getting ready with your old monitors and awaiting the arrival of new ones."

Some 240 shots were thrown at Sumter that Thursday, but there were no casualties and "neither has the injury to the work been serious," Elliott reported. The defenders also were able to relieve a hundred men of the 19th, 23rd, 27th, and 28th Georgia, replaced by the same number of troops from those regiments. In contrast to the beleaguered Rebels, the Yanks not lobbing rounds at enemy positions were observing Thanksgiving, including veterans of the 7th Connecticut Infantry, who had a hand in conquering Fort Pulaski and now were involved in the operations to destroy Sumter. The bluecoats engaged in boat races, music by regimental bands, and a feast of roast pig and beef, pudding, fruit, vegetables, and coffee.[29]

Amid the shell blasts in the city ran a poisonous and backbiting undercurrent at Confederate headquarters that had been getting nastier since it bubbled out in the spring. Not surprisingly, Roswell Ripley was in the center of the storm. It had begun in early May when Ripley was critical of defensive preparations being made on Morris Island, much of his ire directed at the department of engineer David Harris, Beauregard's close friend and confidant. In light of the relative ease with which the Federals seized a foothold against weak Confederate opposition on the south end of Morris, the criticism from Ripley—who was intimately knowledgeable about most of the harbor defenses—appears to have been deserved.

More problems were on the horizon. In late June Beauregard learned that "a portion of this community"—Charleston—was much concerned about Ripley being possibly involved in a "drinking frolic, either in the city, or on a vessel in the harbor." The British officer Arthur Fremantle had added to the party boy portrait of Ripley that June, writing of the general: "He is a jovial character, very fond of the good things of this life; but it is said that he never allows this propensity to interfere with his military duties, in the performance of which he displays both zeal and talent." Still, Beauregard sent two prominent Charlestonians to interview Ripley about the accusations. Based on their inquiry, they assured the general on June 30 that Ripley would "not be intoxicated, nor allow himself . . . to be excited or influenced by liquor so as at any time to interfere with the proper discharge of his duties."

Beauregard ordered the matter closed the next day and even recommended Ripley for promotion in October. But Ripley made waves again in November when he criticized Harris and his engineers for slow progress on fortifications on Sullivan's Island; several high-ranking officers on the island backed his claims. Beauregard, thoroughly rankled by now, would ultimately refuse to hear Ripley's complaints.[30]

The bluecoat gunners blasting Sumter stepped up their cannonade on November 27, hurling 468 projectiles at the fort, the most in a week. A 10-inch Columbiad at Battery Strong did especially destructive work on Sumter's already pulverized southwest angle. The fort's flag was shot down that morning—the sixth time it had happened during this bombardment—and Elliott described what happened next as "a most distinguished display of gallantry." Pvt. James Tupper Jr. of the 27th South Carolina—the Charleston Battalion—made his way along the whole extent of the gorge wall despite the enemy barrage and tried to raise the standard. The staff was too short, however, and Tupper had to find a spar to increase the length. By now, C. B. Foster and Corporals W. C. Buckheister and A. J. Bluett, also of the 27th, had come to his assistance. At one point a shot "cut the flag from their hands," but they managed to splice and rig the staff and hoist the banner again. Two of the men waved their caps at the enemy after they had completed their dangerous task.

At least one of Dahlgren's monitors rejoined the party on the twenty-eighth just long enough to fire 14 of the approximately 267 shells from the Union guns targeting Sumter. Hunkered deep in the ever-increasing ruins, the defenders were unscathed. The bombardment slowed to 152 rounds on November 29; a slave killed by a Parrott shell was the garrison's lone loss. The weather was so rough that for the second night in a row boats could not reach Sumter with the always-needed sandbags or other necessities. On the thirtieth, the shelling was next to nothing, only 24 rounds coming at Sumter. But by now some 18,300 rounds had been fired at the fort since the great cannonade began. "A slow bombardment of Sumter is still maintained by our batteries on Morris Island, which necessarily prevents the garrison from working openly," Dahlgren reported to Welles on the thirtieth.

Regarding the "work to be done"—meaning a naval strike into the harbor—the admiral again balked at the possibility of dealing with the submerged mines unless he had more ironclads. These obstructions were "the unknown element—one that is no doubt very uncertain, but is not to be disregarded," he wrote. Based on earlier correspondence he had received, the admiral was expecting his four new monitors to reach him before mid-December, and "when they do arrive, I wish to enter the harbor immediately, and I have no doubt the Department will find that the result of [an] attack in force will produce more satisfactory results than if made with few vessels." Three of his current monitors were out of service and being repaired.[31]

December 1 was child's play at Sumter, with only six mortar shells hurled at the fort, two missing. But the day also brought victory salutes by the Federals, who had received word of the great Union triumph at Chattanooga a few days earlier. Still, the beleaguered soldiers at Sumter were thankful for the respite from the pounding. "I have the honor to report the fire on this place as having almost totally ceased," Elliott reported on the morning of Wednesday, December 2. No shelling had occurred overnight, allowing a detachment of soldiers from the 19th, 6th, 27th, and 28th Georgia under Capt. J. M. Bateman to relieve 103 other troops from the 19th, 27th, 23rd, and 28th Georgia led by Capt. R. M. Mitchell. But shortly after Elliott noted the lack of shelling that Wednesday, the hail of iron would resume. It was about 10:30 AM when the projectiles began to fall again. It was nothing like the late-October days of seven hundred to a thousand rounds hurtling at the fort when this monumental bombardment began, but every round was as dangerous as the first one fired on October 26, so many tons of metal ago. By sundown, Gillmore's artillerists had thrown a total of 253 shots and shells at Sumter, resulting in one Rebel being slightly wounded. There was no firing that night.

By now Dahlgren was beginning to believe that artillery alone would not be able to extract the defenders. "It is admitted now that the Rebels are snug in the ruins," he wrote in his journal that Wednesday. "Shot and shell will not drive them out." The replacement crewmen he was receiving also were on his mind as winter set in. Many of the officers, as well as the sailors, were not only raw but also not seamen at all. And there were so many foreigners in the mix that one of his captains complained that when he stepped aboard his vessel he thought the English language had been changed.

The bombardment dwindled to only thirty-eight projectiles on Thursday, December 3. The shelling began at 10:00 AM, targeting the southwest angle with mostly Columbiad rounds, but Elliott reported the "damage inflicted [not] considerable." That night, Beauregard and Colonel Rhett inspected Sumter after the Federals had kept up a slow fire on the fort throughout the day. In honor of the visiting officers, Sumter's band ascended to the parapet and played "Dixie" and other tunes. The music lasted about an hour, during which time the Union batteries stopped their shelling, the Richmond papers reported.[32]

On the morning of Friday, December 4, Elliott—promoted to lieutenant colonel less than a week earlier—inspected the fort's greatly shattered exterior. Despite the shocking condition of the once-beautiful structure, he was reassured that the slope of obliterated brick and mortar, along with the uneven footing, would prevent any amphibious landing from succeeding. "The slope is exceedingly steep and the footing very insecure," he noted. "Nothing like a rush can ever be made up these slopes as long as they retain their present inclination." The Yanks launched 149 shots that day, the shelling continuing slowly after nightfall. The limited cannonading did not deter the garrison from relieving more than a hundred officers and men with other troops.

Only six rounds were aimed at Sumter on the fifth, two of which missed. But after forty-one days and nights, the Second Great Bombardment was over. It had been a gargantuan effort. From October 26 to December 5, Union guns on land and sea had hurled almost nineteen thousand projectiles at the fort. The tons of flying death resulted in Confederate casualties of thirty killed and seventy wounded, including the thirteen who died in the Halloween tragedy. Among the slaves, five died and twenty-three were wounded between August 12 and November 24. The Federals' main objective for this bombardment, however, had not been attained. The "three-gun battery" had escaped significant injury, but the fort's right flank, which had borne the brunt of the shelling, had been cut down from a height of forty feet to twenty.[33]

Sumter was still defiant, and for this the Southerners were jubilant; but another event was about to add icing to the celebratory cake and deal a huge blow to Dahlgren's squadron. The *Weehawken*, which had led such a charmed life in its encounters with Sumter and the rest of Charleston's defenses, met a rather inglorious end on December 6. Stationed off Morris Island, a big wave swamped her during a gale, flooding through an open hatch and sinking her with thirty-one sailors. This was glorious news in Charleston, the *Mercury* crowing, "The *Weehawken* has been one of the most active participants in all the recent naval attacks of the iron fleet upon our defences, and it gives us peculiar pleasure to announce that she, like the *Keokuk* and the original *Monitor* of Hampton Roads celebrity, has gone to the bottom." The *Weehawken* had indeed been a workhorse for the squadron, she and the *Nahant* also capturing the vaunted ironclad CSS *Atlanta* on June 17, 1863, near Savannah. From the deck of his flagship, Dahlgren had watched the monitor vanish beneath the waves, his thoughts almost immediately turning to her being raised. "How distressing that such an accident should happen now!" he penned in his journal. "Well, we must get her up in time to aid in the work."[34]

For Sumter, the rest of December was mostly quiet, allowing repairs and "progressive improvement" to be made in the fort instead of filling in mortar craters and patching up masonry. Happy not to be dodging giant pieces of flying iron, the garrison's soldiers sunned themselves on cold days while workmen concentrated on making the troops' quarters more comfortable for the winter. "Everything betokened a sense of relief from troubles past and a brave spirit of endurance for the future," Captain Johnson recalled. Elliott and his engineers also remained active in taking steps to defend the fort in case of another small-boat attack, continuing to bulwark the system of interior defense to be used if the enemy came over the walls. These improvements consisted of barricades and other emplacements made of logs or sandbags, with loopholes for riflemen and openings for howitzers to sweep any part of Sumter's parade "in advantage to us in the last extremity," General Gilmer had noted. As had been outlined in November, the plan was that if the garrison had to take refuge in the casemates and bombproofs they could fight on and be protected while signaling for surrounding Confederate batteries to fire directly on the fort.

On the night of December 7, Lt. John R. Key of the engineers and another soldier, Conrad Wise Chapman, arrived at Sumter. Both men were artists with distinguished pedigrees: Key was the grandson of Francis Scott Key, and Chapman's father, John Gadsby Chapman, was an artist of international renown who was living in Rome. Conrad Chapman had come to Charleston in early September 1863 as a member of Brig. Gen. Henry Wise's brigade sent from Virginia to aid in the city's defense. The men were aching for action, since they had been used primarily as reserves, but they found little excitement on the Carolina coast, posted in a relatively calm sector along the Stono River south of Charleston. Chapman, however, was soon assigned to Beauregard's staff and essentially given a free hand to sketch and paint Charleston at war. His work over the next three months would cement his legacy as the premier soldier-artist of the conflict.[35]

Key and Chapman would spend three days at Sumter, wasting little time in capturing the awesome spectacles of the ruined fortress. Using oils, pencil, and watercolors, Chapman showed various areas of the fort, including the three-gun battery in the northeast face and a panoramic view of Sumter's shell-pocked parade ground, looking east toward the pitiful debris of the right flank at sunrise on December 9. Key did a much starker drawing from the same vantage point, but without the details Chapman provided: men warming by a fire and the Union vessels on the horizon, all set against the vista of a magnificent dawn over the ocean. Another of Chapman's images shows a candlelit chamber at the fort's entrance, Elliott and a telegraph operator working at a desk while a blanket-cloaked soldier stands at the open door.

Chapman had apparently been at Sumter on October 25, because two of his paintings, one among his most famous, were based on sketches made that day. *Evening Gun, Fort Sumter* depicts the Confederate flag being lowered at sundown from a view at the base of the southeast wall. Much of the piece shows the masses of tumbled red brick and other debris, with Charleston's skyline in the distance. Possibly Chapman's most popular—and familiar—rendering is *The Flag of Sumter*. This picture shows a lone sentinel atop the fort's angle, the tattered flag waving insolently at the enemy ships across the waves. "Often he sat on the ramparts of Sumter [and] other forts under a heavy cannonade, while painting these pictures, and those who saw him, said he minded it no more than if he had been listening to the Post band," wrote one of Chapman's Virginia comrades. "Chapman held cannon-balls and shells in great contempt."

*This drawing by Lt. John R. Key shows the entrance to the three-gun battery
and the surrounding devastation as it appeared on December 9, 1863.*
LIBRARY OF CONGRESS

Before leaving Charleston in March 1864, Chapman made sketches and
did other preliminary work for what would amount to thirty-one paintings of the city and its defenses, including Sumter. Many of the actual
paintings based on the drawings were done in Rome, some completed, or
even copied, by his father.[36]

"Affairs here continue quiet," Elliott reported on December 9. He
had to be galled that he had nothing with which to bloody the many
Yankees he watched bolster what were once Wagner and Gregg on Morris Island. Supply wagons trundled unmolested up and down the beach.
The Federals "show themselves in considerable numbers" in and about
these strongholds, he added, "where the work of cutting, hauling and
placing sods continues." The bluecoats amused themselves with a few
light artillery rounds thrown at Sumter that day. Elliott realized the Confederates had to conserve their limited ammunition, but he also knew the
Yanks could not be allowed to work unmolested. "I do not think it is
well for our batteries to suspend their fire when the enemy are silent, as

they are working when not firing; they are then more exposed and vulnerable," he reported on the eighth. Beauregard quickly agreed, issuing orders that same day "that the working parties . . . must not be allowed to work day and night undisturbed; they should be fired upon occasionally, due regard being had to proper economy of ammunition." Two days later Elliott noted, "Enemy continue working, but are seriously interrupted by our shelling when it takes place."[37]

Despite enduring the death, sufferings, and hardships of the Second Great Bombardment, Sumter and its defenders were about to face a more extreme challenge. A "disaster of the most serious and distressing nature" was about to unfold, and the fort's fate would hang by a thread, a sword of Damocles ready to plunge. On the morning of Friday, December 11, it had been several days since the Federals had spent any rounds on Sumter. The outer chamber of the lower southwest magazine had been converted to hold the commissary stores and that morning was crowded with soldiers drawing rations from Capt. Edward D. Frost, assistant quartermaster, who was serving as the post commissary and had recently been assigned to Sumter. The magazine's inner chamber was still being used as the garrison's small-arms magazine, containing an assortment of rifle cartridges, howitzer ammunition, primers, hand grenades, and other weaponry. The magazine was considered one of the most secure points in the fort since it was protected by not only the thick brick and stone walls but also the piled debris along the exterior of the gorge in that area. "The safety of this particular locality from all kinds of shelling had never for a moment been questioned," Johnson noted.

As had been the recent norm, there was no enemy fire that day as the men bunched into the narrow corridors of the commissary. Most of the troops belonged to the 25th South Carolina Volunteers, the 1st South Carolina Artillery, and the 6th, 19th, and 27th Georgia Volunteers. Everything changed in the last heartbeat for some about 9:30 AM, when a powerful explosion ripped through the magazine. In the confined area, there was nowhere for the tremendous energy of the blast and flames to spread except through the passages packed with troops. The fireball incinerated some and burned others to varying degrees. Casemates in the vicinity were immediately filled with dense smoke, driving back anyone who tried to go in as a rescuer or to subdue the flames. Several companies of the garrison were stationed in these casemates and jolted to their feet by the catastrophe. "In total darkness, the occupants rushed from the stifling smoke to the open embrasures, leaving their arms and blankets behind," Elliott later stated. Some of the men suffered burns before they could crawl from their bunks.[38]

Surprisingly, the blast had been so muffled by its depth within the magazine and the layers of rubble that there had been very little effect visible not only to lookouts at other Confederate outposts but also to the Federals. The explosion had resulted in a pit some eighteen feet square and ten feet deep above the magazine, but this could not be seen by the enemy. Smoke from the fire, however, soon seeped into the sky, and within ten minutes of the accident, Union batteries opened with mortar and rifled guns.

In their quarters in a city-front casemate near the magazine, Elliott and Johnson had only been asleep a short time after overnight duties when they were jerked awake by the terrible commotion. In the choking smoke and pitch blackness, they heard the crash of falling debris and initially believed that a Union shell had ignited a chest of hand grenades kept at the top of the nearby spiral stairway for use in repelling attackers. They managed to prop open a heavy oak shutter on one of the embrasures and jumped to the rocky foundation below, which was flooded by a high tide. Barefooted, they slogged around the fort's exterior, looking for another way back inside. The officers clambered through another embrasure and ran across the parade toward the danger point.

By then the Federals were pounding away, and Elliott was slightly wounded in the head and ankle by a shell blast. Nevertheless, the pair entered the narrow entrance to the magazine, the smoke and darkness deepening as they proceeded, stumbling over corpses. Adding to the tumult was a mob of wounded and panicky men gasping for fresh air as they struggled to reach the parade ground. Elliott and Johnson pushed their way through them, no one yet knowing what had triggered the calamity, and discovered an inferno ravaging the commissary area. Like the others, they were soon driven out to the parade by the smoke and flames. The men tried to stifle the fire by erecting barricades of wet sandbags, but it was no use; flames raged up the southwest stairway and through the casemates where some soldiers were trapped. A few of these men, cut off from the stairs, were rescued by long ladders propped below a hole in the wall, from which they were able to climb down.[39]

One of the Rebel ironclads soon sent a small boat with water buckets, but Elliott and his garrison were in serious trouble. The fort's telegraph was down, as operator W. R. Cathcart had to move it to escape the blaze; Sumter's signal officers were desperately trying to contact their counterparts at Fort Johnson and on Sullivan's Island, but to no avail. A number of burned and otherwise wounded men required immediate attention; other Rebels were laboring to quell the fire, and all were subjected to enemy artillery rounds shrieking into the fort.

The Yankees hurled approximately 220 projectiles at Sumter that day, but it would have been worse if they had realized the Confederates were possibly on the brink of being overwhelmed. It would be another lost opportunity for the Federals. As had been the case since November 28, Dahlgren's guns were silent. If the August bombardment had been the worst crisis the garrison had endured, this catastrophe was equally as bad and could have resulted in the fort's surrender if the Yankees had kept up their shelling on the eleventh, according to Johnson: "Through default of such harassing fire as the Federals, combining their land and naval artillery, might have kept up for a week or more at this time, the defense of Fort Sumter was successfully prolonged."

By late afternoon, Sumter's signalmen had reestablished their contacts, the enemy artillery was diminishing, and the initial panic of many of the defenders was gone, despite the fire still charring the fort's innards. Amid the chaos, Lt. L. A. Harper of Company F, 25th South Carolina, "showed great gallantry in rescuing burning bodies from the smoke and flames," Elliott said.[40]

That night Elliott's ankle injury caused him to temporarily relinquish command to Capt. M. H. Sellers of Company F, 25th South Carolina Volunteers. Sellers helped settle the troops, fight the fire, and make defensive arrangements, all as Elliott's minor wound "prevented me from running about," the commander wrote. Elliott would later praise telegrapher Cathcart, who saved his equipment after the initial blast, set up at another spot, and had to relocate again due to the advancing flames. But he was angered and frustrated by the signalmen from the other outposts whom his flagmen had been unable to contact at the height of the crisis. "The Sullivan's Island corps could be seen operating with other points, an inattention when it was known that we were under unusual circumstances and cut off from all communication, seems to me reprehensible in the extreme, and ought, I think, to be looked into," he reported.

The blast killed eleven men and wounded thirty-nine, of which eight were seriously injured. Of this total, the most losses were from the 25th South Carolina, with three dead and seventeen wounded, and the 19th Georgia, with two killed and eight wounded. The 1st South Carolina Artillery also lost three men, along with two injured, all from its Company K. The remains of Frost and some of the others were never recovered. Additionally, Elliott and a Signal Corps officer were injured (the latter severely) in the ensuing bombardment, adding to the wounded total.[41]

Within hours of the explosion, the fire had superheated the bricks in the magazine's sector, and the men struggled into the night to water down and cool the upper casemates. This was crucial since the lower casemates and the nearby sally port were still threatened by the blaze, the sally port's doors having been burned away and the bricks "as hot as though in an oven," Johnson noted. To gain access to the wharf, the Confederates had to plant a ladder there to reach the breach in the wall used earlier for some of the troops to escape from the fire. From that point in the smoky upper casemates, it was necessary to scale another ladder to the top of the mountain of debris which covered these areas. From there, anyone who entered had to descend through a small opening, either by foot or by another ladder, some thirty feet down the tricky and treacherous slope of debris to the parade ground below. By this tenuous route, Sumter that night was reinforced to make up for the casualties and resupplied with arms and ammunition. It was a monumental task, men lugging barrels and boxes up and down the ladders, everyone on the alert for a Federal attack. Fresh water was supplied by a hose run from a water boat outside through an embrasure in the east battery. The fire was still smoldering the next day, but the greatest danger had passed. "The damage done will not materially affect the defenses of the work," Elliott noted on the twelfth. "Captain Johnson . . . was everywhere, doing everything that man could do." To the garrison's surprise, there was no shelling from the enemy at all that Saturday.[42]

By the morning of Sunday, December 13, Elliott was angered that a supply steamer had not docked at Sumter overnight, leaving him with no rations for the next day and without a fire engine that had been promised. The wind had been high for part of the night, and Gillmore's calcium light had been playing on the harbor, but smaller vessels had reached the fort unharmed. Elliott's ire was directed at the steamer's skipper, who had not arrived at Sumter, "alleging as a reason the heavy weather." He also was frustrated and "surprised that movements of importance should be left to the discretion and final decision of irresponsible and timid steamboat captains." Regarding the hazards from the calcium light, Elliott noted the passage to Sumter could be made with "little risk by running down on the Sullivan's Island side until the light is shut in and then turning for the fort and keeping in its shade until the wharf is reached." He added that the "passages are cooling slowly; the gorge wall is much sunken in over the exploded magazine."

The thirteenth also was a bad day for Dahlgren. The *Arago* arrived with mail, including a disheartening dispatch from the Navy Department: The new monitors he was expecting would not be ready before January 1 due to labor strikes by the mechanics. "And yet the papers cry out, 'Why not go ahead?'" he brooded in his journal that night. Like the army, the navy also apparently did not realize Sumter's dire straits, the monitors not having fired a shell at the fort since December 9. Indeed, it would be after the turn of the new year before the blockaders sent a round toward Sumter.[43]

Overnight on December 13–14, a steamer did arrive at Sumter with rations, ordnance, and a relief force of 106 officers and men from four Georgia regiments to replace the same number of troops. During the day on the fourteenth, details from the garrison were assigned to engineer Johnson to help clear rubbish while the labor force made good progress in its repairs of the blast damage. The fact that the fort continued to be unmolested by enemy guns of any sort added to the positive news. "A day of extreme quiet yesterday," Elliott noted of the fourteenth. The fire gradually died out, smothered by the lack of oxygen in the fort's bowels and by sand and sandbags that collapsed into it as the flames burned away timber supports. But it would be days before these areas could be dug out and cooled down so they could be reoccupied by the garrison. Until this happened, the troops and laborers had to use the ladder system every night to get reinforcements and supplies into the fort.

Beauregard, Rhett, and chief engineer Harris inspected Sumter a few nights after the disaster. It was determined that the blast was sparked by a fire that began in the commissary area, but all who could have shed more light on what happened were dead. Nevertheless, the Confederates had already begun vigorous efforts to replace the shattered magazine in the same location, using heavy beams, sand, and brick. The stair tower in the southwest angle also had to have substantial repairs. "Affairs continue quiet," Elliott noted of enemy activity on December 16. "The repair of the damage progressing. Transportation and water were supplied."[44]

The exhaustive, never-ending toil and combat stress took a toll on Johnson. Elliott went to Charleston for a conference on the seventeenth only to return and find the captain suffering from a high fever. With "no comforts here," Elliott sent Johnson into the city to recuperate, his two assistant engineers taking over duties in his absence. On the eighteenth, the commander was finally able to get to the commissary area where the blast originated, writing that "by the use of buckets, the fire will soon be totally extinguished." During this period there were almost nightly rotations of troops—Georgians and South Carolinians—coming or going from Sumter. "We have still been unmolested by the enemy, and the engineer work has progressed as favorably as usual," Elliott wrote on the nineteenth.

The *New York Herald*, meanwhile, was in a spirit of reflection on the eighteenth about not only the accuracy of the artillery against Sumter but also the streaking comet of Union general Ulysses Grant's rise after his war-changing victories at Vicksburg and Chattanooga. "Everything having gone as directly to its mark as Grant always goes to his, and will to the Presidency," the paper said of the sharp-eyed Union gunners. The *Herald* also mentioned the "Swamp Angel" blasting Charleston from more than four miles away. "This achievement renders it certain that the city . . . can be destroyed whenever General Gillmore chooses to do it, just as Fort Sumter has been made to mingle with the dust of her stony and once considered impregnable battlements. And if Gillmore doesn't hurry, Grant will come up in the rear and take the town from the other side."

As the year drew to its end, Gillmore requested some twelve thousand more troops even though his department already had about thirty-three thousand men, most of whom were posted in the Charleston sector. He proposed that these reinforcements would be used for an attack on the city via James Island. He also suggested that a surprise assault be made on Savannah and that a Union force be landed at Bull's Bay, on the coast some twenty miles north of Charleston, to assail the city from that direction. Halleck replied on December 22, telling the general that individual operations within his department were up to him but that he would not be receiving any reinforcements.[45]

The magazine disaster and his minor injuries did not deter Elliott from announcing his intent a few days later for a Christmas celebration at Sumter. "Festivities were rare enough at the fort," related John Johnson, who returned to duty at the fort overnight on December 23–24. "Nevertheless, some extras were arranged for the soldiers, and the messes of the officers were gladdened by the receipt of well-packed boxes and hampers from their homes." On Christmas Day, a feast was spread in the headquarters casemate of the three-gun battery. Despite the Confederacy's ever-mounting supply problems, the men enjoyed a bountiful dinner of roast turkey, wild duck, oysters, and sweet potatoes. A lack of furniture proved to be no problem in the crowded space, as the chassis of a 10-inch Columbiad served as a table. Carpetbags, sandbags, valises, stands of grapeshot, and even cannonballs were used for chairs. Through this holiday cheer "the hardships of life were greatly alleviated," but the banquet's centerpiece was yet another mute reminder of the war: It was a punch bowl made from half of a huge shell, some fifteen inches in diameter and set in a flattened sandbag. The day was not without some bloodshed, however: Two privates in the 1st South Carolina Artillery were slightly wounded when an old shell detonated.[46]

Charlestonians, meanwhile, had been awakened that morning by the worst day of the city's bombardment thus far. Far from a silent night, five guns on Morris Island had erupted shortly after midnight, their shells scarring the heavens in unholy flight. The artillery hurtled in through the morning, damaging several buildings, before ceasing early in the afternoon; about 150 rounds were hurled at the city. There also had been gunfire in the distance that morning as Union gunboats on the Stono River sparred with Confederate artillery.

Most of the Yankee troops on the nearby islands, however, enjoyed a day off and meals of boiled ham and roast turkey. The bluecoats also celebrated the day with sack races, wheelbarrow races, target-shooting contests, and greased pole climbing. Some men opened boxes sent from home, hoping any edible contents weren't spoiled. A few miles away, Admiral Dahlgren spent a quiet holiday, still looking for replacement ironclads to appear on the waves. "No merry Christmas for I am weary with waiting for the new monitors," he scrawled in his journal. Additional monitors or not, the admiral remained in a tough position, much of it created by his own hesitancy to act. Even if he had received the reinforcements by now, it is questionable if he would have attacked, since he faced the unknown element of the harbor obstructions. Also on his mind was Welles's order for him not to take any great risk, as well as the results of the April assault that had scuttled Du Pont's career; he did not want to sail to a similar fate. His renowned colleague, Adm. David Dixon Porter, would later write of the Charleston operation that "It was certainly the hardest task undertaken by the Navy during the war." But this would have been little solace to the despondent Dahlgren that Christmas.[47]

In New York City, readers of *Harper's New Monthly Magazine* flipped to page two of the December issue to read "Twilight On Fort Sumter— August 24, 1863," a poem gloating about the devastating effects of the summer bombardment. The piece included an illustration of the shattered fort with a drooping and tattered flag, as if Satan's minions had taken every Rebel soldier who dared set foot there. The poet, R. H. Stoddard, concluded his work:

> Now—O look at Sumter now,
> In the gloom!
> Mark its scarred and shattered walls,
> (Hark! The ruined rampart falls!)
> There's a justice that appalls
> In its doom;
> For this blasted spot of earth
> Where Rebellion had its birth
> Is its tomb!
> And when Sumter sinks at last
> From the heavens, that shrink aghast,
> Hell will rise in grim derision, and make room![48]

The *Richmond Daily Dispatch*, meanwhile, thanked Beauregard for his defense of Charleston and needled the Yankees for being unable to take the city—not to mention Sumter—despite the finest military technology of the age. Beauregard "has entitled himself to the gratitude and admiration of the country by his magnificent defence," it said.

Under his auspices it has withstood triumphantly such a combination of naval and military engineering as was never before brought to bear upon any fortified place. . . . The boasted skill of the best engineer in the United States army, the terrific armaments with which his fortifications were supplied, and the naval monsters which co-operated with the land forces, have for more than four months expended all their power upon the Palmetto city, and still its flag floats in proud defiance. . . . Where is your Swamp Angel? Where is your Greek fire? Where are your monitors? Where is your Gillmore? And after all, to find out that Charleston cannot be taken. That even Fort Sumter cannot be taken! That all the enormous mass of iron hurled upon it has only made it stronger and more impregnable! We can almost hear the Yankees gnashing their teeth and yelling in impotent rages, as Charleston looks serenely down upon the baffled malice of these fiends in the shape of men.[49]

Elliott, meanwhile, was pushing for an "iron shield" to help protect the casemate battery—better known as the three-gun battery—established in October. So far, his efforts had been futile, even as he planned to mount another battery, this one at the northwest pan coupe. All of these guns would bear on the channel between Sumter and Moultrie, but they would need the iron's extra protection to hopefully withstand the Federals' powerful artillery from land and sea. Elliott had not pressed the issue during the bombardment, but by December 30 he wanted to ensure that this was a priority project. "The application of this armor" would transform a position that could only endure a short cannonade to "one of comparative invulnerability," he wrote, "and by its very moral effect will act most powerfully upon the enemy in our favor. I am perfectly confident that this iron can be procured by vigorous and energetic measures."

Incredibly, the Sumter garrison also completed another back-breaking effort in the year's closing days. For communication purposes, a tunnel, or "gallery" as Johnson described it, was built through the massive mound of debris that lay in a long ridge between the western front, where the fort's headquarters was located, and the ruins of the north and northeast walls, where the three-gun battery was posted. For some four weeks men burrowed through this compact conglomeration of shattered brick, wrecked guns and equipment, splintered wood, twisted iron, and chunks of concrete weighing tons. It was essentially a mining operation, the workers digging, sawing, and chopping a space three feet wide and six feet high and bolstering it with heavy timber and planking. There were delays due to cave-ins, but the gallery was finally finished, running a distance of 275 feet, almost the length of a modern football field. At the same time, the defenders constructed a 50-foot-long tunnel in another area of the fort.[50]

By December 29, the *Montauk* was out of service, yet another blow to the Union fleet. With the *Weehawken*'s loss, this left the seventy-eight or so vessels in the squadron with only five monitors. On a cloudy, rainy New Year's Eve, Dahlgren sat in his cabin reflecting on the past year's momentous events and his life. The pinnacle had obviously been his rise to admiral; the nadir his inability to get by Sumter and smother Charleston's wharves with his ironclads and the rest of his fleet. "Thus endeth the old year 1863," he wrote, "one that has witnessed my highest advancement, but not my happiness, for I have been loaded with responsibilities that no one could hope to lead to a favorable issue; the best possible result of which would ruin the reputation of any man. And now what is there to look forward to?"[51]

CHAPTER 10

"Fort Sumter Can Be Taken at Any Time"—1864

New Year's Day 1864 was one "of unusual quiet," at Sumter, not a gun on either side fired from the islands and batteries as a cold, heavy storm cloaked the coast. The relative calm continued in the following days, only occasional cannon blasts violating the uneasy peace since the end of the Second Great Bombardment. "From her ruins rose the Rebel flag . . . ," a Federal officer at Cummings Point wrote of Sumter's ravaged walls at this time, "while behind it there were stout hearts and arms to defend them; we couldn't take the ruined fort if we would."

An occasional Union round whistled into Charleston in the year's first week or so, and Yankee work parties were active on Morris Island, as always. Rain and fog kept Rebel lookouts from obtaining accurate information about the enemy fleet on some days, and the regular rotation of troops garrisoning Sumter was ongoing. The foul weather caused some concern for Stephen Elliott that the fog would be used as cover for another Federal landing, but this did not occur.

The Confederates were ready, however, having laid a defensive boom in front of the sea and eastern portions of the gorge faces on the night of January 3–4, extending the boom emplaced some six weeks earlier. As this work was done the men were subjected to a few shells of friendly fire from Fort Johnson, based on a jumpy sentinel there, but there was no damage or injuries. Still, the early-morning excitement was not over for Sumter's tired soldiers and laborers. About 4:20 AM, a guard boat sounded the alarm that a monitor and two small boats were approaching the fort. The garrison was turned out, lining the parapet in the bitter cold until day-break illuminated a thick fog but no intruders. The milky conditions were so bad on the night of the fifth that Elliott deployed ten times the number of sentinels usually on duty, but again the Federals did not come.[1]

With the weather gradually getting better and the Union inactivity, Elliott felt he could safely take a week's leave after more than four months of tough and unrelenting duty at Sumter. When he left on the night of January 20, Capt. Francis T. Miles of the Charleston Battalion, assigned to the 27th South Carolina Volunteers, assumed temporary command. The highlight of Miles's tenure was a night visit to the fort by a small group of Charleston belles escorted by an officer. The ladies explored Sumter's labyrinth of destroyed casemates and tottering arch-ways, apparently maintaining their feminine composure as they climbed to the top of the walls. "Favored by mild weather, by a clear moonlight night, and no firing at all, the visit could not have been better timed," Johnson related.

For the Union navy, December had been a miserable month with the bad weather, the loss of *Weehawken*, the further debilitation of the squadron, and the delay in receiving more ironclads. The melancholy shadowed Dahlgren into the new year. On January 1 the admiral wrote that "if the monitors were ready I might get a chance to try an entrance to Charleston. But those here are actually not repaired, and I am at a loss to know why." His son, Ulric, was still with the squadron, going out on scouts with Federal naval patrols in small boats.[2]

For about two weeks after the Christmas Day shelling, Charleston itself was not subjected to a very heavy bombardment. In fact, from August 21, 1863, through January 5, lookouts in the steeple of St. Michael's Church recorded a total of 472 projectiles launched at the city, killing five people. Though the barrages in the early part of January were daily, the most projectiles launched at the city in a day was 45. This changed over the course of nine days beginning on January 12, when the Federals fired a total of some 1,500 rounds at the city. It would be less intense, but still troublesome, for the rest of the month. "Fire of enemy on city for last two days has been almost continuous, doing but little damage," Beauregard wrote on the fourteenth. Over 100 shots had been launched at Charleston both days, but there had been no firing at Sumter.

The shelling of the city had intensified the next day—some projectiles whistling in from guns almost five miles away—but the punishment did not prevent Beauregard from embarking on the sixteenth for Savannah, where he would spend more than two weeks tending to military matters there. Elliott returned to duty at Sumter on the night of January 27 and was impressed by the repair work done since he left. Under Miles, the engineers and laborers had worked on the parade ground, which had been an unhealthy reservoir of water due to the shelling and excavation for sandbags. The water stood in holes and puddles in the parade, which had been dug out some three feet below the high-water mark. Overcrowded quarters due to the December explosion and fire, along with the stagnant pools, contributed to unsanitary conditions that fueled the threat of a meningitis outbreak at the fort. While some of this soggy expanse dried up due to evaporation, the workmen had covered a majority of it with brick and lime in Elliott's absence. Dirt and debris also were added to the parade, raising it about half a foot. "This is an improvement for the present in the sanitary condition of the work," the returning commander reported on the twenty-eighth. A drainage system utilizing a newly dug well and a pump to draw off the tainted water and empty it into the harbor also was constructed.

On a negative note, Elliott was still having trouble with his project to have a protective iron shield built for the three-gun battery. The navy had supplied the necessary iron plating, but a lack of competent mechanics was preventing the work from being done. Contractors in the city were already so busy with other military assignments that they couldn't take on any other tasks. Work also was progressing in mounting three guns in the fort's northwest casemates, and Beauregard wanted a bell alarm system installed at Sumter. When completed, the system would have four stations on the crest of the ruins. Pulling any of the alarms there rang bells deep within the fort, including Elliott's quarters, alerting troops to a threat.[3]

The first twenty-eight days of the year had been comparatively dull for Sumter, the Federals firing at the fort only on eight days during the period. That ceased about 9:00 PM on the twenty-eighth when Union mortars on Morris unleashed a barrage, as if to welcome Elliott back to his post. The shelling was so severe that a steamer whose supplies for Sumter were being unloaded at the dock was ordered to return to Charleston rather than risk being sunk. More than 100 rounds were hurled at the fort, and daybreak on Friday, January 29, would bring even more. Some 150 Parrott and Columbiad projectiles rained in that day, primarily targeting the south angle. The cannonade was conducted despite foggy and misty conditions that prevented Elliott's lookouts from even seeing the Union vessels riding silently at anchor.

The pounding subsided at dark, but there had been some drama that afternoon. About 3:00 PM Sumter's flagstaff was splintered by a shot, but Pvt. F. Schafer of Company A, Lucas's Battalion, didn't allow the flag to be down for very long. He snatched the banner and climbed to the top of a traverse, waving it toward the enemy before he and three other soldiers raised it on another staff while under fire. The men "were exposed to a rapid and accurate fire of shells," Elliott related. "At the close of the scene Schafer, springing from a cloud of the smoke and dust of the bursting shell, stood long waving his hat in triumph. It was a most gallant deed, and the effect upon the garrison was most inspiring." The shelling on the twenty-eighth and twenty-ninth resulted in two Confederates wounded and scant damage to the fort.[4]

"Gregg [actually Battery Strong] has resumed a deliberate fire of single shells at Sumter," Dahlgren wrote on the twenty-ninth. "It is high time." A few days earlier, the admiral had bid farewell to his son, Ully, who was returning north, healed enough to soon be back on active duty. It was near sunset on the twenty-second when the Dahlgrens said their goodbyes on the *Massachusetts*. As the admiral's barge pulled away from the steamer, he waved repeatedly to his son through the fading light. Dahlgren would later write this was "the last time I ever saw my beloved boy."

Sumter's punishment continued on the morning of Saturday, January 30, the blue cannoneers aiming at the west angle with some 160 rounds for the day sent toward the "glorious old ruin," as one newsman described it. Three of Sumter's defenders were wounded in all of this. Again the shelling halted after sundown, but the Federals turned their attention toward Charleston after dark. About 9:00 PM, shells began to pelt the city, the sporadic bombardment lasting through Sunday night; fewer than 200 projectiles reached the city.[5]

Also on the thirtieth, three deserters from the 27th South Carolina reached the Union lines by boat and surrendered. All had served at Sumter at one time or another and gave the Federals more details about the inner workings of the fort. In addition to describing some of the defenses, the deserters spoke about the garrison's rations. The defenders got coffee and a "moderate" supply of hard bread was stored in the bombproofs. On occasion, fresh-cooked beef was brought down from Charleston. There was a permanent garrison of three hundred troops, one-third of whom were changed every twelve days. In general, morale was quite low among the Confederates defending the city, the deserters said. The blockade and other war fortunes were also exacting a heavy price on Charlestonians, with rice at twenty-two dollars a bushel, bacon at four dollars per pound, and corn at eighteen to twenty dollars a bushel.

Sumter received a shipload of lumber and sand overnight on January 30–31 and a 42-pounder was placed in the northwest casemate, ready to be mounted. The west angle was again the Yankees' target on the thirty-first, the labor force having shored it as much as possible before dawn. By day's end, some 130 projectiles had been thrown at Sumter, resulting in little damage and no casualties. There was no firing that night, allowing a steamer and a schooner to reach the fort with full cargoes of sand. The most action overnight as the calendar flipped to February was a mysterious musket shot, which prompted the defenders to temporarily scramble to their posts. January had indeed come in as a lamb and departed like a lion, almost all of the 600 or so shells directed at the fort coming in the last four days of the month.[6]

By mid- to late January, the Confederates at Charleston and Savannah began receiving reports of enemy movements, by land and sea, which pointed to some type of offensive somewhere on the southeastern coast. The objective was unknown, but matters became crystal clear on February 7, when Union infantry went ashore at Jacksonville, Florida, occupying the town. Gillmore was making an effort to regain control of the state, and some five thousand U.S. troops from the Charleston coast were among those shipped south to aid in the operation. Because of this threat, Beauregard—who had returned from Savannah on February 3—had no choice but to send men from Charleston and Savannah to bolster his weak and thinly spread forces in Florida. Compounding his problems was the fact that the enlistments of many Georgia and South Carolina soldiers were about to expire, and he also was being pressed to send men to the Army of Tennessee, recuperating in north Georgia after the Chattanooga debacle. The Union operations in Florida apparently contributed to a lull in the action against Charleston and Fort Sumter during this period.[7]

"There has been no firing on the fort today," Elliott reported on February 1. The highlight of that day, at least for Johnson and his work-force, was the arrival of a steamer and a schooner, both with cargoes of sand. In fact, much of the month would be free of enemy fire, the fort sustaining only an irregular shelling from Morris Island over sixteen days. Much of Elliott's time was spent in observing the Union fleet and report-ing any changes in the number or location of its vessels. Impressed with its "strange, silent grandeur," John Johnson gave a vivid description of Sumter at night during that winter:

> To a beholder looking down from the rim of the ruin, all within seems alike dark and gloomy, save when a chance shower of sparks, blown out from a smouldering fire left in the parade, lights up for a moment some great, rugged blocks of brickwork and the pools of stagnant water into which they were tum-bled. . . . Lanterns here and there glance across the spacious enclosure as, borne by unseen hands, they light the way—some for long files of men toiling with heavy timbers or bags of sand over the roughest footing and up steep, crumbling, dangerous slopes; some to direct the heaping of material over damaged hiding-places, repaired for perhaps the fiftieth time since the fir-ing began . . . ; others, flashing through chance crevices in the ruined casemates, tell of secret galleries of communication bur-rowing deep and mining their way slowly under hills of rub-bish. . . . Halfway up the sloping ruins . . . which resemble most the interior of an ancient amplitheatre [sic], the guards are posted in groups, dimly seen wrapped in blankets, sitting around a little fire allowed to warm, but to give no light. Higher yet are the sentinels peering into the night.

The garrison received a morale boost in early February when the ladies of Aiken, South Carolina, collected two hundred dollars through donations and sent it to Elliott "to be spent on his command as he saw fit." The soldiers had to be touched in learning that eight dollars of the total was raised by "two little girls" who had raffled some of their toys for them.[8]

On February 8, the Richmond government issued thanks to Beauregard and his troops for the defense of Charleston. In contrast, and in mock honor of Lincoln's birthday on February 12, Sumter's garrison completed the mounting of three big guns in the left flank. The pieces, two rifled 42-pounders and a rifled 8-inch Columbiad, were put in casemates next to the northwest angle and the new sally port to guard a portion of the harbor not commanded by artillery at Battery Bee on Sullivan's Island or Fort Johnson on James Island. Now with two three-gun batteries, the Confederates began referring to this new one as the "West Battery" and the other as the "East Battery."

There was minimal artillery activity from the Federals on the thirteenth, but the Confederates were impressed by one well-aimed enemy blast that day. As the garrison was lowering its flag, a Union round clipped the flagstaff near its top, Elliott noting that "it was regarded generally as being a good shot." Yet matters at the fort were generally so calm during this period that Elliott reported the appearance of two ladies seen on the parapet of Fort Putnam on the sixteenth; he added that later in the day they visited the *New Ironsides*. The rotation of infantry units at Sumter continued, but dwindling manpower in Charleston's overall defenses—due to Gillmore's Florida offensive and action elsewhere—necessitated some changes. The 25th and 27th South Carolina had been bearing much of the rotation burden, but as of February 14, the 11th and 21st South Carolina also would be used in garrisoning Sumter.[9]

The Confederate submarine *H.L. Hunley* made naval history on the night of February 17 when it ventured out from Breach Inlet and sank the blockader *Housatonic* with a spar torpedo. Five Union sailors died in what was the first submarine attack in history to sink an enemy warship. Because the torpedo ignited below the surface, there was little noise and no visible flames to alert either the rest of the Union fleet or the Confederates ashore. The *Hunley*, her commander Lt. George Dixon, and her seven crewmen, meanwhile, did not return to port that night. Hazy weather conditions prevented the Southerners from realizing that a Union vessel was down until February 20, the sinking evidently the work of the still-missing sub. The Confederates would not know the identity of the *Hunley*'s victim for more than a week, and Fort Sumter would play a key role in solving the mystery.[10]

The Union strike into Florida, meanwhile, had been blunted with a decisive defeat at Olustee on the twentieth. Over the next few days Gillmore's troops would retreat to the safety of Jacksonville's defenses. February 22 brought a rare day of brief—but distant—harmony as both sides at Charleston celebrated George Washington's birthday with artillery salutes. John Johnson described the interlude as "one of those pleasant incidents which serve to break through the clouds of war as with a gleam of light and peace." The Union fleet—with "all colors flying," Elliott noted—and Morris Island batteries joined the Confederate forts and gunboats in the booming observance, which must have seemed all too familiar to the ears of war-weary Charlestonians. The mutual recognition of Washington's birthday was the first of the war by the opposing sides here, although both had fired salutes in 1861, when Anderson's men held Sumter. But the war did not take a holiday, Rebel mortars on Sullivan's shooting over Elliott's defenders and playing on Battery Strong.

The day also was the anniversary of the organization of the Washington Light Infantry, which had suffered the tragic loss of their comrades at Sumter less than four months earlier. Soldiers from two companies of the W.L.I.—which was now a part of the 25th South Carolina Volunteers—were posted at the fort; James Carson, one of the men's favorite officers, was still on hand as well. With Elliott's permission, these Carolinians held a modest banquet, with music from a favorite brass band, toasts, speeches, and songs. The gathering was held in repaired casemates on the western flank "with more elegance and completeness" than the Christmas dinner in the headquarters mess. The bell alarm system was also in place by now and would be used at Sumter for the remainder of the war.[11]

The enigma of the *Hunley* attack was partially solved on the night of Friday, February 26, when a small boat from the USS *Nipsic* was captured by one of Sumter's picket vessels. From the six Yankee prisoners, the Confederates learned that the enemy vessel sunk by the submarine was the *Housatonic*. While Charleston exhilarated in the dispatch from Colonel Elliott, the celebration was tempered by the fact that Dixon and his brave crew were still unaccounted for. The excitement was also dampened by the "undiminished vigor" of the Yankee shells plowing into the city; the

Mercury reported 106 on the twenty-seventh and 100 the next day. "At midnight the bombardment was still going on very briskly, one shell being thrown every five minutes," the paper said on Monday, February 29. "The report from Fort Sumter is, 'All quiet!'" The boast rang hollow in general, since bluecoat gunners had thrown some 1,727 rounds at Charleston in February.

On orders from the Navy Department, Dahlgren sailed north in the *Harvest Moon* on the night of February 27, heading for Washington to discuss the military situation at Charleston. The squadron would be under the temporary command of Capt. Stephen C. Rowan, the skipper of the *New Ironsides*. "You have had so much experience in the duties at Charleston that it is needless for me to go into detail respecting them," the admiral wrote to Rowan. Essentially, Rowan was to maintain a strict blockade, cooperate with the army, and continue active operations against the enemy if the opportunity arose and odds favored success. Dahlgren and Rowan were not on the best of terms, the admiral believing that Rowan had been hesitant to put the *New Ironsides* into combat during the Charleston campaign. There likely was additional friction since Rowan had more experience but Dahlgren had been promoted to admiral over him.[12]

Wednesday, March 2, would be a devastating day for two enemy commanders from the Charleston sector, personal tragedies hundreds of miles apart haunting them to their graves years later.

Aboard the *Harvest Moon*, Dahlgren steamed up the winding Potomac River that day, going ashore at Alexandria, Virginia. That night he met with Navy Secretary Welles and Gustavus Fox, the department's assistant secretary. As the admiral settled into Washington that evening, Col. Ulric Dahlgren was riding with his troopers through the Virginia countryside—and nearing a deadly ambush. Ully was involved in a Union cavalry raid against Richmond, aiming to take the Rebel capital and free hundreds of Federal soldiers imprisoned there. The raid had been thwarted, and on March 4 Admiral Dahlgren received a note from Lincoln that Ully was missing in action after the ambush and ensuing fight. In the coming days, the admiral conferred with various political and military luminaries, including Lincoln, Secretary of State William Seward, Welles, Fox, and others, but his thoughts were clearly with his son.

Amid the haze of Dahlgren's nervous-father anxiety, Fox told the admiral that he was averse to any attack at Charleston unless it was guaranteed to be successful. Fox also wanted the long-awaited new monitors promised to Dahlgren to be sent to Adm. David Farragut at Mobile. After operations were wrapped up there, the monitors would go to Charleston. His senses already frayed, Dahlgren was unwilling to go along with this, telling Welles that if this were to happen, he wanted to be relieved of squadron command. The secretary, however, told Dahlgren that he wanted him to remain at the helm in Charleston.

Throughout these discussions, Dahlgren still awaited word of Ully's fate. By March 7 there were reports that he had been captured, but these proved false. The next morning, however, Lincoln called for him and broke the terrible news—Ully had been killed. "Merciful Father!" a disbelieving Dahlgren cried in his journal. "Am I to lose my brave son? Not yet, not yet, I pray. Let me see him once more." But Richmond papers received that night confirmed Ulric's death. Salting the family's agony, Ully's body had been mutilated—some ghoul severing one of his fingers to steal a gold ring—and the Confederates contended that papers found on Dahlgren contained instructions for the raiders to kill Jefferson Davis and Confederate cabinet members.[13]

A rival commander in the Charleston sector also was having his heart torn out. Beauregard was in Florida in early March when he received word that his second wife, Caroline, had died in New Orleans on March 2. She had been seriously ill for about two years, and he had not been able to go to her because New Orleans had been in Union hands since late April 1862. Throughout their time apart they had managed to correspond, but Beauregard had not received a letter from Caroline since December 1863. Beauregard immediately returned to Charleston, knowing that her family would write to him there about her passing. Despite his mourning, he still put the Confederacy's cause first, writing in a letter, "Our Independence shall have cost me dearly; but our country is welcome to the sacrifice."[14]

Despite these personal losses, the war had not stopped at Fort Sumter and Charleston, although there was little shelling directed at the fort in early March. Matters were so quiet that on the fourteenth Elliott noted the presence of two ladies and a party of U.S. officers placing a telescope on Battery Strong. During the first week or so of the month, Sumter's commander had been away again, leaving Capt. Samuel H.

Wilds of the 21st South Carolina in charge for several days. All of the infantry at Sumter were relieved overnight on March 12–13. The replacements—troops from the 21st, 22nd, 23rd, 25th, and 27th South Carolina—joined 61 men of the 1st South Carolina Artillery, giving the garrison a strength of 352.

Due to severe damage to the scarp wall at the fort's east angle, the Confederates had spent considerable time during the winter on strengthening this sector. The wall had been bolstered outside by a "cribwork or grillage" that added ten feet to its thickness. It consisted of mounds of debris from the fort fronted by pine timber on the bottom and palmetto logs on top, complete with embrasures for three casemates. The "Palmetto Shield," as the Southerners called this structure, had been erected with as much secrecy as possible, even in such an exposed position.

Several other improvements made in March were noted by the Federals. Union colonel W. H. Davis, the Morris Island commander, reported a traverse built with sandbags had been constructed at the fort's northeast corner, and a large quantity of railroad iron had been embedded close to the water's edge at the same angle. The latter was apparently to serve as an obstacle against small-boat assaults. On the debris of the south face about halfway up were a series of posts some ten feet apart, which were the supports for a wire fence. Davis estimated Sumter's garrison to be 250–300 men who were relieved every fifteen days, based on his observations. By mid-March, the shield was completed and also attracting the attention of Yankee lookouts.[15]

There was a show of artillery might by the Federals against this position on March 15, some 143 projectiles, mostly Parrott rounds, pelting Sumter beginning that morning. Four or five soldiers and a laborer were wounded, and the cribwork sustained some damage before the shelling subsided at sunset. A brief barrage resumed against the east angle the next morning and a scattering of rounds was directed at Sumter over the next few days. A brisk fire was also concentrated on Charleston on March 19, the Confederates recorded. Gillmore that day broached the idea of moving the ten thousand troops of his X Corps to a more active combat zone, an option already being considered by the Union brass.

Wild rumors also abounded among the Southerners that Admiral Farragut was now commanding the Union squadron off Charleston. "There is reason to believe he is on our coast, if he has not already assumed command of the fleet," one newspaper reported. This was

Palmetto logs help reinforce Sumter's channel-side defenses in 1864.
LIBRARY OF CONGRESS

utterly false, since Farragut remained off Mobile. Still in Washington, Dahlgren spent the rest of March grieving and trying to retrieve Ully's remains, but the firestorm kindled in Richmond by the supposed assassination plot against Davis made this extremely difficult. Amid this awful time, the new monitors that he had been expecting for six months were ready in late March. Now, however, it appeared they may not be bound for Charleston *or* Mobile. General Grant was preparing to launch his massive spring campaign, and the ironclads might be needed to support Union movements in Virginia.

Despite the shelling on the nineteenth, the Union bombardment of Charleston dwindled to only 325 rounds in March. Since the previous

November, just under 4,000 projectiles had been thrown at the city, the Confederates estimating that 2,550 had reached their target. Still, some warned that Charleston should not be lulled into complacency by the Federals' lack of offense in the first weeks of the year. "There is danger in the feeling of security excited by the present condition of Charleston," the *Columbia Guardian* reported. "It is very common to hear the opinion expressed that the siege has been virtually abandoned. . . . The Yankees never will give up Charleston while the war lasts. It is the most coveted prize in the Confederacy, Richmond is not as much so."[16]

The early days of April were uneventful at Sumter, although two monitors did steam in and open a slow shelling of the fort about 5:00 PM on the third. But April and May would be a blur of troop movements as war developments on larger stages sapped the Rebels' manpower from Charleston, Savannah, and the Florida outposts. These soldiers were now needed in north Georgia, where a Union army under Maj. Gen. William T. Sherman was knifing south from Tennessee, possibly targeting Atlanta. Reinforcements also had to be sent to Virginia, where the giant Union offensive was soon expected to boil over in blood that spring and summer. The Confederacy needed every man it could get to send to these critical danger points. And since the war was stalemated in the steamy Florida wilds, Savannah's sawgrass marshes, and Charleston's sunbleached islands, Beauregard's department would be among those drastically siphoned of its troops.

Likewise, Gillmore and his forces were affected; the general received orders on April 4 to report to Fort Monroe, Virginia, with as many of his X Corps units as could be spared from the Charleston lines. The troops were to bring with them their "arms, baggage and transportation," not a movement that could be accomplished overnight.[17] The first elements of the X Corps began boarding transports near Hilton Head on the evening of the thirteenth for the voyage north to Virginia, where they would join the U.S. Army of the James. Gillmore hoped to transfer from seven to ten thousand troops over the next week.

Any notion that the Yankees still in their positions were getting lax was dispelled on the thirteenth with a deadly lesson at Sumter. Blue gunners at Cummings Point were sparring with their gray counterparts on James Island—a lethal and long-range "practice" one Southerner noted.

Sumter itself had received only a few shells over the previous few days. The thirteenth, however, was the third anniversary of Major Anderson's submission; that morning, Elliott had requested permission to fire a thirteen-gun salute at noon to mark the occasion. Beauregard had approved the request, and Sumter fired "a defiant salute" to commemorate the event, no doubt incensing the Federals.

Wanting to observe the duel between the islands, a Confederate Signal Corps soldier named Joseph P. Huger ascended to Sumter's southwest angle, always one of the fort's most conspicuous points. Huger had displayed promise as a soldier, but on this day his enthusiasm got the best of him. Seeing a Rebel round make a successful strike, the teenager carelessly waved his cap in celebration. An eagle-eyed Yank at Cummings Point spotted him and a projectile from a 30-pounder Parrott was momentarily winging its way toward Sumter; "the shell exploded with great precision and took off his head." The Huger family already had sacrificed more than most for the cause. Joseph's older brother had been killed at Chickamauga, while another brother had perished from disease in the same campaign. The young signalman "who has yielded up his life amidst the proud ruins of Sumter, will not be forgotten while the memory of the defence lingers in the hearts of our people," the *Mercury* said.[18]

The bombardment of Charleston itself, meanwhile, had dwindled to only about forty-five shots a day, but the lower part of the city was largely a ghost town by now. Residents had either fled inland or found refuge north of Calhoun Street or along the Ashley River, out of range of the enemy guns. Elliott was away from Sumter for about eleven days—whether he was on leave or on assignment elsewhere is unclear—beginning around April 14 or 15. The fort's temporary commander was Capt. John C. Mitchel of the 1st South Carolina Artillery Regiment. Mitchel had been second-in-command during most of Elliott's tenure at the fort.

Also during this time, the Charleston Confederates tried what would be one of the early attempts at photographic intelligence involving Sumter. Beauregard had Charleston photographer George Cook take images of the drawings Lt. John Key had made of the fort's interior the previous December while visiting Sumter with artist Conrad Wise Chapman. On April 17, Beauregard dispatched two of these photographs to Adjutant General Cooper in Richmond to give the Confederate brass a visualization of the fort's devastation. Beauregard explained that the images would have been sent sooner but for the "want of proper materials and instruments" and described Key as "a young artist of great promise." He added that Sumter was "now much stronger for defensive purposes than represented by these views, its interior being well arranged for musketry and light artillery fire." Sumter also had seven guns—five Columbiads and two rifled 42-pounders—mounted in casemates and trained on the Sullivan's Island channel, according to Beauregard, meaning the Confederates had added a gun to the two three-gun batteries, or the general had inaccurate information. It's unclear which was the case. Either way, Cooper received the photographic "views," as he also referred to them, and forwarded them to the Secretary of War, where they were lost to history.[19]

In Washington, Admiral Dahlgren languished in his festering grief, frustration, and inactivity as April faded. He still had been unable to have Ully's remains returned for burial, and the additional monitors he was anticipating to join his squadron were still apparently being sent elsewhere. The lack of these new ironclads meant, to the admiral's thinking, that he would have to "postpone any serious attack on the interior defenses of the harbor," he wrote Gideon Welles on April 21. As an alternative, Dahlgren proposed an army–navy operation against Long Island (present-day Isle of Palms) just north of Sullivan's Island. If the Federals could take Long Island, they could focus on assaulting Fort Moultrie and the other works on Sullivan's without having to face the big guns aimed at the harbor entrance. "If Sullivan's Island can be occupied," the admiral said, "it would enable the ironclads to maintain position in the harbor permanently, and in the end drive the rebels from Charleston."

Dahlgren's plan made the rounds of the highest echelons of the Union brass—navy and army—including Secretary of War Edwin Stanton. Welles noted that the seizure of these islands would provide the fleet access to interior waterways and vital protection during the upcoming hurricane season. Still, there was little enthusiasm otherwise for the proposal, especially since the army's strength on the coast was being significantly weakened by the X Corps' departure. Henry Halleck himself got down to the brass tacks of the matter. "If the ironclads and the large number of troops off Charleston for the last year could not take and hold Sullivan's Island, how can they expect to do it with forces diminished more than one half?" he wrote to Grant on April 24. "I am satisfied that Admiral Dahlgren's letter was intended simply as an excuse in advance for the inability of the ironclads to accomplish anything against Charleston."

Dahlgren met with Welles on the twenty-eighth, telling him "that he could not expect any results unless he sent me the monitors that were promised." Later that day the admiral had a conference with his old friend Lincoln. "I told him also that I had too little force; that he could only expect me to hold on," Dahlgren later wrote. "'O yes,' he [Lincoln] said, that 'was all he expected.'" That night the admiral boarded the *Harvest Moon* for the return voyage to Charleston. He still had been unable to retrieve Ully's body.[20]

Beauregard left Charleston on April 20, ordered north as part of Lee's plans to repel the anticipated Union offensive in Virginia. He had asked for leave due to illness, but promptly withdrew the request so that he could "obey any order for the good of the service." Beauregard was replaced in department command by Maj. Gen. Samuel Jones, a Virginian and career soldier who had seen action from the fighting at First Bull Run to his time heading the Department of West Virginia. Beauregard thanked his men for their service, telling them Jones now deserved their confidence and devotion. He closed by stating: "Should you ever become discouraged, remember that a people from whom have sprung such soldiers as those who defended Wagner and Sumter can never be subjugated in a war of independence." The Creole had not seen the last of Sumter or Charleston.[21]

Elliott returned to Sumter on the night of April 25 to take over from Mitchel and was impressed by the improvements made while he was away. "The defensive arrangements of the fort have during my absence made considerable progress, especially upon the sea face," he wrote on the twenty-sixth.

The sporadic fire from the Federals increased on the afternoon of April 28, some 50 shots thrown at the fort. The shelling intensified to more than 200 rounds the next day and into the night, but no casualties or damage were reported. April 30 saw approximately 170 projectiles launched before the Federals stopped for the night. For the month, the fort was shelled on twelve days. There was scant firing against Sumter on May 1, the main action of the day being the regular rotation of a portion of the garrison. That night about 150 men of the 6th, 19th, and 27th

Georgia relieved the same number of troops from Hagood's brigade. Enemy mortar shelling picked up on the third, with more than 90 rounds thrown, evidently to prevent the Confederates from working on the boom in front of the fort. Sumter's telegraph service was also restored that day after being out for a short time.[22]

Stephen Elliott's service at Sumter ended at this time, as he was ordered to Virginia and assigned to lead the Holcombe Legion, a South Carolina regiment. Elliott was familiar with his new command, especially since some of its troops had been assigned to the fort's garrison in late February. Shells still screeched into Sumter on May 4 as Elliott was replaced at Sumter by twenty-six-year-old John Mitchel, the bantam and battle-wizened captain who already had an admirer in John Johnson. "Few young Confederate officers impressed me more favorably," the engineer wrote. "He was a born soldier, a man of nerve, finely tempered as steel, with habits of order, quick perception, and decision."

Mitchel's father, also named John, was a famous Irish activist and newspaper editor. Convicted of treason against the Crown, the elder Mitchel had been banished to Tasmania, but he and the family managed to immigrate to the United States in 1853. The Mitchels were pro-Southern in their views, and with war looming John and his two brothers had joined the Confederacy. One brother, Willie, was killed during Pickett's Charge at Gettysburg and the other, James, would eventually lose an arm in the fighting around Richmond.

John Mitchel, meanwhile, received a lieutenant's appointment and joined the 1st South Carolina at Fort Moultrie, doing yeoman's work in the 1861 bombardment of Sumter. His company had been among the first Confederate troops to occupy Sumter after Anderson's surrender. Mitchel had served admirably commanding artillery at Fort Johnson and Battery Simkins. "He was considered one of the most vigilant, conscientious and active officers of his splendid regiment," a Charlestonian wrote, adding that he had endured "his full share in all the dangers and fatigues of the siege." Mitchel also had participated in the January 1863 capture of the gunboat *Isaac Smith* on the Stono River and had performed well—though unsuccessfully—in trying to thwart the Union thrust against Morris Island on July 10, 1863. He was a close friend of Alfred Rhett, serving as his second in the bloodless duel with Arnoldus Vanderhorst. "The new commander of Fort Sumter is quite young to have attained so important a position," the *Mercury* said. "Modest as he is brave . . . he lacks but the opportunity, we are sure, to add new laurels to those which he has already won."[23]

Change was in the air for the Federals as well. Gillmore himself sailed north on May 1 to join his troops, relinquishing department command to Brig. Gen. John P. Hatch, a forty-two-year-old New Yorker who graduated West Point in 1845. Hatch was a Mexican War veteran, and after garrison duty at several western outposts in peacetime he was commissioned brigadier general of volunteers in September 1861. He had tasted battle in the Shenandoah Valley and had been seriously wounded at South Mountain in September 1862 while leading a division. Since that time until coming to Charleston, Hatch had served in various administrative posts. He was in temporary command of the department until a higher-ranking and more experienced general could be assigned. "General Hatch is hardly the man for the place, but probably he is the best that can now be spared from the field," Halleck wrote to Grant on April 11.

Gillmore left Hatch with about sixteen thousand troops in the department, including about five thousand on Morris and Folly Islands, another five thousand spread between Port Royal and Fort Pulaski, and the rest in Florida.[24] The steamer carrying Gillmore north literally passed the *Harvest Moon* returning Dahlgren to his squadron, the admiral arriving at Port Royal on May 2. Other than the seasons, little had changed along the Carolina shore during his two-month absence.

Even as Sumter's leadership was in flux, General Jones on May 4 was trying to fill the desperately depleted ranks of Charleston's defenses. The ever-growing war demands in Virginia were such that he had been ordered to send every available man to reinforce Confederate forces there. Jones issued orders to create companies composed of clerks, quartermaster and commissary staff, adjutants, aides, and any other pencil pusher, hanger-on, or warm body who could tote a musket. The situation became so dire in the next two weeks that he called on Charleston's mayor for men from the city's fire battalion. He also asked Flag Officer John Tucker, commander of the naval forces, for help, saying that he could not "muster sufficient men to man all the guns in position."[25]

Also on the fourth, Dahlgren went ashore to confer with Hatch, where he received more fuel for his heightening anger against Gillmore. At the meeting was Brig. Gen. George H. Gordon, a combat-savvy West

Pointer and one of Gillmore's division commanders who was about to embark for an assignment in Florida. According to Dahlgren, Gordon told him that Gillmore encouraged and enjoyed the newspaper attacks on Dahlgren, Gillmore saying that the admiral would be the scapegoat for the Federals' inability to take Charleston. Dahlgren believed Gordon, lauding him in his journal: "His is patriotism, and honor, and honesty!" Gordon did not back off his claims, writing that "many misrepresentations about the navy—false statements, revised and corrected, to prejudice the public" went out from Morris Island on a daily basis. "Day by day these stories were circulated in Northern newspapers; day by day they grew meaner and more contemptible. . . . This senseless and bitter feud among those who ought to have sacrificed all personal feeling for the greater good of their country, paralyzed our efforts." The admiral called his monitor captains together on May 12 to discuss a possible attack on Sumter, but most of them balked, voting seven to two against the assault. The surrounding forts and batteries were too strong, they claimed. Hatch's artillerists were still busy during this period, their mortars occasionally throwing shells at Sumter to hinder any repairs.[26]

One of John Mitchel's first tasks as post commander on May 5 was the attempted recovery of a 7-inch rifle that had sunk near Sumter's wharf, apparently as it was loaded onto a vessel. He dispatched orders to Charleston that he needed two hundred feet of good rope "or Mr. [Adolphus] Lacoste and his appliances." (Lacoste had been the mastermind in salvaging the *Keokuk* guns.) The new commander also needed "some blank morning-report books." Sumter's armament still boasted the three Columbiads and three rifled 42-pounders of its pair of three-gun batteries. Artillery returns also showed the fort contained seven other smaller guns, but most of these pieces apparently were not functioning, weren't mounted, or were still to be removed from the rubble.

As of mid-May, the garrison consisted of 377 troops, the largest contingents including 159 men of the 20th South Carolina Volunteers and 110 soldiers in the 1st South Carolina Artillery. The 6th and 19th Georgia Volunteers rounded out the roster with 54 men each. Among their many duties, these Southerners were now always on alert against Union "boat infantry," which plied the waters close to the fort after nightfall. A howitzer blast usually drove them away, but the constant vigil added to the exhaustive drain on the defenders.[27]

From early to mid-May, the Federal batteries continued to needle Charleston with a few shells each day. This was not intended to do serious damage, but done "with the hope of annoying them and delaying the movements of the railroad trains," Hatch noted on the fourteenth. During the same period, Union mortars on the north end of Morris maintained fire "at intervals" against Sumter. This was punctuated by heavier barrages on May 13–14 when the fort was rocked by mortars, Columbiads, and rifled guns, aided by two of Dahlgren's monitors. A few shells were lobbed at Sumter's east angle on the morning of the thirteenth, and a pair of ironclads joined the fray that afternoon, the cannonade increasing. Mitchel was away temporarily—the reason is unclear—leaving the fort's command to Capt. C. W. Parker, also of the 1st Artillery. The lethal flying metal was annoying as always, but a boat carrying fresh water for the garrison had not come the previous night, leaving the Confederates with only enough water for the day. It was "absolutely necessary that she should be sent tonight," Parker noted.

By about 8:00 PM on the thirteenth, the Union batteries and monitors had combined to send more than four hundred rounds at Sumter. Damage to the interior was "trifling," Parker reported, adding that the lone casualty was a private who lost a foot to a shell fragment. The Confederates on James and Sullivan's Islands tried to protect Sumter, concentrating their rounds at the vessels, which withdrew at dusk. Slow mortar fire against Sumter from Morris Island roared through the night as Mitchel returned.[28]

The Charleston press remained defiantly bitter against the enemy. "The Yankee viper continues gnawing at the file," the *Mercury* said on the eleventh. "It is covered with blood and slaver, but these are from his own jaws. There he sits, squat on Morris Island, and spits his venom at the prey which he dare not approach. Every shell which he hurls against the city costs him one hundred dollars, irrespective of his armament, the personnel he has to feed, the material he has to supply, the watch he has to keep, the sick he has to cure, the dead he has to bury. . . . He batters Sumter into solidity and strength."

The barrage was ongoing on May 14, the bluecoat gunners ashore and two monitors again concentrating on the east angle and the walls in its proximity. In reply, the Rebels rained iron on Fort Putnam and Battery Chatfield, some 450 rounds damaging parapets and traverses but

*Union artillerists man a big gun aimed at Sumter from Battery Chatfield
on Morris Island in December 1864.* LIBRARY OF CONGRESS

inflicting no casualties. Almost 350 Union projectiles had been hurled at
the fort by 7:00 PM, the mortars sending in a few rounds that night. The
overnight firing killed a black laborer, but by 10:00 AM on the fifteenth,
Mitchel was reporting "all quiet" as he kept a wary eye on six warships
inside the bar. Still, the combined army and navy guns had exacted a toll
on Sumter, cracking open two casemates, knocking down some newly
built sections of parapet, and crushing a portion of the wall facing Fort
Moultrie.

All of this pounding of the fort had been prompted by reports of
construction and progress made by the garrison to again mount some
artillery in Sumter. By May's second week, the Federals knew that repairs
at the fort had been ongoing for some time. From deserters, Hatch had
learned on or about May 14 that a few hours of work removing debris
would uncover "a powerful battery on the sea front" where the lower
casemates were still intact. Sumter's defenders also were in the process of

erecting a mortar battery, the deserters claimed. After the shelling on the fourteenth, Union brigadier general Alexander Schimmelfennig, the Prussian-born commander of Hatch's Northern District, composed of Morris and Folly Islands, estimated that he needed one or two more days of this effort to subdue Sumter.[29]

There was spasmodic shelling until the morning of the sixteenth, when the Federals decided to step up their aggression. Two monitors steamed in to punish Sumter about 11:15 AM and a "very pretty little engagement," as Mitchel described it, ensued. The ironclads had been operating with little resistance since this minor bombardment began on the thirteenth, a pair of them coming in each day to aid the army cannoneers. But on this day the Confederates had a surprise for them, unmasking several heavy guns that had been held in reserve at Battery Bee on Sullivan's Island. These pieces boomed away soon after the vessels opened on Sumter. There was a spirited artillery duel from as close as 1,800 yards for about an hour before the monitors retreated with some damage. "The surprise and chagrin of the Federals were very noticeable, as they had been having an easy time during the previous days," engineer Johnson said of the unmasked guns. He added that one of the monitors retired with the conical roof of its pilot house "so wrecked and lifted as to present the appearance of a damaged umbrella on a stormy day." Other than a few random shots, this action marked the last time the Confederates at Sumter would be subjected to shells from the Union navy.

After another fifty rounds from the army batteries on the seventeenth, Schimmelfennig was satisfied that the "repairs recently carried on by the enemy in the fort have again been overthrown." Since then a steady—but not heavy—mortar fire had been maintained against Sumter, Hatch noted on May 22. Hatch himself was unsure if the bombardment had overwhelmed Sumter's latest threat until he received a May 23 dispatch from Schimmelfennig who "considers the bombardment of Sumter as having rendered completely useless the guns lately put into position." Still, the Yanks continued periodic barrages over the next few days.

Dahlgren, meanwhile, continued to be greatly frustrated with the state of his squadron, the overall inactivity of the Federal forces on the coast, and the lack of reinforcements for him as well as the army. On May 17 he sent a dispatch to the Navy Department again asking to be relieved from command. His rationale was that Hatch had barely enough troops for defensive purposes, much less offensive operations, and that the new monitors promised him had now been diverted to the James River in Virginia; this "left me with nothing to do."[30]

Sumter had weathered yet another onslaught, but more trouble was never far off the horizon. Aware of how troops in and around Charleston were being so quickly shipped out, Mitchel was justifiably worried on May 20 when he heard rumors that the 20th South Carolina was to be taken from him. He also needed officers, since at least five were away for various reasons and he had a sergeant absent without leave. Adding to Mitchel's woes, one of the 20th's lieutenants was wounded in the heel by an accidental gunshot overnight on May 19–20 and would require some two weeks' recovery, the fort's surgeon estimated. In addition, a small party of Yanks had tried to cut the submerged or "submarine" telegraph line between Sumter and Fort Johnson about 2:00 AM on the twentieth, but had been repulsed by blasts from Sumter's boat howitzers. But Mitchel was much more concerned about his shrinking force. "I am now, consequently, 6 officers short," he dispatched to Charleston later that day. "Please have some sent." The rumors had been right about the 20th South Carolina; General Jones ordered these troops to be brought into the city and ready to board a train for Virginia two days later.

Keeping up the pressure, Schimmelfennig initiated a "general reconnaissance" along his lines on the night of the twenty-first, the strike stretching into the twenty-second. One objective was to determine if there had been any reduction in Sumter's troop strength. The bluecoats who approached the fort by water soon realized Mitchel's defenders remained defiant and alert. "The enemy was found at Sumter ready to receive us, with a number of men on the walls and on the dock and several row-boats in the rear of the fort," Schimmelfennig noted on May 23. "It appears, therefore, that the garrison . . . has not been reduced."[31]

There was heartening news for Sumter from Virginia about this time that Stephen Elliott had been promoted to brigadier general as of May 24. The Carolinian had been given command of a brigade fighting in the Petersburg sector. What was disheartening was that the garrison's fresh water supply was at a critically low level due to problems with the boat assigned to replenish it. "We have enough water to last until tonight; no more," Mitchel reported on the morning of May 29. "Can you not have the boat fixed today? If not, the water must be sent in some other way." Word also likely reached Charleston during this period that Capt. Thomas China of the 25th South Carolina had died in a Richmond hospital after being wounded in May 14 fighting at Drewry's Bluff. China had briefly commanded Sumter in February.[32]

Despite Schimmelfennig's May 17 optimism, Union reports in the coming days noted considerable repairs at the fort since the bombardment. Intermittent shelling of Sumter and Charleston continued during the period, but this was about to change with the arrival of a new Federal commander. Hatch was succeeded on May 26 by Maj. Gen. John G. Foster, a New Hampshire native who would observe his forty-first birthday the next day. Foster was returning to a seacoast he knew well, since he had been a captain and chief engineer of the Charleston defenses on Robert Anderson's staff in 1861. Sumter's appearance had changed drastically since he and the rest of the despondent garrison watched it shrink as the *Baltic* sailed north that April day after their surrender. Now, more than three years later, one of his priorities would be to capture or destroy the fort he once had risked his life to defend.

Foster had returned to the Charleston sector for a few days in February 1863, only to be embroiled in a heated dispute with Gen. David Hunter. Foster was West Point class of 1846 and had survived a serious wound in the Mexican War. After Sumter's surrender, he was promoted to brigadier general of volunteers in October 1861 and was quite active in Ambrose Burnside's North Carolina expedition. Promoted to major general as of July 1862, he continued his service in North Carolina, fought in the Knoxville campaign, and briefly commanded the Army and Department of the Ohio in December 1863. Foster had to relinquish command in February 1864 due to injuries suffered when his horse fell with him, but he was recovered enough now to return to the Charleston sector with energy, ambition, and aggressiveness. Hatch stayed in the department, relegated to command of the Hilton Head district, while Dahlgren met with Foster on the twenty-seventh to coordinate operations.[33]

The Union fleet, meanwhile, was continuing to deteriorate. Inland expeditions, one in Florida and the other up the Ashepoo River near Charleston, that late spring resulted in the loss of two support vessels, while another steamer was sent north due to a bad boiler. "The squadron is breaking down very fast, and the [Navy] Department sends no reinforcements," Dahlgren penned in his journal on May 31. Making matters worse, the *New Ironsides* was ordered north on June 1, further depleting his warships. He now had seven monitors, two of which were disabled, and a third, the *Passaic*, barely serviceable. Thirteen steamers also were out of action due to needed repairs, and the squadron's coal supply, always an issue, was seriously low. By June 8 there were five monitors off Charleston: the *Catskill*, *Sangamon*, *Passaic*, *Nantucket* and *Lehigh*. The *New Ironsides* was gone by now, and despite his differences with Rowan, Dahlgren missed the leviathan. She was "a large object in the view, and her absence is quickly noticed. . . . The decrease of vessels is so great that we look quite few," he wrote in his journal.

June's arrival saw the continuation of occasional barrages against Sumter primarily by Union mortars and Parrotts. A Parrott round on the morning of June 2 was especially damaging, hitting and dismounting a howitzer that would require major repairs before it could be returned to service. A few projectiles rocked the fort overnight, one severely wounding a crewman aboard a steamboat approaching Sumter. Mitchel was away on June 3, leaving the fort in command of Capt. C. A. Willis of the 32nd Georgia. It is unknown whether Mitchel was on a brief leave or on assignment, but he was back at Sumter the next day. The shelling from May 30 to June 5 amounted to a total of 319 rounds, wounding four laborers, and would be known as the fort's Seventh Minor Bombardment.[34]

Amid all their tribulations, most of the 280 or so soldiers posted at Sumter in mid-June were in decent shape physically. "The health of the garrison is very good," Mitchel reported on the thirteenth. Only eight men were on sick report, none in serious condition. He also noted that for the past month only four soldiers had been considered ill enough to be sent to the city hospital, suffering mainly from "diarrhea and tonsillitis [*sic*]." There was also a unique incident of the campaign that day as one of the monitors came in close enough for the Federal sailors to man a small deck gun and airmail a few rounds at Sumter before leaving.

Almost immediately upon assuming command, Foster ramped up the bombardment of the city as much as his resources would allow. As of June 15, battery fire into Charleston varied from thirty to sixty shots daily, the barrage ongoing night and day and at irregular intervals. By June 22, the army batteries were averaging some fifty shots at the city per day. Foster also wasted little time in taking an even bigger aim at Forts

Sumter and Johnson as the summer baked on. By the fifteenth, he told Halleck that he was waiting for an opportunity to spring a surprise assault on Johnson, adding that "I could take Fort Sumter if it was required, but this will involve some loss, and for it boats and ladders must be provided."

Over the next week or so, his plans to assail Sumter became even more elaborate. He had looked at different options, he wrote to Halleck on the twenty-second, and concluded that the fort "may be taken at any time" if he was given at least six assault craft, each "with a very large scaling ladder, to be lowered upon the top of the wall, so that 5,000 men can scale the walls at the same time." Foster even had a New York ship-builder submit plans "with as much secrecy as possible" for small steamers to be used in the attack. Halleck received Foster's proposal and immediately stonewalled the project. "Unless the iron-clads would advance and capture Charleston, and I think it is now pretty well demonstrated that they will do nothing of the kind, I do not understand the object of capturing that place [Sumter] at the present time," he replied to Foster from Washington on June 29. "As the rebel batteries would concentrate their fire upon it, it could be held only with a great sacrifice of life, if at all. I see no possible good to result from the attempt by land forces." Not yet having received Halleck's response, Foster reiterated his bold assertion the next day, writing, "I am quite sure that, with proper arrangements, Fort Sumter can be taken at any time."[35]

The bluecoats kept up a desultory fire on the fort for much of the rest of June, accomplishing little. But there was some excitement at Sumter about 1:30 PM on June 20 when the second of the Yanks' rounds that day hit the flagpole, its crash injuring a sergeant. Lt. Charles H. Claiborne of the 1st South Carolina Regular Infantry, however, grabbed the fallen banner and climbed to a parapet, whipping it over his head in defiance. He was soon joined by two others, Sgt. N. F. Devereaux and Cpl. B. Brannon of the Engineer Department, the three of them working quickly and under fire to raise the flag on an improvised staff. "Too cowardly to appreciate and too mean to honor a gallant act in a foe, the Yankees at once poured into the gallant trio, a close and rapid fire, but they cooly finished their work, saluted the enemy with a cheer and a wave of their hats, and left their perilous post," the *Charleston Mercury* related, adding that it was "one of the most heroic acts of bravery" in Sumter's battle annals. Mitchel commended the three for their "exceeding gallantry," adding that the flag replacement "took some time to accomplish, under a rapid fire, and at the most imminent personal risk."[36]

War developments elsewhere continued to thin the number of Confederates at Charleston, and by mid-June, Flag Officer Tucker had organized the "Charleston Naval Battalion," based on General Jones's earlier request. These sailors would be equipped to fight as infantry if the need arose, which would be very soon. The manpower drain was not limited to troops; the Southerners were now finding it drastically difficult to get enough slaves, who provided the bulk of the work on the coastal fortifications. Sumter's garrison learned the hard reality of this on the night of June 25, when its entire force of black laborers was removed under orders without a relief shift brought in. Mitchel and engineer Johnson wrote to Jones's headquarters the next day, stating that due to the loss of these men the work at Sumter had "been left in critical condition."[37]

Jones himself had few answers, writing to South Carolina's Governor Bonham on the twenty-ninth about the lack of slaves needed to erect and maintain the state's defenses. The general claimed that in the Charleston district alone, two thousand laborers were needed, while the state had provided only nine. At Fort Sumter, two hundred slaves were required while there currently were no more than twelve, he told Bonham.

The last days of June were reasonably quiet at Sumter, the most lively being the twenty-sixth when thirty-four shots targeted the fort, splintering the flagstaff twice within two minutes. After the pole was brought down the first time, two Confederates were in the process of replacing it when the second staff was shattered. Privates Walter Steele and D. E. Badger still managed to get the banner aloft. With some measure of revenge, Mitchel reported that the U.S. flag at Battery Strong was also shot away that day by a blast from Fort Johnson. Sumter's flagstaff had also been severed on the twenty-fourth, when some forty mortar or Parrott rounds were launched at the fort. On a more serious note from the twenty-sixth, a private in the garrison was severely wounded by a shell fragment. He died an hour later, after the post surgeon amputated his leg in a futile effort to save him.

"All quiet here," Mitchel wrote on June 29, but the relative tranquility was about to end, not only for Sumter but for the other Rebels around Charleston as well.[38]

CHAPTER 11

"They Have Killed Me, Captain . . ."

Foster soon showed his aggressive nature again, launching attacks against Confederate positions on James Island on July 1–2 in cooperation with Dahlgren's squadron. But due to a lack of coordination and support, primarily among the army units, the assaults fizzled. "General Grant will not eat his Fourth-of-July dinner in Richmond," the *Mercury* gloated. "Nor will General Foster eat his in Charleston." Sharp but sporadic fighting crackled on John's and James Islands during the following six days, accomplishing little but more bloodshed on both sides.

Foster was not about to let Sumter escape unscathed, opening a new—and massive—artillery assault against the fort on Thursday, July 7. The guns erupted at 5:00 AM in what would be known as the Third Great Bombardment of Sumter. It would last for two months. "Having become convinced that the enemy were strengthening themselves in Fort Sumter and making arrangements for defense, I have concluded that it is necessary to more effectually demolish the walls of that fort," Foster said of his decision.[1]

The cannonading was focused on the gorge, with mainly rifled guns employed during the day and mortars pounding Sumter at night. "The enemy continue a heavy fire on us," Mitchel wrote to Ripley at 4:00 PM on the seventh. "The fire is quite as damaging as any bombardment since the year commenced. We have no labor to repair." He closed by asking for fifty men, and Ripley was quick to reply that "I have no force of laborers or soldiers to send." The same dispatch from Mitchel, or a similar report, was sent or forwarded to Jones's headquarters, prompting an appeal to Charleston's mayor to assist in providing some slaves for Sumter. "He [Mitchel] has no labor to repair the damage done, and the threatening position of the enemy at other vital points renders it absolutely impossible to send him more men," Jones's assistant adjutant wrote on the seventh. The general was asking the mayor for "50 able-bodied [N]egroes," adding that he felt this impressment would be "cheerfully" submitted to by local residents due to the threat of Sumter being lost. "The small garrison of the fort is unable to do the work required, and we cannot afford to give up the fort which has proved of such importance in . . . the siege of Charleston. It cannot be held unless the damage done by . . . the enemy is constantly and promptly repaired."

The captain believed that the enemy's intent was not only to level the gorge wall but also to destroy the fort's protective boom and weaken its ability to repel an assault. "The fire is quite as damaging as any bombardment since the year commenced," he reported at 4:00 PM on the seventh. By 6:10 PM, Sumter's flag had been shot down three times that day and was "torn to pieces." Mitchel requested a new one.[2]

Foster's cannoneers pumped 438 rounds at Sumter on the seventh, the barrage lifting around midnight. It resumed at daybreak with almost 400 projectiles sent on the eighth. "The smallest favors in the shape of laborers thankfully received," Mitchel wrote that Friday night. By Saturday, July 9, the gorge wall "was successfully cut through in several places," Foster noted, another 350 or so rounds rocking the fort into the night. The tons of iron death slightly wounded one Rebel private, but Sumter's destruction was ongoing with every shell burst. The bluecoats rested somewhat on a humid Sunday, sending only 200 rounds to Sumter throughout the day and night. One of the monitors greeted sunup on the tenth by also lobbing a few shots at the fort.

The Yanks were back at their work on the morning of Monday, July 11, the shelling to "be continued until the fort is thoroughly demolished," Foster told Halleck the next day. Some 239 shots were hurled on the eleventh, followed by 202 on the twelfth, and almost 300 on the thirteenth. The result was two casualties, one of which was serious, and scant damage reported, although the Confederates noted that some of the shells reaching Sumter on the thirteenth contained an "incendiary composition." As usual, most of the firing was from Fort Putnam and Battery Strong. That night Mitchel complained that "very little assistance [is] given us by Sullivan's Island; none by Fort Johnson."[3]

Foster was convinced that many of Sumter's lower casemates remained intact, buried under the mounds of debris. His plan was to use his artillery to make a "breaching cut" along the lower embrasures, allowing him to initiate his second phase of action, which was much more dramatic and creative: Foster wanted to "shake the wall" with rafts carrying large quantities of powder which would explode near the fort. "I shall take these rafts up tomorrow morning," he wrote Halleck on July 12. A few days earlier he had described how he wanted to "explode large torpedoes until the wall is shaken down and the surrounding obstacles are entirely blown away. . . . I am convinced that the fort can, after such a bombardment, be assaulted and taken by boats, and that it can be held without any great loss of life . . . It now serves as a watch-tower to the enemy." He added that the immediate reasons for taking Sumter would be to provide a "shelter or starting point by which boat expeditions" could attack Fort Johnson and Mount Pleasant.[4]

Mitchel, meanwhile, still needed more soldiers and workmen, and Ripley tried to appease him despite having no manpower to send him. "In the present state of things it is impossible to send you either troops or labor," he wrote the captain on July 10. "Both will be furnished as soon as practicable." Ripley said he would also try to get an additional medical officer for the fort and have its boom repaired, both requested by Mitchel. Orders had gone out to the various forts and batteries to support Sumter with artillery fire when needed or requested. "I have no doubt that both yourself and Captain Johnson will do all in your power for the security of the work, with your exceedingly limited means, and shall endeavor to increase the latter, if possible," Ripley told Mitchel.[5]

In addition to Sumter's destruction, Foster had two other major objectives on his mind during this period. First, he was preparing for a raid to try to sever the Charleston & Savannah Railroad, the ever-elusive iron link that had bedeviled the Federals since the war began. Second, he was constructing a prison pen on Morris Island to hold a few hundred captured Confederate officers. The Rebels in Charleston had placed Union POWs of similar rank in areas of the city vulnerable to bombardment by the Federals. In retaliation, the Confederate prisoners would be on exposed terrain where they might be hit by their own friendly fire.

For the first ten days or so of Sumter's pounding, Confederate batteries on Sullivan's and James Islands replied, trying to protect the fort. But their fire eventually slackened and stopped due to a lack of ammunition. Mitchel's undermanned defenders, meanwhile, were doing all they could without artillery to not only survive but also hold the fort. Small work parties struggled every night to keep up with repairs, and obstacles were placed outside the ruins after dark to guard against enemy boat landings.

With the Federal thrust at John's and James Islands now played out, General Jones on July 12 suggested to Ripley that fifty troops be sent to Sumter. These reinforcements would not only bolster the defenders in case the enemy was mulling an assault, but also "strengthen the garrison by the increased confidence it would give to Captain Mitchel and his men." The brain-numbing bombardment, meanwhile, was almost unrelenting, with 400 or so projectiles piercing the air on both the fourteenth and the fifteenth, while another 280 were thrown on the sixteenth and again on the seventeenth. The Rebel guns on Sullivan's and Fort Johnson cranked up during this time, but only after the bluecoats had slackened their barrage. Still, Mitchel noted that this "measurably annoyed" the Yanks and "interfered with their fire." For these few days the fort's casualties amounted to two soldiers killed—along with one laborer—and a handful of wounded.

John Johnson continued his nocturnal efforts to patch up Sumter, taking some eighty men out each night to work on the gorge wall. Other engineers were also active in repairing the fort's boom, but Johnson and his crew had the most hazardous duty. They labored "without any cover, and where they are infinitely more exposed to fire than those other engineers could possibly be in fixing the boom," Mitchel reported on the fifteenth. As usual, much of the fire during this period was directed at the southwest angle.[6]

Ripley tried to raise Sumter's spirits even more on July 16 when he sent a dispatch to Adjutant General Cooper recommending that Mitchel and Johnson both be promoted to major. Mitchel had "served with energy and fidelity" since the war began, much of his record at Sumter. "It is proper that this important position should be commanded by a field officer, and I think that Captain Mitchel, by months of ceaseless vigilance and activity therein, as well as previous service, has fairly earned his promotion," Ripley wrote. Of Johnson he noted that the engineer had been on duty at Sumter since the April 7, 1863, bombardment and his "activity, energy, and skill" had contributed greatly to the garrison being able to hold out. "The possession of Fort Sumter, besides its material necessity, has become a point of honor, and I think there can be no doubt of the propriety of fully recognizing the services of those who are engaged in its gallant defense," Ripley said. General Jones endorsed the recommendation, adding that he had previously requested a promotion for Johnson, "believing as I do that very much of the credit of the defense of Fort Sumter is due to the skill, zeal, and indomitable energy" of the engineer.[7]

"The fire upon Fort Sumter has been kept up, slowly and with marked effect," Foster informed Halleck on the seventeenth. The guns had knocked a breach near the right gorge angle and that day were concentrating on the left gorge angle "where the rebels have their magazine containing the small supply of ammunition left in the fort." The "mine rafts" were still very much in Foster's plans, but he needed to iron out some details before trying them. He continued to believe that Sumter could be easily taken. "I would like very much to receive your sanction to the occupation of this fort, which, I think, can be done with little loss of life," he told Halleck.

Union batteries launched 264 rounds at the fort on the eighteenth, but the heaviest shelling of the Third Major Bombardment thus far was about to take place. On Tuesday, July 19, the bluecoats blasted Sumter with 694 rounds, the most since the shelling began twelve days earlier. "This is the heaviest fire we have been subjected to since the bombardment commenced," Mitchel reported that night, adding however, that many of the rounds were from lighter guns, "30-pounder Parrotts." One laborer was killed and several men, both soldiers and workers, were wounded. "There is not over five minutes during the day or night that a shell is not fired at it," Sgt. W. H. Andrews of the 1st Georgia Regulars wrote of Sumter from his post on James Island at that time. "During the day you can see the puff of smoke as the cannon fires, then if you will look at the sea face of Fort Sumter you will see a cloud of dust and smoke as the shell strikes and explodes. At night . . . you can see the shells from the mortars . . . until they drop into the fort, when you will hear a terrific explosion." Discouraged yet plucky, Andrews added, "How I would like to see gallant old . . . Sumter rise up in her might and hurl defiance at her enemies."[8]

Wednesday, July 20, began as usual for Sumter's garrison with the two 8-inch Parrotts at Fort Putnam opening up at an early hour. Again targeting the southwest angle, the Yankee gunners were doing especially efficient work, the rounds whipping masses of brick and sand into the air on what would be the high-tide day of the Third Great Bombardment. Watching the rounds fly in, Johnson was also focused on his need for more sandbags, among other supplies, writing that day that a "regular supply of at least 1,000 bags every night is considered to be very necessary under such a severe bombardment." He also had to have more lumber.

John Mitchel, meanwhile, had been highly recommended for his promotion to major, an honor his men felt was well deserved. He was expecting this good news at any time; perhaps this would be the day, but he had much more on his mind early on as a mix of mortar and Parrott shells rained on the southwest angle. The almost 250 projectiles thrown at the fort that morning wounded one soldier, killed a workman, and injured seven other laborers, two seriously, Mitchel reported. It would be his last correspondence. That afternoon a sentry on the parapet at the southwest angle sent a request to the captain that he be allowed to leave his post because the enemy shelling was too heavy to endure without the protection of a nearby bombproof sentry box. Mitchel initially refused permission, since it would have set a bad precedent, but he soon received another urgent message from the same soldier. Mitchel then climbed to the ramparts to see if the sentry's pleas were valid. John Johnson offered a different reason for Mitchel's heading to the parapet, stating that after lunch, the commander ascended to the angle to check the position of the blockaders before writing his daily report. It was a clear day and with his "favorite telescope" resting on the parapet, he had a good view of Federal gunners on Morris loading and firing their pieces.[9]

Whatever his reason for going topside about 1:00 PM, Mitchel had only been on the parapet a brief time before a giant mortar shell came rocketing toward him. The round either exploded about eighty feet above him or landed and burst nearby, based on various accounts. Mitchel had not tried to get out of the way, even though he was only a few steps from the protection of the sandbagged sentry post. Why he didn't scramble for

Capt. John C. Mitchel,
Sumter's commander,
killed on July 20, 1864.

cover will never be known, but one version claims that having just admonished the sentinel to stand his ground, Mitchel apparently felt that he himself could do no less and did not head for shelter. An artillerist himself who had been dodging shells since the war began, it is hard to fathom that such a savvy veteran did not see or hear the round cutting the air dangerously close to him on a sunny summer day. If Mitchel wanted to give the sentinel and his men an example of courage and coolness under fire, he succeeded—but it cost him his life. The shell burst drove a large hunk of shrapnel into his left leg just below the hip, causing a ghastly wound. Though Mitchel was slightly built, soldiers had a difficult time getting him down a narrow, winding staircase to the fort's lower level as he bled heavily. "They have killed me, captain, but I ought to have been a major though," he gasped to Johnson as the men lifted him.

Over the next four agonizing hours, Mitchel clung to life as his men quietly filed past the hospital entrance, checking on their commander. At one point he groaned aloud, but quickly stifled himself. He told his officers that the men should not be allowed to pass and re-pass the door since he did not want them to hear him if it should happen again. The captain kept his faculties about him for the most part, but pain continued to intensify despite the stimulants, and later anodynes, given to him. No surgery was attempted since his injuries were obviously mortal. As the torturous hours ticked away, someone asked what could be done for him, Mitchel replied, "Nothing except to pray for me." He finally succumbed about 5:00 PM. At least one account states that his last words were, "I die willingly for South Carolina, but oh that it had been for Ireland!"[10]

Within hours of Mitchel's death, twenty-four-year-old Capt. Thomas A. Huguenin of the 1st South Carolina Regular Infantry was assigned command of Sumter, but he could not immediately reach the fort due to the hazards of getting there by boat. In the intervening hours, Capt. John A. Phillips of the 32nd Georgia Volunteers was in temporary command. "Huguenin will be over as soon as he can cross with safety," Ripley's assistant adjutant general, Capt. W. F. Nance, wrote to John Johnson later in the day. "Keep the garrison in good spirits. There is no danger yet, if all do their duty as you and Mitchel have done. Huguenin will be equal to the emergency." Huguenin's crossing to Sumter that night was dangerous, since the enemy rounds were still falling at random. Mortars sank two of the quartermaster's barges at the wharf that evening; it could just as easily have been the new commander's vessel, but he arrived safely about 8:00 PM. At his request, Johnson gave him a tour of the works and "indicated the plans of defense." Perhaps fittingly, Mitchel had been killed on the day of the heaviest shelling of the third bombardment; 706 projectiles were thrown at Sumter that day.[11]

The captain's body was taken into the city that night and placed in St. Paul's Church, where an honor guard kept silent vigil until the funeral the next afternoon. Charleston was shocked and saddened by Mitchel's loss, and hundreds of citizens joined the military contingent in honoring him. The fort's flag covered the casket, which also was adorned with his sword, white roses, and a laurel wreath. After the service, the band of Mitchel's regiment, the 1st South Carolina Artillery, played dirges while the procession made its way to Magnolia Cemetery. Generals Jones and Ripley were among the most notable in attendance. The striking scene was further heightened by the approach of a heavy thunderstorm, the flashes of lightning and the ground-rumbling thunder reminding one onlooker of the "loud reports of heaven's artillery." Years later, some of Mitchel's old comrades in the 1st Artillery had a granite column placed over his grave. It was a fitting memorial, noted a Charlestonian, "but as long as the waves beat against the ruins of Ft. Sumter, that war-worn fortress will be John Mitchel's best and most enduring monument."[12]

*Capt. Thomas A. Huguenin,
the last Confederate
commander at Fort Sumter.*

Thomas Huguenin, meanwhile, had been cast into the cauldron. By the twenty-first, the enemy's use of incendiary shells had forced him to remove ammunition from the southwest magazine for fear that some flammable material could reach the ordnance through a ventilator shaft. Johnson was still requesting more sandbags, the fort's boom had been broken in two places, and the fort needed more signalmen. About 375 projectiles, mostly mortar, pelted Sumter that Thursday, killing a workman; despite all this, Huguenin reported, "The garrison appears to be in good spirits."

Born near Beaufort, Huguenin had graduated with high honors from South Carolina Military Academy in 1859 and was appointed to its faculty as an assistant professor of mathematics. When the war began he was commissioned a first lieutenant in the 1st South Carolina and had participated in the 1861 bombardment of Sumter and the defense of Sullivan's and Morris Islands. Promoted to captain later that year, Huguenin was indeed a veteran who was not one to flinch at artillery bursts or men being blown apart. He had certainly seen both in combat while serving as chief of artillery at Wagner and had been the last Confederate off Morris Island when the fort was evacuated in September. After the main garrison left Wagner that night, Huguenin led a small party to spike the guns and was charged with destroying the main magazine. Finishing with

most of the cannon, he lit the fuse to the magazine and left the fort with
the other men, the last to wade out to the boats. Unfortunately for the
Rebels, Union troops discovered the burning fuses at Wagner and Battery
Gregg's magazine and snuffed them. Huguenin later commanded Battery
Beauregard on Sullivan's Island. "The military authorities have shown
their appreciation of his gallantry and ability, in conferring upon him the
honor of so important a command," the *Mercury* said of him. "We trust
that his career in his new post will be such as to add new distinction to
his present reputation."[13]

Unaware of Sumter's loss, Dahlgren late on the twentieth was
focused on the results of the fourteen days of shelling. He was not
impressed. "Our cannon have been pounding Sumter, but the effect is
not very evident to a hasty glance," he noted in his journal. The admiral
had also met with Foster that day to discuss possible offensive action
against the fort. Foster wanted monitors to lay off the channel walls and
simply blast them down. When this was done, the monitors would send
in landing parties of fifty men each while the army assailed Sumter from
the other sides. Knowing Halleck opposed such an operation in general,
Dahlgren also expressed doubt about its success, telling Foster that
artillery fire from Moultrie and Fort Johnson would likely cause heavy
casualties among the attackers. He advised Foster to keep blasting the
fort, and they would see how matters stood in a few weeks. Dahlgren also
was still awaiting a decision about his request to be relieved of squadron
command and who would replace him. "I have labored hard to serve the
country," he confided in his July 22 journal entry after receiving a vague
and noncommittal reply from the Navy Department that day. "But the
public will only be satisfied with victory; and they will find *that* is not to
be had, under the conditions here."

The bombardment reached the two-week mark on July 21 and continued, the staggering weight of iron hurled at Sumter increasing hourly.
From Fort Putnam and Batteries Strong, Chatfield, Barton, and Seymour,
Union cannoneers had launched 5,525 projectiles of varying calibers
against Sumter during the period. But the long-term shelling, as always,
was exacting a serious toll on many of the Federal pieces. "So many of the
guns used in breaching have been disabled," Schimmelfennig's artillery
chief, Lt. Col. William Ames, noted on July 27. The bombardment also
had been hindered by premature shell explosions, although casualties were
apparently minimal.[14]

There was another army–navy attempt to float a mine raft against Sumter on the night of the twenty-first, but Dahlgren noted, "As in all combined operations, things did not work well." The monitor *Nahant* was to position the raft within a thousand yards of the fort before veering away. Yet by 6:00 PM, the powder had not been loaded on the raft, and the admiral sent an aide to check on the holdup. Shortly afterward the skies burst, rain falling in torrents accented by angry lightning. The raft would have to wait for another opportunity. The stormy weather that had blanketed the coast for several days certainly was a factor in delaying use of the mine rafts (also described as powder rafts), but Foster also was disappointed with the navy's involvement in this project and voiced his frustration to Halleck on the twenty-fifth: "I hoped to have received aid from the monitors in floating these rafts against the fort, but I found, after some delay, that the officers entertained so many objections to going as near the fort as I judged necessary for effect, say 1,000 yards, that I was forced to give up the idea of their assistance. I then turned the rafts over to the boat infantry on shore to operate. I do not think that Admiral Dahlgren intends to undertake, on his own responsibility, any offensive operations with the ironclads."[15]

In Sumter, the bombardment entered its sixteenth day on Friday, July 22, with the artillery as usual targeting the southwest angle. Stretching into the night, some 386 rounds fell in and around Sumter, with no more significant damage and no casualties. Huguenin was more concerned that no quartermaster boats had come down the previous night, adding there was "no reason why they should not." The Confederates did add 18 slaves to the workforce, bringing the total to 160 men. The cannonade was less severe on the twenty-third, Parrott crews firing 237 rounds while the mortar squads took a break. The southwest and southeast angles were again the targets, but there were no casualties.

The shelling slackened to 161 projectiles on Sunday the twenty-fourth, and one soldier was slightly wounded. One round knocked down a portion of an arch and a section of wall along the gorge, a mass of brick and mortar falling onto the heavy, log-covered roof of a blockhouse used as quarters for the slaves. Rather than a danger, this added to the security of the structure, the Confederates noted. They also became aware of the fact that the Yankees' mortar fire had almost stopped, engineer Johnson writing: "The enemy seemed to have run out of mortar shells." The laborers were engaged at night in repairing the shattered angles while details of soldiers were put to work during the day filling in some case-mates.[16]

The shelling of Charleston and Sumter continued on July 25, the mortars returning to action as the bombardment heightened again. Some 440 rounds were thrown at the fort, though it was at a slow rate as the Federals tried to conserve their guns and ammunition. The southeast angle was their main focus, and they damaged the ceiling and supports of the east magazine. Johnson had revised his work schedule by now; the laborers were employed from 7:00 PM to 5:00 AM, while the soldiers were assigned to two three-hour shifts of forty men each during the afternoon. The shelling wounded one Rebel and a slave.

General Foster also was focused on extending Battery Putnam so that it connected with Battery Chatfield, allowing the bluecoats to bring even more guns to bear on the fort and the harbor channel. From deserters, Foster also had culled a fairly accurate description of Sumter's condition and its garrison, which he sent to Halleck on the twenty-fifth: The lower tier casemates were generally intact and being used for quarters and store-rooms. The tops of the arches of these casemates, as well as their ends, were so buried by debris that they were essentially shell-proof. The Con-federates had a communications system throughout the ruins, and dirt had been taken from the parade ground to fortify the arches and bombproofs and to erect traverses. Water was some four feet deep in the parade area that had been dug out, and a plank walk extended across this crater from the sally port; the drainage improvements made months ear-lier had been negated by the myriad additional shell holes since then and continued digging to fill sandbags. A large bombproof, constructed of earth and timber, had been built on the parade. The defenders had five guns in casemates and four light field pieces—probably 12-pounder how-itzers—the deserters claimed. The lighter cannon were wheeled atop the ruins at night in case of enemy assault. The deserters said Captain Mitchel commanded the garrison (their information obviously outdated by several days) of about 250 men, which was relieved every two or three weeks. To thwart night assaults, the defenders—in addition to the howitzers—kept a guard of a hundred troops on the alert, men on the walls armed with hand grenades "of the improved pattern." Temporary obstructions were placed at key positions at night and taken in before daylight. No buried torpedoes were believed to be around the fort at that time.[17]

Foster wanted to try to close Sumter's access to reinforcements and supplies by bringing guns to bear on the sally port and the rest of the fort's left flank. He sent orders to Schimmelfennig on Tuesday, July 26, to make this happen by repairing the Swamp Angel's emplacement and posting a 30- or 100-pounder Parrott there. He also wanted the brigadier's opinion regarding a boat attack on Sumter and his report on the mine raft operations. Schimmelfennig likely had not received this dispatch the next day when he informed Foster that he had requested a number of "clock-work torpedoes" from the fleet. He wanted to use these weapons, which detonated based on a timing device, to destroy the boom around much of Sumter, adding that until this was accomplished, "no mines can be brought properly in contact with the fort."

While all of this was happening, Sumter's bombardment had resumed for the twentieth straight day, another 440 or so rounds searing across the sky at its ragged silhouette. The parapet of the southeast angle was blown away, primarily by the big rounds from a 300-pounder Parrott. "For five successive days they have swept away by noon the work it took all the previous night to reconstruct," a frustrated but determined John Johnson reported. The rain of iron injured a Georgia private and five laborers. Overnight on July 26–27, artillery killed one workman and wounded two others. The water boat also was sunk at the wharf but was repaired in time to send it back to Charleston by the next night.[18]

Sumter was getting viciously pummeled, but the Federals' big guns were continuing to wear out due to the onslaught. From July 20 to 27, a 200-pounder Parrott at Fort Putnam burst upon firing its 1,300th round; a second Parrott at Putnam and another at Battery Chatfield needed new vents; and a Columbiad had more than a foot of its muzzle blown off by a premature ignition but could still be used for short-range firing. Colonel Ames noted that the only reserve guns in his command were two Parrotts, one with no carriage or chassis. Still, the Yanks managed to send 341 rounds at the fort on Wednesday, July 27.

In addition to 270 incoming shells, Sumter absorbed another blow on the twenty-eighth with the wounding of chief engineer Johnson. About 3:45 AM, he had been checking the eastern angle of the gorge when he was seriously injured by a mortar fragment that gashed his head. Johnson, who had been on almost continuous duty at the fort since November 8—a period of eight months and twenty days—was immediately evacuated to Charleston for treatment. The *Mercury* described the captain's loss as a "distressing casualty" that would "for a time at least, deprive the country of the services of the accomplished and indefatigable engineer." Johnson was temporarily succeeded by Lt. Ralph S. Izard, who came off sick leave to take the assignment, before the arrival of Lt. Edwin J. White on the night of the thirtieth. White had served at Sumter previously, had assisted in the construction of fortifications around the harbor, and had been recommended as a replacement by the wounded Johnson. He would be the fort's last Confederate chief engineer.

Another soldier had been killed in the overnight shelling of July 27–28. On the twenty-ninth, 359 projectiles fell in and around Sumter, injuring a private and two workmen. This was followed by 281 rounds the next day and another 359 on the thirty-first; one soldier was wounded.[19]

Charleston received more news from Virginia regarding Stephen Elliott, but this time the dispatches were dire. Little more than two months after being promoted to brigadier, he had been badly wounded at the Battle of the Crater near Petersburg on July 30, a bullet piercing his left lung. The wound was believed to be mortal, based on Richmond newspaper accounts. Another Sumter veteran and officer had met his end at the Crater. David Fleming, formerly of the 1st South Carolina Artillery, had been promoted to colonel of the 22nd South Carolina Infantry in early June, his troops posted in the Petersburg sector. Fleming was at Sumter with his company of cannoneers in May when he was transferred to Virginia and reassigned to the 22nd. He had been a civil engineer before the war and was thirty-two when he disappeared in the titanic explosion—instrumented by Union soldiers who were miners—that gave the battle its name. His body was never found.

On the same day as the Crater, Foster tried to replenish his guns by asking Dahlgren to loan him six 100-pounder Parrotts for a new battery at Cummings Point. The general added that he would also need ammunition for these pieces since he had none. Dahlgren replied the next day that he had the Parrotts available whenever Foster wanted them. In another development, General Hatch was assigned to head the District of Florida on July 31, replaced at Hilton Head by Brig. Gen. Edward E. Potter.[20]

From July 21 to August 1, Union batteries threw 3,333 projectiles of various sizes and calibers at Sumter, enlarging the breach in the gorge wall by about seven feet and cutting down the seawall by some five feet, reported Ames, the artillery chief. But the toll on the Federal guns was unabated as well. A 200-pounder Parrott at Putnam cracked on July 30 and was disabled; at Battery Chatfield on August 1, a 300-pounder blew off about two feet of its muzzle after firing some 1,200 rounds.

From deserters, the Federals learned that rumors had been flying in Charleston that General Grant had been killed and Sherman had been repulsed at Atlanta. The deserters also claimed Sumter had a garrison of 250 men "considered capable of holding it," Schimmelfennig reported.

At Sumter on August 1, the defenders marked the twenty-fifth day of the bombardment; Huguenin reported more than 8,800 rounds fired at the fort since the artillery onslaught opened on July 7. The majority had been from Parrotts of various calibers, but mortars and Columbiads had also taken their toll. By far, most of the shelling had occurred during the day, with the highest total at night 194 shells on July 20. "Repairs have been in proportion to damages, which may not be considered severe, when the number and kind of projectiles are considered," Huguenin noted.[21]

Also on the first, Schimmelfennig informed Foster that he would be ready to proceed with the mine raft operation against Sumter within two or three days. He had received a number of the clockwork torpedoes from the navy, and Dahlgren had sent an officer to explain the workings of these devices. Schimmelfennig still intended to use the torpedoes to destroy Sumter's protective boom so that the rafts could float close to its walls. The Prussian also wanted to send a boat patrol around the fort to determine the damage to the left and right faces. In the fort that day, Huguenin noted that the garrison had been under Parrott and mortar fire overnight, wounding a laborer, and requested more sand and timber. The mortars stepped up their efforts by sunrise, slightly injuring a soldier.

The Union "boat infantry" conducted its daring reconnaissance of Sumter on the night of August 2, Capt. Richard Allison of the 127th New York leading a few men in three rowboats. The party embarked about 8:00 PM, passing quietly between Johnson and Sumter near one of the Rebels' telegraph poles in the channel. The Yanks rowed close enough to Sumter's dock to see a sentinel and a lit lantern there. Allison counted nine casemates on the left face "through which the light could be plainly seen," but as they drifted on the tide they saw no other signs of life. As they continued around the fort, the Federals saw the Confederate iron-clads in the distance, one of which was moving toward the harbor's mouth. Faint light flickered from several other casemates, but the patrol went entirely around Sumter without being challenged. Allison wrote a report of his exploit and included a drawing showing the outline of the jagged walls as seen from his boats—and his soldiers had a story to regale their families for years to come. This little operation had come on the heels of the relentless shelling that day, the Confederates reporting 126 rounds hurled at Sumter—plus 45 mortar shells—killing a laborer and slightly wounding the post physician, a Dr. McCauley.[22]

While they contemplated the next move with the mine rafts, the fact that much of Sumter had been knocked down by now presented the Federals with another issue, which Schimmelfennig also addressed to Foster on August 1. The rifled guns had done "excellent service" in breaching the walls but "are not as effective in clearing away the debris and combing down the slope" as large-caliber smoothbore cannon could be. In other words, the rifles were great at boring through brick walls, but their shells burrowed in and were buried by the immense mounds of blasted material they had created. Schimmelfennig had learned that some 11- and 15-inch Dahlgrens could be loaned from the navy and asked Foster to obtain six or so of them to be brought to Morris Island "for use against Sumter."

The pounding of the fort continued on the third "as far as the supply of ammunition and the condition of the guns in the batteries will allow," Schimmelfennig related. Still, the Prussian was optimistic, adding: "The result for the past eight days has been most favorable, and gives more hope of an ultimate demolition of the fort than ever before." On the negative side, his gunners were out of mortar powder, despite his ordnance officer having made a requisition ten days earlier. Because of this, Schimmelfennig had to borrow a hundred barrels of powder from the navy to keep up his mortar fire.[23]

"The slow and careful firing upon Fort Sumter is beginning to exhibit a marked effect," Foster informed Halleck on August 4. "The immense mass of debris . . . is being smashed up and blown away by our shells." Foster had complete confidence that the cannonading would soon allow the Federals to seize Sumter without much opposition. "In a reasonable time the fort will be rendered untenable, and if still held by the enemy can be taken by our troops at any time we choose," he told Halleck. "I prefer, however, before doing this to wait until the preparations are completed, so as to avoid loss of life." The story was much the same on the eighth, Foster stating that he could see results "although our fire is very slow and unfrequent [*sic*], in consequence of the stock of ammunition having given out and none being received. The rebels are calculating how many days they can hold the fort, expecting that we will assault." Due to his lack of cannon and ammo, Foster had accepted an offer from Dahlgren for six 11-inch guns with not only ample rounds but also officers and seamen to serve them. The troops would soon have this naval battery built and functioning, no doubt to "prove very effective."

Foster also was disappointed that his plan for constructing "assaulting arks" had not been approved by the army brass. He told Halleck that he planned to build two of them and gave a description that more resembled a siege machine of the Roman Empire than any war marvel of the 1860s. The arks would be "simply modern row galleys" with fifty oars on each side, and would draw twenty-six inches of water when loaded with a thousand troops. They would have at least one tower for sharpshooters and an "assaulting ladder or gang-plank" fifty-one feet long and operated by machinery. These vessels "will be very useful anywhere, in assaulting a fort or landing troops in shoal water," Foster explained. The general also wanted to construct a light-draft ironclad and already was making inquiries about having captured railroad iron from Florida converted into armor plating for it. These were Caesar-like plans indeed, but Foster was about to be jolted by the war's meat grinder in Virginia. On August 11 he received a dispatch from Halleck stating that Grant needed "all the troops you can possibly spare." Foster was to remain "purely on the defensive" to make up for this loss of manpower.[24]

In Charleston on the fifth, General Jones readied a dispatch to Secretary of War Seddon regarding Sumter's bombardment, including a daily tally of the shelling: "The conduct of the officers and men of the garrison during this, the heaviest bombardment to which the fort has been subjected, has been all that could be desired." Seddon forwarded the report to Jefferson Davis who replied, "The conduct of the garrison is praiseworthy." The president's economy of words was likely due to his focus on the critical fighting ongoing around Petersburg and its supply lines so vital to the Confederacy.

Overnight on August 2–3, Sumter endured thirty-five Parrott shells and more than a hundred mortar rounds smacking the fort, two soldiers and a slave receiving slight injuries. Ironically, the shelling did not deter a flag of truce arranged in the channel off Sumter for the exchange of fifty Union and Confederate officers. Huguenin asked for permission early on the morning of the third to offer a salute to the Confederates as they passed the fort.[25]

From August 3 to 14, Union guns threw 3,180 rounds at Sumter, including Parrotts and mortars, Ames noted on the sixteenth. Three 200-pounder Parrotts had been lost in the process. That same day, Schimmelfennig noted that he had been forced to borrow an additional 450 barrels of powder and 1,000 30-pounder shells from the navy to maintain even a minimal fire on Sumter. "I have thus managed to keep the fort in about the state it was a fortnight ago," he reported, adding that he could do no more until his guns and ammunition were replenished. The Prussian also had not given up on his plans for the mine rafts but admitted that he was "progressing slowly in this matter" due to the inexperience of the men working on the project and the heavy swell in the harbor channel, even on calm nights.

Still, Foster seemed happy with the rate of Sumter's reduction, despite the fact that he still had not been able to dislodge its defenders. "We have so knocked Fort Sumter that it is almost insupportable to the small garrison," he told Halleck on the eighteenth. "The closeness of their bomb-proofs, the breach which the sea makes at high tides into the fort, and the abundance of rats and other vermin make the garrison often come out on the open ramparts, exposed to our fire, in preference to remaining in their casemates. We shall soon render the fort an easy prey." Despite this bravado, Foster expressed dismay during this period that his department had been so picked over that he lacked enough troops for any offensive action. In another message to Halleck on the eighteenth, Foster said the bombardment of Sumter was "progressing slowly but surely" and that Dahlgren had "kindly consented" to loan six of the fleet's heaviest guns to the army, along with officers and men to work them.[26]

"The fire from our batteries is still kept up on Sumter and the city, slowly, but with most gratifying accuracy," the New York Herald said on August 19. "A deserter who came in recently informs us that our firing does great execution . . . directed at the weakest points . . . a fact attributable to General Foster's knowledge of it while stationed there." Through the twenty-third the pounding of Sumter was continual, but slackening, as the Federals still tried to conserve their ammunition and preserve their cannon.

As if they didn't have enough problems to deal with, the Charleston Confederates added another major worry to their list in August. Union rear admiral David Farragut garnered more laurels on the fifth with his hallmark victory at Mobile Bay, damning the torpedoes, battling past the outlying forts, and defeating the Rebel naval squadron there. The immediate speculation among the Confederate brass was that Farragut would bring his conquering fleet from the Gulf of Mexico to the south Atlantic that fall and join Dahlgren's squadron for a grand assault on Sumter and Charleston itself. "Renew rope obstructions near Sumter and put down new ones" at the mouths of the Cooper and Ashley Rivers, Beauregard wrote to Samuel Jones on August 30 from near Petersburg. "Farragut may soon pay you a visit." This didn't happen, but the Rebels were far from optimistic that they could stop such an armada from blasting its way up to the city's wharves if Farragut and Dahlgren united.[27]

While the summer sizzled toward its end, Foster finally made at least two other attempts to put his mine rafts into play against Sumter, apparently without the navy's help. On the night of Sunday, August 28, Huguenin reported that a torpedo had been floated down and exploded near the fort's wharf, throwing up a giant geyser of water, but Sumter was unscathed. The Confederates were initially unclear about the source of this blast, believing that either the Federals had brought a large torpedo by boats through the creeks behind Morris Island and allowed it to float down toward Sumter, or an enemy vessel had taken advantage of the very dark night to convey the bomb close to the walls. The garrison was kept on alert all that night but there was no other disturbance. Daybreak brought no visual evidence of what had caused the explosion. This attack had been made by men of the 127th New York, led by Lt. G. F. Eaton, who filled a "pontoon-boat" with powder and sent it toward the fort's left flank. The New Yorkers miscalculated the current and the boat detonated before reaching the walls.

Overnight on August 31–September 1, another effort was made to "blow up the fort," as one account stated. The Federals constructed six torpedoes, "made of barrels set in frames" and each containing a hundred pounds of powder. On the flood tide, these were set afloat from Morris, bobbing toward Sumter, but they erupted about three hundred yards from Sumter's east angle. There was apparently some minor damage to the boom surrounding the fort, but this was the last of Foster's experiments with the powder rafts.

The fort had suffered terribly at the beginning of the bombardment due to a shortage of men in the workforce, but as the pounding progressed the fort actually became stronger. This was due to the fact that whenever the shelling stopped or slowed, day or night, laborers scrambled out to bolster the fort's defenses, according to engineer Johnson; the sporadic shelling emboldened the squads to toil around the clock. These men were particularly employed filling in the sea face with debris hauled from other sections of the fort. A new blockhouse was also laid out to provide quarters for a company and to allow infantry fire on the parade ground if necessary.[28]

The Third Great Bombardment of Sumter ended on September 4, after sixty days. It had varied in ferocity, but there had been few intermissions, night or day. During that time, 14,666 rounds were rained on Sumter, resulting in sixteen killed—including John Mitchel—and sixty-five wounded.

Schimmelfennig, meanwhile, was relieved due to illness on September 1 and replaced a few days later by Brig. Gen. Rufus Saxton as commander of the department's Northern District. Saxton spent his first few days sizing up his troops, fortifications, and armament, finding that through attrition he had only one gun—a 100-pounder Parrott—capable of sending shells into Charleston. Still, he was convinced that the city could be destroyed if he were given twenty or thirty Parrotts, ample ammunition, and orders to blast the place off the map. "If then the navy could be induced to sail in, I am confident the city would be completely destroyed or surrendered," he wrote Foster on September 8. "I have no faith in the impregnability of Charleston, and I trust that our Government will determine ere the fall campaign is over the headquarters of the Department of the South shall be in Charleston or where it was." Foster replied that while he liked Saxton's idea and his moxie, he had just received orders "to remain strictly on the defensive, hence the fire on Sumter and the city cannot be increased at this time."[29]

Despite this, the Federals kept up a minor bombardment of Sumter from September 6 through the eighteenth. Saxton also maintained a regular fire on Charleston with his 100-pounder Parrott "with most excellent effect," he claimed. Deserters scooped up by the navy on the sixteenth claimed that the bombardment over the prior week had been "more destructive than ever before to the city," Saxton wrote to Foster. By now,

Union shells were hurtling more than two blocks above Calhoun Street, in areas where most of the remaining civilians had relocated. "The city is completely within the range of our guns and can be destroyed," Saxton stated on the seventeenth.

That morning, Saxton had ventured out to inspect the naval battery being built on Morris and well within reach of Sumter's marksmen. Construction of this battery had been delayed not only by a lack of material but also by Huguenin's snipers, and the general himself had apparently come under fire. "Within the last two days the work . . . has been greatly interfered with by . . . sharpshooters which the enemy has stationed on Fort Sumter," he told Foster on the seventeenth. "The bullets came in very thick when I was at the front this morning." Saxton requested that "any telescopic rifles" be sent to him immediately to quell this threat, adding, "I think I can use them to great advantage." Huguenin that day also noted the performance of his snipers, stating, "The Yankees have done no work today at Gregg [Strong] because of our sharpshooters," and that the Federals had maintained a "brisk fire with small arms" in reply.[30]

Foster noted on the nineteenth that the reason for the cease-fire was a lack of ordnance, his supply of powder and rounds growing increasingly dire with each shot launched. "We are about out of ammunition . . . in the front batteries of Morris and Folly Islands," he reported that day, the shortage forcing him to slacken his fire against Sumter and other enemy targets. Sumter's defenders had reacted to the bombardment's decline by making repairs "with great energy," he said. That same day, Foster told Halleck that ammunition shortages had forced him to "decrease the fire from the batteries on Morris. The fire on Sumter has almost entirely ceased in consequence and the rebels are now taking advantage of the quiet by repairing that work." He also mentioned the fort's snipers and their "telescopic rifles, who annoy working parties very much, so much so that but little work can be done in the daytime in the front batteries on Morris Island." The artillery's supplies were suffering in other ways as well. "No powder for the mortars; no suitable fuses for the fire on Charleston; no shells for the 30-pounder Parrotts . . . no material for making cartridge bags, or grease for lubricating the projectiles," Saxton lamented on the seventeenth. "I shall do all in my power with what I have."[31]

By September 27, Saxton still had been unable to suppress Sumter's pesky riflemen. "His sharpshooters continue to annoy my working parties," he reported that day. The marksmen "are very industrious, and retard my work somewhat." The *Port Royal Palmetto Herald*, a Union newspaper, also noted this ongoing menace, adding that the Rebel snipers "have burned a great deal of powder and thrown away quantities of lead, without accomplishing a single result" other than to pock the nearest Union flagstaff with Whitworth bullets. "A few well directed shells generally smoked these fellows out, and drove them into the fort."

Yellow fever ravaged Charleston that fall, but while it was a serious scourge in the city and the Confederates' interior line, the Union forces were not largely affected due to a strict quarantine and stringent sanitary regulations, Foster related in early October. Federal rounds continued to crash into the city despite the Yanks' dearth of ordnance. "Our fire . . . is now far more effective than ever before," Foster told Halleck on October 4. "Our shells reach the arsenal and the whole upper part of the city." This new devastation was due to the addition by early October of several 200-pounder Parrotts to Fort Putnam, one to be used against Charleston and the others to target Sumter and Sullivan's. "The 200-pounder now in use is by far the most effective gun ever brought to bear upon the city," Saxton said during this time. "I think it is very destructive, as nearly the entire city can be covered by its fire. I am anxious to experiment with a 300-pounder," he added in requesting more and heavier guns to bedevil Charleston.[32]

A flare-up and shake-up among senior Confederate commanders at Charleston in late September festered into November, with Roswell Ripley again at center stage. Beauregard was immersed in the fighting around Petersburg when he received verbal orders from Jefferson Davis about September 25 to return to Charleston, and did so within a few days. Beauregard was to look into a dispute between Jones and Ripley involving one of Jones's staff officers, Maj. John F. Lay. Ripley questioned actions and orders given by Lay as being unauthorized by Jones, and the bitterness between the generals had deepened.

Beauregard also reopened his scrutiny of Ripley's drinking habits, with the end result that he recommended Ripley be transferred from Charleston, "which offers such great temptations and facilities for indulging in his irregular habits." In a dispatch to Davis on September 29, Beauregard suggested that Ripley be sent to Petersburg to lead Elliott's brigade. He also wanted Col. David B. Harris, the trusted and highly capable engineer, to be promoted to brigadier and to replace Ripley in commanding the First District. Harris was one of Beauregard's closest friends and comrades, and his engineering skills had been instrumental in making the city's defenses so formidable, including Fort Sumter. Unknown to Beauregard, Harris had succumbed to the fever on September 26 at Summerville, a few miles inland from Charleston. This was a grievous blow to the Louisianan who, in a letter to Harris's widow, described Harris as "one of my best and most valued friends."

Harris's loss and the command problems aside, Beauregard was taken aback by what he saw in and around the city. The appearance of Charleston and its defenses were in a worse state than when he left in April, and nowhere was the destruction and deterioration more shockingly evident than at Fort Sumter. "The parapets . . . formed partly of the debris and ruins of its former magnificent walls and casemates, had crumbled down, and were being gradually washed away by the rains and the waves . . . thus rendering parts of the parade visible to the sentries in the rigging of the enemy's blockaders," stated Lt. Col. Alfred Roman of Beauregard's staff.[33]

An even greater threat loomed—well to the west now, but one which the entire Confederacy was watching with much trepidation. Union major general William T. Sherman and his veteran army of some sixty-two thousand had captured Atlanta on September 1 after a summer of battle and maneuver across northern Georgia. What Sherman intended next was anyone's guess, but he and his Yanks were a significant menace that had to be dealt with.

By September's end, little was being accomplished by either blue or gray on the Carolina coast, although the battle lines were far from quiet. Charleston was still being shelled, as were the Confederate works on James Island occasionally. "Fort Sumter is rarely pounded, unless there are evidences of the rebels . . . attempting to strengthen its defences at all, when their improvements are speedily demolished and the garrison kept snugly in their ratholes," the *New York Herald* said on September 30. "It was discovered . . . that no commensurate results were obtained by the expenditure of ammunition . . . upon Sumter, as the debris became more and more pulverized and compact as the process of disintegration went on." The fort's parade still contained a "large pond" formed by shell fire and excavation by the Confederates for the defenses.

*Union major general
William T. Sherman.*
PHOTOGRAPHIC HISTORY OF THE CIVIL WAR

Without big guns facing Morris, the extent of Sumter's offensive power were the sharpshooters who pelted the Yankees at Cummings Point. With their telescopic Whitworth rifles, the Rebels burrowed into pits outside Sumter and triggered "bolts"—or bullets—at the Federals from a range of about 1,400 yards, a distance the bluecoats grudgingly admired. "The bolts reach Putnam with enough velocity to perforate any respectable thick head," the *Herald* correspondent noted. "This is regarded as an exceedingly good range, surpassing perhaps that of the best arm we have in our service." Despite being a continuing annoyance, the gray snipers inflicted few, if any, casualties.

Amid all this, Foster still believed he could level Charleston if provided a few more big guns. "I am confident that the city can be destroyed entirely by the fire of a large number of 100- and 200-pounder Parrott rifles, say twenty in number," he informed Halleck on October 13. The waters had been roiling around Dahlgren's flagship as well. The admiral had been informed by Gideon Welles that David Farragut would be in Port Royal by late September with a naval force to attack the Confederate defenses guarding Wilmington, North Carolina, a key Southern port. Discussions of a Wilmington offensive had been bantered about since the summer, but now the popular Farragut was finally coming, and Dahlgren would be under his orders. Yet while Farragut had indeed been Welles's first choice to lead the Wilmington expedition, he ultimately declined due to ill health. By the end of September, Rear Adm. David D. Porter had been assigned to command the strike force.[34]

Like the Confederates the previous April, the Federals were using photographs of Sumter to convey the varying degrees of damage to their respective high commands hundreds of miles to the north. Gillmore had dispatched sketches of the fort on two occasions, while Foster in early September had sent a photo to Brig. Gen. Richard Delafield, chief of engineers in Washington. The illustrations allowed Delafield to examine the artillery effects on the masonry walls based on the various calibers, numbers of rounds, and distances of the batteries. "If through your engineer and artillery officers you can give me detailed information and forward me several copies of the best photograph of the actual condition of Sumter, taken with the best light upon it, you will still further oblige me, and promote the interest of our service," he wrote to Foster on September 29.[35]

The swirl of the ongoing Jones and Ripley controversy, meanwhile, was briefly swept aside when Lt. Gen. William J. Hardee arrived in Charleston on October 5, replacing Jones as commander of the Department of South Carolina, Georgia, and Florida. Hardee, nicknamed "Old Reliable" by his troops, was a tough-as-nails Georgian with a long and distinguished record who had led a corps in the Army of Tennessee before he was reassigned to his new post on September 28. This would be a much-needed fresh start for Hardee, since there had been bad blood between him and Lt. Gen. John Bell Hood, who had taken the reins of the Army of Tennessee in July, and it was a promotion Hardee believed he had earned and deserved. In greeting Hardee, the *Mercury* stated that "all of our people, civil and military, we are sure, will be glad to welcome him amongst them. He brings with him the reputation of an able, gallant and experienced soldier, who in many a hard fought battle, has won a fame worthy of the great cause. . . . In the new field of duty, which the defence of our stout old city imposes, may he earn, and we delight to crown him with new and fadeless laurels of victory." Hardee spent several weeks familiarizing himself with his new post, making inspection tours and trying to strengthen its defenses. He had only some 12,500 scattered troops to defend the vast reaches of his department, most of them concentrated around Charleston and Savannah.

*Confederate lieutenant general
William J. Hardee.*
AUTHOR'S COLLECTION

Meanwhile, Beauregard in early October assumed command of the newly formed Military Division of the West. His position was mainly as an adviser, but he held vague authority over Hardee and Hood, his command extending from the Georgia and South Carolina coast to the Mississippi River. Jones was to head the District of South Carolina, a new post which encompassed much of the state and was headquartered in Mount Pleasant. Jones, however, was absent from duty for at least a portion of November due to sickness and was replaced by Maj. Gen. Robert Ransom Jr., who was ordered to Charleston early that month. But Ransom's own bad health caused him to leave his post just after Christmas, and he never returned to active duty.

Amid this unsettled situation, Ripley remained on duty in Charleston, but this was about to change. A petition supporting the Ohioan was signed by a number of prominent Charlestonians and leaders from adjoining areas, endorsed by Governor Bonham, and sent to Secretary of War Seddon in late November. By then, however, Ripley had been furloughed. Despite the petition's claim that his removal would be a "public calamity," his service in defense of Charleston was over.[36]

By November's first week, Union guns on Morris were launching one shell every fifteen minutes at Charleston from at least two 100-pounder pieces at Fort Putnam, some of the other guns there apparently disabled by then. Sumter was also still a target, enduring some mortar rounds from Battery Chatfield.

At Sumter, Capt. Huguenin by now had settled into as much of a routine as possible in holding the fort. He arose every day at 4:00 AM and required the garrison to be ready instantly from that time until sunrise, the hours he believed Sumter was most likely to be attacked. "The feeling of responsibility that weighed upon me was very great, and I endeavored to exercise a constant vigilance and to be prepared to meet any attempt which might be resorted to by the enemy," he said in a postwar account.

The intrepid Charleston photographer George Cook also returned to Sumter amid this period. He took pictures of Rebels cooking a meal in a huge shell crater and soldiers making sandbags, all against the backdrop of the moonscape that had become the fort's surreal interior. Despite the dire conditions in Charleston, Cook still was able to obtain chemicals from Anthony & Co., which also supplied the more widely known Mathew Brady and his team of photographers. (Cook and Brady had been colleagues in New York before the war.) Cook had his chemicals smuggled through the lines labeled as quinine, sometimes on orders "signed" by Lincoln himself.[37]

Sherman's army torched much of Atlanta on November 15 and was on the move again. After considering several objectives, Grant and Sherman had decided on a "march to the sea" through the heart of Georgia. Encountering scant opposition, the Yankee troops marched in two wings, wrecking railroads, burning hundreds of buildings, looting, and pillaging along a sixty-mile-wide swath. Sherman had vowed to "make Georgia howl," and he did just that. In an effort to aid Sherman, a Union force led by General Hatch and assisted by Dahlgren's squadron attempted to cut the Charleston & Savannah Railroad. The expedition was thwarted when Hatch's troops were defeated at Honey Hill on November 30, but this did nothing to delay Sherman's boys from plunging ahead toward the ocean. "I am more than ever convinced that Sherman is moving by the most direct routes to the Atlantic coast, as a base whence to attack Charleston or Savannah, or to reinforce Grant in Virginia," Beauregard wired Hardee on November 27.[38]

In the Charleston sector on Sunday, December 4, a truce flag was observed by both sides for a possible exchange of prisoners. The rival batteries ceased fire for the rest of the day, and for a few precious hours tranquility reigned over the war-ravaged city. The truce was in effect through the fifth, but through miscommunication, Fort Sumter was not aware of this. Who was at fault has never been traced, but early on Monday morning, the fort's sharpshooters began spraying the Federal batteries on Morris Island's north end. Union colonel E. N. Hallowell, the commander on Morris, tolerated this sniping for about an hour before ordering his guns and mortars to open on Sumter and James Island. After an hour or so of shelling, the Federals saw a small boat displaying a white flag emerge from Sumter. The soldiers aboard had a message from Huguenin to Hallowell: "Sir: Having just been informed by the proper authorities of the continuance of the truce . . . I beg leave to offer an apology for having fired upon the batteries . . . this morning with sharpshooters." Hallowell replied shortly afterward: "Sir: Your communication of this a.m., in explanation of the firing from Fort Sumter is received. The explanation is satisfactory. The firing from the batteries on this island will be discontinued." In reporting this incident on the sixth, Hallowell wrote that since the correspondence, there had "been an entire cessation of firing on both sides," a rare display of civility from the enemies.[39]

From September 18 when the last bombardment ceased, to the end of the year, a total of about 430 rounds was thrown at Sumter, but the roles of Huguenin's men were being shaped by events elsewhere. By December 12, Sherman's bluecoats were coiling around Savannah and concentrating on Fort McAllister, the strong earthwork south of the city which Du Pont's first monitors had engaged almost two years earlier. There was a brisk and bloody little fight for McAllister on the thirteenth before Union infantry overpowered its defenders and the Federals began entrenching to besiege or assault Savannah. The Yankees also were again menacing the Charleston & Savannah Railroad, causing the suspension of train traffic between the cities.

Dahlgren met with Sherman on the fourteenth to work out logistics for his troops, McAllister's fall allowing the navy to reach his army with much-needed supplies. Realizing the hopelessness of trying to hold Savannah and outnumbered about six to one, Hardee evacuated the city overnight on December 20–21, the sullen Rebels marching across a makeshift pontoon bridge over the Savannah River and leading into South Carolina. Some of the Savannah troops were sent to the Charleston area, while others were deployed in defensive positions and strategic points across the lower part of the state, expecting Sherman to eventually strike north into South Carolina.

Within days of his December 22 arrival in Charleston from Savannah, Hardee had clear instructions from Beauregard about how the city should be defended: "You will apply to the defense of Charleston the same principle applied to that of Savannah," Beauregard wrote on December 31, "that is, defend it as long as compatible with the safety of your forces. Having no reason at present to expect succor from an army of relief, you must save your troops for the defense of South Carolina and Georgia. The fall of Charleston would, necessarily, be a terrible blow to the Confederacy; but its fall with the loss of its brave garrison would be still more fatal to our cause."[40]

Including the ten thousand or so troops evacuated from Savannah, Hardee had only about twenty thousand men to defend the entire state, many of them posted at river crossings and other remote crossroads that could easily be bypassed or outflanked by the bluecoats. He desperately needed every soldier he could get, and if Charleston were abandoned, men like the troops of Sumter's garrison would find themselves in much different circumstances than defending a fort. To this end, Hardee soon began reorganizing his Charleston forces, equipping and drilling the artillerymen as infantry and organizing them into brigades in the extreme case that they would have to march and fight in open country. The city itself, meanwhile, continued to deteriorate, with burglaries, thefts, and muggings on the rise. The Union shelling was ongoing; streets in the now-desolate lower part of the city were overgrown with grass and weeds and lorded over by rabbits and rats. The once-grand avenues and picturesque courtyards were now a canvas of shell-shattered houses, crumpled chimneys, and broken windows.

Ironically, among the worst offenders were some of the soldiers assigned to defend the city. Charlestonian W. F. G. Peck wrote that "of all the thieves, burglars, and highwaymen who were ever brought together . . . these were the worst." They plundered homes, dug up lead pipes, and stole copper pumps, locks, and keys to sell, roaming the streets like common thugs. "For a season no one ventured out after nightfall, in any part of the city, without secreting a revolver about his person."[41]

Charleston was unraveling.

CHAPTER 12

"God Has Laid Us Very Low"—1865

The new year debuted with little cheer across the dying Confederacy as its territories shriveled and shrank on the secession vine. Sherman's veterans resting and refitting at Savannah were girding for an avenging strike into South Carolina and beyond. Indeed, Grant and Sherman were planning for Sherman's troops to march north through the Carolinas, possibly joining Grant's armies in Virginia. The offensive would be launched despite heavy winter rains that were swelling the swamps, rivers, and creeks in the bluecoats' path. With Federal successes across the board, the *New York Herald* predicted the war would be over by early spring and called on the "loyal states" to re-energize their troop recruitment efforts so that "the anniversary of the first bombardment of Fort Sumter may dawn upon the complete triumph of the Union arms."

On the Carolina coast, the cold and rain resulted in fog often blanketing the Atlantic, making it difficult for sentinels at Sumter and the other defenses to watch enemy movements, either by land or sea. The dire weather "made the difficulties of our situation extremely hard and guard duty a ceaseless and most imperative necessity," Huguenin noted. "Indeed, when I lay down to rest I fancied myself upon the ramparts and that I was peering into the darkness and the gloom." Stephen Elliott, meanwhile, had survived his supposedly mortal wound at the Crater on July 30 and returned to Charleston in early January. It had been an agonizing few months for Sumter's former commander. After being shot he had spent almost three weeks in a Petersburg hospital, where his wife and father came to comfort him. His left arm had been paralyzed for some time, and although he had been resting and recuperating, he was still far from healthy when he took command of a brigade in the Charleston defenses.[1]

Sherman and Dahlgren met in Savannah on January 13 to discuss how the squadron could assist Sherman's strike into South Carolina by keeping the Charleston Confederates occupied. The general told the admiral then that his troops would march through the state's interior, destroying the railroads, and would not target Charleston. With this in mind, the admiral met with his monitor captains on the fifteenth and proposed three attack options: an assault against Sullivan's Island, a rush into the harbor aimed at Charleston itself, or blasting into the harbor and assailing Fort Johnson. His skippers only showed interest in the Sullivan's Island operation, which disappointed Dahlgren, despite the fact that Sherman had advised him not to needlessly risk his men and ships against Charleston so late in the game. Sherman felt that a diversionary thrust at Bull's Bay on the coast north of the city was the best move; Gillmore had proposed a strike there in late 1863. But with the war winding down—and with it the opportunity for battle glory—Dahlgren suddenly became more daring, proposing the three attack options and that same day ordering an aggressive search-and-destroy operation against the obstructions and torpedoes barring him from Charleston Harbor.

In confidential instructions issued that day, the monitors would take the lead but would be assisted by all available support vessels. The objective was to finally neutralize the harbor obstacles by a variety of means. "The preliminary to removal will be by explosion," the admiral said. Union-made torpedoes and "boats filled with powder floated up with the tide" would be used to detonate enemy mines. Small boats would have grapnels, hooks, and long, slender pine poles to ward off floating torpedoes. Dahlgren described this as "the first measure" to "examine the channel and make sure of the obstructions, their nature and position." He realized his time to capture Charleston—and the American legend he would earn in doing it—were rapidly melting away. Thus, this new drive to get rid of the harbor defenses would be around the clock. "It is expected that each day and night will furnish its share of results," he closed in the confidential orders.[2]

The "results" were not long in coming, though not what Dahlgren had envisioned. That night, monitors *Patapsco* and *Lehigh* were sent toward the harbor mouth to probe obstructions between Sumter and Sullivan's Island. The ironclads also were to cover three scout boats whose crews were equipped with grapnels to search for torpedoes and other obstacles. With the *Lehigh* in reserve, *Patapsco* reached a position almost between Sumter and Moultrie. At Sumter, a lookout spotted the lead monitor, and Captain Huguenin was awakened. He ascended the watchtower and through his field glass also saw the low-slung craft. "This stealthy visitor, I surmised, was nothing less than a monitor, and I presumed that, coming in so unusually close, she must have some evil intent," he recalled. Only one of the three-gun batteries—the "East Battery"—could be brought to bear on the ironclad at the time, and Huguenin used a speaking tube, which ran from the ramparts to the position, to alert its commander, Capt. Hal Lesesne of the 1st South Carolina Artillery. He told Lesesne to fire on his order after the monitor had been allowed to get closer.

Silently, the *Patapsco* continued in, and several minutes later Huguenin yelled into the tube, "Fire!" There was no response, and Huguenin repeated the order, still getting no answer from his guns. Exasperated, he called into the tube a third time, exclaiming, "Lesesne, in God's name, why don't you fire?" Lesesne replied that he had lost sight of the ship. "Almost beside myself with excitement and disappointment, I hurried below, raised my field glass, and gazed seaward, but nothing could I see of this unfriendly visitor, the ghostly ship having vanished as completely as if she had been an optical illusion," Huguenin related.

The *Patapsco* had indeed disappeared, but there was no black magic involved. She had hit a submerged mine on her port side, the damage so extensive that she sank in less than a minute, carrying some sixty officers and men down with her. Scanning the ocean for the phantom ship the next morning, Sumter's lookouts spotted only the top of the monitor's smokestack some eight hundred yards out. "She had struck a torpedo and had gone down . . . as silently as a spirit," Huguenin recalled. He added that the monitor's destruction was "of great service to us . . . as it made an approach to our works to be regarded as an extremely hazardous enterprise, and not one to be lightly undertaken." The monitor's loss also sank Dahlgren's planned thrust into the harbor.[3]

For the Charleston Confederates, the blow against the *Patapsco* would soon be tempered by the bigger news from North Carolina that Fort Fisher, the huge bastion guarding the port of Wilmington, had fallen that same day, the fifteenth. Fisher had been the keystone of Wilmington's defenses, and its capture—after a desperate and bloody fight—meant that Wilmington likely would soon be in Federal hands as well. With some elements of his army already moving into South Carolina, Sherman left Savannah on January 21 on a steamer bound for Beaufort, South Carolina. He was ready to take the field again, and many Confederates believed Charleston and Fort Sumter were in his crosshairs.

As January closed, Sumter's garrison consisted of about three hundred troops—three companies of the 32nd Georgia Volunteers led by Col. George P. Harrison Jr., and two companies of the 1st South Carolina Regular Infantry, commanded by Col. William B. Butler. These Georgians had been heavily engaged at Olustee, where Harrison had been wounded, and in the earlier fighting on Morris Island. Butler, thirty-three, was the brother of Confederate major general Matthew C. Butler, and his men had been bloodied at Battery Wagner and elsewhere in the Charleston operations. Now these Carolinians and Georgians would constitute the last garrison of Fort Sumter.[4]

By February 2, Sherman's entire army had left Savannah and was spearing into South Carolina with a vengeance. To confuse the Confederates, Sherman divided his troops into two prongs with two apparent objectives—Charleston, and Augusta, Georgia. This proved to be a very effective strategy since it forced the Southerners to split their meager forces to guard both points, preventing them from mounting strong opposition to the Federals' advance. Augusta and Charleston were secondary targets for Sherman, knowing that both would be isolated as he carved the state in half with his sword. He knew well that Charleston was the more glittering prize, a fact that Halleck had reinforced even before the Yanks marched into Savannah. "Should you capture Charleston," Halleck wrote on December 18, 1864, "I hope that by some accident the place may be destroyed, and if a little salt should be sown upon its site it may prevent the growth of future crops of nullification and secession."

To Sherman, however, Charleston was essentially already conquered. Its defenders held in place by Foster and Dahlgren, and with no significant force to oppose his march well inland, the city was no longer of great military value to him, despite its symbolism. Over the coming weeks, he could always change his mind, turning his tough legions again toward the coast and assailing Charleston from the west—where its defenses were weakest—without having to face the harbor forts and batteries. But there were still battle laurels to be won and railroads to be wrecked, especially with "Charleston being a dead cock in the pit altogether," the general wrote on December 31, 1864. Sherman had friends in Charleston and knew the city, since he had been posted at Fort Moultrie in the early 1840s and savored its social scene. None of that mattered now as he aimed to crush the Rebel forces standing in his way, a move that would bypass Charleston.[5]

Sumter's old antagonist, Quincy Gillmore, returned to the Carolina coast on February 6, replacing John Foster as commander of the U.S. Department of the South, Foster taking a leave of absence "on account of disability from wounds," including the lingering effects of his Mexican War injuries incurred almost twenty years earlier. He also had been forced to relinquish command of the Department of the Ohio a year earlier due to injuries suffered when his horse threw him. "With a lameness which would have long ago amounted to disability with many, he has been one of the most active commanders the department ever had," the *New York Herald* said of Foster. At age forty-one he was suffering, although his leave was described as temporary.

Like Beauregard's return to Charleston in late summer 1862, Gillmore was not riding a crest of victory back to the southern coast. His record in Virginia had been mediocre at best, and he had been relieved of X Corps command the previous June for a lack of aggression in a coordinated attack near Petersburg. Still, he was returning to familiar ground. "General Gillmore finds a host of friends and admirers here, where he was so popular during his command of the department in 1863–4," the *Herald* said of the change. Not counted among them was a shocked Admiral Dahlgren, who had worked more efficiently with Foster only to now see the "unexpected passenger"—the despised Gillmore—return. "I have an entire contempt for Gillmore because of his conduct last year—harboring scribblers to lampoon me and denying their assertions to my face," the admiral wrote that day in his diary. Dahlgren was so incensed that he again requested to be relieved since the "public interests must suffer where want of harmony would not insure perfect concord of action" between Gillmore and him. He added, "I shall lose some prize money . . . but I will keep my self-respect which is better." On his part, Gillmore, about two weeks shy of his fortieth birthday, was still recovering from a fall he had taken with his horse the previous July during Confederate Jubal Early's raid on Washington.[6]

If Dahlgren had any second thoughts about again asking to be relieved, these were likely doused the next day when one of his officers brought him a copy of Gillmore's just-released book, *Engineer and Artillery Operations Against the Defences of Charleston Harbor In 1863, Comprising The Descent Upon Morris Island, The Demolition of Fort Sumter, The Reduction of Forts Wagner and Gregg*. The admiral thumbed through the work, finding himself mentioned many times and not liking what he saw. He immediately dismissed the book as Gillmore penning "a vindication of himself . . . at my expense." After his anger cooled a bit in the coming days, Dahlgren withdrew his relief request about a week later, telling Gideon Welles that he wanted to continue to cooperate with Sherman's operations, especially if Sherman changed his mind and decided to attack Charleston. The squadron already was heavily involved in Sherman's campaign, gunboats and other vessels operating on inland creeks and rivers to provide firepower, supplies, and ferrying for the troops.

The Federals' penetration into the state caused Robert Barnwell Rhett Jr., editor of the *Mercury*, to "temporarily" relocate the newspaper after publication on February 11. Rhett cited interruption of mail service and circulation due to the enemy's disruption of the South Carolina Railroad, plus problems in getting sufficient paper as reasons for the decision. No doubt the much-deserved reputation of the Rhett family as hard-shelled secessionists who did much to instigate the conflict also figured in the move. "For a few days, therefore, the issue of The Mercury will be suspended; but soon, we trust, it will revisit all our readers," the paper said in its last edition. It would be almost two years before the paper returned to Charleston.[7]

Despite unrelenting cold, rainy weather and flooded rivers, the Union columns kept plodding ever deeper into the South Carolina interior, brushing aside mostly weak resistance and leaving the frazzled Confederates still stymied as to their objectives. By Wednesday, February 15, Sherman's forces had slogged to within four miles of Columbia, the state capital, panicking many of the city's civilians. Some Union units reached

Columbia's outskirts on the sixteenth, lobbing shells into it, some crashing into the unfinished statehouse.

In Charleston, about 110 miles distant from the capital, Hardee had been ill and bedridden for two days by the sixteenth, but events were unfolding so quickly that there was no time for a restful recuperation for him. Beauregard, arriving in Charleston by train from Columbia on the fourteenth, issued orders detailing the roads the troops should use in leaving their positions in and around the city and where they would regroup.

Huguenin received orders on the sixteenth to begin evacuation preparations at Sumter. More detailed instructions about this movement soon followed, and that night the fort's sick, its black workmen and servants, and its officers' baggage were shipped to the city. Charleston and its defenses, including Fort Sumter, were to be abandoned by the Confederates overnight on February 17–18. There would be no magnificent last stand amid the brick rubble or hand-to-bayonet fighting in the casemates. Huguenin's men were more valuable to the Confederacy than the crumbling fortress they defended—despite its historic prominence. The star of secession was one with the sea; she couldn't be removed and was about to be left behind by brave soldiers whose cause was fading hard and fast.

On the morning of Friday, February 17, a new battle flag was hoisted over Sumter. Among the three hundred or so Carolinians and Georgians, orders and word spread quickly about the withdrawal. Some of the despondent and angry Rebels said they would rather die in the fort's ruins than relinquish it to the enemy whom they and so many others had battled for so long. "The day passed wearily and sadly to all who felt the crisis of the cause they had perilled [*sic*] their lives to maintain, and who understood the significance of abandoning such a post in the defense of Charleston," engineer Johnson wrote.[8] It was the 585th day of the siege of Charleston. No one in the city knew that Confederate troops had evacuated Columbia early that morning. Whether the capital still held out or not was immaterial to the Charleston Rebels, since the advance of Sherman's bluecoats already threatened to hem in any retreat by the forces there.

Also that Friday morning, Union troops waded ashore at Bull's Bay, on the coast about twenty miles north of Charleston, driving out the few Rebels posted there in the feint that Sherman had requested. Gillmore made a "special visit" to these Federals during the day, telling them that

Charleston would surrender if and when they gained a firm foothold there. Both Gillmore and Dahlgren, however, were expecting an imminent evacuation—possibly that night—based on rumors, observations from the trenches, and intercepted telegrams. The admiral wrote one of his officers on the seventeenth that "the movements of the rebels at all points of the harbor shall be closely and vigilantly watched, and . . . measures be . . . taken to apprise me by signal of the first appearance of any abandonment of the city or harbor defenses." One of the monitors or a picket boat should regularly attempt to draw fire from Moultrie to see if it was still occupied, Dahlgren ordered. The fleet should also be alert to any traffic between Sumter and Fort Johnson.[9]

As the sun slipped behind Charleston's silhouette, the Carolinians and Georgians at Fort Sumter went about their duties as if it were just another day at war. The new flag was lowered and the evening gun boomed its last salute over the harbor. The defensive barriers—including the wire entanglements and rows of wooden pikes—were placed around Sumter's perimeter. The light howitzers were run up the ramps and posted on the crest. Shutters on the casemate embrasures were closed and fastened and sentinels posted on the walls. Every hawkeyed Yank lookout needed to believe this was business as usual in order for the Rebels to successfully disguise their withdrawal. Different on this night, however, a soldier was posted on the wharf to watch for the vessels to remove the command. After dark, the soldiers, other than the sentinels, were formed up so they would be ready to leave quickly when the ships came. Huguenin made his own personal preparations to leave, burning some "valuable military books" in the fireplace of his quarters and sewing a batch of "official records" into a pair of underwear to be carried on the march. He also poured some whiskey into the water, "for fear the men might get hold of it during the retreat and create a disturbance."

About 10:00 PM, two small steam transports arrived at the dock. These vessels, whose names are apparently lost to history, were commanded by Lt. Thomas L. Swinton of the quartermaster department. There was a roll call and orders were quietly given for the boarding of the steamers, which was done without incident. The gloomy scene was accented by the throaty growl of Union guns in the distance, two monitors and a mortar schooner giving cover fire from the Stono River to

Gillmore's troops, who were probing Rebel positions on James Island. But no shells were sent toward Sumter.[10]

Huguenin and two lieutenants—E. J. White, his chief engineer, and W. G. Ogier, the post adjutant—watched the troops begin to board and then hurried to complete their duties before joining them. It was about midnight when the three climbed to the ramparts and personally relieved the sentinels, who were sent to the boats. They then made a final round of the now cold and empty fort. There would be no bone-jarring eruption to try to destroy Sumter, as the Confederates had attempted at Wagner. Orders were for the fort to be left intact. While Wagner was wrecked even before Huguenin lit the match to try to blow it up, Sumter was a magnificent ruin, four years of devastation creating a tapestry of bold, stark images. The soldiers and laborers had done their best to spruce her up, as if costuming a stately old dame for a last waltz. "At Fort Sumter ruin had wellnigh been covered up and concealed," noted John Johnson. "[T]rim ranks of gabions held up the slopes of sand or debris . . . the parade even looked swept and garnished; the casemates, either armed or turned to useful purposes, still recalled the old brick fort."

Despite the urgency of the evacuation, this was a solemn few minutes for Huguenin and his lieutenants, the last armed Confederates who would ever tread Sumter's tomblike passages and quarters. "The eye of the commander took in all these things for the last time as he went the rounds . . . pacing the deserted chambers, which only echoed to his footfall, or walking through the deep shadows of the long gallery, until he emerged at length through the sally-port . . . where the boats were waiting for him," Johnson wrote. Huguenin later acknowledged he had made the last rounds with "a heavy heart" but could not describe the myriad emotions engulfing him. Preparing to board the steamer, he knew that "many a heart clung to those sacred and battle scarred ramparts. . . . I felt as if every tie held dear to me was about to be severed; the pride and glory of Sumter was there, and now in the gloom of darkness we were to abandon her, for whom every one of us would have shed the last drop of his blood." The captain, assisted by Swinton and White, cast off the lines, and the last transport pushed away from the wharf. "Fort Sumter loomed grandly before their lingering eyes for a few minutes longer," Johnson added, "then the dark night enveloped it and they saw it no more."[11]

At least one account states that in the hours before their departure, the garrison was ordered to leave the fort cleanly swept and in the best order possible "as a monument of Southern skill, perseverance, industry and endurance." Emma Holmes made this claim in her April 7, 1865, journal entry based on conversations with her first cousin, John Holmes, a doctor assigned to Sumter at the time of its evacuation. Of the fort, she added, "500 men could have held it against 10,000, but alas, God has laid us very low and abased our pride. Every earthly support has been struck from beneath our trembling feet."

As at Sumter, other Confederate units began crawling out of their rifle pits and earthworks around Charleston after dark on the seventeenth. In the James Island defenses, two of Sumter's former commanders, Brig. Gen. Stephen Elliott and Col. Alfred Rhett, readied their troops for the evacuation. Both led patchwork brigades containing artillerymen and infantry and were a part of Brig. Gen. William B. Taliaferro's division.[12] Within hours, the Rebel forces, including Huguenin's men and those of Elliott and Rhett, were streaming away from the city. Their immediate objective was the hamlet of St. Stephen, some forty miles to the north, where they would board trains and try to unite with the Confederates who had fled Columbia.

Many terrible days had blotted the Confederacy's brief existence—Fort Donelson, Gettysburg, and Vicksburg included—but the banshees of war were dancing over South Carolina that night. As the Charleston troops tramped along the swampy roads out of the city, Columbia itself was cloaked in flames, each side later blaming the other for igniting the holocaust of ammunition and cotton bales that would level much of the capital. As at Savannah, Hardee had done a masterful job in evacuating Charleston—although he was criticized by Beauregard for being hesitant—but it was a forlorn and desperate accomplishment in the overall picture. Everyone from generals to drummer boys knew this as the sullen ranks plunged north on roads out of the city in a comatose effort to try to repel Sherman's hosts.

Overnight, Union seamen saw scattered fires and heard occasional heavy explosions coming from Charleston and James Island, before a dense haze that settled in before dawn on Saturday the eighteenth obscured almost everything. Union cannoneers at Cummings Point had banged away at enemy positions on the west end of Sullivan's Island during the night, and unconfirmed reports of Charleston's evacuation continued to heighten suspicions in the predawn hours.

Through the morning mist, Lt. Cmdr. George E. Belknap, of the recently arrived monitor *Canonicus*, scanned the coastline as closely as he could to determine what, if anything, was happening. Was this a ruse or were the Confederates actually abandoning the city? His ironclad had advance picket duty that morning, and Belknap got underway at daybreak, feeling his way toward Fort Moultrie. Because of the *Patapsco's* demise and Moultrie's big guns, his progress was cautiously slow, lookouts aboard peering into the murkiness to spot floating mines or other obstacles. By about 7:45 AM, the sun began to sear away the fog, and Belknap could see Rebel banners still crowning Moultrie and Castle Pinckney and in the city itself, apparently to give the impression that the Confederates were still there. Seeing no movement in or around Moultrie, the *Canonicus* lobbed two rounds at the fort from long range, receiving no reply. The vesuvian eruption of the magazine at Battery Bee on Sullivan's about this time was the most dramatic sign to the Yankees that something was amiss. The *Mahopac*, another monitor new to the squadron, soon came up near *Canonicus*, and an army boat was seen leaving Cummings Point and pulling toward Fort Sumter.[13]

Gillmore's men were indeed on the move this historic morning. Lt. Col. Augustus G. Bennett, of the 21st U.S. Colored Troops on Morris Island, had received word that the Charleston defenses might have been abandoned. From Cummings Point, Bennett sent a few soldiers in a small boat toward Moultrie to determine the situation. These were the men seen by Belknap. Some forty yards east of Fort Sumter, the Yanks encountered a boat from Sullivan's Island containing a group of Confederate musicians who had been left behind amid the evacuation chaos. The bandsmen confirmed that the Rebels were indeed gone.

With no troops immediately available, Bennett ordered Maj. John A. Hennessy of the 52nd Pennsylvania Infantry to head to Sumter "and there replace our flag." Wary that the fort's approaches were mined, Hennessy and a handful of soldiers gingerly climbed the parapet. In the now eerie quiet of this heart of secession, they waved the 52nd's regimental colors over the fort's southeast angle at 9:00 AM, sailors on the nearby monitors heartily cheering. "The sight of the old flag [actually the 52nd's banner] on Sumter was an assurance that the enemy had evacuated all their works, and it was hailed by every demonstration of joy by all, on ship and on shore," said one account.

Within a few minutes, another massive blast rent the morning air, the Rebel ironclad *Chicora* blown apart at her mooring. The *Palmetto State* already had met a similar end that morning as the Confederates destroyed their warships rather than leave them to the enemy. By now *Canonicus* and *Mahopac* had launched boats, their seamen stroking hard in a race with the army to plant colors on each of the grimly silent enemy outposts. The soldiers had a head start, but the tars managed to raise flags over Batteries Bee and Beauregard on Sullivan's Island. Belknap seized the blockade runner *Celt*, which had run aground near Moultrie on the night of the fourteenth with a cargo of cotton. Federals also boarded the wrecked Rebel ironclad *Columbia*, which had crashed into rocks in Moultrie's vicinity in January and not been refloated.[14]

Bennett, meanwhile, headed toward Charleston, accompanied by five officers and the armed crews of two small boats—twenty-two men in all. Some of these troops first landed at Fort Ripley and then Castle Pinckney, tearing down Rebel banners and showing an American flag in their place. Bennett's party, including a few soldiers of the 52nd Pennsylvania, reached the wharf near the foot of Broad Street about 10:00 AM and learned that a scattering of Johnnies were still in the city. Civilians also told them that mounted patrols were torching some property and abandoned supplies. His little command volunteered to press ahead from the wharf, but Bennett, without reinforcements available, decided against such a move. Instead, he penned a brief note to Mayor Charles Macbeth, demanding the city's surrender.

As the soldiers cautiously waited at the wharf, they could see smoke from about twenty fires and hear several more explosions. One of the blasts was especially terrific in its power: The Northeastern Railroad depot was detonated, killing some 150 people. It had been packed with a large amount of gunpowder and others supplies that the Confederates left behind. Some children playing with fire and handfuls of gunpowder outside the station accidentally triggered the devastation that also engulfed nearby homes and other buildings. Another mighty roar marked the doom of the ironclad *Charleston*, blown up by the Rebels at her anchorage on the Cooper. Amid all this, Bennett received a note—not in response to his earlier demand—from Macbeth stating that the

Confederates had evacuated and that he had remained to "enforce law and preserve order" until U.S. troops took over. "The city of Charleston and its defenses came into our possession this morning," Gillmore wrote to Halleck later that day.

More Federal units filtered into the city in the hours after Bennett's landing, and with no Rebs to fight, their duties turned to battling the blazes and policing the streets. Shortly thereafter, General Schimmelfennig, who had recently returned to duty after recovering from malaria, was placed in charge of securing the city. There was diehard gloom from other quarters. "When the sun rose next morning [Saturday], illuminating the old city, shining gayly [*sic*] on the white seas and the glittering waves, the siege had ended, for the forts were all empty and silent, and the way was left open for the enemy, who sailed cautiously in and took possession of the batteries and cannon that they had never been able to capture," Charlestonian Claudine Rhett recalled.[15]

John Dahlgren finally managed to get past Sumter that Saturday afternoon, arriving from the Stono where he had been directing operations. Despite the ongoing threat of torpedoes and obstructions, his flagship, the *Harvest Moon*, glided into the inner harbor, with the barely trusted mate from a blockade runner guiding the way. "Now came the getting in. I had made up my mind to do so, torpedoes or not," he would write. They passed the abandoned forts and the other now mute batteries and docked quietly at a city wharf on the Cooper River. "Not a shot was fired for the place, not a blow struck," he had dispatched Gideon Welles hours earlier. The "navy's occupation has given this pride of rebeldom to the Union flag and thus the rebellion is shut out from the ocean and foreign sympathy," he wrote later that day to his friend, Rear Adm. David D. Porter. "They [the Confederates] went from it unheralded by a shot." By then, Dahlgren had even taken a stroll through the city, finding "every house shut up; the few persons in the streets were foreigners and negroes. As they have made their beds, so let them lie," he told Porter. Dahlgren's exuberance continued later as he described the historic day in his journal: "And thus was deserted, without firing one shot or the loss of one life that 'city by the sea' that the proud chivalry had sworn to burn before we should enter; that we should only walk on its ashes, and they would die for. . . . The whirlwind came; blood and treasure flowed as if they were water. . . . At last comes fate—ignominy and disgrace."

At some point during the day, Union forces did get around to hoisting a U.S. flag over Sumter's stoic battlements, an anticlimactic event since Hennessy had snatched the glory that morning. The Stars and Stripes twisting in the air was different now, adorned by thirty-five stars, including the new states of Kansas and West Virginia as well as those of the sinking Confederacy, still stitched to the Union with bayonets and a sea of gore whose tide had first roiled against Sumter's walls.[16]

A few days after Charleston was restored to the Union, Gillmore, accompanied by his staff and a party of civilians, boarded the steamship *W. W. Coit* and went to Sumter for a tour. "The fort was found to be in a very strong condition for defence," wrote a *New York Herald* correspondent. The group noted nine guns there, "iron entanglements," abatis, and other obstructions designed to wreak havoc among assaulting troops. "The work could have been taken only by a heavy loss of life," the *Herald* reported. "It is stronger than when we fired the first gun against it."

Including Sumter's artillery, the Federals captured more than 450 pieces of ordnance in Charleston's defenses, more than double what Gillmore had initially believed to be the haul when the city was evacuated. Bennett added the Confederate flags from Forts Moultrie and Ripley and Castle Pinckney, along with seventeen signal pennants found in the city. "It appears that her [Charleston's] humiliation was in reserve for the day when her valiant fire-eating sons should abandon her without a fight," the *Herald* crowed.

Despite the city's fall, some Confederates remained unimpressed with the Union victory and were confident Charleston would be retaken, a forlorn hope at best. "After three years of immense and superhuman effort to take that place by regular siege; after burning more powder and throwing more weight of iron ball and shell than ever was expended in any siege since the world began, and all in vain; at length, finding the back door of the place purposely left open, they slip in," the *Richmond Examiner* noted. "How triumphantly they will display their felon flag upon the glorious ruins of Sumter!"[17]

Gen. Joseph E. Johnston returned to command of the Army of Tennessee and the other fragmented Rebel units in late February and attempted to concentrate his scattered troops near Fayetteville, North Carolina, in early March, after the Rebels failed to block Sherman's burning path through South Carolina. Under John Bell Hood, the Army of

Interior view of the fort in April 1865, weeks after it was evacuated by the Confederates. The many gabions emplaced by the Rebels were essential to bolster the crumbling walls. LIBRARY OF CONGRESS.

Tennessee had been wrecked in battle at Franklin and Nashville in Tennessee in November–December 1864 and in the hellish wintry retreat into Mississippi that followed. Now piecemeal units of its troops were being sent to the Carolinas to join other Confederates, including Hardee's men, under the feisty Johnston. Elliott, Rhett, and Huguenin—three of Sumter's surviving Confederate commanders—reached North Carolina with Hardee, but it was an awful journey for them and their men. The artillerists in the ranks, not used to marching long distances, suffered terribly on the bad roads worsened by winter weather, their misery heightened by minimal rations and exposure to the elements. There were numerous desertions among not only these soldiers but also all of Hardee's troops, many realizing the war was essentially over and that they were needed more by suffering loved ones at home.[18]

The regiments of Sumter's last garrison, meanwhile, had been assigned to two different brigades in Hardee's corps. The reunited 32nd Georgia was posted in a brigade led by its own Colonel Harrison in Maj. Gen. Lafayette McLaws's division, while William Butler's 1st South Carolina Regular Infantry was placed in Rhett's brigade under Taliaferro. Captain Huguenin was among Butler's officers, and Elliott's brigade also was a part of Taliaferro's division. Most of these men would see a great deal of combat on March 15–16, as Hardee and his troops tried to halt the advance of a portion of Sherman's forces near the village of Averasboro, North Carolina. Rhett, however, was captured on the rainy morning of the fifteenth after mistakenly approaching enemy horsemen he mistook for Confederates. He would spend the rest of the conflict and a few months more as a Union prisoner of war.

Averasboro would be quite eventful for Huguenin. With Rhett's loss, Butler became the brigade commander on the fifteenth, and Huguenin rose to the regiment's second-in-command. On the sixteenth, the 1st South Carolina's acting commander, Lt. Col. Robert DeTreville, was killed in action; Huguenin led the regiment for the rest of the battle. Amid some of the heaviest combat, a Carolinian recalled Huguenin's coolness as he slowly walked just behind their battle line, "smoking his pipe as calmly as if he had been at home."[19]

Elliott also led his troops at Averasboro, but the arduous campaign was aggravating his previous injuries—and the worst was yet to come. He and Huguenin both fought in the battle of Bentonville on March 19, as Johnston again tried to blunt the bluecoats. This was a bloodier, larger-scale, and more desperate clash than Averasboro, and Elliott, despite his weakened condition, exposed himself to enemy artillery while regrouping his men. The Carolinian had survived Fort Sumter with barely a scratch despite the tons of metal hurled at it, but his luck ran out here. A nearby shell burst sent shrapnel tearing into his leg. It was not a life-threatening wound, but combined with his earlier injuries and debilitated state, this was a devastating blow to not only his military career but also his health.

There were spasms of fighting the next day and on the twenty-first, but by now Johnston was outnumbered three to one as most, if not all, elements of Sherman's army of sixty thousand had now reached the field. The Confederates retreated overnight on March 21–22, and Elliott almost immediately left the army because of his wounds, his arm worsening due to the campaign's rigors.[20]

Meanwhile, Sumter's first Confederate commander, Roswell Ripley, had joined Johnston's forces amid the Bentonville struggle. This was his first active duty since his furlough the previous November. Though records are vague, he apparently briefly led Brown's Division, composed of four vastly understrength brigades of the Army of Tennessee, during the fighting. The division's commander, Brig. Gen. Mark P. Lowrey, had resigned his commission a few days earlier on March 14 due to bad health and exposure. Within days, Ripley was ordered back to South Carolina for duty, though his assignment is unclear. He had just arrived in Chester, South Carolina, when he learned of the Confederacy's imminent collapse.[21]

In Charleston, the Federals had spent several weeks in late February and early March inspecting and removing the Confederate defenses and preparing the city for a return to peacetime. For Admiral Dahlgren, this meant dealing with the dreaded obstructions and torpedoes that had played such a vital part in his squadron's inability and reluctance to blast its way into the harbor for all those months. There was some irony in the fact that he narrowly avoided death or serious injury on March 1 when the *Harvest Moon* struck a mine and sank off Georgetown, South Carolina, after he had taken such pains to successfully avoid these devilish devices for so long. For the Charleston operation, he used his seamen—along with ex-Confederates who had actually worked on these defenses—to locate and recover the infernal machines and the other barriers.

The reality of the situation had to be a jolt to the admiral, although he would never admit it. The only obstructions he had found by March 11 were two anchored lines of rope and wood obstacles stretching fifty feet apart from Sumter to Sullivan's Island. There also had been a chain barrier across the channel here, but it was removed by his tugboats and sailors shortly after the city fell. Two floating torpedoes were discovered nearby, although one of the captured Rebels claimed that 160 had been in the harbor waters by the previous May. "The small number of torpedoes found is probably due to the fact that they were easily put down, and that they were put down always previous to an expected attack, because keeping them in the water was injurious to the powder and there was a steady loss from being washed away," Dahlgren reasoned. A number of these weapons were also found on the city wharves, ready to be floated.[22]

"I see no reason to alter my opinion as to the entrance of this harbor," he wrote to Gideon Welles on the eleventh. "It could only have been effected by such a number of ironclads as might have suffered loss or damage from the obstructions and torpedoes and then preserved sufficient to engage [Fort] Johnson then pass on to the city batteries, then get out as well as they could." The admiral maintained that the interior harbor forts could not have been taken unless troops assailed them from the rear while the ironclads attacked in a coordinated effort between the navy and army. He then gave Welles his assessment of Fort Sumter in the grand scheme: "I judged rightly also in regard to the value of Sumter. If we had held that, then no obstructions could have remained in the channel, and all difficulty of foul screws avoided. As long as the rebels held it they could obstruct the channel in any way they deemed best."[23]

Quincy Gillmore would not place any stock in the admiral's explanation, instead blasting Dahlgren without naming him directly. "In point of fact there were no formidable obstructions in Charleston harbor," he wrote after the war, alluding to the scene of ships and boats reaching the city on the day of its capture without being blown out of the water or snarled by submerged rope or chain. A "novel spectacle was presented of a large fleet, comprising gun-boats, army and navy transports, a coast-survey steamer, dispatch boats, tugs, sutlers' and traders' vessels, passing up to the city . . . without encountering any of those hidden objects of terror . . . the question naturally arose whether at any previous time during the war the various channel obstructions, mines, and torpedoes had in reality been in a more efficient condition than we found them at that time." Gillmore contended that Roswell Ripley, Stephen Elliott, and other Confederates responsible for Charleston's defense claimed the strength of the barriers and torpedoes was "a huge fiction" to intentionally mislead the Federals. "From their statements, some of which are written, it appears to have been the constant and studied practice of the Confederate commanders to spread exaggerated and incorrect reports concerning this special means of defense," the general noted.

Backing Gillmore's stance was Whitelaw Reid, a war correspondent who would become editor of the *New York Tribune* in 1872. The silencing of Sumter by the bombardments and the seizure of Morris Island "opened the way for the navy to Charleston," Reid wrote. "Only unsailor-like timidity prevented the squadron from entering it. . . . On Admiral Dahlgren rests the full responsibility of the delay. Nor is there any disposition to question the skill or courage of that officer. But he lacked the warlike disposition that was required in the post he filled; and would have been better employed at his old work—casting giant iron smooth-bores at the Washington Navy Yard."[24]

Gillmore and Reid were correct in stating the perceived threat of the harbor obstructions was much greater than the obstacles the Confederates had in the water. But on March 13, two days after Dahlgren wrote to Welles, sailors found three large "boiler torpedoes" submerged in the channel between Sumter and Battery Bee, with detonation wires leading to the battery. A smaller mine was located near the wreck of the *Patapsco* and was hauled in and disarmed by emptying its powder onshore. And during the period from February 19 to March 17, an ex-Confederate named M. Martin Gray, now in Union service due to his knowledge of the city's harbor defenses, recovered or located approximately thirty-three torpedoes, although his search area covered not only the harbor but also portions of the Cooper, Ashley, Wando, and Wadmalaw Rivers. Gray was a shadowy character, supposedly the head of the Charleston Torpedo Service but more than willing to cooperate with the Federals as the war flickered out.[25]

Apparently for the first time, Dahlgren strode into Fort Sumter on March 13 and was surprised at the neat condition of the work despite the battle carnage. "I found that no account received gave me a proper idea of Sumter," he wrote in his journal. "The area is level and clear of rubbish. . . . The ruins—that shapeless mass is limited to the walls. The material pulverized, and thrown down in slopes from the walls inside and outside on the faces toward our guns. But I could not discern that impregnability to assault which rendered it certain death to get inside, as was pretended." He went on to describe the galleries loopholed for rifle fire, but added these could have been "easily" blocked and the defenders driven out by dropping a shell or two down the chimney.[26]

By late March between fifty and sixty torpedoes had been fished from the waters around Charleston, the *New York Herald* reported. It was an ongoing and delicate process to recover others of these infernal machines, but the operations had proceeded with scant casualties and little damage to the Union seamen and vessels involved. The Yanks also were sounding the channel and repairing the harbor lights. There were initial reports that Robert Anderson would be returning to Fort Sumter for a symbolic ceremony to end the war where it began, "replacing the identical old flag lowered from its ramparts four years ago at the dictation of South Carolina traitors," the paper said.[27]

If the war had temporarily bypassed Charleston and Sumter by early April as both sides fought through the end game, some facts and figures were immediately eye-opening. The Confederates had held Sumter during almost daily assaults of various kinds from April 1863 to February 1865. No place in American history would be involved in combat longer, no fort as famous. It would endure three major bombardments and eight minor bombardments, plus naval punishment by the most lethal Poseidons of the age. The Union army and navy hurled an estimated total of 46,000 projectiles at Sumter during the siege, some 3,500 tons of artillery metal. Incredibly, the resulting Confederate casualties were 319, including 52 killed and 267 wounded—hardly a field hospital full compared to a few hours in the volcanoes of The Wilderness or Chickamauga. Casualties among the slaves were apparently never recorded but likely at least as high as those of the Rebel defenders. These brave men would forever sleep in unmarked graves unheralded by grand monuments.

Total Union losses on the islands were never tallied, especially those among troops engaged in besieging Sumter, but about 2,400 Federals fell in the fighting on Morris Island, primarily against Battery Wagner. Certainly the navy sustained the most casualties in tackling Sumter itself, including almost 100 sailors who went down with the *Weehawken* and *Patapsco*; 16 wounded aboard the doomed *Keokuk*; and 130 or so killed, wounded, or captured in Dahlgren's failed amphibious assault in September 1863. John Johnson noted that from Du Pont's attack on April 7, 1863, to February 17–18, 1865, when the fort was evacuated, Sumter was under fire for 280 days, there being three months in 1863 and January–February 1865 when the fort was not shelled.[28]

All of these numbers would mean little—at least for a time—as an earthquake of events catapulted the war toward a close. Just before noon on Good Friday, April 14, 1865, Robert Anderson indeed returned to Fort Sumter four years to the day after his humbling departure. Joe Johnston's grim army was still defying Sherman in North Carolina, and there were scattered Confederate forces still on the map elsewhere. But the surrender of Robert E. Lee and the Army of Northern Virginia at Appomattox Court House on April 9 had cut off the head of the secessionist serpent; the war was essentially over. The steamer *Oceanus* had arrived in Charleston on the thirteenth with word of Lee's capitulation, the news crackling like a wildfire of euphoria among the Northerners who had come to the city for the Sumter flag-raising ceremony. Celebrating crowds cavorted in the streets and packed the parlors of the Charleston Hotel, all giving "vent to the wildest jubilation over the great event," a New York reporter noted. Regimental bands played patriotic tunes, lusty toasts and cheers for Lincoln and Grant rang out, and the joyous revelry swirled well into the night.[29]

That Friday, Anderson reluctantly stepped back into the national limelight as he and his family made their way onto Sumter's wharf. Not until Douglas MacArthur returned to the Philippines almost eighty years later—and perhaps not even then—would any general in American history make such a dramatic return to the site of his worst defeat, and now ultimate victory. But Anderson was far from a triumphant hero. Now a few weeks shy of his sixtieth birthday, he had not been on active duty since October 1863 due to age, illness, and the rigors of all he had endured at this very place. Still, the Republic certainly never forgot him, and in February 1865 he had been brevetted major general for his "gallant and meritorious service" in defending Sumter. He walked into the fort with Peter Hart, an ex-sergeant who was a carpenter and had served heroically during the 1861 bombardment. Hart had been among several men who risked their lives to replace the garrison flag after it was shot down by the Confederates that April 13 so long ago.[30]

An energized crowd of about five thousand had come to Sumter for this victory celebration, and others jammed onto various ships and boats in the harbor to try to get a glimpse of the proceedings. Many people clambered about the fort, "examining the immense ruin and groping

Soldiers and civilians begin to gather at Sumter as U.S. Navy vessels,
festooned with banners, cluster nearby for the April 14, 1865,
flag-raising ceremony. LIBRARY OF CONGRESS

through the dark passages, peering into the bombproofs and magazines, looking into the throats of the big guns, collecting pieces of exploded shells," the *New York Herald* related. From Sumter's jagged or demolished ramparts, visitors gazed about the harbor at the myriad ships and boats of all sizes dotting the water, including the now-famous *Planter*, crowded with many of Charleston's black citizens.

Dahlgren's warships were the most impressive, however, their rigging resplendent with an array of colorful banners. The vista from Sumter also included U.S. flags flying above all the former Confederate forts and batteries ringing the harbor. The admiral's monitors had steamed up to Charleston for the first time that morning and joined other Union vessels in firing a twenty-one-gun salute while anchored near the city wharves. Many people, including Charlestonians, had never seen the ironclads up close, and "the curiosity to see these terrors was very great," the *Herald* noted. Adding to the electricity, word continued to spread about Richmond's fall and Lee's surrender. "Mighty was the enthusiasm created by this news in the already stirred audience . . . who had assembled in the battered and shapeless fortress lying like some monster of the deep in the center of the harbor." said one account.

Among the notables present was Henry Ward Beecher, a leading abolitionist, whose sister, Harriet Beecher Stowe, had written *Uncle Tom's Cabin*, the powerful antislavery novel of the 1850s. Gillmore and Dahlgren were also in attendance. Hart carried the same flag that had been hauled down when the fort was surrendered. A military band played "Rally Round the Flag" and "Victory at Last," everyone singing along. A new flagpole had been erected in the center of the parade ground for the ceremony and Hart, assisted by three sailors, attached the banner to its halyards.[31]

The most poignant moment of the day was now at hand. Anderson, the pale and gray-haired old soldier, rose to speak on a platform decorated with flowers and greenery. He had not wanted this hoopla, but the Union needed closure to Fort Sumter's saga, and Secretary of War Edwin Stanton had pushed him to participate in it. "Had I observed the wishes of my heart it should have been done in silence," he told the hushed audience about the flag raising. "I restore to its proper place this dear flag, which floated here during peace before the first act of this cruel rebellion. I thank God that I have lived to see this day, and to be here to perform this, perhaps the last act of my life, of duty to my country." Anderson then hoisted the banner, with a garland of roses attached, to its pinnacle, the throng roaring in approval. Soon, Sumter's guns joined others in the forts and batteries around the harbor in a booming salute to the flag, the man, and the hour.

But not everyone was jubilant that day. Emma Holmes spoke for many diehard Rebels by turning a poison pen on the historic event: "The Y[ankee]s had a grand Union glorification, 'Bob Anderson' returning to raise the old flag over the glorious old fort which he had been compelled to surrender—then a long procession of his colored brethren to a hall where Beecher held forth—various other fooleries . . ."[32]

As the Stars and Stripes rose and danced in the ocean breeze over Sumter, a few hundred miles to the north in Washington Abraham Lincoln was attending to his daily functions and anticipating a Friday night out at Ford's Theatre to enjoy a performance of the comedy *Our American Cousin*. Learning of the president's evening plans, actor John Wilkes Booth also was plotting his next move.

The big crowd boarded vessels back to Charleston, and the shadows gradually deepened until the harbor was bathed in darkness, setting the stage for the next act of the historic day. On a signal, all of the navy ships were brilliantly illuminated, flashes flickering off Sumter's crumbled walls as if an attack by phantoms was unfolding. "Every vessel and transport and monitor was ablaze with many-colored fires," said one account. "Each mast and sail and rope was aglow with light. From every deck came the roar and glare of rockets, darting in quick procession to the sky, then turning and descending in showers of golden rain." Hundreds of lanterns glowing red, green, and white glowed from the vessels' rigging, reflecting on the water in a "scene of rare enchantment."

Shortly after this display, Anderson was a guest of honor at a military ball in the city and raised a toast to the president—"the good, the great, and honest man, Abraham Lincoln." Less than an hour later, about 10:15 PM, Lincoln was shot and mortally wounded by Booth at Ford's Theatre. The president lingered until 7:22 AM on Saturday; the ball in Charleston had finally broken up shortly before.[33]

After Bentonville, Joe Johnston's army withdrew to the vicinity of Smithfield and later to Hillsboro, North Carolina, farther to the northwest, always trying to thwart Sherman's advance. With Alfred Rhett a prisoner of war, Stephen Elliott again wounded, and Ripley apparently on his way to South Carolina, Thomas Huguenin was the last of Fort Sumter's immediate commanders still with the army. He was apparently promoted to major during this time, but it was a cheerless accomplishment with the war all but lost.

Through the final days of March and into early April, the rival armies sized each other up across the North Carolina countryside, Sherman settling in at Raleigh, the state capital. Other than some skirmishing, however, there was a lull in the fighting which lasted into the second week of April. Richmond's fall and Lee's surrender were numbing blows to Johnston and his war-weary troops, who now composed the largest

Confederate army still in the field. It was a hopeless situation, and Johnston finally capitulated to Sherman on April 26.

For Huguenin and the remaining Georgians and Carolinians who evacuated Sumter on February 18, the long struggle was finally over. Beauregard also laid down his sword here, the general who had first fired on the fort joining its last defenders in opening a new chapter of tempestuous reconstruction before a lasting peace.

The Postwar Years

For almost five years after the April 1865 ceremony, Sumter faded into the past, untouched and forgotten as the nation healed and tried to rise from the ashes of war. No repairs or renovations occurred at the fort—except to clear the parade ground and build a review stand for the triumphant flag-raising event—until January 1870. In a fascinating twist of history, the man charged with rebuilding Sumter was Quincy Gillmore, who had done more to destroy the fort than any other man in the Union army or navy. Gillmore commanded the U.S. Department of the South until the war's end and was returned to the rank of major of engineers in the peacetime army. The initial work under his supervision was little more than clearing debris, constructing a new wharf, and preparation to rebuild portions of the walls; operations were suspended in 1871 and took place on and off for the next few years.

From 1876 to 1897, the fort did not have a garrison, serving primarily as a lighthouse station. It was essentially forgotten and neglected over those years, with guns corroding, artillery platforms rotting, and much erosion by the relentless sea and storms. Old soldiers occasionally visited the fort; among them was C. H. Wessells, who had served in the 127th New York Infantry on Folly and Morris Islands. He was in a group that made its way out to Sumter in the summer of 1884, finding the only occupants the lighthouse keeper, his family, and an artillery sergeant.

"Aside from repairs to walls . . . and the removal of rubbish that was the chief feature of the place when the old flag was again raised in 1865, little had been done to give it the appearance of a fortress, and as we walked around its walls the wonder was that it had so long and successfully withstood attacks and capture," Wessells recalled.[1]

Gillmore was long gone from the fort by then, settling into civilian life in New York City, writing several other books, and engineering the Kings County Elevated Railroad along Fulton Street in Brooklyn, his last major achievement. The Ohio farmer's son had earned quite a name for himself, but the hardships of waging war in the Carolina heat and humidity were not yet done with him. While the railroad project was nearing completion in early spring 1888, the retired general had been suffering greatly for about two weeks due to a "combined liver and kidney complaint," the *New York Times* said. Gillmore had contracted the disease during the Charleston campaign, and "his sufferings have been constant, and compelled his retirement from very active business," the paper claimed. He was sixty-three when he died at his Brooklyn home on April 7, 1888, the twenty-fifth anniversary of Du Pont's attack on Fort Sumter. Trains began moving on the Brooklyn rail line a few days later, shortly after Gillmore's remains were taken by steamer up the Hudson River to West Point where he was buried with full military honors.[2]

Escalating tensions between the United States and Spain in 1897 prompted more focus on America's weak defenses on the East Coast, especially since the Spanish controlled Cuba. This impacted Sumter, and plans for a massive two-gun concrete artillery battery there were soon in the works. The battery would occupy almost two-thirds of Sumter's parade ground and be named for Isaac Huger, a Revolutionary War general. By the time the short-lived Spanish-American War ended in August 1898, construction on Battery Huger was just getting started, but work continued and was mostly completed in late 1899. Fort Sumter became a national monument in 1948.[3]

Sumter's last Confederate commander, Maj. Thomas Huguenin, returned to Charleston after the war. He was a farmer and cattleman and did railroad survey work before being elected a Charleston County commissioner in 1878. Beginning two years later, he served as superintendent of the city's street department for about fifteen years, his tenure spanning the terms of four mayors. Under Huguenin's guidance, Charleston began paving its streets. He was also very active in the state militia; he reached the rank of general and served as boarding officer for the U.S. Customs House before his death in summer 1897.[4]

Stephen Elliott returned to Beaufort after the war and in November 1865 received a pardon from President Andrew Johnson based on the efforts of his old adversary, Union general Quincy Gillmore. Impoverished, Elliott was reelected to the state legislature, but his war ravages soon overcame him. He died in February 1866 at the age of thirty-five.[5]

Roswell Ripley went to England after the war and was involved in a manufacturing enterprise, which soon folded. He returned to the States and resided in Charleston, although he spent considerable time in New York City. It was there on March 29, 1887, at age sixty-four, that he suffered a fatal stroke after having breakfast in the dining room of the New York Hotel. His body was returned to Charleston, where his passing was front-page news. His pallbearers included Alfred Rhett and Thomas Huguenin. He was buried in Charleston's Magnolia Cemetery.[6]

Alfred Rhett spent several months as a prisoner of war at Fort Delaware in the Delaware River after he was captured at the battle of Averasboro. Upon his release in late July, he returned to the Charleston area and married Alicia Middleton Sparks, Ripley's stepdaughter, in August 1866. He also resumed his rice planting, but later served as Charleston's police chief under two mayors. Controversy dogged Rhett even after the war. In 1872, a letter by Beauregard was published in a New Orleans newspaper, implying that Rhett had wanted to evacuate Fort Sumter prematurely amid the siege in 1863. The old general endured a barrage of criticism from Rhett's brother Robert and others who came to Alfred's defense, the furor eventually subsiding. Rhett died on November 12, 1889, a few weeks after his sixtieth birthday.[7]

Adm. Samuel Du Pont's career was harpooned by his failed assault on Fort Sumter in April 1863. He is a tragic and heroic figure who had not wanted to attack Charleston in the first place without the army's cooperation, but had been overruled by the blind ambition and aggressiveness of

Welles and, especially, Gustavus Fox. The various reasons for the delays of the monitors getting to Charleston in spring 1863 allowed the Rebels to further fortify an already formidable defensive position. No navy commander in history had ever led such a force into battle—this was a major event—and he had no idea how the monitors would perform, although their actions against the earthwork Fort McAllister had given him plenty to think about.

The broad-daylight attack on April 7 was as bold—or foolish—as could be envisioned, and likely reflected the unabashed confidence that Fox in particular placed in the invincibility of the monitors. The ironclads, with their low-to-the-water profiles, probably would have been much more effective in a night assault. But even if several had shot their way past Sumter in darkness, there were obstructions, including torpedoes, to be dealt with, and the harbor itself possibly would have become a shooting gallery, the slow-moving and slow-firing monitors basically surrounded by enemy cannon unless they immediately captured Charleston.

When the April 7 attack failed, Du Pont polled his trusted, veteran captains and tallied the damage inflicted on his vessels before deciding not to go in again. This decision was made as his newest monitor, *Keokuk*, was settling into her grave, torn apart after an hour of combat in her first fight. Realizing that the most modern warships on the planet were essentially outgunned and overmatched, Du Pont, backed by his senior officers, would not renew the assault.

Thus Du Pont faced a dead-end situation that ruined him, not only in terms of his career but also physically. Relegated to desk duties, he served on various boards and commissions for the war's duration. In poor health at age sixty-one, he died suddenly during a trip to Philadelphia on June 23, 1865. The *New York Times* was gracious in its brief obituary of the admiral, describing him as "the hero of one of the earliest and most brilliant naval victories of the war" at Port Royal in 1861. He had "followed up his advantage with vigor at different points along the Southern coast, the naval operations . . . invariably attended with success." There was no mention of the April day in 1863 that led to his downfall.[8]

John Dahlgren retained command of his squadron off Charleston until the war's end, despite his lackluster performance and his several requests to be relieved. Like Du Pont, he stepped into a position in which he had no experience: the handling and command of monitors. His dearth of battle savvy also worked against him, and when his September 1863 amphibious assault on Sumter failed terribly, he became even more cautious, fearing another debacle if he acted without the promised new ironclads which were always expected to appear. Gillmore's supposed betrayal, though always denied by the general, also engulfed him. But nothing else haunted and obsessed him like the death of his son, Ulric, the mutilation of the corpse, and the ensuing and ongoing firestorm about the documents found with the body during the Richmond raid. The inability to recover Ully's remains wore on him for more than a year and was not remedied until hostilities ceased. Ully was finally brought home and laid to rest in Washington, D.C., in October 1865.

Dahlgren held command of the U.S. South Pacific Squadron for a brief stint before again returning to duties at the Ordnance Bureau and the Washington Navy Yard in the autumn of his career. His feud with Gillmore was apparently never resolved before the admiral's death in July 1870 at age sixty. In his last years, however, Dahlgren was more focused on clearing Ulric's name—he and his second wife, Madeleine, worked on a memoir of his son's life. The admiral did not live to see it printed, but Madeleine completed the task; the *Memoir of Ulric Dahlgren By His Father, Rear-Admiral Dahlgren* was published in 1872.[9]

After Johnston's surrender, Beauregard returned to New Orleans, a widower with one silver dollar to his name. He considered going abroad to fight as a soldier of fortune, but never did so. His wartime popularity soon jumpstarted his peacetime fortunes, the aging general serving as a railroad president for about five years and then becoming a commissioner with the Louisiana lottery. He also employed his former staff officer, Alfred Roman, to write his biography; the extensive, two-volume work was published under Roman's name but was really an autobiography.

Beauregard died in New Orleans in February 1893 at age seventy-five, but his story doesn't end there. In his will, Beauregard requested that a sword given to him by a group of New Orleans ladies after his 1861 victory at Fort Sumter be given to the City of Charleston. A delegation of Carolinians, including Thomas Huguenin and John Johnson, journeyed to the Crescent City to accept the sword from the Beauregard family. It was formally presented to the Charleston City Council on March 27, 1893.[10]

Major John Johnson, Sumter's longtime engineer, saw action at Averasboro and Bentonville before surrendering with Johnston's army. Before the war he had been studying to become an Episcopalian minister, and upon returning to South Carolina he resumed his studies. Ordained in 1866, he was minister of Grace Episcopal Church in Camden, South Carolina, for several years before becoming assistant minister of St. Philip's in Charleston in 1871. He is best known to history, however, for writing *The Defense of Charleston Harbor: Including Fort Sumter And The Adjacent Islands, 1863–1865*. Published in 1890, it was the definitive eyewitness account of the Charleston campaign. Johnson died at age seventy-seven on April 7, 1907, the forty-fourth anniversary of Du Pont's failed attack on Sumter. He rests in the cemetery of St. Philip's church.[11]

Fort Sumter Odds and Ends

A number of other interesting aspects of Fort Sumter's saga have long been covered in the dust of time.

LINCOLN VERSUS DAVIS

Some historians have concluded that Lincoln's decision to send the naval relief expedition to Sumter in early April 1861 was one of the most brilliant decisions of his presidency. To wit, it placed the choice of keeping the peace or going to war squarely on Jefferson Davis and his advisers. If the Southerners blasted away at unarmed supply ships, they faced the stigma of starting a war. If the provisions were allowed to reach Sumter, who knew how long Anderson's men might hold out, which would be an embarrassing scenario for the Southerners.

More likely, as other scholars contend, Davis already had decided to go to war. The Confederates realized that as long as Union troops held Sumter and Fort Pickens in Pensacola Bay, Florida, the momentum of their cause would be stalled and possibly fail in its infancy. They needed a signature victory, but the Rebel forces in Florida were not yet strong enough to capture Fort Pickens. Thus Charleston and Fort Sumter would take center stage and never relinquish it.

THE "ANDERSON FLAG" QUESTION

After the repulse of the Union amphibious attack against Sumter in September 1863, the Confederates were convinced and ecstatic that they had captured the "Anderson flag" that the U.S. garrison had lowered in April 1861. The Federals contended that it was not the historic banner, and after Charleston's evacuation in 1865, Anderson returned the supposedly original flag. This standard is on display at Fort Sumter National Monument, while the whereabouts of the flag captured by the Rebels are unknown, if the flag still exists.

The army and navy had independent and mostly uncoordinated attacks planned against Sumter that night. Since Anderson was an army officer, it would have made more sense for Colonel Osborn's soldiers to have carried the authentic flag in their assault boats rather than allowing Dahlgren's seamen the chance for renown in raising it in victory, especially with the rivalry between the services and the ambitious Union commanders at Charleston in 1863. And since the army boats never reached the fort, the flag captured from the naval force apparently was not the original article. Thus, despite Beauregard's examination of the banner and his exultation in sending it to Governor Bonham as a war prize, it seems the Confederates were likely mistaken.

OLD FOES CORRESPONDING

In the years after the war, U.S. Navy rear admiral Thomas H. Stevens and Beauregard corresponded about the amphibious attack on Sumter in September 1863. Stevens, then a commander who skippered the monitor *Patapsco*, had led the failed strike. Beauregard wrote that the Rebels had expected an assault on Sumter after the fall of Morris Island and that the interception of signals and the gathering of armed vessels around Dahlgren's flagship on September 8 confirmed their beliefs. The old Confederate, however, lamented that Sumter's defenders had been impatient. "If our guns had not opened so soon and fired so rapidly, we would have captured or destroyed your whole command," Beauregard wrote, a claim with which Stevens agreed. Beauregard, through his biographer and former staff officer Alfred Roman, basically expressed the same sentiment in stating, "Had our batteries remained silent until the whole Federal detachment had left the barges, it is probable that the 500 or 450 'picked men' alluded to by Admiral Dahlgren would have fallen into our hands." Stevens also reflected on the brief but furious firefight on Sumter's shattered slopes, his words a testament of courage to the men on both sides who clashed there. "There was material in the command, both in officers and men, that would have insured success, had this been within the range of human endeavor," he said of the bluejackets. "Five thousand men could not have captured the fort that night."[12]

THE PLOT TO CAPTURE GENERAL GILLMORE

As shot and shell plastered Sumter on August 22, 1863, during the First Great Bombardment, at least one Confederate was intent on a daredevil and covert scheme to capture Union general Gillmore. Capt. Samuel L. Hammond of the 25th South Carolina Volunteers was devising a plan to snatch Gillmore from his quarters in a daring night raid and bring him to Charleston. Hammond made his proposal to Brig. Gen. W. B. Talia-ferro, his commander on James Island. "I desire to attempt an enterprise, which, it is true, will require much labor and some risk," the captain wrote that day. "It is nothing more or less than to visit Folly Island, some dark, rainy, disagreeable night, with 3 or 4 resolute men, take General Gillmore out of bed, and transfer him . . . that he may enjoy the hospitality of 'our city by the sea,' which he seems so anxious and determined to reach. Of course such an undertaking will require time; its issue doubtful. Plans must be formed, schemes invented, energy employed." Taliaferro wasted little time in rejecting Hammond's proposal that same day, noting tersely, "The scheme believed altogether impracticable."[13]

A FINAL GATHERING OF COMMANDERS

On July 20, 1914, the fiftieth anniversary of Capt. John Mitchel's death at Fort Sumter, a group of aging veterans and others gathered at his gravesite in Charleston's Magnolia Cemetery. They unveiled an impressive addition to honor him: a low, stone replica of Sumter's parapet, commissioned by a group called the John C. Mitchel Memorial Association. There had been at least one earlier formal remembrance of the captain. In October 1896, Mitchel's mother had presented to the city the sword her son was wearing the day he died, as well as his regimental flag.[14]

In addition to Mitchel, Magnolia Cemetery is the burial ground for three other Sumter commanders: Roswell Ripley, Alfred Rhett, and Thomas Huguenin.

A FLAG'S AMAZING ODYSSEY

When the Confederates evacuated Charleston in 1865, the troops of the 1st South Carolina Artillery left behind the regiment's flag. The beautiful silk banner had been presented to the soldiers in the war's early days by some of the city's most prominent ladies, including Mrs. Roswell Ripley. It had flown at Fort Sumter during some of the worst of the bombardments and in fighting elsewhere in which the Carolinians were engaged on the coast. After the regiment surrendered with Johnston's army, its commander, Lt. Col. Joseph A. Yates, returned to Charleston and tried to retrieve the flag, but met with sad news: He was told that the banner had been hidden in an attic for safekeeping from the Federals and had been destroyed by rats. That was the apparent end of the story for more than a quarter century.

In early 1893 the ragged banner was found to be in possession of a relic collector and was bought by two former officers of the regiment for one hundred dollars. Learning of the discovery, Yates's widow and daughter—the latter named Belle Sumter to honor her father's service in capturing and defending the fort—claimed the right to represent the colonel and sent money to the officers to purchase the banner for the city of Charleston. This storied flag was presented to the Charleston City Council on November 14, 1893, and displayed with honor near a full-length portrait of General Beauregard and one of the general's swords, bequeathed to the people of Charleston after Beauregard's death earlier that year.[15]

AN ENDURING TRIBUTE

On October 20, 1932, some eight thousand people crowded onto The Battery at White Point Garden for the dedication of a monument to the Confederate defenders of Fort Sumter. The most honored guest for the ceremony was William Robert Greer, who at age eighty-eight was the lone surviving Confederate veteran of the fort still living in Charleston, having served in the Washington Light Infantry.

The impressive monument was unveiled by four young ladies who were descendants of some of the best known of Sumter's heroes in gray. They included the granddaughters of Alfred Rhett, Thomas Huguenin, and engineer John Johnson, as well as the grandniece of Gen. Stephen Elliott. Despite his age, Greer rose to speak, thanking philanthropist

Andrew B. Murray for his gift of $100,000 to the city to help fund the memorial. He then spoke of Sumter's defense, saying there was never "at any time any lack of courage, but a determination unalterable that this great Gibraltar of Charleston should never be captured or surrendered."

The work had been created by Hermon A. MacNeil, one of America's preeminent sculptors of the period, who also was on hand and briefly described what he had tried to capture in shaping the monument: "Its motif in brief, is that the stalwart youth, standing in front with sword and shield symbolizes by his attitude the defense not only of the fort, but also of the fair city behind the fort in which are his most prized possessions, wife and family. And she, the wife, glorified into an Athena-like woman, unafraid, stands behind him with arms outstretched toward the fort, thus creating an inseparable union of the city and Fort Sumter."

Greer did not linger long, passing away in December 1932 and joining so many of his comrades in Magnolia Cemetery. MacNeil's masterful creation endures, however, as the exquisite centerpiece of The Battery.[16]

GLOSSARY

Berm. A narrow shelf between a fort's wall and the ditch or other obstructions outside the stronghold.

Bombproof. A structure designed and constructed to resist destruction from enemy bombardment.

Casemate. A fortified enclosure for artillery.

Chevaux-de-frise. Defensive obstacle of sharpened spikes attached to a wooden frame.

Columbiad. Large seacoast guns or howitzers first used in the War of 1812.

Dahlgren. Smoothbore guns invented by Union admiral John A. Dahlgren. These cannon were known for their distinctive shape and were made in various bore diameters.

Gabion. A barrel-shaped wicker basket filled with dirt, rocks, or other material and used in building fortifications.

Gorge. A narrow entrance into a fortification.

Merlon. The parapet section between two embrasures—or openings—in a fort.

Mortar. Artillery with a high, arcing trajectory suitable for firing over a fort's walls and into its interior.

Parapet. A protective wall of a fort to protect soldiers from enemy fire.

Parrott. Rifled, muzzle-loading artillery of various sizes invented by R. P. Parrott.

Pounder. Caliber of a cannon firing a shot of that weight; for example, a 200-pounder Parrott.

Revetment. A facing, or barricade, to support defensive works or to guard against exploding artillery rounds.

Rifled gun. A cannon with spiral grooves cut in the bore. When the cannon is fired, the grooves make the projectile spin, increasing its velocity and accuracy.

Smoothbore. An older-style cannon with no rifling in the bore.

Terreplein. Horizontal platform behind a parapet where heavy guns are mounted.

Torpedo. A floating or submerged explosive device—also called a mine. Other types of these weapons were used primarily by the Confederates to defend land forts and were sometimes buried along roads or other approaches.

Traverse. A defensive barrier built to protect against enfilade fire, i.e., fire from the rear or flanks.

FORT SUMTER
TIMELINE OF EVENTS

1829

Construction begins on Fort Sumter in Charleston Harbor.

1860

December 20—South Carolina votes to secede from the Union.
December 26—Union troops under Maj. Robert Anderson evacuate
　　Fort Moultrie and occupy Fort Sumter.

1861

January 9—Southerners open fire on the steamer *Star of the West*
　　attempting to bring supplies and troops to the Union garrison at
　　Sumter; the vessel turns back.
March 1—Brig. Gen. P. G. T. Beauregard arrives in Charleston to take
　　command of Southern forces there.
April 12–13—Carolinians open bombardment of Fort Sumter, igniting
　　the war. On the afternoon of the thirteenth, Anderson agrees to a
　　truce and hours later decides to surrender the garrison.
April 14—Anderson and his soldiers march out of Sumter;
　　Confederates occupy the fort.
April 18—Anderson and his troops reach New York City and are
　　greeted as heroes.
April 19—Lincoln issues proclamation ordering a blockade of Southern
　　ports.
May 11—The first Union blockader, the USS *Niagara*, arrives off
　　Charleston.

November 7—Union fleet under Adm. Samuel Du Pont wins the battle of Port Royal, South Carolina. Gen. Robert E. Lee arrives to take command of Confederate forces in South Carolina, Georgia, and eastern Florida.

December 11–12—Massive fire destroys much of downtown Charleston.

December 20—The first "Stone Fleet" is sunk off Charleston in an attempt to block one of the shipping channels.

1862

March 3—Lee ordered to Virginia and replaced by Maj. Gen. John C. Pemberton. Union major general David Hunter assumes command of newly created U.S. Department of the South about this time.

May 13—Robert Smalls and other slaves take the Confederate vessel *Planter* out to the Union fleet.

May 26—Brig. Gen. Roswell Ripley transferred from Charleston to Virginia.

June 16—Battle of Secessionville on James Island results in a Confederate victory.

July 16—Lt. Col. Thomas Wagner, one of Sumter's commanders, mortally wounded in artillery mishap.

August 9—Duel between Alfred Rhett and Arnoldus Vanderhorst.

September 5—Duel between Rhett and William Ransom Calhoun, who is killed.

September 17—Union major general Ormsby Mitchel replaces Hunter in departmental command.

September 24—Beauregard replaces Pemberton in departmental command.

October 16—Roswell Ripley resumes command of First Military District of South Carolina after being wounded at Antietam.

1863

January 31—Ironclads *Chicora* and *Palmetto State* attack Union fleet, temporarily lifting the blockade off Charleston.

March 28—Union forces occupy Coles and Folly Islands.

April 7—Du Pont's much anticipated naval attack on Sumter is repulsed. Monitor *Keokuk* sinks the next morning due to battle damage.

June 12—Brig. Gen. Quincy Gillmore relieves Maj. Gen. David Hunter as commander of U.S. Department of the South.

July 6—Admiral Du Pont relieved by Adm. John A. Dahlgren as commander of South Atlantic Blockading Squadron.

July 11—Attack on Battery Wagner repulsed.

August 17—Opening of the First Great Bombardment of Fort Sumter.

September 1–2—First Great Bombardment ends.

September 4—Maj. Stephen Elliott relieves Col. Alfred Rhett in command of the fort.

September 6–7—Battery Wagner and other positions on Morris Island evacuated by the Confederates.

September 9—Early-morning amphibious assault by Union naval forces repelled.

October 14—Three heavy cannon mounted in Sumter's northeast casemates.

October 26—Opening of the Second Great Bombardment of Sumter.

November 24—Death of Capt. Frank H. Harleston at the fort.

December 5—The Second Great Bombardment of Sumter ends after forty-one days and nights.

December 6—Monitor *Weehawken* sinks in heavy swells off Morris Island.

December 11—Explosion in fort's magazine area kills eleven men and wounds some forty others.

1864

February 12—Sumter's defenders establish second three-gun battery.

February 17—Confederate submarine *Hunley* sinks USS *Housatonic* off Sullivan's Island in night attack. The *Hunley* and her crew are lost in the history-making event.

July 7–8—Third Great Bombardment of Sumter begins.

July 20—Capt. John C. Mitchel, the fort's commander, mortally wounded and replaced by Capt. Thomas A. Huguenin that night.

September 4—Third Great Bombardment ends after sixty days.

December 20–21—Confederate garrison under General Hardee evacuates Savannah overnight; Sherman's army occupies city the next morning.

1865

January 15—Monitor *Patapsco* hits a submerged torpedo and sinks near the fort.

February 17–18—Fort Sumter evacuated as Confederate troops abandon Charleston overnight. Columbia, the state capital, is occupied by Sherman's army early on the seventeenth.

February 18—Union forces occupy Fort Sumter and Charleston.

April 14—Robert Anderson returns to the fort for the ceremonial flag-raising to return Sumter to the Union. President Abraham Lincoln is shot in Ford's Theatre that night and dies the next morning.

1898

Construction of Battery Huger begins amid defensive preparations for the Spanish-American War; battery completed the following year.

1948

Fort Sumter designated a national monument.

NOTES

INTRODUCTION

1. *Mobile Register*, March 14, 1900.

PROLOGUE

1. Ezra J. Warner, *Generals in Blue: Lives of the Union Commanders* (Baton Rouge: Louisiana State University Press, 1964), 7–8; Brian McGinty, "Robert Anderson: Reluctant Hero," *Civil War Times Illustrated* (hereafter cited as *CWTI*), 31, no. 2 (May/June 1992): 46–47; Frank Moore, ed. *Fort Sumter Memorial—The Fall of Fort Sumter, A Contemporary Sketch From Heroes and Martyrs* (New York: Edwin C. Hill, 1915), 59–60.

2. John Johnson, *The Defense of Charleston Harbor: Including Fort Sumter and the Adjacent Islands, 1863–1865* (Charleston, SC: Walker, Evans & Cogswell Co., 1890), 17–21; Albert Castel, "Fort Sumter—1861," *CWTI*, 15, no. 6 (October 1976): 47.

3. *Charleston Mercury*, December 28, 1860; Castel, "Fort Sumter—1861," 7, 12, 19; Mark M. Boatner III, *The Civil War Dictionary* (New York: David McKay Company, 1987), 729.

4. Anonymous, "Charleston Under Arms," *Atlantic Monthly*, 7, no. 42 (April 1861): 488–89.

5. Alfred Roman, *The Military Operations of General Beauregard in the War Between the States* (New York: Harper & Brothers, 1884), 1:25.

6. Gerard A. Patterson, "Gustave," *CWTI*, 32, no. 3 (July/August 1992): 31.

7. John G. Nicolay and John Hay, "Abraham Lincoln: A History—Lincoln's Inauguration," *The Century*, 35, no. 2 (December 1887), 283; Francis H. Kennedy, ed., *The Civil War Battlefield Guide* (Boston: Houghton Mifflin Co., 1990), 3–4.

8. U.S. War Department, *The War of the Rebellion: A Compilation of the Official Records of the Union and Confederate Armies* (Washington, DC: U.S. Government Printing Office, 1880–1901), series 1, vol. 1, 291 (hereafter cited as *OR*); McGinty, "Robert Anderson: Reluctant Hero," 47; Kennedy, *The Civil War Battlefield Guide*, 4–6; Castel, "Fort Sumter—1861," 38–39.

9. Ibid; C. Vann Woodward, ed., *Mary Chesnut's Civil War* (New Haven, CT, and London: Yale University Press, 1981), 46.

10. U.S. War Department, *Official Records of the Union and Confederate Navies in the War of the Rebellion* (Washington, DC: U.S. Government Printing Office, 1894–1922), series 1, vol. 4, 251–54 (hereafter cited as *ORN*); E. Milby Burton, *The Siege of Charleston—1861–1865* (Columbia: University of South Carolina Press, 1970), 48–49.

11. Ibid.

12. Abner Doubleday, *Reminiscences of Forts Sumter and Moultrie in 1860–61* (New York: Harper & Brothers, 1876), 166, 173.

13. *ORN*, series 1, vol. 4, 251–54.

CHAPTER 1

1. "Charleston Under Arms," *Atlantic Monthly*, 488–89.

2. Doubleday, *Reminiscences of Forts Sumter and Moultrie*, 166, 173.

3. Samuel Wylie Crawford, *The Genesis of the Civil War: The Story of Fort Sumter, 1860–1861* (New York: Charles L. Webster & Co., 1887), 447; Burton, *The Siege of Charleston*, 56; *Charleston Mercury*, April 16, 1861.

4. Burton, *The Siege of Charleston*, 56–57; *New York Times*, April 19, 1861; Crawford, *The Genesis of the Civil War*, 470, 447; Doubleday, *Reminiscences of Forts Sumter and Moultrie*, 171–72.

5. Ibid; C. A. Bennett, "Roswell Sabin [*sic*] Ripley: Charleston's Gallant Defender," *South Carolina Historical Magazine*, 5, no. 3 (July 1999): 227–28; *ORN*, series 1, vol. 4, 252, 263.

6. *Charleston Mercury*, April 16, 1861, and May 2, 1861; *OR*, series 1, vol. 1, 28, 56.

7. Crawford, *The Genesis of the Civil War*, 447; Doubleday, *Reminiscences of Forts Sumter and Moultrie*, 173; Burton, *The Siege of Charleston*, 56–57; *Charleston Mercury*, April 16, 1861, and May 2, 1861; *OR*, series 1, vol. 1, 56; Edmund Ruffin, "The First Shot At Fort Sumter (Extract from the Unpublished Diary of Edmund Ruffin)," *William and Mary College Quarterly Historical Magazine*, 20, no. 1 (October 1911): 90.

8. *ORN*, series 1, vol. 4, 255; *Charleston Mercury*, April 16, 1861, and May 2, 1861; *New York Times*, April 19, 1861.

9. *OR*, series 1, vol. 1, 28, 314; *ORN*, series 1, vol. 4, 255; Doubleday, *Reminiscences of Forts Sumter and Moultrie*, 174; *Charleston Mercury*, April 16, 1861.

10. Ibid.

11. Ibid; Ruffin, "The First Shot At Fort Sumter," 90; *New York Herald*, April 16, 1861.

12. *Yearbook—1883, City of Charleston, South Carolina* (Charleston: The News and Courier Book Presses, 1883), 483–88; *OR*, series 1, vol. 1, 56, and series 1, vol. 53, 175; *Charleston Mercury*, April 15 and 17, 1861. Some accounts say Galway died on April 19, which appears erroneous. He also is variously identified as Edwin Galway, Edward Gallway, Sgt. James E. Galway, and Edward Galloway, all apparently inaccurate. There was a Sgt. James E. Galway serving at the fort at this time, but he belonged to the 1st Artillery Regimental Band and survived the bombardment.

13. William Howard Russell, *My Diary—North and South* (Boston: T. O. H. P. Burnham, 1863), 98; McGinty, "Robert Anderson: Reluctant Hero," 58; *New York Times*, April 19, 1861; Warner, *Generals in Blue*, 7–8; *New York Herald*, April 19, 1861.

14. *OR*, series 1, vol. 53, 160; Ezra J. Warner, *Generals in Gray: Lives of the Confederate Commanders* (Baton Rouge: Louisiana State University Press, 1959), 22; Patterson, "Gustave," 31; Russell, *My Diary—North and South*, 99.

15.   *OR*, series 1, vol. 1, 28; Roman, *The Military Operations of General Beauregard*, 1:50; Russell, *My Diary—North and South*, 108–9.

16.   Ibid; *New York Times*, April 30, 1861.

17.   Robert M. Browning Jr., *Success Is All That Was Expected—The South Atlantic Blockading Squadron during the Civil War* (Washington, D.C.: Brassey's Inc., 2002), 8; Douglas W. Bostick, *Charleston Under Siege: The Impregnable City* (Charleston: The History Press, 2010), 12.

18.   *Charleston Mercury*, May 6, 1861.

19.   Ibid., May 7, 1861.

20.   Woodward, *Mary Chesnut's Civil War*, 128; A Prominent Secessionist (no other author listed), "Stories of a Confederate," *The National Magazine*, 10, no. 1 (April 1899), 51–52; *Yearbook—1883, City of Charleston, South Carolina*, 487–88; C. Russell Horres Jr., "An Affair of Honor at Fort Sumter," *The South Carolina Historical Magazine*, 102, no. 1 (January 2001): 6, 9; *OR*, series 1, vol. 53, 177–78.

21.   John F. Marzalek, ed., *The Diary of Miss Emma Holmes—1861–1866* (Baton Rouge: Louisiana State University Press, 1994), 60–61; Claudine Rhett, "Frank H. Harleston—A Hero of Fort Sumter," *Southern Historical Society Papers* (hereafter cited as *SHSP*), 9 (1882): 316; Bennett, "Roswell Sabin [*sic*] Ripley: Charleston's Gallant Defender," 226; Warner, *Generals in Gray*, 257; Jack D. Welsh, M.D., *Medical Histories of Confederate Generals* (Kent, OH, and London: Kent State University Press, 1995), 184–85; *Charleston Mercury*, June 24, 1861.

22.   *Charleston Mercury*, July 6–9, 1861.

23.   Ibid, July 29, 1861, and October 12, 1861; Patterson, "Gustave," 32.

24.   Marzalek, *The Diary of Miss Emma Holmes*, 66–67, 69; *Charleston Mercury*, July 27, 1861.

25.   Woodward, *Mary Chesnut's Civil War*, 128; A Prominent Secessionist (no other author listed), "Stories of a Confederate," 51–53; *Yearbook—1883, City of Charleston, South Carolina*, 487–88; Warner, *Generals in Gray*, 257; *OR*, series 1, vol. 53, 193; Horres, "An Affair of Honor at Fort Sumter," 7; William C. Davis, *Rhett—The Turbulent Life and Times of a Fire-Eater* (Columbia: University of South Carolina Press, 2001), 265, 315, 349–50, 354, 475.

26.   Browning, *Success Is All That Was Expected*, 21–22.

27.   *Charleston Mercury*, September 25, 1861.

28.   J. Thomas Scharf, *History of the Confederate States Navy From Its Organization to the Surrender of Its Last Vessel* (New York: Grammercy Books, 1996), 663–65.

29.   Mark Grimsley, "Robert E. Lee: The Life and Career of the Master General," *CWTI*, 24, no. 7 (November 1985): 20; *OR*, series 1, vol. 6, 312.

30.   *OR*, series 1, vol. 6, 312–13, 326.

31.   *Charleston Mercury*, November 15, 1861; W. F. G. Peck, "Four Years Under Fire at Charleston," *Harper's New Monthly Magazine*, 31, no. 183 (August 1865): 359.

32.   *OR*, series 1, vol. 6, 320; *Charleston Mercury*, July 19, 1862. Benjamin referred to Wagner as a captain in his dispatch, apparently unaware of his recent promotion to major.

33.   *Yearbook—1883, City of Charleston, South Carolina*, 483–87; *Charleston Mercury*, July 19, 1862; *OR*, series 1, vol. 53, 191.

34.   Horres, "An Affair of Honor at Fort Sumter," 9.

35. *Charleston Mercury*, November 28, 1861.

36. Bennett, "Roswell Sabin [*sic*] Ripley: Charleston's Gallant Defender," 230; *OR*, series 1, vol. 6, 352; Stanley F. Horn, *The Robert E. Lee Reader* (Indianapolis: Bobbs–Merrill Company, 1949), 131–32.

37. Burton, *The Siege of Charleston*, 81–84; Robert N. Rosen, *Confederate Charleston—An Illustrated History of the City and the People During the Civil War* (Columbia: University of South Carolina Press, 1994), 86–89; *Charleston Mercury*, December 12–14, 1861; *Recollections and Reminiscences, 1861–1865, Through World War I* (South Carolina Division, United Daughters of the Confederacy, 1992), 2:372.

38. *New York Herald*, December 23, 1861; Scharf, *History of the Confederate States Navy*, 662–63.

39. Woodward, *Mary Chesnut's Civil War*, 128; Warren Ripley, ed., *Siege Train—Journal of a Confederate Artilleryman in the Defense of Charleston* (Columbia: University of South Carolina Press, 1986), 285; Horres, "An Affair of Honor at Fort Sumter," 9; Bennett, "Roswell Sabin [*sic*] Ripley: Charleston's Gallant Defender," 230–31; *OR*, series 1, vol. 6, 351, 363–64.

40. Ibid.

CHAPTER 2

1. Burton, *The Siege of Charleston*, 88–89; Scharf, *History of the Confederate States Navy*, 662–63; Boatner, *The Civil War Dictionary*, 801; *OR*, series 1, vol. 6, 354.

2. Claudine Rhett, "Sketch of John C. Mitchel, of Ireland, Killed Whilst in Command of Fort Sumter," *SHSP*, 9 (1882): 270; *OR*, series 1, vol. 6, 248; Quincy Gillmore, "The Army Before Charleston In 1863," *Battles and Leaders of the Civil War* (New York: Century Company, 1887), 4:55; Clement A. Evans, ed., *Confederate Military History* (Atlanta: Confederate Publishing Company, 1899), 5:40.

3. Horres, "An Affair of Honor at Fort Sumter," 9–10; *Charleston Mercury*, July 19, 1862; Bruce S. Allardice, *Confederate Colonels—A Biographical Register* (Columbia: University of Missouri Press, 2008), 87, 321; *OR*, series 1, vol. 14, 515; Woodward, *Mary Chesnut's Civil War*, 277; Ripley, *Siege Train*, 285.

4. Derek Smith, *Civil War Savannah* (Savannah: Frederic Beil, 1997), 76–78; Quincy A. Gillmore, "Siege and Capture of Fort Pulaski," *Battles and Leaders of the Civil War* (New York: Century Company, 1887), 2:9.

5. Marzalek, *The Diary of Miss Emma Holmes*, 144; Smith, *Civil War Savannah*, 91; *New York Times*, May 15, 1862; *Recollections and Reminiscences, 1861–1865*, 2:179.

6. Horres, "An Affair of Honor at Fort Sumter," 10; Scharf, *History of the Confederate States Navy*, 668; Rosen, *Confederate Charleston*, 90–92; Burton, *The Siege of Charleston*, 94–95; Howard Westwood, "Mr. Smalls—A Personal Adventure," *CWTI*, 25, no. 3 (May 1986): 21–22; *OR*, series 1, vol. 14, 563. Sixteen slaves escaped on the *Planter*.

7. *OR*, series 1, vol. 14, 484, 563; A Prominent Secessionist, "Stories of a Confederate," 51–53; Allardice, *Confederate Colonels*, 87; *Yearbook—1883, City of Charleston, South Carolina*, 487–88; Bennett, "Roswell Sabin [*sic*] Ripley: Charleston's Gallant Defender," 230–31. Bennett states Coles Island was ordered to be abandoned in March 1862, which is inaccurate.

8. *OR*, series 1, vol. 14, 503–4, 508; Boatner, *The Civil War Dictionary*, 592. The three Carolinians were William Porcher Miles, W. D. Porter, and A. G. Magrath. Obviously, Lee no longer held departmental command on the southeast coast, but he had the respect of most Charlestonians and, just as importantly, the ear of Jefferson Davis in his role as military adviser through May 1862.

9. *OR*, series 1, vol. 14, 515–17; Horres, "An Affair of Honor at Fort Sumter," 26. Pickens refers to "Major" Wagner and "Captain" Rhett in his dispatch to Lee, but both officers had been promoted by this time. The governor's assertion that Ripley and Rhett were close is supported by the fact that Rhett married Ripley's stepdaughter after the war and was a pallbearer at the general's funeral.

10. Ibid. The soldier was Pvt. John Aiken of Company I, 1st South Carolina Artillery (Regulars).

11. *OR*, series 1, vol. 14, 484, 519–20, 523–24; *Charleston Mercury*, May 31, 1862.

12. *OR*, series 1, vol. 14, 516, 527, 562–65. Letter from Pickens to Lee in Richmond, May 23, 1862.

13. Ibid.

14. *New York Herald*, June 8, 1862; Iredell Jones, "Letters From Fort Sumter in 1862 and 1863," *SHSP*, 12 (1884): 6; Davis, *Rhett*, 506–7.

15. *OR*, series 1, vol. 14, 569; Woodward, *Mary Chesnut's Civil War*, 128; A Prominent Secessionist, "Stories of a Confederate," 51–53; *Yearbook—1883, City of Charleston, South Carolina*, 487–88; Horres, "An Affair of Honor at Fort Sumter," 6–7; *Charleston Mercury*, July 19, 1862.

16. *ORN*, series 1, vol. 13, 131; Stephen R. Wise, *Lifeline of the Confederacy—Blockade Running During the Civil War* (Columbia: University of South Carolina Press, 1988), 71–72.

17. *New York Herald*, June 8, 1862; *OR*, series 1, vol. 14, 366–67. Hunter's department had a total of 16,200 men present for duty as of July 31, 1862.

18. *OR*, series 1, vol. 14, 560, 580–81, 590, 597–98. Lee to Davis, June 25, 1862.

19. *Charleston Mercury*, July 19, 1862; Stephen R. Wise, *Gate of Hell—Campaign for Charleston Harbor, 1863* (Columbia: University of South Carolina Press, 1994), 14–17; *OR*, series 1, vol. 14, 552. Battery Wagner was originally called the Neck Battery. At least one account erroneously states Wagner was mortally wounded on July 17.

20. Patterson, "Gustave," 32–35; Boatner, *The Civil War Dictionary*, 59; *OR*, series 1, vol. 14, 601; T. Harry Williams, *P. G. T. Beauregard—Napoleon In Gray* (Baton Rouge: Louisiana State University Press, 1955), 161. Benjamin replaced Leroy Walker as Secretary of War in September 1861. Benjamin became Secretary of State in March 1862. Benjamin Huger and G. W. Smith had been among the generals discussed to replace Pemberton before Beauregard was chosen.

21. Roman, *The Military Operations of General Beauregard*, 2:436–437; *OR*, series 1, vol. 14, 600, 608–611, 622.

22. Woodward, *Mary Chesnut's Civil War*, 37, 110; William C. Davis, *Rhett*, 350, 506–7; Allardice, *Confederate Colonels*, 87; Horres, "An Affair of Honor at Fort Sumter," 18–19; Marzalek, *The Diary of Miss Emma Holmes*, 196.

23. A Prominent Secessionist, "Stories of a Confederate," 51–54; Allardice, *Confederate Colonels*, 87; *Yearbook—1883, City of Charleston, South Carolina*, 487–88; Horres, "An Affair of Honor at Fort Sumter," 19–21.

24. Ibid; William C. Davis, *Rhett*, 507; Marzalek, *The Diary of Miss Emma Holmes*, 196; *Richmond Daily Dispatch*, October 24, 1862.

25. Ibid.

26. *Richmond Daily Dispatch*, October 24, 1862; *Sacramento Daily Union*, November 19, 1862.

27. *Southern Presbyterian* (no date), republished in *Southern Christian Advocate*, September 24, 1862. Dueling would not be outlawed in South Carolina until 1880.

28. *OR*, series 1, vol. 14, 604–5; A Prominent Secessionist, "Stories of a Confederate," 52; Boatner, *The Civil War Dictionary*, 678–79; Warner, *Generals in Gray*, 252. George Randolph was Confederate Secretary of War from March to mid-November 1862.

29. John Johnson, *The Defense of Charleston Harbor*, 17–21; John Johnson, "The Confederate Defense of Fort Sumter," *Battles and Leaders of the Civil War* (New York: Century Company, 1887), 4:24; Hobart G. Cawood, *Combat History of Fort Sumter, 1863–1865* (Charleston: Fort Sumter National Monument, U.S. Department of the Interior, National Park Service, 1962), 1–2; James N. Ferguson, *An Overview of the Events at Fort Sumter, 1829–1991—Historic American Buildings Survey, Field Recording Project* (Denver: National Parks Service, 1991), 11.

30. *ORN*, series 1, vol. 13, 808–9; *OR*, series 1, vol. 14, 516, 600, 610, 622, 653, 712; Roman, *The Military Operations of General Beauregard*, 2:436–37; Burton, *The Siege of Charleston*, 116–17; Ben L. Bassham, *Conrad Wise Chapman—Artist and Soldier of the Confederacy* (Kent, OH: The Kent State University Press, 1998), 118–19; P. G. T. Beauregard, "Torpedo Service in the Water Defences of Charleston," *SHSP*, 5, no. 4 (April 1878): 147.

31. *OR*, series 1, vol. 14, 380, 382, 637; Smith, *Civil War Savannah*, 86–87, 95–96; Warner, *Generals in Blue*, 243–44, 327; *ORN*, series 1, vol. 13, 324. Mitchel was assigned to department command on September 1, but did not reach the South Carolina coast until about the middle of the month.

32. C. R. P. Rodgers, "Du Pont's Attack At Charleston," *Battles and Leaders of the Civil War* (New York: Century Company, 1887), 4:32; Browning, *Success Is All That Was Expected*, 130.

33. Bennett, "Roswell Sabin [*sic*] Ripley: Charleston's Gallant Defender," 233; Warner, *Generals in Gray*, 285–86; Roman, *The Military Operations of General Beauregard*, 2:26; Welsh, *Medical Histories of Confederate Generals*, 202; *OR*, series 1, vol. 14, 624–25, 633, 635, 641. Ripley replaced Brig. Gen. William D. Smith in command of the recently created First Military District. Smith died of yellow fever on October 4 after being ill for about two months. In point of fact, Ripley actually replaced Brig. Gen. S. R. Gist, who had temporary command of the district during Smith's illness and after his death until Ripley was assigned to head the district on October 16. At this time there were four districts in the department, including the District of Georgia.

34. *OR*, series 1, vol. 14, 613; *ORN*, series 1, vol. 13, 811; Horres, "An Affair of Honor at Fort Sumter," 14. Horres states that in his September 29 dispatch to Beauregard, Pickens refers to the death of General Smith. This is erroneous since Smith did not die until October 4. Horres also states Beauregard assumed department command on September 29, when it was actually September 24.

35.   *OR*, series 1, vol. 14, 380, 388; Smith, *Civil War Savannah*, 95–96; Warner, *Generals in Blue*, 42–43, 327; Horres, "An Affair of Honor at Fort Sumter," 21–22.

36.   *Charleston Mercury*, November 1, 1862; *New York Times*, November 18, 1862.

37.   Horres, "An Affair of Honor at Fort Sumter," 21–22; *OR*, series 1, vol. 14, 689, 715, 735–36.

38.   *Charleston Mercury*, December 10, 1862.

CHAPTER 3

1.   Horres, "An Affair of Honor at Fort Sumter," 22–23; *OR*, series 1, vol. 14, 689; Evans, *Confederate Military History*, 5:188; Marzalek, *The Diary of Miss Emma Holmes*, 222.

2.   Kevin J. Weddle, *Lincoln's Tragic Admiral—The Life of Samuel Francis Du Pont* (Charlottesville and London: University of Virginia Press, 2005), 183; Smith, *Civil War Savannah*, 103, 106–7.

3.   Scharf, *History of the Confederate States Navy*, 676–80.

4.   *OR*, series 1, vol. 14, 760, 768–69, 783; *New York Herald*, February 18, 1863; *Charleston Mercury*, February 12, 1863.

5.   *OR*, series 1, vol. 14, 396, 400, 404.

6.   Ibid, 781–782.

7.   Ibid, 749–50, 769–70.

8.   *Richmond Enquirer* (no date), republished in *Charleston Mercury*, February 28, 1863; *Richmond Daily Dispatch* (no date), republished in the *Mercury*, January 6, 1863; Browning, *Success Is All That Was Expected*, 150–51.

9.   Scharf, *History of the Confederate States Navy*, 685–86; Cawood, *Combat History of Fort Sumter*, 4–5; *OR*, series 1, vol. 28, pt. 2, 219, and series 1, vol. 14, 769; Craig L. Symonds, ed., *A Year on a Monitor and the Destruction of Fort Sumter* (Columbia: University of South Carolina Press, 1987), 46.

10.   *OR*, series 1, vol. 14, 802–4.

11.   Ibid.

12.   Smith, *Civil War Savannah*, 109–110; Weddle, *Lincoln's Tragic Admiral*, 183; *Charleston Mercury*, February 12, 1863; *ORN*, series 1, vol. 13, 709. William N. Still Jr., "Technology Afloat," *CWTI*, 14, no. 7 (November 1975): 42, 45.

13.   R. Adm. Daniel Ammen, *The Navy In The Civil War: The Atlantic Coast* (New York: Charles Scribner's Sons, 1883), 123; Boatner, *The Civil War Dictionary*, 252.

14.   Derek Smith, "Guns of the *Keokuk*," *North & South*, 9, no. 3 (June 2006): 80–81.

15.   Rodgers, "Du Pont's Attack At Charleston," 34–35; Browning, *Success Is All That Was Expected*, 153; *OR*, series 1, vol. 14, 427, 432.

16.   John Johnson, *The Defense of Charleston Harbor*, 37–39; John Johnson, "The Confederate Defense of Fort Sumter," 23.

17.   Ibid; Samuel Jones, *The Siege of Charleston and the Operations on the South Atlantic Coast in the War Among the States* (New York: The Neale Publishing Company, 1911), 166–70; Smith, "Guns of the *Keokuk*," 65; *OR*, series 1, vol. 14, 436–37, 564–65.

18.   *ORN*, series 1, vol. 14, 9; Rodgers, "Du Pont's Attack At Charleston," 33, 35.

19.   *ORN*, series 1, vol. 13, 823 and vol. 14, 95; Symonds, *A Year on a Monitor*, 46; *Charleston Mercury*, April 6 and April 8, 1863.

20. Symonds, *A Year on a Monitor*, 46; Claudine Rhett, "Frank H. Harleston," 312; Peck, "Four Years Under Fire at Charleston," 359; Ammen, *The Navy In The Civil War*, 102–3.

CHAPTER 4

1. Bostick, *Charleston Under Siege*, 61; Symonds, *A Year on a Monitor*, 46–48; Edgar Holden, "The First Cruise of the 'Monitor' *Passaic*," *Harper's New Monthly Magazine*, 27, no. 161 (October 1863): 593.

2. *ORN*, series 1, vol. 14, 95–97; Browning, *Success Is All That Was Expected*, 173; *Charleston Mercury*, April 11, 1863; Evans, *Confederate Military History*, 5:199. The current South Carolina state flag, with its crescent moon and palmetto tree, was adopted in January 1861, little more than a month after the state seceded from the Union.

3. Rodgers, "Du Pont's Attack At Charleston," 37; Holden, "The First Cruise of the 'Monitor' *Passaic*," 594; *Charleston Mercury*, April 11, 1863.

4. William M. Fowler Jr., *Under Two Flags—The American Navy In The Civil War* (New York and London: W. W. Norton & Company, 1990), 255; Wise, *Gate of Hell*, 30; Samuel Jones, *The Siege of Charleston and the Operations on the South Atlantic Coast*, 171; John Johnson, *The Defense of Charleston Harbor*, 50, 53–57; Rodgers, "Du Pont's Attack At Charleston," 37.

5. Symonds, *A Year on a Monitor*, 53; Weddle, *Lincoln's Tragic Admiral*, 193; Rodgers, "Du Pont's Attack At Charleston," 39. Rodgers reported the quartermaster's death and other carnage was caused by a 78-pound piece of iron blown away from the pilothouse.

6. *ORN*, series 1, vol. 14, 23; Samuel Jones, *The Siege of Charleston and the Operations on the South Atlantic Coast*, 171; *Charleston Mercury*, April 8, 1863.

7. *ORN*, series 1, vol. 14, 27, 95–97; Rodgers, "Du Pont's Attack At Charleston," 39–40.

8. Ibid; Browning, *Success Is All That Was Expected*, 180; Ammen, *The Navy In The Civil War*, 102–3.

9. *Charleston Mercury*, April 8, 1863; John Johnson, *The Defense of Charleston Harbor*, 50; Burton, *The Siege of Charleston*, 140; Claudine Rhett, "Frank H. Harleston," 312; *OR*, series 1, vol. 14, 263.

10. John Johnson, "The Confederate Defense of Fort Sumter," 24; Holden, "The First Cruise of the 'Monitor' *Passaic*," 594; *OR*, series 1, vol. 14, 257.

11. Smith, *Civil War Savannah*, 122; Wise, *Gate of Hell*, 30; Burton, *The Siege of Charleston*, 138; *OR*, series 1, vol. 14, 257.

12. *ORN*, series 1, vol. 14, 24, 95–97; Johnson Hagood (U. R. Brooks, ed.) *Memoirs of the War of Secession* (Columbia, SC: The State Company, 1910), 116; *OR*, series 1, vol. 14, 263.

13. *Charleston Mercury*, April 8 and 9, 1863; *OR*, series 1, vol. 14, 241; Dana Wegner, "The Port Royal Working Parties," *CWTI*, 15, no. 8 (December 1976): 24.

14. Browning, *Success Is All That Was Expected*, 180; Holden, "The First Cruise of the 'Monitor' *Passaic*," 594–95.

15. *OR*, series 1, vol. 14, 437–38, 442.

16. *ORN*, series 1, vol. 14, 37–38.

17. Browning, *Success Is All That Was Expected*, 180; Holden, "The First Cruise of the 'Monitor' *Passaic*," 594–95; *Charleston Mercury*, April 8, 1863; John Johnson, *The Defense of Charleston Harbor*, 76; *OR*, series 1, vol. 14, 897–98.

18. *New York Herald*, April 7 and April 14, 1863.

19. *OR*, series 1, vol. 14, 440–41; *New York Herald*, May 8, 1863.

20. Ibid. 901–2; Beauregard, "Torpedo Service in the Water Defences of Charleston," 160–61; *Recollections and Reminiscences, 1861–1865*, 2:205.

21. John Johnson, *The Defense of Charleston Harbor*, 65; Smith, "Guns of the *Keokuk*," 82–83.

22. *OR*, series 1, vol. 14, 241, 926; *Charleston Mercury*, May 6, 1863; John Johnson, *The Defense of Charleston Harbor*, 71; Burton, *The Siege of Charleston*, 146–47.

23. Rodgers, "Du Pont's Attack At Charleston," 38–39; *OR*, series 1, vol. 14, 455–457.

24. Wise, *Gate of Hell*, 36–37; John Johnson, *The Defense of Charleston Harbor*, 71–75; *OR*, series 1, vol. 25, pt. 1, 830, 833. Cuthbert and his men were in the 2nd South Carolina Infantry in Brig. Gen. Joseph Kershaw's brigade at Chancellorsville.

25. Sir Arthur James Lyon Fremantle, *Three Months in the Southern States: April–June 1863* (Mobile: S. H. Goetzel, 1864), 92–96, 101. Entry on June 14, 1863.

26. Quincy A. Gillmore, *Engineer and Artillery Operations Against The Defences of Charleston Harbor In 1863, Comprising The Descent Upon Morris Island, The Demolition of Fort Sumter, The Reduction of Forts Wagner and Gregg* (New York: D. Van Nostrand, 1865), 12–14, 21; *OR*, series 1, vol. 28, pts. 2, 3; *OR*, series 1, vol. 14, 459; *OR*, series 1, vol. 28, pt. 1, 5–7.

27. Lewis R. Hamersly, *The Records of Living Officers of the U.S. Navy and Marine Corps; With A History of Naval Operations During the Rebellion Of 1861–5* (Philadelphia: J. B. Lippinscott & Co., 1870), 14–15; Smith, *Civil War Savannah*, 121–22; Boatner, *The Civil War Dictionary*, 218; John A. and Madeleine Vinton Dahlgren, *Memoir of John A. Dahlgren, Rear-Admiral, United States Navy* (Boston: J. R. Osgood & Company, 1882), 381, 390, 396; Wise, *Gate of Hell*, 37; Browning, *Success Is All That Was Expected*, 216; Still, "Technology Afloat," 45.

28. *OR*, series 1, vol. 28, pt. 2, 288–89; *Confederate Veteran* 1:372.

29. *OR*, series 1, vol. 28, pt. 1, 288–89; Gillmore, *Engineer and Artillery Operations*, 21; *New York Herald*, July 18, 1863.

30. Whitelaw Reid, *Ohio In the War: Her Statesmen, Her Generals, and Soldiers* (Cincinnati: The Robert Clarke Company, 1895), 1:131, 654–55; Warner, *Generals in Blue*, 176–77; *New York Times*, April 8, 1888.

31. *Confederate Veteran*, 1:372; Wise, *Gate of Hell*, 81–82; *OR*, series 1, vol. 28, pt. 2, 204, 288–89.

32. Ibid.

33. *OR*, series 1, vol. 28, pt. 1, 572; Cawood, *Combat History of Fort Sumter*, 20; Iredell Jones, "Letters From Fort Sumter in 1862 and 1863," 139.

34. Iredell Jones, "Letters From Fort Sumter in 1862 and 1863," 161–62; Wise, *Gate of Hell*, 144.

35. *OR*, series 1, vol. 28, pt. 1, 573–77; John Johnson, *The Defense of Charleston Harbor*, 108–9; *OR*, series 1, vol. 28, pt. 2, 238, 253.

36. Dahlgren, *Memoir of John A. Dahlgren*, 404–5; *ORN*, series 1, vol. 14, 682.

CHAPTER 5

1. *OR*, series 1, vol. 28, pt. 1, 16, 576; *Confederate Veteran*, 1:372; Cawood, *Combat History of Fort Sumter*, 22–23; John Johnson, "The Confederate Defense of Fort Sumter," 24; Iredell Jones, "Letters From Fort Sumter in 1862 and 1863," 161–62.

2. Ibid; *New York Herald*, July 22 and July 27, 1863; *OR*, series 1, vol. 28, pt. 1, 16, 576–78.

3. Wise, *Gate of Hell*, 145–46; *OR*, series 1, vol. 28, pt. 1, 21–23, 214–217; *New York Herald*, August 8, 1863; Gillmore, *Engineer and Artillery Operations*, 51.

4. *OR*, series 1, vol. 28, pt. 1, 18–19, 21–23, 212–15; Dahlgren, *Memoir of John A. Dahlgren*, 406–7.

5. Reid, *Ohio In the War*, 1:655; Gillmore, *Engineer and Artillery Operations*, 55–56; *New York Herald*, August 30, 1863.

6. *Mobile Tribune* (no date), republished in *New York Times*, September 12, 1863; Fitzgerald Ross, *A Visit To The Cities and Camps of the Confederate States* (Edinburgh and London: William Blackwood and Sons, 1865), 108–9.

7. *OR*, series 1, vol. 28, pt. 1, 608; *New York Herald*, August 20, 1863; Frederic Denison, *Shot and Shell—The Third Rhode Island Heavy Artillery Regiment In The Rebellion, 1861–1865* (Providence, RI: J. A. & R. A. Reid, 1879), 174–75.

8. Cawood, *Combat History of Fort Sumter*, 22; Iredell Jones, "Letters From Fort Sumter in 1862 and 1863," 161–62; *OR*, series 1, vol. 28, pt. 1, 608, 578.

9. Charles H. Olmstead, "Reminiscences of Service in Charleston Harbor in 1863," *SHSP*, 20 (January–December, 1882): 165–66.

10. *OR*, series 1, vol. 28, pt. 1, 609, 659.

11. *New York Times*, August 14, 1863; *New York Herald*, August 20, 1863.

12. *ORN*, series 1, vol. 14, 448–49; *OR*, series 1, vol. 28, pt. 1, 609.

13. Ross, *A Visit To The Cities and Camps of the Confederate States*, 114; Dahlgren, *Memoir of John A. Dahlgren*, 407; *ORN*, series 1, vol. 14, 472.

14. *OR*, series 1, vol. 28, pt. 1, 21, 609–610 and series 1, vol. 28, pt. 2, 287.

15. Ibid; Cawood, *Combat History of Fort Sumter*, 23; John D. Pelzer, "The Second Bombardment of Fort Sumter," *America's Civil War*, 9, no. 2 (May 1996): 26; *OR*, series 1, vol. 28, pt. 1, 215. Rhett stated that seven guns opened on Sumter at 5:00 AM. Col. John W. Turner, Gillmore's artillery chief, reported that Battery Kirby's two mortars joined in the shelling of Sumter on August 17, but this may be inaccurate due to the long range for these pieces.

16. Ibid; Burton, *The Siege of Charleston*, 185; John Johnson, *The Defense of Charleston Harbor*, 119.

17. Ibid; Browning, *Success Is All That Was Expected*, 236–37; *ORN*, series 1, vol. 14, 450, 472; Samuel P. Bates, *History of the Pennsylvania Volunteers, 1861–65, Prepared In Compliance With Acts of the Legislature* (Harrisburg, PA: B. Singerly, State Printer, 1869), 2:57; George H. Gordon, *A War Diary of Events in the War of the Great Rebellion, 1863–1865* (Boston: James R. Osgood and Company, 1882), 183.

18. John Johnson, *The Defense of Charleston Harbor*, 120–21; *OR*, series 1, vol. 28, pt. 1, 610–11; Browning, *Success Is All That Was Expected*, 237–38; *ORN*, series 1, vol. 14, 458, 472.

19. Ibid; Iredell Jones, "Letters From Fort Sumter in 1862 and 1863," 212–13.

20. *OR*, series 1, vol. 28, pt. 2, 288; Marzalek, *The Diary of Miss Emma Holmes*, 294–95.

21. *OR*, series 1, vol. 28, pt. 1, 215, 596, 610–11.
22. Ibid; 598; *Philadelphia North American* (no date), republished in *New York Times*, August 30, 1863.
23. Ibid; Iredell Jones, "Letters From Fort Sumter in 1862 and 1863," 213.
24. John Johnson, "The Confederate Defense of Fort Sumter," 24; Claudine Rhett, "Frank H. Harleston," 314; Dahlgren, *Memoir of John A. Dahlgren*, 408; *OR*, series 1, vol. 28, pt. 1, 611.
25. *Philadelphia North American* (no date), republished in *New York Times*, August 30, 1863; *OR*, series 1, vol. 28, pt. 1, 215, 611–12. The Union gun added on August 19 was at Battery Stevens.
26. Ibid; Cawood, *Combat History of Fort Sumter*, 24; *ORN*, series 1, vol. 14, 462.
27. *OR*, series 1, vol. 28, pt. 1, 612; John Johnson, *The Defense of Charleston Harbor*, 124; *Charleston Mercury*, August 20, 1863.
28. Iredell Jones, "Letters From Fort Sumter in 1862 and 1863," 213; *OR*, series 1, vol. 28, pt. 1, 217; *ORN*, series 1, vol. 14, 462.
29. *OR*, series 1, vol. 28, pt. 1, 19, 214–15, 220, 222; Stephen Walkley, *History of the Seventh Connecticut Volunteer Infantry, Hawley's Brigade, Terry's Division, Tenth Army Corps—1861–1865* (no publisher listed, 1905), 100; John Johnson, *The Defense of Charleston Harbor*, 135–36; Gordon, *A War Diary*, 189. Gordon described the Parrott's fire, saying it was on August 21, which appears to be in error.
30. *OR*, series 1, vol. 28, pt. 1, 612–13. Initial reports that day said 35,000 pounds of powder were shipped with "between 300 and 400" 32-pounder shells. Also, the usually reliable Johnson states this shipment was done overnight on August 20–21, which is inaccurate.
31. Ibid.
32. Peck, "Four Years Under Fire at Charleston," 361; Iredell Jones, "Letters From Fort Sumter in 1862 and 1863," 214.
33. Ibid.
34. Browning, *Success Is All That Was Expected*, 240–41; Dahlgren, *Memoir of John A. Dahlgren*, 409; *OR*, series 1, vol. 28, pt. 1, 222; Walkley, *History of the Seventh Connecticut Volunteer Infantry*, 96–99.
35. *ORN*, series 1, vol. 14, 498–99; Iredell Jones, "Letters From Fort Sumter in 1862 and 1863," 255.
36. *OR*, series 1, vol. 28, pt. 1, 613.

CHAPTER 6

1. *Charleston Mercury*, August 21, 1863; *OR*, series 1, vol. 28, pt. 1, 614.
2. John Johnson, *The Defense of Charleston Harbor*, 124; Claudine Rhett, "Frank H. Harleston," 314; *ORN*, series 1, vol. 14, 471–72.
3. *OR*, series 1, vol. 28, pt. 1, 615; *ORN*, series 1, vol. 14, 465–66, 470; Wise, *Gate of Hell*, 164–65; Iredell Jones, "Letters From Fort Sumter in 1862 and 1863," 253–54; Browning, *Success Is All That Was Expected*, 241.
4. Roman, *The Military Operations of General Beauregard*, 2:140; *OR*, series 1, vol. 28, pt. 1, 19, 219; James Goldy, "The Swamp Angel," *CWTI*, 28, no. 2 (April 1989): 24; Wise, *Gate of Hell*, 169–70; Burton, *The Siege of Charleston*, 185. Gillmore said the range to "the lower end of Charleston City" was 7,000 yards; his artillery chief, Col. John W. Turner, calculated the distance at 7,900 yards to St. Michael's. Both are essentially accurate.

5.   *OR*, series 1, vol. 28, pt. 1, 615; Iredell Jones, "Letters From Fort Sumter in 1862 and 1863," 253–54.

6.   Roman, *The Military Operations of General Beauregard*, 2:141, 511; Wise, *Gate of Hell*, 171; Burton, *The Siege of Charleston*, 255.

7.   Iredell Jones, "Letters From Fort Sumter in 1862 and 1863," 253–54.

8.   *ORN*, series 1, vol. 14, 466–67, 470.

9.   John Johnson, *The Defense of Charleston Harbor*, 129–30; *OR*, series 1, vol. 28, pt. 1, 615; Dahlgren, *Memoir of John A. Dahlgren*, 409–410.

10. Ibid; Burton, *The Siege of Charleston*, 186–87; Browning, *Success Is All That Was Expected*, 241–42.

11. Olmstead, "Reminiscences of Service in Charleston Harbor in 1863," 165–66; John Johnson, *The Defense of Charleston Harbor*, 131, 133–34; Claudine Rhett, "Frank H. Harleston," 316–17; Cawood, *Combat History of Fort Sumter*, 26; Iredell Jones, "Letters From Fort Sumter in 1862 and 1863," 255–57.

12. Ibid; *OR*, series 1, vol. 28, pt. 1, 615–16.

13. Ibid.

14. Ibid.

15. *New York Herald*, August 28, 1863; Goldy, "The Swamp Angel," 25–27; *OR*, series 1, vol. 28, pt. 1, 219.

16. *OR*, series 1, vol. 28, pt. 1, 216, 598–600; Gillmore, *Engineer and Artillery Operations*, 65–66.

17. Ibid.

18. Roman, *The Military Operations of General Beauregard*, 2:144–146, 512; *OR*, series 1, vol. 28, pt. 1, 616.

19. Ibid.

20. Iredell Jones, "Letters From Fort Sumter in 1862 and 1863," 256–57; *New York Herald*, August 24, 1863.

21. Roman, *The Military Operations of General Beauregard*, 2:145–48, 513; Warner, *Generals in Gray*, 105. Gilmer was promoted to major general directly from colonel on August 25. Captain Warthen is incorrectly identified as "Wharthen" or "Worthen" in various accounts.

22. Ibid; *OR*, series 1, vol. 28, pt. 1, 222, 616–17; John Johnson, *The Defense of Charleston Harbor*, 131, 135–36; Walkley, *History of the Seventh Connecticut Volunteer Infantry*, 96–99; *Charleston Mercury*, August 26, 1863. Johnson states the transfer of these troops occurred on August 25–26, which does not jibe with the *Official Records* or Rhett's report in Roman, volume 2.

23. *Charleston Mercury*, August 25, 1863; Iredell Jones, "Letters From Fort Sumter in 1862 and 1863," 257–58.

24. Ibid; *OR*, series 1, vol. 28, pt. 1, 600, and series 1, vol. 28, pt. 2, 305–6.

25. *OR*, series 1, vol. 28, pt. 1, 600–2, 617; Iredell Jones, "Letters From Fort Sumter in 1862 and 1863," 258; *ORN*, series 1, vol. 14, 517–18; Browning, *Success Is All That Was Expected*, 244.

26. Iredell Jones, "Letters From Fort Sumter in 1862 and 1863," 544; Dahlgren, *Memoir of John A. Dahlgren*, 410–411; *OR*, series 1, vol. 28, pt. 1, 617, 654, and series 1, vol. 28, pt. 2, 306; *Charleston Mercury*, August 26, 1863, and *New York Herald*, August 26, 1863.

CHAPTER 7

1. Roman, *The Military Operations of General Beauregard*, 2:147–48; *OR*, series 1, vol. 28, pt. 2, 309.

2. Ibid, 311; Dahlgren, *Memoir of John A. Dahlgren*, 411; Marzalek, *The Diary of Miss Emma Holmes*, 305.

3. *OR*, series 1, vol. 28, pt. 1, 617–18.

4. *New York Herald*, August 28, 1863.

5. *OR*, series 1, vol. 28, pt. 1, 618.

6. Iredell Jones, "Letters From Fort Sumter in 1862 and 1863," 543–44; James V. Murfin, *The Gleam of Bayonets: The Battle of Antietam and the Maryland Campaign of 1862* (Baton Rouge: Louisiana State University Press, 1965), 371; *New York Herald*, August 29, 1863.

7. Roman, *The Military Operations of General Beauregard*, 2:515; *Charleston Mercury*, August 30, 1863; *ORN*, series 1, vol. 14, 524–25.

8. Iredell Jones, "Letters From Fort Sumter in 1862 and 1863," 544–45; *OR*, series 1, vol. 28, pt. 1, 600–2, 616, 619.

9. Ibid; *Charleston Mercury*, August 30, 1863.

10. Olmstead, "Reminiscences of Service in Charleston Harbor in 1863," 165–66; *OR*, series 1, vol. 28, pt. 1, 619.

11. Burton, *The Siege of Charleston*, 180–82; Wise, *Gate of Hell*, 177–78.

12. Iredell Jones, "Letters From Fort Sumter in 1862 and 1863," 544; *OR*, series 1, vol. 28, pt. 1, 619.

13. *OR*, series 1, vol. 28, pt. 1, 602; Dahlgren, *Memoir of John A. Dahlgren*, 412.

14. *ORN*, series 1, vol. 14, 529–30; Gordon, *A War Diary*, 202; John Johnson, *The Defense of Charleston Harbor*, 146–47; *OR*, series 1, vol. 28, pt. 1, 602, 621–22. Johnson says Companies B and C of the 1st South Carolina Artillery, along with only the 27th Georgia, composed the garrison then, which is inaccurate.

15. Burton, *The Siege of Charleston*, 189; *ORN*, series 1, vol. 14, 530–33; *OR*, series 1, vol. 28, pt. 1, 602; *Charleston Mercury*, September 3, 1863.

16. Ibid.

17. Ibid.

18. John Johnson, *The Defense of Charleston Harbor*, 146–47; Roman, *The Military Operations of General Beauregard*, 2:519–20; *OR*, series 1, vol. 28, pt. 1, 620–21; *ORN*, series 1, vol. 14, 532.

19. Welsh, *Medical Histories of Confederate Generals*, 60–61; Warner, *Generals in Gray*, 81–82; Roman, *The Military Operations of General Beauregard*, 2:152; *OR*, series 1, vol. 28, pt. 1, 621–22.

20. Roman, *The Military Operations of General Beauregard*, 2:152; *OR*, series 1, vol. 28, pt. 1, 621–22, 666; W. Chris Phelps, *Charlestonians in War; The Charleston Battalion* (Gretna, LA: Pelican Publishing Company, 2004), 139–40.

21. Ibid; *New York Herald*, September 10, 1863.

22. John Johnson, *The Defense of Charleston Harbor*, 154–55; *Augusta Constitutionalist* (no date), reprinted in *Charleston Mercury*, September 5, 1863; *OR*, series 1, vol. 28, pt. 1, 28, 123, 623; Jacob Newton Cardozo, *Reminiscences of Charleston* (Charleston: Joseph Walker, Stationer and Printer, 1866), 127; Dahlgren, *Memoir of John A. Dahlgren*, 412.

23. Burton, *The Siege of Charleston*, 190–94; Wise, *Gate of Hell*, 205–6; Milton F. Perry, *Infernal Machines: The Story of Confederate Submarine and Mine Warfare* (Baton Rouge and London: Louisiana State University Press, 1965), 61; *OR*, series 1, vol. 28, pt. 1, 38, 219.

24. Ibid; *OR*, series 1, vol. 28, pt. 1, 623.

25. Ibid; John Johnson, *The Defense of Charleston Harbor*, 155–59; *ORN*, series 1, vol. 14, 549–51, 553–54, 606–7.

26. Francis Trevelyan Miller, ed. *Photographic History of the Civil War* (Springfield, MA: Patriot Publishing Co., 1911), 1:24, 100; John Johnson, *The Defense of Charleston Harbor*, 166–67; Conley L. Edwards III, "The Photographer of the Confederacy," *CWTI*, 13, no. 2 (June 1974): 29–32.

CHAPTER 8

1. *OR*, series 1, vol. 28, pt. 1, 623, 667; Roman, *The Military Operations of General Beauregard*, 2:156; Phelps, *Charlestonians in War*, 139–40; Hagood, *Memoirs of the War of Secession*, 173–74.

2. *ORN*, series 1, vol. 14, 606–7.

3. Thomas H. Stevens, "The Boat Attack on Sumter," *Battles and Leaders of the Civil War* (New York: Century Company, 1887), 4:64; *OR*, series 1, vol. 28, pt. 1, 89.

4. *ORN*, series 1, vol. 14, 607–8; Scharf, *History of the Confederate States Navy*, 699–700.

5. Stevens, "The Boat Attack on Sumter," 49; *ORN*, series 1, vol. 14, 627–28.

6. *ORN*, series 1, vol. 14, 608–9.

7. Ibid; *New York Times*, September 16, 1863.

8. Stevens, "The Boat Attack on Sumter," 49; *Charleston Mercury*, September 10, 1863.

9. *ORN*, series 1, vol. 14, 623–24, 626.

10. Stevens, "The Boat Attack on Sumter," 50; Scharf, *History of the Confederate States Navy*, 700; *OR*, series 1, vol. 28, pt. 1, 726.

11. *ORN*, series 1, vol. 14, 623, 625, 626–29; Stevens, "The Boat Attack on Sumter," 50; *OR*, series 1, vol. 28, pt. 1, 726.

12. *ORN*, series 1, vol. 14, 613, 618, 623–24, 626, 630.

13. Ibid; *OR*, series 1, vol. 28, pt. 1, 727; *Philadelphia North American* (no date), reprinted in *New York Times*, September 16, 1863.

14. Ibid; Scharf, *History of the Confederate States Navy*, 700; Stevens, "The Boat Attack on Sumter," 50; Phelps, *Charlestonians in War*, 146–48; *Charleston Mercury*, September 10 and September 12, 1863.

15. *ORN*, series 1, vol. 14, 610–11; Roman, *The Military Operations of General Beauregard*, 2:157; *Charleston Mercury*, September 12, 1863.

16. *OR*, series 1, vol. 28, pt. 1, 28; Gillmore, "The Army Before Charleston In 1863," 64.

17. *New York Times*, September 13 and 14, 1863; *New York Herald*, September 17, 1863.

18. *Charleston Mercury*, September 19, 1863; *Richmond Enquirer*, September 11, 1863.

19. *OR*, series 1, vol. 28, pt. 1, 724–25; *ORN*, series 1, vol. 14, 630.

20. *ORN*, series 1, vol. 14, 641, 660, 679.

21. *OR*, series 1, vol. 28, pt. 1, 39–40.

22. Cawood, *Combat History of Fort Sumter*, 31; Denison, *Shot and Shell*, 188; *OR*, series 1, vol. 28, pt. 1, 123, 625, 654–55; Walkley, *History of the Seventh Connecticut Volunteer Infantry*, 113–14.

23. *OR*, series 1, vol. 28, pt. 1, 133–34; Dahlgren, *Memoir of John A. Dahlgren*, 415.

24. Denison, *Shot and Shell*, 189; Gordon, *A War Diary*, 247–48; Dahlgren, *Memoir of John A. Dahlgren*, 415; *ORN*, series 1, vol. 14, 674–75; 680–83.

25. Ibid.

26. *ORN*, series 1, vol. 14, 684; *OR*, series 1, vol. 28, pt. 1, 136.

27. *OR*, series 1, vol. 28, pt. 1, 136, 626; Cawood, *Combat History of Fort Sumter*, 31–32; *Charleston Mercury*, September 29, 1863, and October 1, 1863. See *OR*, series 1, vol. 28, pt. 1, page 627, for particulars about these few days.

28. *OR*, series 1, vol. 28, pt. 1, 93; *Charleston Mercury*, September 29, 1863.

29. *OR*, series 1, vol. 28, pt. 1, 16, 627–29, 654–55; Scharf, *History of the Confederate States Navy*, 758–60; Evans, *Confederate Military History*, 5:294, 297; Maj. James A. Hamilton, "General Stephen Elliott, Lieutenant James A. Hamilton, and Elliott's Torpedoes," *SHSP*, 10 (January–February 1882): 184–85.

30. Ibid; Dahlgren, *Memoir of John A. Dahlgren*, 418–19; Cawood, *Combat History of Fort Sumter*, 32; John Johnson, *The Defense of Charleston Harbor*, 170; Gillmore, "The Army Before Charleston In 1863," 62.

31. Ibid.

32. *New York Herald*, October 26, 1863; Cawood, *Combat History of Fort Sumter*, 32; *OR*, series 1, vol. 28, pt. 1, 602.

CHAPTER 9

1. *New York Herald*, November 8, 1863; Denison, *Shot and Shell*, 195; *OR*, series 1, vol. 28, pt. 1, 630, 649, 668–69; Dahlgren, *Memoir of John A. Dahlgren*, 420–21.

2. *OR*, series 1, vol. 28, pt. 1, 630–31; *ORN*, series 1, vol. 15, 88.

3. *OR*, series 1, vol. 28, pt. 1, 604; *New York Herald*, November 8, 1863; Dahlgren, *Memoir of John A. Dahlgren*, 421.

4. *OR*, series 1, vol. 28, pt. 1, 631–32, 649; Maj. John G. Pressley, "The Wee Nee Volunteers of Williamsburg District, S.C., in the First (Hagood's) Regiment," *SHSP*, 16 (January–December, 1888): 174; *ORN*, series 1, vol. 15, 91.

5. John Johnson, *The Defense of Charleston Harbor*, 182; Hagood, *Memoirs of the War of Secession*, 173–74.

6. Pressley, "The Wee Nee Volunteers of Williamsburg District, S.C., in the First (Hagood's) Regiment," 174–75; *Confederate Veteran*, 10: 419–20; Burton, *The Siege of Charleston*, 201; John Johnson, *The Defense of Charleston Harbor*, 171–72; *Charleston Mercury*, November 2, 1863; *OR*, series 1, vol. 28, pt. 1, 631–632; *Charleston Courier* (no date) in Denison, *Shot and Shell*, 203. Which Mathewes brother was the victim is uncertain.

7. Denison, *Shot and Shell*, 197; Dahlgren, *Memoir of John A. Dahlgren*, 421–22; *ORN*, series 1, vol. 15, 89, 91; *OR*, series 1, vol. 28, pt. 1, 632; *Confederate Veteran*, 18:113; *Charleston Mercury*, November 2, 1863. The Georgians who raised the flag on both occasions were Sgt. James Garahan, Cpl. W. M. Hitt, and Pvt. R. J. Swain of Company F, based on reports written at the time. In an account written more than forty years later, the battalion commander, Lt. Col. Henry D. Capers, identified the men as a Sgt. Hopps, Pvt. Garland Sneed, and "Pvt." Hitt.

8. Dahlgren, *Memoir of John A. Dahlgren*, 421–22; *OR*, series 1, vol. 28, pt. 1, 633, 649, 669–70; *Confederate Veteran*, 18:113.

9. Burton, *The Siege of Charleston*, 202; Bostick, *Charleston Under Siege*, 105; Smith, *Civil War Savannah*, 124–26; *Charleston Mercury*, November 3, 1863; Dunbar Rowland, *Jefferson Davis—Constitutionalist—His Letters, Papers and Speeches* (New York: J. J. Little & Ives Company, 1923), 6:76.

10. *OR*, series 1, vol. 28, pt. 1, 633; *ORN*, series 1, vol. 15, 88.

11. *OR*, series 1, vol. 28, pt. 1, 633–34; Dahlgren, *Memoir of John A. Dahlgren*, 422–23.

12. *OR*, series 1, vol. 28, pt. 1, 634–35, 649; Denison, *Shot and Shell*, 196, 200; William V. Izlar, *A Sketch of the War Record of the Edisto Rifles: 1861–1865* (Columbia, SC: The State Company, 1914), 42–43. Initial reports indicated the bulk of the casualties were from the 27th Georgia, which were apparently erroneous. The men who replaced the flag were Sgt. N. D. Currie and Cpl. S. Montgomery.

13. John Johnson, *The Defense of Charleston Harbor*, 173; *OR*, series 1, vol. 28, pt. 1, 604–5; *New York Herald*, November 8, 1863.

14. *OR*, series 1, vol. 28, pt. 1, 635–37, 649.

15. Ibid; *ORN*, series 1, vol. 15, 91.

16. John Johnson, *The Defense of Charleston Harbor*, 175; John Johnson, "The Confederate Defense of Fort Sumter," 25; *OR*, series 1, vol. 28, pt. 1, 637–39.

17. Ross, *A Visit To The Cities and Camps of the Confederate States*, 175–76.

18. *OR*, series 1, vol. 28, pt. 1, 604–5, 638.

19. Ibid, 639–69.

20. *ORN*, series 1, vol. 15, 114, 117–19, 142; John Johnson, "The Confederate Defense of Fort Sumter," 26; *OR*, series 1, vol. 28, pt. 1, 638.

21. Burton, *The Siege of Charleston*, 256–57; W. Chris Phelps, *The Bombardment of Charleston, 1863–1865* (Gretna, LA: Pelican Publishing Company, 1999), 64; *Richmond Enquirer*, November 13, 1863; *OR*, series 1, vol. 28, pt. 1, 638.

22. *OR*, series 1, vol. 28, pt. 1, 605–6, 639, 641, 649, 742–743; Burton, *The Siege of Charleston*, 204–5; Evans, *Confederate Military History*, 5:295–96.

23. Ibid. Conyngham is listed as Cunningham in some Union reports. At least one postwar Southern history of the war erroneously portrayed this episode as another failed attempt by the Federals to make a landing, Elliott's men preventing them from reaching Sumter. Burton states this attack was on November 30, which appears to be inaccurate since Elliott makes no mention of enemy offensive action—other than the shelling—between November 28 and December 1.

24. *Charleston Mercury*, November 21, 1863; *OR*, series 1, vol. 28, pt. 1, 655–58. These officers' reports were from November 13 and 15–16.

25. *OR*, series 1, vol. 28, pt. 1, 605–6, 639–40; *Charleston Daily Courier*, November 11, 1863; *Charleston Mercury*, November 21, 1863.

26. John Johnson, *The Defense of Charleston Harbor*, 172; *OR*, series 1, vol. 28, pt. 1, 639–40; *Recollections and Reminiscences*, 1861–1865, 2:221.

27. *Charleston Mercury*, November 25, 1863; Claudine Rhett, "Frank H. Harleston," 318–19; *OR*, series 1, vol. 28, pt. 1, 743; John Johnson, *The Defense of Charleston Harbor*, 178. Miss Rhett's account makes no mention of Houston and states that Harleston lay on the cold, slippery rocks for about fifteen minutes before he was missed, his comrades coming to find him.

28. Marzalek, *The Diary of Miss Emma Holmes*, 326–27; *OR*, series 1, vol. 28, pt. 1, 640, 649; Dahlgren, *Memoir of John A. Dahlgren*, 427, 477.

29. Dahlgren, *Memoir of John A. Dahlgren*, 427; *OR*, series 1, vol. 28, pt. 1, 605–6, 641, 649; *ORN*, series 1, vol. 15, 136; Walkley, *History of the Seventh Connecticut Volunteer Infantry*, 116.

30. Bennett, "Roswell Sabin [*sic*] Ripley: Charleston's Gallant Defender," 234–37; *OR*, series 1, vol. 35, pt. 2, 634; Fremantle, *Three Months in the Southern States*, 90–91.

31. *OR*, series 1, vol. 28, pt. 1, 641–42, 649; *ORN*, series 1, vol. 15, 142, 145. The monitors out of action were the *Patapsco, Catskill*, and *Lehigh*.

32. Ibid; Dahlgren, *Memoir of John A. Dahlgren*, 428, 430; *New York Times*, December 8, 1863. Elliott does not mention this visit or the band incident in his official reports. The reports also do not record any enemy rounds falling on the night of the third.

33. *OR*, series 1, vol. 28, pt. 1, 642, 649–50; John Johnson, *The Defense of Charleston Harbor*, 181–82, 184–85; Ripley, *Siege Train*, 68.

34. *Charleston Mercury*, December 15, 1863; *ORN*, series 1, vol. 15, 163; Dahlgren, *Memoir of John A. Dahlgren*, 429.

35. John Johnson, *The Defense of Charleston Harbor*, 186–88; John Johnson, "The Confederate Defense of Fort Sumter," 26; *OR*, series 1, vol. 28, pt. 1, 656–58; Bassham, *Conrad Wise Chapman*, 119, 126–28.

36. Bassham, *Conrad Wise Chapman*, 112–113, 131, 133, 151–52. *The Flag* painting is dated October 20, but Bassham states it is based on the October 25 sketch.

37. *OR*, series 1, vol. 28, pt. 1, 642.

38. Ibid, 643–44, 649; John Johnson, *The Defense of Charleston Harbor*, 188–90, 192–95; John Johnson, "The Confederate Defense of Fort Sumter," 25–26.

39. Ibid; Burton, *The Siege of Charleston*, 207–8; *Charleston Mercury*, December 15, 1863.

40. Ibid. The Confederates would describe the shelling on December 11 as Sumter's Second Minor Bombardment.

41. Ibid.

42. Ibid.

43. *OR*, series 1, vol. 28, pt. 1, 645, 649; Dahlgren, *Memoir of John A. Dahlgren*, 430; *ORN*, series 1, vol. 15, 146. The dispatch on the *Arago* was apparently a December 3 message from Welles saying the *Onondaga, Tecumseh*, and *Canonicus* wouldn't be ready.

44. *OR*, series 1, vol. 28, pt. 1, 646.

45. Ibid; *New York Herald*, December 18, 1863; Browning, *Success Is All That Was Expected*, 281; Dahlgren, *Memoir of John A. Dahlgren*, 434.

46. John Johnson, *The Defense of Charleston Harbor*, 194–98; *Charleston Mercury*, December 28, 1863; *OR*, series 1, vol. 28, pt. 1, 647.

47. Burton, *The Siege of Charleston*, 257–58; Phelps, *The Bombardment of Charleston*, 64; Franklin McGrath, *The History of the 127th New York Volunteers—'Monitors'—in the War For the Preservation of the Union—September 8, 1862–June 30, 1865* (no publisher, 1898), 86–87; Dahlgren, *Memoir of John A. Dahlgren*, 432; Browning, *Success Is All That Was Expected*, 282; David Dixon Porter, *The Naval History of the Civil War* (New York: The Sherman Publishing Co., 1886), 375.

48. R. H. Stoddard, "Twilight On Fort Sumter—August 24, 1863," *Harper's New Monthly Magazine*, 28, no. 163 (December 1863), 2.

49.   *Richmond Daily Dispatch* (no date), republished in *Charleston Mercury*, December 18, 1863.

50.   *OR*, series 1, vol. 28, pt. 1, 647–48; John Johnson, *The Defense of Charleston Harbor*, 195–97.

51.   Dahlgren, *Memoir of John A. Dahlgren*, 433; Ripley, *Siege Train*, 104.

CHAPTER 10

1.   *OR*, series 1, vol. 35, pt. 1, 129–33, 135–36, 177–78, 180; Gordon, *A War Diary*, 276; Ripley, *Siege Train*, 105.

2.   *OR*, series 1, vol. 35, pt. 1, 181; John Johnson, *The Defense of Charleston Harbor*, 194–98; Dahlgren, *Memoir of John A. Dahlgren*, 434.

3.   Phelps, *The Bombardment of Charleston*, 71–73; Burton, *The Siege of Charleston*, 258; *OR*, series 1, vol. 35, pt. 1, 109, 183, 501, 504–6; Gillmore, "The Army Before Charleston In 1863," 62; Cawood, *Combat History of Fort Sumter*, 38; John Johnson, *The Defense of Charleston Harbor*, 205.

4.   *OR*, series 1, vol. 35, pt. 1, 183–85; *Charleston Mercury*, February 1, 1864. The men assisting Schafer were Cpl. L. Bressentiam and Pvt. Charles Banks of Lucas's Battalion and H. B. Middleton of the Signal Corps.

5.   Dahlgren, *Memoir of John A. Dahlgren*, 437; *Charleston Mercury*, February 1, 1864.

6.   *OR*, series 1, vol. 35, pt. 1, 109, 185–86, 190, 462, 606; Cawood, *Combat History of Fort Sumter*, 38.

7.   Ibid; Smith, *Civil War Savannah*, 129–30; John Johnson, *The Defense of Charleston Harbor*, 176–77, 205.

8.   Ibid; *Charleston Daily Courier*, February 3, 1864.

9.   Ibid.

10.   *ORN*, series 1, vol. 15, 336; Wallace Shugg, "Prophet of the Deep; The *H. L. Hunley*," *CWTI*, 11, no. 10 (February 1973): 46–47.

11.   John Johnson, *The Defense of Charleston Harbor*, 201–2; *OR*, series 1, vol. 35, pt. 1, 190–91. Carson himself commanded Sumter for at least one day in February, the sixteenth, when Elliott was away. Capt. Thomas A. China, also of the 25th South Carolina, was in charge at the fort on February 25.

12.   *Charleston Mercury*, February 29, 1864. This issue also said the *Hunley* crew was "now safe," which was totally untrue. Burton, *The Siege of Charleston*, 258; *OR*, series 1, vol. 28, pt. 1, 687; *ORN*, series 1, vol. 15, 345, 466; Dahlgren, *Memoir of John A. Dahlgren*, 442; Browning, *Success Is All That Was Expected*, 242.

13.   Dahlgren, *Memoir of John A. Dahlgren*, 442–44. Controversy still swirls as to whether the documents were planted by the Rebels, but some leading experts believe the papers were authentic.

14.   Williams, *P. G. T. Beauregard*, 203–4; Patterson, "Gustave," 35, 52.

15.   *OR*, series 1, vol. 35, pt. 1, 193–97, 196; John Johnson, *The Defense of Charleston Harbor*, 202; *OR*, series 1, vol. 35, pt. 2, 23–24, 40–41. Elliott still referred to the battery as Gregg in his report.

16.   Ibid; *OR*, series 1, vol. 28, pt. 1, 687; Browning, *Success Is All That Was Expected*, 307–8; *Columbia Guardian* (no date), reprinted in *Charleston Mercury*, March 28, 1864; Dahlgren, *Memoir of John A. Dahlgren*, 448.

17.   *OR*, series 1, vol. 35, pt. 1, 199; *OR*, series 1, vol. 35, pt. 2, 34.

18.   *OR*, series 1, vol. 35, pt. 1, 201; *OR*, series 1, vol. 35, pt. 2, 51; John Johnson, *The Defense of Charleston Harbor*, 206–7; Evans, *Confederate Military History*,

5:300; *Charleston Mercury*, April 19, 1864; Ripley, *Siege Train*, 313. Huger was seventeen and needed parental consent to join the army when he enlisted in January 1864.

19. Phelps, *The Bombardment of Charleston*, 92; *OR*, series 1, vol. 35, pt. 1, 115–16, 204. It is unclear when Cooper received the photos or when they were forwarded.

20. *OR*, series 1, vol. 35, pt. 2, 67–68; Dahlgren, *Memoir of John A. Dahlgren*, 451.

21. Patterson, "Gustave," 52; Warner, *Generals in Gray*, 166; *OR*, series 1, vol. 35, pt. 2, 445.

22. *OR*, series 1, vol. 35, pt. 1, 205–7; Cawood, *Combat History of Fort Sumter*, 39.

23. Claudine Rhett, "Sketch of John C. Mitchel, of Ireland, Killed Whilst in Command of Fort Sumter," 271–72; *OR*, series 1, vol. 35, pt. 2, 589–90; Horres, "An Affair of Honor at Fort Sumter," 19; *Charleston Mercury*, May 6, 1864.

24. Warner, *Generals in Blue*, 216–17; *OR*, series 1, vol. 35, pt. 2, 48, 51.

25. Dahlgren, *Memoir of John A. Dahlgren*, 451, 453–54; *OR*, series 1, vol. 35, pt. 2, 474, 489.

26. Ibid; Warner, *Generals in Blue*, 177–78; Gordon, *A War Diary*, 255–56.

27. *OR*, series 1, vol. 35, pt. 2, 465, 468–69, 473, 485; *OR*, series 1, vol. 35, pt. 1, 55–57. The entire Department of South Carolina, Georgia, and Florida contained approximately 472 mounted and working guns as of May 3, 1864.

28. *OR*, series 1, vol. 35, pt. 1, 5–7, 138, 209–11.

29. *Charleston Mercury*, May 11, 1864; *OR*, series 1, vol. 35, pt. 1, 5–7, 55–57, 138, 209–11; *OR*, series 1, vol. 35, pt. 2, 485.

30. Ibid; John Johnson, *The Defense of Charleston Harbor*, 210; Browning, *Success Is All That Was Expected*, 307–8; Dahlgren, *Memoir of John A. Dahlgren*, 454.

31. *OR*, series 1, vol. 35, pt. 2, 494–96; *OR*, series 1, vol. 35, pt. 1, 58, 213.

32. *OR*, series 1, vol. 35, pt. 1, 214–15; Warner, *Generals in Gray*, 81–82; Welsh, *Medical Histories of Confederate Generals*, 60–61; Ripley, *Siege Train*, 305. One source states Elliott was promoted to brigadier general on May 20, which appears to be wrong.

33. Warner, *Generals in Blue*, 157–58; *OR*, series 1, vol. 35, pt. 2, 203; Dahlgren, *Memoir of John A. Dahlgren*, 455–58.

34. Ibid; *OR*, series 1, vol. 35, pt. 1, 215; Cawood, *Combat History of Fort Sumter*, 39.

35. Ibid; *OR*, series 1, vol. 35, pt. 1, 13, 217, 219; *OR*, series 1, vol. 35, pt. 2, 130, 144, 156–58; *Charleston Mercury*, June 25, 1864.

36. Ibid. It should be noted that Mitchel said the flag incident occurred under a "rapid fire," but also reported at 9:10 PM that night that twenty-six Parrott shots—and nothing else—were thrown at Sumter that day.

37. *OR*, series 1, vol. 35, pt. 2, 534, 541.

38. Ibid, 242–43; *OR*, series 1, vol. 35, pt. 1, 219–20.

CHAPTER 11

1. Cawood, *Combat History of Fort Sumter*, 39–40; Dahlgren, *Memoir of John A. Dahlgren*, 463–68; *Charleston Mercury*, July 4, 1864; *OR*, series 1, vol. 35, pt. 1, 15.

2. *OR*, series 1, vol. 35, pt. 1, 221; *OR*, series 1, vol. 35, pt. 2, 566–67.

3. *OR*, series 1, vol. 35, pt. 1, 15–17, 222–24, 232. The Confederates still referred to these strongholds as Wagner and Gregg.

4. Ibid.

5. *OR*, series 1, vol. 35, pt. 2, 575–76.

6. Ibid, 588; *OR*, series 1, vol. 35, pt. 1, 232, 224–25.

7. *OR*, series 1, vol. 35, pt. 2, 589–590.

8. *OR*, series 1, vol. 35, pt. 1, 16–17, 226, 232, 244; W. H. Andrews, *Footprints of a Regiment: A Recollection of the 1st Georgia Regulars, 1861–1865* (Atlanta: Longstreet Press, Inc., 1992), 146, 148.

9. Ibid; Claudine Rhett, "Sketch of John C. Mitchel, of Ireland, Killed Whilst in Command of Fort Sumter," 271–72; John Johnson, *The Defense of Charleston Harbor*, 227–28; Burton, *The Siege of Charleston*, 298.

10. Ibid.

11. *OR*, series 1, vol. 35, pt. 2, 593; *OR*, series 1, vol. 35, pt. 1, 227, 232, 245.

12. *Confederate Veteran*, 4:6–7.

13. *OR*, series 1, vol. 35, pt. 1, 227; *Confederate Veteran*, 5:421, 162; Wise, *Gate of Hell*, 200–1; *Charleston Mercury*, July 27, 1864. Some accounts state that a bursting shell may have smothered the lit fuse at Wagner.

14. Dahlgren, *Memoir of John A. Dahlgren*, 469–71; *OR*, series 1, vol. 35, pt. 2, 181–82, 190–91.

15. Ibid; *OR*, series 1, vol. 35, pt. 1, 18.

16. *OR*, series 1, vol. 35, pt. 1, 228–29, 232, 246–47.

17. Ibid.

18. *OR*, series 1, vol. 35, pt. 2, 187, 190–91; *OR*, series 1, vol. 35, pt. 1, 229–30, 232, 247.

19. Ibid; John Johnson, *The Defense of Charleston Harbor*, 231; *Charleston Mercury*, July 29, 1864.

20. Welsh, *Medical Histories of Confederate Generals*, 60; *Richmond Daily Dispatch*, no date, reprinted in *Charleston Mercury*, August 8, 1864; *OR*, series 1, vol. 35, pt. 2, 200–3, 468–69; Allardice, *Confederate Colonels*, 148. Foster's department had more than 19,000 troops present for duty in July 1864.

21. *OR*, series 1, vol. 35, pt. 2, 197, 207–8; *OR*, series 1, vol. 35, pt. 1, 232–33.

22. *OR*, series 1, vol. 35, pt. 2, 206, 210–11; *OR*, series 1, vol. 35, pt. 1, 69, 233. Lt. G. F. Eaton of the 127th New York had led a similar operation around Sumter a few nights earlier.

23. Ibid.

24. *OR*, series 1, vol. 35, pt. 1, 19–21, 26.

25. Ibid, 232–34.

26. *OR*, series 1, vol. 35, pt. 2, 248, 241; *OR*, series 1, vol. 35, pt. 1, 21, 72.

27. *New York Herald*, August 19, 1864; *OR*, series 1, vol. 35, pt. 2, 615–17.

28. *OR*, series 1, vol. 35, pt. 1, 75, 238–40; *Charleston Mercury*, August 30, 1864; Burton, *The Siege of Charleston*, 299; John Johnson, *The Defense of Charleston Harbor*, 232–36; Browning, *Success Is All That Was Expected*, 328. Some sources state there was a raft attack on July 28, but this appears incorrect based on Huguenin's and Schimmelfennig's reports about the August 28 incident.

29. Ibid; Cawood, *Combat History of Fort Sumter*, 41; *OR*, series 1, vol. 35, pt. 2, 264, 276.

30. Ibid; *OR*, series 1, vol. 35, pt. 1, 80–81, 242.

31. *OR*, series 1, vol. 35, pt. 2, 295–96; *OR*, series 1, vol. 35, pt. 1, 23.

32. *OR*, series 1, vol. 35, pt. 1, 25–26, 80–81, 242; *OR*, series 1, vol. 35, pt. 2, 308–310; *Port Royal Palmetto Herald* (no date), reprinted in *Charleston Mercury*, October 6, 1864; *Charleston Mercury*, November 2, 1864.

33. Roman, *The Military Operations of General Beauregard*, 2:275–76; Bennett, "Roswell Sabin [*sic*] Ripley: Charleston's Gallant Defender," 237–38; *OR*, series 1, vol. 35, pt. 2, 632–33; Cardozo, *Reminiscences of Charleston*, 121–23.

34. *New York Herald*, September 30, 1864; *OR*, series 1, vol. 35, pt. 1, 26; Rod Gragg, *Confederate Goliath—The Battle of Fort Fisher* (New York: HarperCollins, 1991), 32–33; Browning, *Success Is All That Was Expected*, 328; John G. Barrett, *The Civil War In North Carolina* (Chapel Hill: The University of North Carolina Press, 1963), 262–63.

35. *OR*, series 1, vol. 35, pt. 2, 305.

36. *Charleston Mercury*, October 5, 1864; Nathaniel Cheairs Hughes Jr., *General William J. Hardee—Old Reliable* (Baton Rouge and London: Louisiana State University Press, 1965), 250–51; Williams, *P. G. T. Beauregard*, 241; Patterson, "Gustave," 53; Warner, *Generals in Gray*, 253–54; Welsh, *Medical Histories of Confederate Generals*, 123, 182–83; *OR*, series 1, vol. 35, pt. 2, 646–47. Seddon's response to the leadership problems in Charleston shows the communications and command breakdowns already infecting the Confederacy in late 1864. "Has General Ripley been relieved or furloughed?" he wrote on December 2. "I am not aware that any orders affecting his position have been entered. Was General Ransom ordered to Charleston to relieve General Jones or anyone else, or for any general assignment?"

37. *OR*, series 1, vol. 35, pt. 1, 83; *Confederate Veteran*, 5:422–23; Miller, *Photographic History of the Civil War*, 3:170; Edwards, "The Photographer of the Confederacy," 29. General Potter had assumed command of the Northern District on October 27, replacing Saxton.

38. Smith, *Civil War Savannah*, 146, 160–61; Roman, *The Military Operations of General Beauregard*, 2:610.

39. *OR*, series 1, vol. 44, n.p., 83.

40. Cawood, *Combat History of Fort Sumter*, 41; *Charleston Mercury*, December 12, 1864; *OR*, series 1, vol. 44, n.p., 1009–10.

41. Hughes, *General William J. Hardee*, 273–74; *Charleston Mercury*, December 31, 1864; Peck, "Four Years Under Fire at Charleston," 365.

CHAPTER 12

1. Smith, *Civil War Savannah*, 146, 230–31; *New York Herald*, January 1, 1865; *Confederate Veteran*, 5:422–23; Welsh, *Medical Histories of Confederate Generals*, 60; Helen P. Trimpi, *Crimson Confederates—Harvard Men Who Fought for the South* (Knoxville: The University of Tennessee Press, 2010), 69–70.

2. *ORN*, series 1, vol. 16, 169, 364–65.

3. Ibid, 171, 173–74; *Confederate Veteran*, 5:422–23. Five officers and thirty-eight enlisted men escaped from *Patapsco*.

4. Cawood, *Combat History of Fort Sumter*, 43; Burton, *The Siege of Charleston*, 314–315; John Johnson, *The Defense of Charleston Harbor*, 256–57; Allardice, *Confederate Colonels*, 85; Smith, *Civil War Savannah*, 130; Evans, *Confederate Military History*, 6:422–23. Burton says 1st South Carolina Artillery, which is in error. Harrison may have been promoted to brigadier general in February, but it never came through channels as the Confederacy languished. A few weeks shy of his twenty-fourth birthday, Harrison himself appears to have been posted with the rest of his regiment in the Charleston defenses but apparently spent little, if any, time at Sumter in January–February 1865.

5. Robert L. Crewdson, "Burning Columbia," *CWTI*, 20, no. 6 (October 1981): 12; *OR*, series 1, vol. 44, n.p., 741, 843.

6. *New York Herald*, February 22, 1865; *OR*, series 1, vol. 47, pt. 2, 369; Dahlgren, *Memoir of John A. Dahlgren*, 494–95; Warner, *Generals in Blue*, 157, 176–77; *ORN*, series 1, vol. 16, 367; Denison, *Shot and Shell*, 294. Some accounts claim Foster tried to cover his disappointment about the command change by saying he was leaving due to the old wounds, but this does not appear to be the case.

7. Dahlgren, *Memoir of John A. Dahlgren*, 495; Browning, *Success Is All That Was Expected*, 342; *ORN*, series 1, vol. 16, 244; *Charleston Mercury*, February 11, 1865.

8. *OR*, series 1, vol. 47, pt. 2, 1179–80; Roman, *The Military Operations of General Beauregard*, 2:346–47; Hughes, *General William J. Hardee*, 277–78; John Johnson, *The Defense of Charleston Harbor*, 256–57. Beauregard headed back to Columbia on the night of February 14, arriving the next day.

9. *ORN*, series 1, vol. 16, 240, 247–48.

10. Burton, *The Siege of Charleston*, 318; Cawood, *Combat History of Fort Sumter*, 43; John Johnson, *The Defense of Charleston Harbor*, 256–57, 259. Neil Kagan and Stephen G. Hyslop, *Eyewitness To The Civil War: The Complete History From Secession To Reconstruction* (Washington, DC: National Geographic Society, 2006), 357.

11. Ibid.

12. Marzalek, *The Diary of Miss Emma Holmes*, 431; Warner, *Generals in Gray*, 297–98; Trimpi, *Crimson Confederates*, 69–70. Taliaferro is listed as a major general by some sources, but this appears to be inaccurate.

13. *ORN*, series 1, vol. 16, 258; Burton, *The Siege of Charleston*, 318; Browning, *Success Is All That Was Expected*, 344–45; McGrath, *The History of the 127th New York Volunteers*, 149. *Mahopac* was skippered by Lt. Cmdr. A. W. Weaver.

14. *OR*, series 1, vol. 47, pt. 1, 1018–20; *New York Herald*, February 28, 1865; *ORN*, series 1, vol. 16, 258; Scharf, *History of the Confederate States Navy*, 701, 706–7.

15. Ibid; *OR*, series 1, vol. 53, n.p., 60–61; *OR*, series 1, vol. 47, pt. 2, 483–84; Claudine Rhett, "Sketch of John C. Mitchel, of Ireland, Killed Whilst in Command of Fort Sumter," 271; Warner, *Generals in Blue*, 423–24.

16. *ORN*, series 1, vol. 16, 250, 370; Dahlgren, *Memoir of John A. Dahlgren*, 500. Porter commanded the North Atlantic Squadron. He was a friend of Dahlgren's and had sent him a letter after Porter had been instrumental in the January 1865 capture of Fort Fisher near Wilmington.

17. *OR*, series 1, vol. 47, pt. 1, 1008, 1020 (Gillmore to Halleck); *New York Herald*, February 21, 1865, and February 28, 1865; *Richmond Examiner* (undated), reprinted in *New York Times*, February 25, 1865.

18. Trimpi, *Crimson Confederates*, 69–70; Thomas L. Connelly, *Autumn of Glory: The Army of Tennessee, 1862–1865* (Baton Rouge: Louisiana State University Press, 1971), 520–22. Hood had replaced Johnston in army command in July 1864.

19. Sion H. Harrington III, and John Hairr, *Eyewitness To Averasboro—Volume 1: The Confederates* (Erwin, NC: Averasboro Press, 2001), 38–39; Arthur P. Ford, *Life in the Confederate Army, Being Personal Experiences of a Private Soldier in the Confederate Army* (New York and Washington: The Neale Publishing Co., 1905), 51.

20. Trimpi, *Crimson Confederates*, 69–72; Welsh, *Medical Histories of Confederate Generals*, 60–61. Some accounts say Elliott was wounded in the arm at

Bentonville, which is in error. His brother, William Elliott, was also wounded in this battle and survived.

21. Welsh, *Medical Histories of Confederate Generals*, 145; Warner, *Generals in Gray*, 195–96, 257; Bennett, "Roswell Sabin [*sic*] Ripley: Charleston's Gallant Defender," 240. Bennett has more information about Ripley's activities from November 1864 to this time.

22. *ORN*, series 1, vol. 16, 374–75.

23. Ibid.

24. Gillmore, "The Army Before Charleston In 1863," 67–68; Reid, *Ohio In the War*, 1:646.

25. *ORN*, series 1, vol. 16, 376–77; Perry, *Infernal Machines*, 171.

26. Dahlgren, *Memoir of John A. Dahlgren*, 504–5.

27. *New York Herald*, March 26, 1865.

28. John Johnson, *The Defense of Charleston Harbor*, 265, 267, 273; Kennedy, *The Civil War Battlefield Guide*, 300–2; Smith, "Guns of the *Keokuk*," 81; *OR*, series 1, vol. 28, pt. 1, 727.

29. *New York Herald*, April 18, 1865.

30. W. A. Swanberg, *First Blood—The Story of Fort Sumter* (New York: Charles Scribner's Sons, 1957), 335–36. MacArthur returned on October 20, 1944.

31. Castel, "Fort Sumter—1861," 49–50; *New York Herald*, April 18, 1865; McGinty, "Robert Anderson: Reluctant Hero," 45–46; Moore, *Fort Sumter Memorial—The Fall of Fort Sumter*, 36–38.

32. Ibid; Marzalek, *The Diary of Miss Emma Holmes*, 441.

33. McGinty, "Robert Anderson: Reluctant Hero," 58; Moore, *Fort Sumter Memorial—The Fall of Fort Sumter*, 44; *New York Herald*, April 18, 1865.

EPILOGUE

1. Ferguson, *An Overview of the Events at Fort Sumter*, 42–44; Warner, *Generals in Blue*, 176–77; *Fort Sumter Official Park Guide* (Fort Sumter National Monument, SC, National Park Service, Department of the Interior, 1997); *New York Times*, April 8, 1888; McGrath, *The History of the 127th New York Volunteers*, 174.

2. Ibid.

3. Ferguson, *An Overview of the Events at Fort Sumter*, 48–49.

4. *Yearbook—1914, City of Charleston, South Carolina* (Charleston: Walker, Evans & Cogswell Company, 1915), 449–50; Harrington and Hairr, *Eyewitness To Averasboro—Volume 1*, 38–39; *Confederate Veteran*, 5:421.

5. Trimpi, *Crimson Confederates*, 69–70; Warner, *Generals in Gray*, 81–82; Welsh, *Medical Histories of Confederate Generals*, 60–61.

6. Warner, *Generals in Gray*, 257; Welsh, *Medical Histories of Confederate Generals*, 184–85; Bennett, "Roswell Sabin [*sic*] Ripley: Charleston's Gallant Defender," 241.

7. Horres, "An Affair of Honor at Fort Sumter," 24; Allardice, *Confederate Colonels*, 321; H. Newcomb Morse, "General Beauregard And The Colonel Rhett Controversy," *The South Carolina Historical Magazine*, 78, no. 3 (July 1977): 184. The wife is also identified in some accounts as Marie Alice Sparks.

8. Boatner, *The Civil War Dictionary*, 252; *New York Times*, June 24, 1865.

9. Hamersly, *The Records of Living Officers of the U.S. Navy and Marine Corps*, 14–15; Browning, *Success Is All That Was Expected*, 355; Boatner, *The Civil War Dictionary*, 218; Dahlgren, *Memoir of John A. Dahlgren*, 274.

10. Williams, *P. G. T. Beauregard*, 326–27; Patterson, "Gustave," 54; *Yearbook—1914, City of Charleston, South Carolina*, 461.

11. Edward McCrady Jr. and Samuel A. Ashe, *Cyclopedia of Eminent and Representative Men of the Carolinas of the Nineteenth Century with a Brief Historical Introduction on South Carolina by General Edward McCrady Jr. and on North Carolina by Hon. Samuel A. Ashe* (Madison, WI: Brant & Fuller, 1892), 1:512.

12. Stevens, "The Boat Attack on Sumter," 50; Roman, *The Military Operations of General Beauregard*, 2:157.

13. *OR*, series 1, vol. 28, pt. 2, 300–1.

14. *Yearbook—1914, City of Charleston, South Carolina*, 461.

15. Ibid, 460; *Confederate Veteran*, 2:126.

16. Rosen, *Confederate Charleston*, 158; Charleston *News & Courier*, October 21, 1932; John R. Young, *A Walk in the Parks* (Charleston: Evening Post Books, 2010), 37. Some accounts identify the sculptor as "Herman" MacNeil, an error.

BIBLIOGRAPHY

Allardice, Bruce S. *Confederate Colonels—A Biographical Register*. Columbia: University of Missouri Press, 2008.

Ammen, Rear Admiral Daniel. *The Navy In The Civil War: The Atlantic Coast*. New York: Charles Scribner's Sons, 1883.

Andrews, W. H. *Footprints of a Regiment: A Recollection of the 1st Georgia Regulars, 1861–1865*. Atlanta: Longstreet Press, 1992.

Atlantic Monthly. "Charleston Under Arms," 7, no. 42 (April 1861).

Baker, Gary R. *Cadets in Gray—The Story of the Cadets of the South Carolina Military Academy and the Cadet Rangers in the Civil War*. Columbia, SC: Palmetto Bookworks, 1989.

Barnes, Frank. *Fort Sumter National Monument, South Carolina*, Historical Handbook Series 12. Washington, DC: National Park Service, 1961.

Barrett, John G. *The Civil War In North Carolina*. Chapel Hill: University of North Carolina Press, 1963.

Bassham, Ben L. "Conrad Chapman's Charleston." *Civil War Times Illustrated* 16, no. 1 (April 1977).

———. *Conrad Wise Chapman—Artist and Soldier of the Confederacy*. Kent, OH: Kent State University Press, 1998.

Bates, Samuel P. *History of the Pennsylvania Volunteers, 1861–65, Prepared In Compliance With Acts of the Legislature*. 5 vols. Harrisburg: B. Singerly, State Printer, 1869.

Beauregard, P. G. T. "The Defense of Charleston." *Battles and Leaders*. Vol. 4. New York: 1887.

———. "Torpedo Service in the Water Defences of Charleston." *Southern Historical Society Papers* 5, no. 4 (April 1878).

Bell, Jack. *Civil War Heavy Explosive Ordnance—A Guide to Large Artillery Projectiles, Torpedoes, and Mines*. Denton: University of North Texas Press, 2003.

Bennett, C. A., M.D. "Roswell Sabin [*sic*] Ripley: Charleston's Gallant Defender." *South Carolina Historical Magazine* 5, no. 3 (July 1999).

Black, Robert C., III. *The Railroads of the Confederacy*. Chapel Hill: University of North Carolina Press, 1998.

Boatner, Mark M., III. *The Civil War Dictionary*. Rev. ed. New York: David McKay, 1987.

Bostick, Douglas W. *Charleston Under Siege: The Impregnable City*. Charleston: History Press, 2010.

Browning, Robert M., Jr. *Success Is All That Was Expected—The South Atlantic Blockading Squadron during the Civil War*. Washington, DC: Brassey's, 2002.

Bruce, Robert V. *Lincoln and the Tools of War*. Indianapolis: Bobbs-Merrill, 1956.

Buel, Clarence C., and Robert V. Johnson. *Battles and Leaders of the Civil War: Being for the Most Part Contributions by Union and Confederate Authors*. 4 vols. New York: Century, 1887.

Burton, E. Milby. *The Siege of Charleston—1861–1865*. Columbia: University of South Carolina Press, 1970.

Campbell, R. Thomas. *The CSS* H. L. Hunley—*Confederate Submarine*. Shippensburg, PA: Burd Street Press, 2000.

———. "Raising the Blockade—The Nighttime Attack of the CSS *Palmetto State* and the CSS *Chicora*." *North & South* 9, no. 1 (March 2006).

Cardozo, Jacob Newton. *Reminiscences of Charleston*. Charleston: Joseph Walker, Stationer and Printer, 1866.

Castel, Albert. "Fort Sumter—1861." *Civil War Times Illustrated* 15, no. 6 (October 1976).

Catton, Bruce. *This Hallowed Ground—The Story of the Union Side of the Civil War*. Garden City, NY: Doubleday, 1956.

Cawood, Hobart G. *Combat History of Fort Sumter, 1863–1865*. Charleston: National Park Service, 1962.

Coffin, Charles C. *Freedom Triumphant: The Fourth Period of the War of the Rebellion From September, 1864, To Its Close*. New York: Harper & Brothers, 1890.

Connelly, Thomas L. *Army of the Heartland: The Army of Tennessee, 1861–1862*. Baton Rouge: Louisiana State University Press, 1967.

———. *Autumn of Glory: The Army of Tennessee, 1862–1865*. Baton Rouge: Louisiana State University Press, 1971.

Cox, General Jacob D. *Sherman's March to the Sea—Hood's Tennessee Campaign & The Carolina Campaigns of 1865*. New York: Da Capo, 1994.

Crawford, Samuel Wylie. *The Genesis of the Civil War, The Story of Sumter, 1860–1861*. New York: Charles L. Webster, 1887.

Crewdson, Robert L. "Burning Columbia." *Civil War Times Illustrated* 20, no. 6 (October 1981).

———. "In A Bottle Strongly Corked." *Civil War Times Illustrated* 23, no. 8 (December 1984).

Cunningham, Tim. "Prisoners Under Fire." *America's Civil War* 15, no. 6 (January 2003).

Dahlgren, John A., and Madeleine Vinton Dahlgren. *Memoir of Ulric Dahlgren By His Father, Rear-Admiral Dahlgren*. Philadelphia: J. B. Lippincott, 1872.

Dahlgren, Madeleine Vinton. *Memoir of John A. Dahlgren, Rear-Admiral, United States Navy*. Boston: J. R. Osgood, 1882.

Davis, Burke. *The Long Surrender*. New York: Random House, 1985.

Davis, William C. *Battle at Bull Run—A History of the First Major Campaign of the Civil War*. Baton Rouge: Louisiana State University Press, 1977.

———. *Rhett—The Turbulent Life and Times of a Fire-Eater*. Columbia: University of South Carolina Press, 2001.

Denison, Frederic. *Shot and Shell—The Third Rhode Island Heavy Artillery Regiment In The Rebellion, 1861–1865*. Providence, RI: J. A. & R. A. Reid, 1879.

Doubleday, Abner. *Reminiscences of Forts Sumter and Moultrie in 1860–'61*. New York: Harper & Brothers, 1876.

Draper, John William. *History of the American Civil War*. 3 vols. New York: Harper & Brothers, 1870.

Edwards, Conley L., III. "The Photographer of the Confederacy." *Civil War Times Illustrated* 13, no. 3 (June 1974).

Evans, Clement A., ed. *Confederate Military History*. 12 vols. Atlanta: Confederate Publishing, 1899.

Extract From the History of the Third Regiment, Rhode Island Heavy Artillery, Published in the Adjutant General's Report of the State of Rhode Island. Providence, RI: E. L. Freeman & Son, 1894.

Ferguson, James N. *An Overview of the Events at Fort Sumter, 1829–1991*. Denver: National Park Service, 1991.

Ford, Arthur P. *Life in the Confederate Army, Being Personal Experiences of a Private Soldier in the Confederate Army*. New York and Washington: Neale, 1905.

Fort Sumter Official Park Guide. Fort Sumter National Monument, SC: National Park Service, 1997.

Fowler, William M., Jr. *Under Two Flags—The American Navy In The Civil War*. New York: W. W. Norton, 1990.

Freeman, Douglas Southall. *Lee's Lieutenants: A Study in Command*. Abridged by Stephen W. Sears. New York: Simon & Schuster, 2001.

Fremantle, Sir Arthur James Lyon. *Three Months in the Southern States: April–June, 1863*. Mobile, AL: S. H. Goetzel, 1864.

Gillmore, Quincy A. *Engineer and Artillery Operations Against The Defences of Charleston Harbor In 1863, Comprising The Descent Upon Morris Island, The Demolition of Fort Sumter, The Reduction of Forts Wagner and Gregg*. New York: D. Van Nostrand, 1865.

———. "The Army Before Charleston In 1863." *Battles and Leaders*. Vol. 4. New York: 1887.

———. "Siege and Capture of Fort Pulaski." *Battles and Leaders*. Vol. 2. New York: 1887.

Goldy, James. "The Swamp Angel." *Civil War Times Illustrated* 28, no. 2 (April 1989).

Gordon, George H. *A War Diary of Events in the War of the Great Rebellion, 1863–1865*. Boston: J. R. Osgood, 1882.

Gragg, Rod. *Confederate Goliath—The Battle of Fort Fisher*. New York: HarperCollins, 1991.

Grimsley, Mark. "Robert E. Lee: The Life and Career of the Master General." *Civil War Times Illustrated* 24, no. 7 (November 1985).

Hagood, Johnson. *Memoirs of the War of Secession*. Edited by U. R. Brooks. Columbia, SC: The State Company, 1910.

Hamersly, Lewis R. *The Records of Living Officers of the U.S. Navy and Marine Corps; With A History of Naval Operations During the Rebellion Of 1861–5*. Philadelphia: J. B. Lippincott, 1870.

Hamilton, Major James A. "General Stephen Elliott, Lieutenant James A. Hamilton, and Elliott's Torpedoes." *Southern Historical Society Papers* 10 (January–February 1882).

Harrington, Sion H., III, and John Hairr. *Eyewitness To Averasboro—Volume 1: The Confederates*. Erwin, NC: Averasboro Press, 2001.

Holden, Edgar. "The First Cruise of the 'Monitor' *Passaic*." *Harper's New Monthly Magazine* 27, no. 161 (October 1863).

Horn, Stanley F. *The Robert E. Lee Reader*. Indianapolis: Bobbs-Merrill, 1949.

Horres, C. Russell, Jr. "An Affair of Honor at Fort Sumter." *The South Carolina Historical Magazine* 102, no. 1 (January 2001).

Hughes, Nathaniel Cheairs, Jr. *General William J. Hardee—Old Reliable*. Baton Rouge: Louisiana State University Press, 1965.

Izlar, William V. *A Sketch of the War Record of the Edisto Rifles: 1861–1865*. Columbia, SC: The State Company, 1914.

Johnson, Clint. *Touring the Carolinas' Civil War Sites*. Winston-Salem, NC: John F. Blair, 1996.

Johnson, John. "The Confederate Defense of Fort Sumter." *Battles and Leaders*. Vol. 4. New York: 1887.

———. *The Defense of Charleston Harbor: Including Fort Sumter and the Adjacent Islands, 1863–1865*. Charleston: Walker, Evans & Cogswell, 1890.

Johnston, Joseph E. *Narrative of Military Operations, Directed, During the Late War Between the States*. New York: D. Appleton, 1874.

Jones, Iredell. "Letters From Fort Sumter in 1862 and 1863." *Southern Historical Society Papers* 12 (1884).

Jones, John B. *A Rebel War Clerk's Diary at the Confederate States Capital*. 2 vols. Philadelphia: J. B. Lippincott, 1866.

Jones, Samuel. *The Siege of Charleston and the Operations on the South Atlantic Coast in the War Among the States*. New York: Neale, 1911.

Kagan, Neil, and Stephen G. Hyslop. *Eyewitness To The Civil War: The Complete History From Secession To Reconstruction*. Washington, DC: National Geographic, 2006.

Keith, Willis J. "Fort Johnson." *Civil War Times Illustrated* 14, no. 7 (November 1975).

Kennedy, Frances H., ed. *The Civil War Battlefield Guide*. Boston: Houghton Mifflin, 1990.

Martin, Isabella D., and Myrta Lockett Avary. *A Diary From Dixie, as written by Mary Boykin Chesnut, wife of James Chesnut, Jr., United States Senator from South Carolina, 1859–1861, and afterward an Aide to Jefferson Davis and a Brigadier General in the Confederate Army*. New York: D. Appleton, 1905.

Marzalek, John F., ed. *The Diary of Miss Emma Holmes—1861–1866*. Baton Rouge: Louisiana State University Press, 1994.

McCrady, General Edward, Jr., and Hon. Samuel A. Ashe. *Cyclopedia of Eminent and Representative Men of the Carolinas of the Nineteenth Century with a Brief Historical Introduction on South Carolina by General Edward McCrady Jr. and on North Carolina by Hon. Samuel A. Ashe*. 2 vols. Madison, WI: Brant & Fuller, 1892.

McGinty, Brian. "Robert Anderson: Reluctant Hero." *Civil War Times Illustrated* 31, no. 2 (May–June 1992).

McGrath, Franklin. *The History of the 127th New York Volunteers—'Monitors'—in the War For the Preservation of the Union—September 8, 1862–June 30, 1865*. 1898.

Miller, Francis Trevelyan, ed. *Photographic History of the Civil War*. 10 vols. Springfield, MA: Patriot, 1911

Moore, Frank, ed. *Fort Sumter Memorial—The Fall of Fort Sumter, A Contemporary Sketch From Heroes and Martyrs*. New York: Edwin C. Hill, 1915.

Morse, H. Newcomb. "General Beauregard And The Colonel Rhett Controversy." *The South Carolina Historical Magazine* 78, no. 3 (July 1977).

Murfin, James V. *The Gleam of Bayonets: The Battle of Antietam and the Maryland Campaign of 1862*. Baton Rouge: Louisiana State University Press, 1965.

Nicolay, John G., and John Hay. "Abraham Lincoln: A History—Lincoln's Inauguration." *The Century* 35, no. 2 (December 1887).

Oleland, Glenn. "Secret Weapon of the Confederacy." *National Geographic* 202, no. 1 (July 2002).

Olmstead, Charles H. "Reminiscences of Service in Charleston Harbor in 1863," *Southern Historical Society Papers* 20 (1882).

Olmsted, Frederick Law. *The Cotton Kingdom—A Traveller's Observation on Cotton and Slavery in the American Slave States*. Edited by Arthur M. Schlesinger Sr. New York: Random House, 1984.

Patterson, Gerard A. "Gustave." *Civil War Times Illustrated* 32, no. 3 (July–August 1992).

———. *Rebels From West Point*. New York: Doubleday, 1987.

Peck, W. F. G. "Four Years Under Fire at Charleston." *Harper's New Monthly Magazine* 31, no. 183 (August 1865).

Pelzer, John D. "The Second Bombardment of Fort Sumter." *America's Civil War* 9, no. 2 (May 1996).

Perry, Milton F. *Infernal Machines: The Story of Confederate Submarine and Mine Warfare*. Baton Rouge: Louisiana State University Press, 1965.

Phelps, W. Chris. *The Bombardment of Charleston, 1863–1865*. Gretna, LA: Pelican, 1999.

———. *Charlestonians in War: The Charleston Battalion*. Gretna, LA: Pelican, 2004.

Plum, William R. *The Military Telegraph During the Civil War With An Exposition of Ancient and Modern Means of Communication, And Of The Federal and Confederate Cipher Systems; Also a Running Account of the War Between the States*. 2 vols. Chicago: Jansen, McClurg, 1882.

Porter, David Dixon. *The Naval History of the Civil War*. New York: Sherman, 1886.

Pressley, Major John G. "The Wee Nee Volunteers of Williamsburg District, S.C., in the First (Hagood's) Regiment." *Southern Historical Society Papers* 16 (1888).

A Prominent Secessionist. "Stories of a Confederate." *The National Magazine* 10, no. 1 (April 1899).

Ragan, Mark K. "Union and Confederate Submarine Warfare." *North & South* 2, no. 3 (March 1999).

Recollections and Reminiscences, 1861–1865, Through World War I. 6 vols. South Carolina Division, United Daughters of the Confederacy, 1992.

Reid, Whitelaw. *Ohio In the War: Her Statesmen, Her Generals, and Soldiers*. 2 vols. Cincinnati: Robert Clarke, 1895.

Rhett, Claudine. "Frank H. Harleston—A Hero of Fort Sumter." *Southern Historical Society Papers* 10 (1882).

———. "Sketch of John C. Mitchel, of Ireland, Killed Whilst in Command of Fort Sumter." *Southern Historical Society Papers* 10 (1882).

Ripley, Warren, ed. *Siege Train—The Journal of a Confederate Artilleryman in the Defense of Charleston*. Columbia: University of South Carolina Press, 1986.

Rodgers, C. R. P. "Du Pont's Attack At Charleston." *Battles and Leaders*. Vol. 4. New York: 1887.

Roman, Alfred. *The Military Operations of General Beauregard in the War Between the States*. 2 vols. New York: Harper & Brothers, 1884.

Rosen, Robert N. *Confederate Charleston—An Illustrated History of the City and the People During the Civil War*. Columbia: University of South Carolina Press, 1994.

Ross, Fitzgerald. *A Visit To The Cities and Camps of the Confederate States*. Edinburgh: William Blackwood and Sons, 1865.

Rowland, Dunbar. *Jefferson Davis—Constitutionalist—His Letters, Papers and Speeches*. 10 vols. New York: J. J. Little & Ives, 1923.

Ruffin, Edmund. "The First Shot At Fort Sumter (Extract from the Unpublished Diary of Edmund Ruffin)." *William and Mary College Quarterly Historical Magazine* 20, no. 1 (October 1911).

Russell, William Howard. *My Diary—North and South*. Boston: Burnham, 1863.

Sandburg, Carl. *Abraham Lincoln*. 4 vols. New York: Harcourt, Brace, 1939.

Scharf, J. Thomas. *History of the Confederate States Navy From Its Organization to the Surrender of Its Last Vessel*. New York: Gramercy Books, 1996.

Shugg, Wallace. "Prophet of the Deep; The *H. L. Hunley*." *Civil War Times Illustrated* 11, no. 10 (February 1973).

Smith, Derek. "Ambush on the Stono." *North & South* 8, no. 5 (September 2005).

———. *Civil War Savannah*. Savannah: Frederic Beil, 1997.

———. *The Gallant Dead: Union and Confederate Generals Killed in the Civil War*. Mechanicsburg, PA: Stackpole Books, 2005.

———. "Guns of the *Keokuk*." *North & South* 9, no. 3 (June 2006).

———. *In The Lion's Mouth: Hood's Tragic Retreat From Nashville, 1864*. Mechanicsburg, PA: Stackpole Books, 2011.

———. "The Stand at Ft. McAllister." *Army* (May 1989).

Smith, Mark A., and Wade Sokolosky. *"No Such Army Since the Days of Julius Caesar"—Sherman's Carolinas Campaign from Fayetteville to Averasboro*. Fort Mitchell, KY: Ironclad, 2005.

Stevens, Thomas H. "The Boat Attack on Sumter." *Battles and Leaders*. Vol. 4. New York: 1887.

Still, William N., Jr. "Technology Afloat." *Civil War Times Illustrated* 14, no. 7 (November 1975).

Stoddard, R. H. "Twilight On Sumter—August 24, 1863." *Harper's New Monthly Magazine* 28, no. 163 (December 1863).

Swanberg, W. A. *First Blood—The Story of Fort Sumter*. New York: Charles Scribner's Sons, 1957.

Swinton, William. *The Twelve Decisive Battles of the War: A History of the Eastern and Western Campaigns, in Relation to the Actions That Decided Their Issue*. New York: Dick & Fitzgerald, 1871.

Symonds, Craig L., ed. *A Year on a Monitor and the Destruction of Fort Sumter*. Columbia: University of South Carolina Press, 1987.

Thompson, Benjamin W. "Back to the South—The Benjamin W. Thompson Memoir—Part III." *Civil War Times Illustrated* 12, no. 7 (November 1973).

Trimpi, Helen P. *Crimson Confederates—Harvard Men Who Fought for the South*. Knoxville: University of Tennessee Press, 2010.

U.S. War Department. *Official Records of the Union and Confederate Navies in the War of the Rebellion*. 303 vols. Washington, DC: U.S. Government Printing Office, 1894–1922.

U.S. War Department. *The War of the Rebellion: A Compilation of the Official Records of the Union and Confederate Armies*. 128 vols. Washington, DC: U.S. Government Printing Office, 1880–1901.

Walkley, Stephen. *History of the Seventh Connecticut Volunteer Infantry, Hawley's Brigade, Terry's Division, Tenth Army Corps—1861–1865*. 1905.

Warner, Ezra J. *Generals in Blue: Lives of the Union Commanders.* Baton Rouge: Louisiana State University Press, 1964.

―――. *Generals in Gray: Lives of the Confederate Commanders.* Baton Rouge: Louisiana State University Press, 1959.

Weber, John Langdon. *Fifty Lessons in the History of South Carolina.* Boston: Ginn, 1891.

Weddle, Kevin J. *Lincoln's Tragic Admiral―The Life of Samuel Francis Du Pont.* Charlottesville: University of Virginia Press, 2005.

Wegner, Dana. "The Port Royal Working Parties." *Civil War Times Illustrated* 15, no. 8 (December 1976).

Welsh, Jack D., M.D. *Medical Histories of Confederate Generals.* Kent, OH: Kent State University Press, 1995.

Westwood, Howard. "Mr. Smalls―A Personal Adventure." *Civil War Times Illustrated* 25, no. 3 (May 1986).

Williams, T. Harry. *P. G. T. Beauregard―Napoleon In Gray.* Baton Rouge: Louisiana State University Press, 1955.

Wise, Stephen R. *Gate of Hell―Campaign for Charleston Harbor; 1863.* Columbia: University of South Carolina Press, 1994.

―――. *Lifeline of the Confederacy―Blockade Running During the Civil War.* Columbia: University of South Carolina Press, 1988.

Woodward, C. Vann, ed. *Mary Chesnut's Civil War.* New Haven: Yale University Press, 1981.

Yearbook―1883, City of Charleston, South Carolina. Charleston: News and Courier Book Presses, 1883.

Yearbook―1914, City of Charleston, South Carolina. Charleston: Walker, Evans & Cogswell, 1915.

Young, John R. *A Walk in the Parks.* Charleston: Evening Post Books, 2010.

NEWSPAPERS AND MAGAZINES

America's Civil War
Army
Atlanta Appeal
Atlantic Monthly
Augusta Constitutionalist (Georgia)
The Century
Charleston Daily Courier (South Carolina)
Charleston Mercury (South Carolina)
News and Courier (Charleston)
Post and Courier (Charleston)
Charlottesville Chronicle (Virginia)
Chicago Tribune
Civil War Times Illustrated
Columbia Guardian (South Carolina)
Confederate Veteran
Daily Richmond Enquirer
Harper's New Monthly Magazine
Military Heritage
Advertiser (Mobile)
Mobile Register

Mobile Tribune
National Geographic
New York Herald
New York Times
New York Tribune
World (New York)
North & South
Philadelphia North American
Port Royal Palmetto Herald (South Carolina)
Daily Dispatch (Richmond)
Richmond Enquirer
Richmond Examiner
Richmond Sentinel
Sacramento Daily Union
Southern Christian Advocate
Southern Presbyterian
Times (London)

INDEX

Page numbers in italics refer to illustrations

Allison, Richard, 275–276
Ames, William, 270, 273, 275, 278
Ammen, Daniel, 69, 72, 74, 81
Anderson, Eliza, 2
Anderson, Richard, 1–2
Anderson, Richard H., 23, 27
Anderson, Robert, 246
  background of, 1–2
  Beauregard and, 5, 6, 14
  flag, 178, 181–182, 323
  occupation and surrender of Sumter, 1,
    2, 3, 7, 9, 11–13, 14, 15–16, 18
  return to Sumter, 310, 311, 313
Andrews, W. H., 265–266
Army of Northern Virginia, 43, 56, 311
assault on Sumter, failed, 170, 171–179,
  182, *176*
Atlanta, 220
Averasboro, North Carolina, 306

Baltic, 6, 7, 9, 16, 18
Barton, Battery, 270
Beauregard, Caroline, 242
Beauregard, P. G. T., *15*, 287, 289, 315
  abandonment versus holding of
    Sumter, 142–143, 144, 148, 188–
    189
  Anderson and, 5, 6, 14
  background of, 19
  bombardments, comments on, 97–98,
    100, 110, 111, 112, 113, 127, 138,
    139, 143, 197, 200, 206, 223, 235
  Bull Run (Manassas), First, 26
  in command of Military Division of
    the West, 286
  conflicts with Davis, 48–49, 202
  death of wife, 242
  dissension of men, 56–57
  Gillmore's surrender demand, 129–130
  letters of commendation from, 17–18
  naval attacks, comments on, 79, 83–
    84, 87–88, 179
  occupation of Sumter, 15, 16–17
  photographic views of Sumter, 246–
    247, 285
  postwar years, 321–322
  replaced by Jones, 248
  response of people toward, 19, 230–
    231
  Rhett and, 147–148
  in Richmond, 23
  Ripley and, 216–217, 282–283
  rumors of attacks on Charleston or
    Savannah, 63–66
Bee, Battery, 66, 89, 301
Beecher, Henry Ward, 313
Belknap, George E., 301, 302
Ben De Ford, 182
Bennett, Augustus G., 301, 302
Blake, Julius A., 160–161, 169, 179
Blanding, Ormsby, 67, 71, 138
blockades of Southern ports, 21–22, 27–
  29, 34, 46–47, 55, 91
bombardment of Charleston, 128, 129–
  130, 136, 137–138, 210, 215–216,
  229, 234–235, 236, 240–241, 244–
  245, 246, 252, 256, 257, 280–281,
  282, 286–287
bombardments of Fort Sumter, *166*
  during Anderson's occupation, 6–9
  in April 1864, 245–246, 248
  assessment of fort's condition following
    bombardments, 138–139, 140
  August 13, 1863, 107–154

in August 1864, 276, 277–278, *279*
bell alarm system, 235, 240
in February 1864, 238, 239
First Great Bombardment, 110–112
in January 1864, 236, 237
in July 1863, 98–108
in July 1864, 261–264, 265–266, 270,
    271–275
in June 1864, 257–259
in March 1864, 243
in May 1864, 249, 252–255, *253*, 256
October 26–December 5, 1863, 195–
    232
preparations for, 96, 97, 101–108
Second Great Bombardment, 189, 195,
    219
in September 1863, 155–159, 188
in September 1864, 280
Seventh Minor Bombardment, 257
Third Great Bombardment, 261, 265,
    266, 280
tunnel, creation of, 231–232
Booth, John Wilkes, 314
Brady, Mathew, 287
Bragg, Braxton, 17, 27, 48, 201, 202
Brannan, John M., 57, 63
Bull's Bay, 228, 292, 297–298
Bunce, Francis M., 171, 175
Butler, William B., 294, 306

Calhoun, John C., 22
Calhoun, William Ransom, 22–23, 27,
    46, 47
  dissension of men under, 41, 42–45
  duel with Rhett, 50–52, 57–58, 61–62
  feud with Rhett, 31–32, 34, 35, 38,
    40–41, 49–52
Canandaigua, 72, 172
Canonicus, 301, 302
Carson, James M., 187–188, 199, 240
Castle Pinckney, 66, 120, 302
casualties
  Charleston, 234
  Confederate, 310
  Sumter, 153–154
  Union, 126, 137, 157, 179, 191, 203,
    239, 293, 310

casualties at Fort Sumter
  during Anderson's occupation, 7, 9, 12,
    83
  from Foster's bombardments, 259, 264,
    265, 266–268, 273, 274, 280
  from Gillmore's and Dahlgren's bom-
    bardments, 111, 112, 115, 116,
    117, 118–119, 122, 132, 133, 134–
    135, 157, 195, 196, 197, 198–199,
    200, 202, 204, 207, 209, 213, 214–
    215, 219
  from Hatch's bombardments, 252
  magazine explosion, 223–226, 227–
    228
Catskill, 72, 80, 109, 112, 130, 157,
    196, 202, 257
Celt, 302
Champneys, John T., 158, 169, 196, 204
Charleston, 302
Charleston, South Carolina
  after the surrender of Sumter, 17, 18
  attacks, rumors and plans for, 63–66,
    191
  blockade of, 21–22, 28, 40, 91
  bombardment of, 128, 129–130, 136,
    137–138, 210, 215–216, 229, 234–
    235, 236, 240–241, 244–245, 246,
    252, 256, 257, 280–281, 282, 286–
    287
  conditions in, 289
  Confederate forces honored in, 22–23
  evacuation of, 300–301, 304
  Federal views of, 55–56
  fire of December 11, 32–34
  food prices, 40, 237
  joint attack preparations, 70–71, 72
  land defenses, 66
  Lee at, 29–30
  naval attacks, 62, 68–69, 73–74, 75, 79
  prewar view of, *2*
  Second District, 32
  Sherman and, 294–295
  Stone Fleets, 34, 37
  truce, 287–288
  Union troops enter, 302–303, 307–308
Charleston & Savannah Railroad, 29, 57,
    93, 96, 263, 287, 288

Charleston Battalion, 160–161, 178, 183
Chatfield, Battery, 191, 252, 270, 272, 275
Chesnut, Mary, 6–7, 35, 38
Chesterfield, 154
Cheves, Battery, 66, 120, 184
Chicora, 62, 88, 89, 154, 171, 174–175, 302
Cleburne, Pat, 23
Clinch, 16
Coles Island, 41, 45, 47
Colhoun, Edmund R., 163, 165
Columbia, 4, 302
Columbia, South Carolina, 296–297, 300
Conyngham, John B., 210–211
Cook, George S., 165–167, 246, 247, 287
Cummings Point, 6, 7, 13, 66, 76, 161, 195
Cuthbert, George B., 13, 14, 15, 17, 22, 91

Daffodil, 173, 174
Dahlgren, John A., 93, 94–95, *95*, 100, 215, 229–230, 254–255, 288
   assault on Sumter, 170, 171–179, 182, *176*
   bombardments, comments on, 104, 110, 116, 119, 122, 130–131, 132, 143–144, 155, 158, 196, 203, 206, 218, 236, 270
   Charleston, arrival in, 303
   Charleston, attack on, 191
   death of son, 241–242, 247, 248
   Gillmore, relations with, 185–187, 190, 191–192, 200, 250–251, 295–296, 308
   harbor obstacles, removing, 292–293, 307–308, 309
   Long Island proposal, 247–248
   monitors, 111, 112, 114, 127, 130–131, 132, 134, 144, 148, 150–151, 152–153, 156–157, 163–165, 195, 196, 200, 202–203, 207, 209, 217–218, 220, 227, 232, 234, 244, 256–257, 271, 312
   postwar years, 320–321, 323–324
   Rowan and, 241
   Sumter, arrival at, 309, 313
Dahlgren, Ulric, 100, 104, 215, 234, 236, 241–242, 247, 248, 321
Dahlgren guns, 68, 70, 88–90, 94
Dandelion, 83
Dan Smith, 172
David, 189
Davis, Jefferson, 4, 19, 29, 38, 48, 201–202, 277, 322
Davis, W. H., 243
Delafield, Richard, 285
Dixon, George, 239
Doubleday, Abner, 7, 9, 11, 14, 16
Downes, John, 72, 78
Drayton, Percival, 72
duels
   Rhett-Calhoun, 50–52, 57–58, 61–62
   Rhett-Vanderhorst, 49–50
Du Pont, Samuel F., 27–29, 55, 56, *57*, 62, 68–70, 72, 73, 76–77, 84, 85, 90–91, 94, 95, 319–320

Edisto Island, 65, 73
Elliott, Stephen, Jr., *160*, 164, 174, 175, 176, 178, 179, 188, 189, 191, 196, 198, 201, 202, 203, 205, 206, 207–208, 211, 213, 214, 216, 218, 219, 222–223, 228, 238, 240, 248, 300, 305, 306, 307
   bomb proofing of quarters, 190
   demands of Sumter's surrender and, 163, 169
   injury of, 274, 291–292
   iron shield proposal, 231, 235
   magazine explosion, 224, 225, 226–227
   postwar years, 319
   promoted to brigadier general, 255
   replaced by Mitchel, 249
   as replacement to Rhett, 147, 159–160
Engineer and Artillery Operations Against the Defences of Charleston Harbor in 1863 (Gillmore), 296
Etiwan, 117, 120, 144, 149, 154

evacuation
  of Charleston, 300–301, 304
  of Sumter, 297, 298–300, *305*
Evening Gun, Fort Sumter (Chapman),
  221

Fairfax, Donald M., 72
Farragut, David, 242, 243–244, 279,
  284–285
Ferguson, Samuel, 12, 14
Fisher, Fort, 294
Flag of Sumter, The (Chapman), 221
Fleming, David G., 143, 150, 161, 274
floating boom between Maffitt's Channel
  and Sumter, 53–54, 58, 66
Folly Island, 66, 95
Foote, Andrew H., 90–91, 93, 94
Foster, John G., 15, 64, 256, 257–258,
  261, 262, 263, 265, 271, 276–277,
  278, 281, 282, 284, 295
Fox, Gustavus V., 6, 7, 9, 16, 56, 70, 85,
  242
Fremantle, Arthur J. L., 91–92, 216–217
Frost, Edward D., 223, 226

Galena, 40
Georgia Battalion, 12th, 196, 199, 200,
  201
Gillmore, Quincy A., 39, 92–93, *93*,
  96–97, 206, 228
  assault on Sumter, 170–171, 172–173,
    180
  batteries, 103–104, 105–106
  bombardments, comments on, 104–
    105, 110, 114, 115, 127–128, 137,
    143, 151, 152, 155, 183, 197, 204–
    205, 208, 213, 215–216
  Bull's Bay, 228, 292, 297–298
  Dahlgren, relations with, 185–187,
    190, 191–192, 200, 250–251, 295–
    296, 308
  Foster, as a replacement for, 295
  harbor obstacles, removing, 308, 309
  plot to capture, 324
  postwar years, 317, 318
  promotion to major general, 184–185
  replaced by Hatch, 250
  Sumter, arrival in, 304, 313
  surrender demand, 129–130

Gilmer, Jeremy F., 127, 138, 140, 184,
  212
Glassell, W. T., 189
Glover, Battery, 66
Goldsborough, Louis M., 27
Gordon, George H., 250–251
Grant, Ulysses, 228, 244, 287, 291
Gray, Sylvester H., 122, 141
Greer, William Robert, 325–326
Gregg, Battery, 66, 99, 101, 110, 111,
  161, 191

Hall, F. Marion, 158, 159
Halleck, Henry W., 63, 229, 247–248,
  250, 258, 294
Hallonquist, James H., 13, 17
Hallowell, E. N., 288
Hammond, Samuel L., 324
harbor obstacles, removing, 292–293,
  307–309, 310
Hardee, William J., 285, *286*, 288, 289,
  297, 300, 305–306
Harleston, Frank H., 138, 143, 150,
  207, 214–215
Harriet Lane, 7
Harris, David B., 54, 88, 113, 127, 138,
  140, 216, 217, 282–283
Harris, J. C., 174, 176–178, 184, 212
Harrison, George P., Jr., 294
Harvest Moon, 241, 303, 307
Haskell, Battery, 120, 184
Hatch, John P., 250, 252, 256, 274, 287
Haviland, John, 179
Hays, Battery, 104
Hennessy, John A., 301
Heyward, James S., 134–135
Hibben, 106
Higginson, F. J., 172, 174, 177
Hilton Head, 29, 65, 72
Holbrook, Henry, 118–119, 137
Holden, Edgar, 76, 77, 82, 84, 86
Holmes, Emma Edwards, 23–24, 26, 39,
  50, 51, 62, 113–114, 148, 215,
  300, 313
Holmes, John, 300
Hood, John Bell, 285, 304
Housatonic, 72, 172, 239, 240
Houston, John H., 214
Huger, Isaac, 318

Huger, Joseph P., 246
Huguenin, Thomas A., 268, 269–270,
    269, 275, 278, 279, 281, 287, 291,
    293, 297, 298, 299, 305, 306, 314,
    318–319
H. L. Hunley, 239–240
Hunter, Alvah, 75, 75, 81
Hunter, David, 38, 47, 54–55, 63–64,
    70–71, 72, 85, 87, 90, 92, 256
Huron, 55, 72

Inglesby, Charles, 81
Ingraham, Duncan, 31
ironclads. *See* monitors
Isaac Smith, 71, 249
Isabel, 9, 11, 13, 14, 15, 16
Izard, Ralph S., 274
Izlar, William, 204

Jackson, Thomas J. "Stonewall", 23, 91
James Island, 6, 41, 45–46, 55, 66, 70,
    96, 99, 100, 120, 129, 197, 261,
    264, 283, 300
Johnson, Fort, 6, 66, 164, 258, 264
Johnson, John, 71, 111, 113, 115–116,
    132, 133, 134, 135, 138, 158, 162,
    198, 204, 206–207, 209, 214, 220,
    223, 224, 225, 226, 228, 229, 234,
    238, 240, 249, 297, 299, 310
  postwar years, 322
  Ripley's recommendation that Johnson
    be promoted to major, 264–265
  wounding of, 273–274
Johnston, Albert Sidney, 48
Johnston, Joseph E., 26, 304, 305, 306–
    307, 314–315
Jones, Iredell, 106, 113, 118, 121–122,
    123, 126, 127, 128–129, 130, 134,
    135–136, 139, 142, 143, 144, 150,
    151, 152, 154
Jones, Samuel, 248, 250, 277, 282, 285,
    286
Jordan, Thomas, 147, 163

Kearny, Battery, 104
Keokuk, 69–70, 72, 79, 82, 83–84, 85,
    310
  use of guns from, 88–89, 90, 91, 92,
    113, 118, 126, 132, 134, 138, 158,
    251

Key, John R., 220–221, *222*
Keystone State, 62

LaCoste, Adolphus W., 88, 89, 251
LaCoste, James, 88, 89
Lee, Robert E., 23, 91, 311, 313
  command on the southeastern coast,
    29–30, 31, 32, *33*, 34, 35–36, 38
  dissension of men under Calhoun, 41,
    42–45
  Ripley-Pemberton feud, 42
  transfer of Pemberton, 47
  transfer of Ripley to the Army of
    Northern Virginia, 43
Lehigh, 156, 165, 173, 177, 196, 200,
    202, 209, 257, 293
Lincoln, Abraham, 1, 5–6, 18, 21, 54,
    86–87, 248, 313–314, 322
Lodona, 172
Long Island proposal, 247–248

MacNeil, Hermon A., 326
Maffitt's Channel (Sullivan's Island), 37
  floating boom between Fort Sumter
    and, 53–54, 58, 66
  magazine explosion at Sumter, 223–226,
    227–228
Mahaska, 172
Mahopac, 301, 302
Mary Francis, 107
Massachusetts, 215
Mathewes, J. Fraser, 158, 184
Mathewes, William, 158, 159
McAllister, Fort, 62, 65, 68, 288
McCawley, C. G., 174, 176, 177
McClellan, George, 45
Memphis, 46–47, 172
Mercedita, 62
Mercury, 13, 16, 17
Milan, 59
mine/powder rafts, 271, 275–276, 278,
    279
Mitchel, James, 249
Mitchel, John, Sr., 249
Mitchel, John C., 13, 37–38, 246, 249–
    250, 251, 255, 257, 261, 262, *267*,
    324
  injury and death of, 266–268

Ripley's recommendation that Mitchel be promoted to major, 264, 265, 266

Mitchel, Ormsby M., 54, 55, 57, 63

Mitchel, Willie, 249

Monitor, 39, 40, 62, 68

monitors, 39–40, 62, 68–71, 72, 76, 75–91, 111, 112, 114, 127, 130–131, 132, 134, 144, 148, 150–151, 152–153, 156–157, 163–165, 191, 195, 196, 200, 202–203, 206, 207, 209, 217–218, 220, 227, 232, 234, 244, 254, 256–257, 271, 292–293, 312

Montauk, 62, 65, 72, 80, 109, 130, 131, 165, 173, 206, 232

Morris Island, 3, 4, 13, 15, 34, 46, 48, 66, 77, 161, 183, 188, 310

bombardments from, 90, 95–96, 97, 98–100, 101–122, *192*, 200, 202

Moultrie, Fort, 1, 2, 6, 30–32, 66, 77

Nahant, 68, 72, 73, 75, 76, 78–79, 80, 81, 109, 130, 131, 165, 209, 220, 271

Nance, W. F., 268

Nantucket, 72, 80, 100, 257

naval attacks against Fort Sumter
assault on Sumter, 170, 171–179, *176*
damage following, 82, 87, 91–92
initial, 68–69, 73–74, 75–91, *80*, 95
monitors, 39–40, 62, 68–71, 72, 76, 75–91, 254
monitors (Dahlgren's), 111, 112, 114, 127, 130–131, 132, 134, 144, 148, 150–151, 152–153, 156–157, 163–165, 195, 196, 200, 202–203, 207, 209, 217–218

Naval Battery, 104, 126

navies
Rebel, 62, 239–240
U.S., 21–22, 27–29, 34, 39–40, 62, 68–74, 75–91, *80*

New Ironsides, 72, 73, 77–78, 79, *80*, 82–83, 99, 109, 111, 112, 114, 120, 123, 126, 138, 150, 156, 164, 165, 172, 173, 189–190, 241, 257

New Jersey, 116

Niagara, 21

Nipsic, 240

Olmstead, Charles H., 39, 107, 133, 153

Osborn, Francis A., 170, 173, 178

Palmetto Guard, 13–14, 17, 22, 43, 91

Palmetto Shield, 243, *244*

Palmetto State, 62, 88, 154, 163, 302

Passaic, 68, 72, 76, 77, 79, 80, 82, 84, 109, 111, 114, 116, 127, 130, 131, 156, 165, 206, 257

Patapsco, 68, 72, 74, 80, 81, 109, 111, 130, 131, 165, 171, 172, 196, 200, 202, 203, 293, 309, 310

Pawnee, 7, 9, 14, 16

Peck, W. F. G., 73–74, 121, 289

Pemberton, John C., 35, 38
dissension of men under Calhoun, 41, 42–45
relations with Ripley, 32, 41–43
transfer of, 47, 48

Philadelphia, 122, 171, 173

photography, 165–167, 246, 247, 285, 287

Pickens, Francis W., 6, 35, 38, 42–43, 45

Planter, 40–41

Pocahontas, 7, 9

Port Royal, South Carolina, 28–30, 65, 68, 97

Port Royal Palmetto Herald, 282

Porter, David Dixon, 230, 285

Powhatan, 7, 9, 172, 175, 179

Preston, Samuel W., 171, 172, 182

prisoners
exchange of, 287–288
Rebel, 263
Union, 178, 179, 240, 263–264

Pulaski, Fort, 39, 97, 107

Putnam, Battery, 272, 275

Putnam, Fort, 190–191, 252, 270

Racer, 172

Rattlesnake, 65

Reid, Whitelaw, 96, 309

Remey, G. C., 172, 177, 182

Rhett, Alfred Moore, 17, 24, 27, 28, 30, 44, 47, *53*, 300, 305, 306
bombardments/preparations, comments on, 96, 98, 105, 107, 108, 111–112, 113, 114, 115, 116, 117, 119–120, 123, 125, 138, 157, 159, 212

duel with Calhoun, 50–52, 57–58, 61–62

duel with Vanderhorst, 49–50

escapes from injuries, 133, 135, 157

feud with Calhoun, 31–32, 34, 35, 38, 40–41, 49–51

naval attacks, comments on, 73, 81, 82, 83

postwar years, 319

recognition of performance, 147–148

return to command at Sumter, 61–62, 71

surrendering versus holding of Sumter, 149–150

transfer to command Charleston's inner ring of fortifications, 159

Rhett, Claudine, 73, 303

Rhett, Edmund, 40, 49

Rhett, Julius M., 88

Rhett, Robert Barnwell, Jr., 27, 296

Rhett, Robert Barnwell, Sr., 27

Rhett, Robert W., 46

Rhind, Alexander C., 69, 70, 72, 79, 83

Ripley, Fort, 66, 302

Ripley, Roswell S., 13, 24, *25*, 27, 37, 38, 263, 286, 307

Beauregard and, 216–217, 282–283

bombardments, comments on, 100, 118

Harris, criticism of, 216–217

naval attacks, comments on, 73, 83

postwar years, 319

recommendation that Mitchel and Johnson be promoted to major, 264–265

relations with Pemberton, 32, 41–43

return to Charleston and Sumter, 56, 58, 67

Rhett-Calhoun duel, 57–58

transfer to the Army of Northern Virginia, 43–44, 56

Rodgers, C. R. P., 68, 69, 81

Rodgers, George W., 72, 112, 157

Rodgers, John, 72, 76, 77

Roman, Alfred, 19, 20, 66–68, 140, 283, 323

Ross, Fitzgerald, 105, 109–110, 207

Ruffin, Edmund, 13, 14, 17

Russell, William Howard, 18, 19–20

Salvor, 205

Sangamon, 257

Savannah, 130

Saxton, Rufus, 280–282

Schimmelfennig, Alexander, 254, 255, 273, 275, 276, 278, 280, 303

Secessionville, 45–46, 47, 55

Seneca, 46

Seymour, Battery, 270

Sherman, William T., 245, 283, *284*, 287, 288, 291, 292, 294–295, 314, 315

Simkins, Battery, 120, 164, 184

Sonoma, 196

South Carolina Artillery Battalion, 1st, 13, 17, 22, 23, 24, 27, 31, 34–35, 38

South Carolina Artillery Regiment, 1st, 38, 71

South Carolina Regular Infantry, 1st, 71

South Carolina's Companies A and G, 44

Spaulding, 140

Star of the West, 3, 4, 5

Stevens, Thomas H., 171–172, 173, 174, 175, 177, 179, 323–324

Stoddard, R. H., 230

Stowe, Harriet Beecher, 313

Strong, Battery, 104, 119, 122, 191, 236, 270

Stuart, J. E. B., 23

Sullivan's Island, 1, 3, 4, 8, 15, 37, 77, 98, 100, 164, 184, 197, 264

floating boom between Fort Sumter and, 53–54, 58, 66

Sumter, 117, 120, 153–154

Sumter, Fort

Anderson's occupation and surrender of, 1, 2, 3, 7, 9, 11–13, 14, 15–16

Anderson's return, 310, 311, 313

banner (regiment's flag), 325

civilians tour and celebration at, 311–313, *312*

Confederate occupation of, after Anderson's, 13–17

construction of, 2–3, 5

dissension of men, 41, 42–45, 56–57

evacuation of, 297, 298–300, *305*

last garrison of, 294, 305–306

layout of, *8*

name of, 2
postwar years, 317–326
prewar, 4, 5
rebuilding and fortification of, 19–21,
    23–24, 49, 52–53, 54, 56, 58, 65,
    71, 101–102, 105, 108, 110
Roman's description of, 67–68
timeline of events, 329–332
Union troops take over, 301–302, 304
Sumter, Thomas, 2
surrendering versus holding of Sumter,
    142–143, 144, 148–167
Swamp Angel (Parrott), 127, 128, 130,
    136, 142, 228

Torch, 123
Tucker, John, 250, 259
Turner, John W., 136–137, 141
Turner, Thomas, 72
"Twilight On Fort Sumter—August 24,
    1863" (Stoddard), 230

Unadilla, 72
Uncle Tom's Cabin (Stowe), 313
U.S. Colored Troops, 54th Massachusetts
    regiment, 99
U.S. Department of the South, 38, 54,
    92, 295

Vandalia, 28
Vanderhorst, Arnoldus, 49–50
Virginia, 62

Wabash, 104
Wagner, Battery, 66, 95–96, 98–99, 112,
    115, 161, 184, 188, 190–191
Wagner, Thomas M., 30, 31, 32, 34, 35,
    38, 47–48
Washington Light Infantry, 198–199,
    240
weapons
    assaulting arks, 277
    Columbiad, 81–82, 99, 106
    Dahlgren guns, 68, 70, 88–90, 94
    hot shot projectiles, 7, 8
    mine/powder rafts, 271, 275–276, 278,
        279
    Parrott rifle, 119, 122–123
    rifled ordnance at long range, effects of,
        39, 65
    searchlights (calcium light), 206–207,
        226, 227
    Swamp Angel (Parrott), 127, 128, 130,
        136, 142, 228
    torpedoes, 190
    underwater mines, 82–83
Weehawken, 72, 76, 77, 79, 80, 109,
    114, 130, 131, 132, 156, 157, 163–
    165, 206, 220, 310
Williams, E. P., 172, 175, 176, 178, 182
Wilmington offensive, 284–285, 294
Wissahickon, 72, 172
Worden, John L., 62, 72

Yates, Joseph A., 28, 44, 67, 71, 325